Date Due

YOUNG LADY RANDOLPH

LADY RANDOLPH CHURCHILL

Young Lady Randolph

THE LIFE AND TIMES OF JENNIE JEROME

AMERICAN MOTHER OF WINSTON CHURCHILL

BY RENÉ KRAUS

G·P·PUTNAM'S SONS

NEW YORK

COPYRIGHT, 1943, BY RENÉ KRAUS

Designed by Robert Josephy

MANUFACTURED IN THE UNITED STATES OF AMERICA

To

AUDREY

in deep gratitude for her invaluable inspiration and help.

CONTENTS

Part One: JENNIE

Part Two: LADY RANDOLPH

ILLUSTRATIONS

Part One: JENNIE

CHAPTER I *Family Chronicle*

"*Néve!*" said the nurse, a dark-eyed, kindly peasant woman, pointing out the peak of Mont Cenis. "*Falda di néve!*" she added, excited as southern people are at the unaccustomed aspect of a glacier.

The family was on one of these short land expeditions which used to interrupt a cruise along the Mediterranean so pleasantly. They had not seen snow-capped mountains for almost four years, ever since Mr. Jerome had been appointed U. S. Consul in Trieste, the Adriatic seaport. It was good to see a snowfield again. It reminded one of the Berkshires in winter, of home.

"A glacier!" sighed Mr. Jerome comfortably. Almost four years of uninterrupted sunshine and blue skies had been too much for him. Nothing is harder to bear than a constant flow of beautiful days. One gets listless and lazy dividing one's days between sunshine and office hours. Leonard W. Jerome had at length become most anxious for a little fresh air and rough going. "A glacier!" he repeated with gusto.

"*Ghiacciájo!*" the nurse translated for the benefit of the baby.

The child looked first at her nurse, then at her father. Evidently, she had to make her choice. A choice is easily made at the tender age of four. Her oversized, pitch-black eyes in the round, peach-colored face, crowned with clusters of dark

3

little curls, were illuminated by a happy smile. *"Ghiacciájo!"* she repeated, clapping her fat little hands.

"Glacier!" Mr. Jerome said sternly.

"Néve! ... Falda di néve!" the baby insisted stubbornly.

"She will never learn English," Mr. Jerome sighed once more, this time not so comfortably. The prospect of bringing home an Italian daughter did not elate him. "I will not have an Italian child!" he grumbled. In the year of the Lord 1854 New York was prone to regard Italians primarily as Sicilian cutthroats or ice-cream vendors. At best, their gangs were sewer workers for Irish bosses. Of course, they could be opera singers, too.

"One day she will be a famous prima donna," his wife tried to comfort him. Now it was her turn to sigh a little. Clarissa Jerome, née Hall, before her marriage the most beautiful girl in Palmyra, New York, had herself been born for the stage; or so she believed. But such a career had been out of the question for a distinguished up-state belle, a modest heiress. Instead, she and her sister had duly married—on the same day, the fifth of April, 1849—their cousins, two of the innumerable brothers Jerome, Leonard and Lawrence, respectively. Thus the dowry remained in the family; besides, a double wedding was so romantic. The newlyweds started their married lives under the most promising auspices. Leonard Jerome, then an assiduous young lawyer in Rochester, was patently destined for a splendid future, a prospect that his young bride found delightful. But the doors of the great world, it seemed, were prematurely closing, as her husband's first appointment in the consular service led nowhere but to an unceremonial return to the United States. Clarissa, however, was determined to open these doors very wide indeed to her little girls. *"Fanciulla!"* she said tenderly, caressing Jennie, the second, the favorite baby. The mother, too, had to muster her few words of broken Italian to be understood by the child.

"Néve!" answered Jennie. *"Falda di néve!"* she persisted.

Almost half a century later Lady Randolph Churchill recalled the first impression of her turbulent life. "The deep snow on the Mont Cenis," she wrote, "filled my childish mind with awe and astonishment." And she still maintained that Italian was the most melodious of all languages.

Both little Jennie's obstinacy and inclination to disagree were part of her heritage from her father which she, in turn, bequeathed to the next generation. Leonard Jerome, a most conspicuous man throughout his sixty-seven blessed and sometimes harassed years, had been already remarkable as a boy. On the paternal side he was a Huguenot; his mother was of Scottish descent. His grandfather, a clergyman, had married Betsy Ball, a distant relative of George Washington; by this marriage the Jerome family gained access to polite society. Yet the reverend gentleman preferred to remain tucked away in his village. He bequeathed his rural inclination to his son Isaac, who bought a tract of land in the Berkshire Hills, between Lenox and Stockbridge, Massachusetts. There he settled down, and married Aurora Murray. Like all the ladies of the Jerome tribe, Aurora developed into a memorable character. Oldsters of the Berkshires still remember the countless tales and legends centering around "Aunt Bora," her nickname in her advanced years.

True to the prolific habits of her time, Bora gave birth to nine children, eight boys and one girl. America was full of opportunity, and the boys could choose their calling. The two elder, Aaron and Allen, both Princeton graduates, became Presbyterian clergymen, whereas brothers Addison and Lawrence—"Larry"—became men of affairs. At the peak of his achievements Mr. Addison Jerome was a well-known society lion in New York, a wit and *bon vivant* and a favorite of the international set, then in the making. Larry established himself as a prosperous Wall Street broker. Three other brothers preferred to stick to the soil. They remained farmers. But in Leonard all the contradictory qualities of the amazing Jeromes were embodied. A survey of his career, spectacular as it was, cannot adequately describe him. Throughout the ups and downs of his life, he was, above all, a gambler, a freebooter, and a patriot. His principal claim to posthumous fame lies in the fact that he was to become the grandfather of Winston Churchill. But to regard Leonard W. Jerome only as a fore-runner—admittedly the ancestor of one of the greatest men of our century—is doing grave injustice to his memory. He was, indeed, in his own right the perfect embodiment of the chaotic era of American giants.

He started as a farmboy at Pompey Hill, Onanda County, N. Y., where he had been born in 1818. He was a silent young-ster, who, tilling the soil, soon acquired habits of self-reliance. The monotonous farm work, however, was not entirely to his taste, nor did an early knowledge of crops and cows fully satisfy his hunger for information, the passion that spurred him on throughout the busy years. His genuine Yankee trading instinct was early developed. While still in short trousers, he quit his father's farm and made good as an apprentice in the village store. He saved every penny of his salary, which rapidly increased from a dollar a week to a dollar fifty, and finally to two dollars. He was determined to amass sufficient capital to get a higher education.

At fourteen he entered Princeton. But opportunities to work one's way through the fashionable college were scant. So he shifted to Union College, where it was easier to earn a few dollars on the side. Three years later he graduated with high marks.

For another three years he read law at Albany with John C. Beach and Marcus T. Ronalds. At the age of 22 he was ad-mitted to the bar. His uncle, Judge Hiram K. Jerome, took him as a junior partner into his law office in Palmyra. A couple of years later, some time between 1842 and 1844, Leonard Jerome had saved enough money to establish his own law office in Rochester, on the corner of Exchange and Buffalo (now Main) Streets. His practice flourished, but the exercise of the legal profession in a small town did not satisfy his ambition.

He was always in a hurry; both his daughter and his grandson inherited this trait.

Brother Larry, himself somewhat erratic, approached Leonard with an excellent idea: Why not enter the publishing business? A newspaper might well become a formidable weapon in a small town. Moreover, it could be tied up with a printing office, for which there should be good chances in expanding Rochester. Leonard needed not much persuasion. Quick of decision, but careful in the execution of his plans, as he was in his youth—paradoxically, this inherent caution failed him in later life—he entered into negotiations with the *Rochester Daily American*. In the second part of 1845 the brothers Jerome took over the newspaper. For a time—again the strangely unyouthful caution!—Leonard regarded his paper strictly as a business enterprise. While he developed the printing shop into the finest in the city, he refrained even from entering the editorial room. His province was the counting room only, whereas gay brother Larry, a born super-salesman, procured subscriptions and advertisements. Some of the elder citizens smiled at the young brothers, the lords of the local press. Leonard, after all, was only an attorney of a few years' standing in town, and Larry still gave his regular profession as a law student. Mr. Samuel Wilder, described as a gentleman always entertaining and usually accurate, spoke haughtily of the "know-nothing paper, the local *American*."

This, of course, was challenging a man who spent most of his subsequent career himself looking for a fight. As if to silence his deriders, Leonard Jerome plunged into politics. The neighborhood paper developed into a hard hitting Whig organ that soon achieved a degree of national importance, particularly by its manner of sharply attacking the Democrats. Leonard never wrote an editorial, either in Rochester or later on, when an infinitely greater opportunity in the newspaper field came his way. He confined himself to whistling the tune to which his editors danced, a tune that occasionally gave the Democratic foe the St. Vitus dance. The thirty-two-year-old chief's personal respectability had to be kept out of feuds, the more so after his marriage.

The young Jeromes moved into a comfortable apartment in smart Fitzhugh Street. The mortgage on the newspaper was repaid out of the bride's dowry. The first two little girls arrived with clockwork precision; Jennie, the second daughter, incidentally, in Brooklyn, when her parents were already about to leave for Europe.

Leonard Jerome was satisfactorily settled. Still his restless ambition drove him on. He had saved thousands, but he dreamed of millions. The memory of the hard sledding he had undergone in his youth never released him from its grip. The way to the millions was clearly indicated. There were different ways in booming, roaring America. The most promising, if not the cleanest, led through the marsh of politics.

The *Rochester Daily American* stressed more and more strongly its allegiance to the Whigs. In 1850 their candidate, Mr. Millard Fillmore, became President of the United States. For Larry Jerome this entailed the unassuming but juicy post of a Rochester port collector; to Leonard it brought the U. S. Consulate in Trieste. Naturally, this modest assignment was intended only as a first stepping-stone on the way to a brilliant diplomatic career. The brothers entrusted their paper to the management of Messrs. Lee, Mann & Co., and embarked upon their promising new duties.

For almost four years Leonard Jerome was mildly bored in far-away Trieste. But his time was not entirely wasted. In his official position he learned to deal with men of many nationalities, and his beautiful wife acquired the old-world polish that her second daughter was later to develop to its highest, late-Victorian perfection. A cosmopolitan family, yet American to the core, they returned, when the next Presidential election was won by the Democrats. The assumption of power by Mr. Franklin Pierce brought about sweeping changes among port collectors and consuls. Leonard Jerome did not mind the homecoming. He had been yearning for the excitement of America.

He was at that time, and long remained, a tall, straight, hand-some man with a sharply-cut face, embellished, according to the taste of the period, by a walrus-mustache, and with a certain military bearing. He possessed a little money, he had gained a lot of early experience, and he felt entitled to nurse great expectations. Only with politics he was definitely through. Subsequently, he tried to imbue his children with his disgust of this dirty game. But children do not learn from their parents' experience. All the three Jerome girls married, in due course, British men of politics.

Some people do not learn from their own experience either. Immediately upon his return to Rochester, Jerome plunged again into the political turmoil. Railroads were the fashion. Their sudden development was tremendously popular, and gave scope to vast speculations. The New York and New Haven Railroad Co., as well as the Harlem Railroad Co., were then involved in terrific scandals. They had sold forged stock, a practice that exceeded even the accepted business habit of over-issuing stock in which at that time many companies indulged. Instantly Leonard Jerome took a hand in the rail-road battle. For ten years he remained a leading speculator in the field. Finally he succeeded in persuading his good friend Mr. Freeman Clark, Congressman for Rochester, to secure the passage of a railroad reform bill which would not be quite unprofitable to its sponsors.

Gambler's blood flowed in the veins of most of the Jerome family. While a theology student in Princeton, Leonard's eldest brother Aaron had taken a flier in the memorable mulberry tree speculation, and had made $40,000 in a single coup. He used this money to build a home for deserving fellow-students whom he housed and entertained for the remainder of his collegiate career. Another older brother, Addison G. Jerome, had already established himself as a successful Wall Street operator, by the time Leonard returned from Europe. Brother Addison had built a fine residence at 33 W. 20th Street. In this mansion he received his brother Leonard one evening late in 1854; after an elaborate dinner it was decided that Leonard should join the firm. William R. Travers, a friend of brother Larry's, was taken in as a third partner. And so the "three musketeers," as they were soon to be called, prepared their attack on the Street.

The first attack backfired. Leonard Jerome's initial venture ended in disaster. On a sure-fire "tip" from a friend, the treasurer of the Cleveland and Toledo Co., he put up a margin of $2,000 on 500 shares of that stock. But the stock crashed, and Leonard discovered that his supposed friend, the treasurer, had unloaded on him. Another man, double-crossed in this treacherous way, might have raged with fury. Not so Leonard Jerome. The volcano did not erupt. Quietly he retired from active business, since he had lost his entire capital, and devoted a whole year to studying the ways and people of Wall Street. Then he tried his hand a second time in buying $500 calls, risking a modest sum, but, as it was, his last penny. Inside a month he pocketed ten times his investment. His success began.

Wall Street did not welcome the lucky newcomers. Their operations were too bold for conservative tastes. They sometimes startled the most hard-bitten speculators. Moreover, the three musketeers were persistently on the short side. Their methods were new and merciless. A striking example of Leonard Jerome's originality and fertility of combative tactics, by the same token a proof that he was by instinct a journalist, was his invention, the "observatory," a luxuriously furnished room he rented on the upper floor of a building at Pine and Nassau Streets. In this setting exquisite luncheons with plenty of champagne were served to intimate friends, primarily to Messrs. Hudson and Snow, financial editors of the *Herald* and the *Tribune,* respectively. Having satisfied himself by careful research that the Cleveland and Toledo was rotten to the core, Jerome, ever persuasive, and aided and abetted by streams of champagne, convinced the gentlemen from the financial press that it was their patriotic duty, or that it would be at least a sure-fire scoop, to debunk the above-mentioned company. In due course a press campaign started, Cleveland and Toledo stock crashed, and the bank accounts of Jerome and Travers mounted correspondingly. The same procedure was repeated in the case of the ill-fated Michigan Southern. Again the three musketeers cleaned up, but they had the perfect excuse that they were simultaneously cleaning up the Street.

The panic of 1857 was a godsend to the bears. While countless millions evaporated in the fog of speculation and many an old established operator put a bullet through his head, Leonard Jerome harvested a golden crop. Over night he became the rival of Vanderbilt and Drew. Now the newcomer could dictate his terms to the Street. One lucky stroke had endowed him with a fortune. But he did not hoard it. He scattered it with lavish hands.

Leonard W. Jerome was never a true capitalist, with the latter's inborn worship of finance. Certainly, in an era of dancing around the golden calf he was one of the fastest dancers. But money was not his ultimate aim; to him it remained, throughout the years, merely a means to establish his leadership in whatever sphere he chose and to satisfy his ambition. He prided himself on being progressive in his methods, but conservative in his manner. He dressed very much *vieux jeu,* preferably in a black, silk-faced, high-buttoned morning-coat, wearing paper collars and cuffs and the fashionable "dickey" of white linen that covered the vest opening and hid the blue flannel shirt underneath. The coat stopped short at the hips. The "spring bottom" trousers were slim and tight. A flat pancake derby hat crowned the outfit. Leonard Jerome was never seen without his pocket toothpick, in the fifties an indispensable adjunct to the well-dressed man. To possess an inherited toothpick was a mark of lineage.

In his sartorial splendor, he jealously watched over the fashionable appearance of his wife. Mrs. Leonard Jerome, Clarissa to her friends, was an outstanding beauty in her day. A little

on the plump side, her classic figure was well suited to the
Grecian bend, much affected by society ladies. The Grecian
bend demanded long, trailing skirts, bustles, bosom pads of
inflated rubber or stuffed with horsehair, and formidable
corseting. Beneath the layers of petticoats and skirts white
cotton stockings were universally worn, later adorned with
horizontal green, yellow and red stripes which, of course,
remained invisible to others, but pleased their wearers. The
same argument was used to defend the introduction of fine
lingerie—both a new term and a new necessity at about the
time Clarissa established her salon in New York. Many a penny-
wise husband received the news that lingerie would now form
a new budget item with the skeptical question: "Why spend
money on what nobody is going to see?"

American women were just about to establish their independence in the realm of fashion. Clarissa Jerome, keen to
be recognized as a leader, wore tremendous hoop skirts. She
approved the bell sleeve, loose about the wrist, and supported
by delicate undersleeves of mull or lace. Another innovation
she popularized was the re-introduction of the fichu, the most
flattering of neckwear. Ruffles, sashes and fringe trimmed her
dresses. Clarissa was a wife to be proud of. She was never
seen without all the paraphernalia of a gentlewoman: fresh lace
at throat and wrists, shining boots, a crisp handkerchief, and
spotless gloves. Her daughter studied *belissima mammina* with
an expert's admiration. Jennie was six at the time.

Jennie was an anxiously guarded and rather spoiled child.
Soon after their return to New York the Jeromes had been
grieved by the sudden death of one of their daughters. The
two surviving little girls, and another that came later, were
carefully protected from the dangers of the world. "Unlike most
American children we were seldom permitted to go to boy and
girl dances," Lady Randolph recollected, decades later.

The upbringing of the Jerome girls was well in advance of
the customs of those days. Exercise and fresh air for women
and children was almost a subversive idea in the early Fifties,

when female frailty was considered a delicate attraction. Again the Jeromes were among the first to challenge the accepted rules. In spite of her expanding hip-line Clarissa gave up wearing tight corsets. The windows in airless bedrooms were opened wide. Dietetic rules, which Jennie subsequently adhered to throughout her life, long before the age of vitamins and calories, were first introduced by Clarissa. Hard mattresses replaced the soft featherbeds. Another startling innovation was the bathtub which allowed of more comfortable and hence more frequent bathing. The baths were followed by "home exercises" and "lessons in calisthenics for young ladies." These new and rigid methods of upbringing brought about many hardships and privations. But Jennie picked up her mother's words. They deeply impressed her, and remained unforgotten: "Strong women are more beautiful." In her seventh year she was entirely determined to become a strong woman.

In spite of Clarissa's progressive ideas, the Jerome household maintained the old-fashioned ways. The family dinner was a solemn affair. Everyone dressed. Little Jennie was early introduced to the mysteries of fashion. The family was assembled in the drawing room to await the head of the house. Usually a few of Jerome's friends with healthy appetites were present. Grace was said before the solid meal. Blessed with a trim figure, Leonard could afford to smile at his wife's dietetic fads. They were all very well at breakfast and lunch which the ladies partook of by themselves. But at the dinners over which Leonard Jerome presided, eating was still written with a very big E. Drinking was not neglected either. The children retired immediately after the meal. The parents sat down in the drawing room, reading books from the Society Library or, if there were guests, engaging in a game of whist.

Clarissa, a pioneer of healthy and hygienic education, tenderly supervised Jennie's growth—incidentally a slow process, for Jennie never reached above middle height. Her father imbued her, while still almost a baby, with his sporting instinct, above all his passionate love of horses. But it is doubt-

ful whether she would ever have become one of the leading
hostesses of her time, had it not been for Mr. Ward McAllister's
patient exertions.

The "snob of snobs," who had coined this title for himself,
the only one he ever aspired to, was a close companion of
Leonard Jerome, although a good deal younger. He enjoyed
tutoring his friend's remarkable daughter. He saw in Jennie
a great opportunity to perpetuate his theories on fashion,
perfect manners, and good eating. He visualized the perfect
lady, before Jennie had quite outgrown the nursery.

Once she was grown up and married, he told her when she
was eight, she would have to spend much of her time in the
kitchen. (Here the prophet erred.) The kitchen was a full-time
job. Not the best French chef could relieve a hostess from her
personal duties. "I do not give any attention to the details of
my dinners. Nine times out of ten I simply tell my chef how
many people there are to be." Disdainfully McAllister quoted
these words of a well-known hostess as a horrible example.
Then he smiled in slightly self-satisfied memory. "My comeback was: 'Nine times out of ten, Madam, this is apparent in
your dinners!' "

Little Jennie nodded earnestly. This was a lesson to be
remembered. Another lesson followed immediately: "Baroness
Rothschild, who, of course, gives the best dinners in Paris . . ."
(evidently Mr. McAllister was familiar with Parisian hostesses)
"personally supervises every dish. So does the Duchess of
Sutherland, Queen Victoria's intimate friend."

Jennie listened attentively. She became familiar with the
social register of the three cities that counted: New York,
London, Paris. But her education was not confined to fashion-
able nonsense. "To improve their minds," her parents used to
send the children frequently to the matinee in the Opera House.
Usually their mother accompanied the little flock. Only when
Adelina Patti sang, Mr. Jerome, too, took the afternoon off.
On these occasions his business cares were not so important.
He was an avowed admirer of the prima donna. He felt more

than just admiration for her voice, he felt a sort of paternal
affection for her as well, he frankly admitted. In a way she
strongly resembled his own little Italian baby, whose gibberish
in a foreign language he no longer discouraged. Who had ever
dared to say that all Italians were Sicilian cutthroats or ice-
cream vendors? Indeed, it was a pity that Jennie now chattered
in plain English. Something of her earliest charm was lost.
This girl Adelina reflected it.

Adelina Patti was six years older than Jennie. At the age
of ten, she had been the craze of New York. Her debut on
September 22, 1853, at a concert at the Tripler Hall had caused
a sensation. Overnight she became the "nightingale." A year
later, when the Jeromes came back to America, they soon
heard the nightingale's song. By that time La Patti had already
joined the distinguished company of Mmes. Sontag, Staffanone,
and Salvi who graced Signor Maretzek's Italian *stagione* at
Castle Garden.

As the years went on, Leonard Jerome's zest for the opera
increased. Now he went repeatedly alone to the evening performances. He was still convinced that he was admiring the
image of his child on the stage. But when Adelina had grown
to the respectable age of fourteen—and Jennie was eight—the
young prima donna received for the first time an enormous
bouquet in her dressing room, sent by an unknown admirer.
La Patti waved and kissed the orchids, a comparatively new
and very *chic* flower, just before the last curtain. She received
the unknown admirer after the show. She was a little exhausted
and terribly thirsty. A glass of champagne at Delmonico's? Why
not? *Mammina cara* would enjoy it. Unmindful of her increasing bulk, La Patti's mother enjoyed, indeed, a twelve-
course dinner. Then Mr. Jerome squired the ladies home. He
was proud of his four-in-hand, one of the first in New York.
But La Patti found the carriage a little too conspicuous. In
view of her tender age, which was constantly stressed by
mammina, she preferred, she said, a modish little barouche
with ponies.

Before the door of the Patti abode Leonard Jerome lifted
his silk hat. When alone, he whistled a few bars of "Twenty
Years Ago," the hot tune of the period, partly to encourage
his horses, partly to encourage himself. "Twenty Years Ago..."
he was still whistling as he stood before the mirror at home.
Why twenty years ago? he asked his image. He was still
going strong, and if his hair was receding a little, his mustache
was certainly flourishing. The tune changed to another ditty:
"Kissing a man without a mustache is like eating an egg without salt...."

When Adelina awoke next day toward three o'clock, a
barouche with two white ponies stood in front of her door.
Clarissa was very silent on this day. She did not even answer
when her husband explained to her in detail the business conference that had kept him the night before. But the family
peace was completely preserved. Strictly to maintain its semblance, at least, was obligatory in polite society. Only Jennie
brought a discordant note to the family dinner. When her
father entered the drawing room, she looked at him, long and
silently, and then refused to kiss him. She was a terribly moody
child.

She was allowed to do pretty much as she liked. One day
she returned from the dancing class, relating with tears:
"Georgina spit at me!"

"Georgina—who?" asked her father sternly.

"Georgina Rivage!"

"A Southerner, of course! Why did she...er...behave so
outrageously?"

"Because I pinched her," Jennie replied, frankly assuming
full responsibility for the incident. She was entirely unafraid.

Amazingly her father chuckled: "You are quite right, my
dear! Nowadays Southerners must be pinched."

The year of 1858 was closing. But New York disregarded
the signs of the times. The grave depression of the year before
gave way to riotous gaiety. Fun was all-important. The great

P. T. Barnum sold fun at a dime. With the slogan: "There's a sucker born every minute," he soon all but monopolized the amusement business. In deference to old prejudices which were only slowly waning, he cloaked his performances with the mantle of respectability. His shows were given in so-called lecture rooms. He covered the whole town with posters, inviting everyone to visit his spectacles. The public came by the thousands. Signs directed them through the halls. They read: "This way to the Fat Lady." Or: "This way to the Happy Family." One inscription said mysteriously: "This way to the Egress." The way led out to the street, and the human specimen, born every minute, had to pay another dime to gain re-entry.

Such popular amusements were strictly forbidden to the Jerome children. They were not even allowed to skate in Central Park, where enormous crowds gathered enjoying the new mass amusement. Instead, Leonard bought a large area near Fordham, enclosed and flooded it, and called it Jennie's Playground. It was a strictly private ice-rink, but the only way Mr. Jerome could envision strict privacy was to invite to the opening three trainloads of guests who found two pretty cottages full of conveniences and comforts, with a good band playing, while they lunched, chatted, and skated.

Soon after Jerome built his stables on Madison Square. Only the Emperor's mews in Paris could compare with them. They were of red brick, faced with marble, three stories high, with a mansard roof, housing thoroughbred horses and carriages of the finest makes. The building was lavishly decorated with black walnut paneling, plate glass and richly carpeted floors. On the second floor was an enormous hall, the scene of the opening ball to which invitations were at a premium. All the wealth, fashion and beauty of the metropolis danced. There were two fountains, one spouting Eau de Cologne, the other champagne. The entrance to the stables was carpeted in crimson. The front of the building was flood-lit by the new illuminating gas. It was a great evening. Total expenses: $7,536, Mr. Jerome noted.

The children were still too young for such parties. The youngest guest was Adelina Patti. As she surveyed the wide ballroom, she exclaimed: "What a marvelous place this would be to give an opera!" Indeed, a few weeks later the ballroom in the Jerome stables was converted into a private theater, more brilliant in decoration than Niblo's and Wallack's, the leading theaters of the day. Duly, Patti became the star of the troupe which was otherwise made up of amateur singers, society ladies and stage-struck young Wall Street brokers. La Patti herself had chosen this ensemble. Perhaps she did not care for competition. However, rivals there were. The horses downstairs out-neighed the arias upstairs. It was a strange duet: Adelina Patti and "Kentucky," the most famous race-horse of his period. Jerome enjoyed the dissonance tremendously. He soon built a palatial home opposite the stables.

For many years the Jerome mansion on Madison Square was a center of New York's fashionable set. Ceremoniously, the host left it every Sunday afternoon in his four-in-hand. The neighbors thronged the streets. They themselves profited from the spectacle, for Mr. Jerome had spent a great deal of money in improving the streets in the vicinity. The people cheered when he made his appearance. They cheered still more loudly when Jennie gravely mounted the place of honor next to her driving father. Gracefully she nodded her curly head. At eight, she was already perfectly accustomed to the admiration of the crowd. She smiled enchantingly. People thought the dark little girl in her white lace dress must be enjoying the ovation. What she really enjoyed was being allowed to sit next to her father, while her mother and sister sat tamely behind.

The children had their own social circle. The season for this youngest set included three outstanding entertainments. One was the surprise party. Gentlemen in their teens received the following invitation: "You are cordially invited to attend a sur-

MRS. LEONARD JEROME AND
HER DAUGHTER JENNIE

THE JEROME CHILDREN

(*Left to right:* Jennie, later Lady Randolph
Churchill; Clara—Mrs. Moreton Frewen;
Léonie—Lady Leslie)

prise party to meet at the residence of Miss . . . on . . . at . . .
Please bring oranges (candy, cake, fruit, lemons). Yours truly,
The Committee." The young people gathered at the address,
and trooped off to "surprise" some girl in her home. Since the
intelligence service in her dancing-class was highly developed,
Jennie used to know beforehand when the palatial building on
Madison Square would be the goal of such an invasion. But she
was inimitable in concealing her advance knowledge and in
feigning the most innocent surprise when the uninvited guests
arrived.

Another accepted occasion for merrymaking was the New
Year's call, an old Dutch custom. Toward the middle of December boys in their first long trousers got invitations from
the young ladies bearing the address at which they would be
received on New Year's Day. Mostly, three or four young ladies
received together. The point was, of course, who would attract
the greatest number of callers. Amazingly, Jennie did not
score. The family chronicle, carefully kept by Clarissa, expressed the suspicion that "the boys were too shy to present
themselves to little Jennie." Many of the would-be visitors
hesitated at the red-carpeted entrance to the Jerome mansion,
and decided instead to leave their New Year's cards—some
lavishly sprinkled with powdered tinsel to represent glistening
snow, others in gorgeously embossed floral designs—with the
liveried doorman.

More democratic were the grotesque parades on Thanksgiving Day, the only time in the year when the Misses Jerome,
thanks to the emphatic patriotism of their father, were permitted to stroll the streets. Thousands of children from every
social stratum dressed up in their parents' clothes, wearing masks
over their faces. They made the rounds of their neighborhood,
collecting a few pennies in a tin cup. This peculiar custom, Mr.
McAllister insisted, had its origin in the English Guy Fawkes
day.

Ward McAllister was a connoisseur of people, manners, and
things English. He imbued Jennie with her first images of

London. In his opinion the English gentleman was the first gentleman in the world. He did not make such statements lightly. He had traveled a good deal. He was a globe-trotter, always eager to bring home to America the experience he collected in the old world. He had recently been in London for a few months. But a little village had impressed him much more than the Empire's capital: Windsor, the site of the Royal Castle.

He had used his preferred methods of surveying Windsor. He was not actually presented at court. This privilege was, at that time and for a few more years, rarely granted to American sight-seers. Yet he had made friends at Windsor. "It was my great pleasure to meet Her Majesty's chef, who frequently dined with me at the village inn," he reminisced. "Soon he allowed me to inspect the kitchen," Mr. McAllister's principal interest. "I saw roasts for all living in the castle—at least twenty pieces turning on spits. I had a welcome opportunity carefully to examine the large hot steel table on which any cooked dish would stay hot for an indefinite period. It was thrilling. I entered the dining room, of course not as a dinner guest, only to admire the gold bowl, the size of a small bathtub, in which the Prince of Wales had been baptized. I was finally admitted in Her Majesty's model farm; I had just to say: 'I am an American landed proprietor.' I observed that all the flax-seed for the cattle was imported from America...."

But the Prince of Wales, it appeared, was foremost on Mr. McAllister's mind. Speaking of Edward, he said: "Everyone loves the Prince. The chef admitted unblushingly that he reserved his talents for the dinners the Prince honored. I, too, have my modest dinner-recollections with Edward. In the village inn I dined off pheasants which the Prince of Wales himself had shot. Two or three times I even had the opportunity to see him shooting...."

"I want to dance with the Prince!" exclaimed Jennie determinedly.

It was not childish arrogance. It was a perfectly legitimate

ambition. In the last year before the Civil War the Jeromes
were already the American counterparts of British aristocratic
society. On the far side of forty but still slim and spare, Jennie's
father was climbing the social ladder. In September, 1860,
he bought, in company with Mr. Raymond, the majority of
the shares of the *New York Times* from Mr. Wesley. Although
Jerome modestly contented himself with the unassuming title
of "consulting director," and as in the days of his first newspaper venture in Rochester, he never exercised any direct editorial influence, he was now generally accepted as a leading
citizen. He was also one of the wealthiest. Before the general
profiteering that followed in the wake of the Civil War, and
before the boom of the ensuing era of reconstruction, there
were only five or six taxpayers in New York with incomes of
$60,000 a year or more. Leonard W. Jerome was one of them.
In spite of his occasional escapades, he was an excellent family
man, and, above all, a deeply loving father. If Jennie wanted
to dance with the Prince—well, in ten years or so, after her
debut in Madison Square, he would take his ladies to London.

In the meantime, in New York, he preferred them to confine their social activities to the upper set. The riotous gaiety
in the early summer of 1860 was not to his taste. This unbridled
gaiety reached its height when the first Japanese delegation
ever to visit New York arrived on June 16th. The delegation
was led by three high commissioners, representing their Tycoon,
as the Emperor of Japan was then called. They were princes
of the blood, attended by a retinue of 74 courtiers. New York
had never seen anything like the group of little yellow gentlemen in stiff kimonos, wearing two swords apiece and with
tonsured skulls. As they arrived aboard the "Alida," cheering
crowds almost mobbed them; the entire police force of 1,100
men struggled to keep back the masses. This excess merry-
making boded ill. "We do hope," editorialized James Gordon
Bennett's *Herald,* "that at least our aldermen will school themselves in good manners when acting as hosts. They will find
that by taking fewer chews of tobacco, and smoking less bad

cigars, their sanitary condition will be improved." But it was the same dignified Mr. Bennett who gave a sumptuous reception at Washington Heights for the Japanese guests—a reception climaxed by the ball sponsored by the Corporations at the Metropolitan Hotel, where the little yellow men were staying.

The day was Monday, June 25th. The night of the ball was the wildest, and the most expensive, New York had thus far witnessed. Ten thousand guests, invited or uninvited, partook of the dinner; some had come from the most distant parts of the United States. Five bands played until dawn. Yet the gala affair ended in disaster. Contemporary critics called the ball miserably and vulgarly conducted. "Thousands of bottles of champagne had been wasted on a class of people whose ordinary drink was whisky. This gentry handed champagne bottles by the dozens unashamed to their friends and voters crowding the streets, to people who thus far had only tasted New England rum. The most costly ornaments in the ballroom were either broken or 'abstracted' by persons who had surreptitiously gained entry to the supper. The scene was little better than a civic orgy." The costs of the evening exceeded $100,000, to say nothing of costs of a very different sort which the *New York Times* summed up with the words: "The Japanese take back complete models of our best howitzers and Dahlgren guns, with full instructions as to their manufacture and use.... We can only hope that we may not find ourselves among the earliest victims of our overzealous and mistaken benevolence."

Just as suddenly public enthusiasm turned to complete indifference. Without even an official farewell the Japanese mission slipped away aboard the U. S. S. "Niagara" on June 30. Most newspapers did not even bother to announce their departure. Perhaps the people of New York felt a little ashamed of themselves. But the main reason why the departure of the Tycoon's emissaries went unsung and unheralded was a bombshell that had burst while the Japanese officials roamed Niblo's Garden, the popular Music Hall, and while the Academy of Music still announced a Japanese Gala Matinee without at-

tracting the slightest interest. Washington published the text
of a letter, received via the Atlantic cable, the newest great
invention.

The letter was addressed to President Buchanan. It read:
"Buckingham Palace, June 22, 1860. My Good Friend: I have
been much gratified at the feelings which prompted you to
write to me, inviting the Prince of Wales to come to Washington.
He intends to return from Canada through the United States,
and it will give him great pleasure to have an opportunity
of testifying to you, in person, that these feelings are fully
reciprocated by him. He will thus be able at the same time to
mark the respect which he entertains for the Chief Magis-
trate of a great and friendly State and a kindred nation. The
Prince of Wales will drop all Royal State on leaving my
Dominions, and travel under the name of Baron Renfrew, as
he has done when traveling on the continent of Europe. The
Prince Consort wishes to be kindly remembered to you. I remain, ever your good friend, Victoria R."

The letter created a sensation, mingled, however, with a
certain dissatisfaction. Buckingham Palace had evidently de-
creed that the Prince should drop his exalted state during his
stay in America in order to respect this country's republican
feelings. President Buchanan, a former U. S. ambassador to
the Court of St. James, appreciated the gesture. Public opinion
did not. "A prince is a thing we don't see every day. And we'd
rather not see him than see him half way!" R. J. deCordova,
the popular Broadway rhymster, expressed public opinion.

The upper set was above such petty considerations. Newspapers teemed with offers of mansions whose owners desired
to place their residences at his Royal Highness' disposal. A
certain "brownstone-front" house on Fifth Avenue splashed its
invitation across a whole page in every respectable morning
paper. Besides, every hotel-keeper turned his establishment
upside down. He would make a fortune if the Prince would
only sleep a single night in his house. All sorts of suggestions
appeared in the papers. The "Rainbow," in Beekman Street,

a modest but disguised hostelry in the heart of the business section, yet in the close neighborhood of the filthy, dilapidated slums (a most unlikely quarter for the Prince of Wales) entered the race with the claim that its owner was an Englishman; hence he was the natural host for His Royal Highness. Most discussed was an elaborate epistle Mr. Gorham Abbott, a gentleman of high literary ability, wrote to the papers. Mr. Abbott was the head of the Springler Institute, one of the first and most respectable academic institutions in the country. It was, beyond doubt, the leading finishing school for young ladies. From this fact Mr. Abbott derived his right to claim: "The Prince has a mother. Consequently, no house in New York would so fitly receive him as a ladies' school."

It so happened that the eldest Jerome daughter was, at that time, a pupil in the Springler Institute. Elated, she conveyed to her family the news that the Prince would be their school's house-guest. Leonard was skeptical, Clarissa mildly excited; only Jennie did not lose her poise. "The Prince comes to dance with me," the ten-year-old beauty said confidently.

The Prince's journey through the United States was a highly successful re-affirmation of Anglo-American friendship, due largely to Edward's engaging personality and unaffected friendliness. He had, in fact, come not as the British Empire's traveling salesman—usually the principal task of globe-trotting heirs to the throne—but to make a serious study of the U. S. Presidential campaign, which, in the autumn of 1860, was approaching its climax. True, the Prince was not supposed to display his deep political interest. It was not tolerated at home, and had strictly to be suppressed abroad. Edward had to confine himself to playing the role of the royal charmer, whose remarkably handsome appearance, well-cut face with blue eyes and light hair, agreeable countenance and gracious manner, set many an American heart aflame. Never before had a young gentleman of nineteen years scored such a complete triumph. Conversely, it was on this journey that Edward acquired that predilection for the men, and perhaps still more for the women of the U. S. A. to which he remained so faithful as King.

Edward made hundreds of friends in New York City. He shook hands with all the notables who were waiting in City Hall to be introduced to him during his triumphal entry into New York. When the crowd jammed outside found the ceremony too prolonged and expressed this feeling with their healthy American vocal cords, the Prince stepped out on the balcony and waved his hand, beaming, a happy boy. Uproarious cheers answered.

The Prince established his headquarters in the Fifth Avenue Hotel. For three days the hotel was besieged by masses, patiently staring at the lifeless walls. Then the plans for "The Prince's Ball" were worked out. On Friday, the twelfth of October, at nine o'clock in the evening, the General Committee of Arrangements gathered. Messrs. Peter Cooper, Charmor, and M. B. Field, the secretary of the General Committee, formed the inner council. They were concerned whether white waistcoats should be *de rigueur* for the men's apparel. It would have been the most natural thing, but many guests from all parts of the States were expected, and it was dubious whether all these out-of-towners would be suitably equipped. Since this was an important matter of protocol, the inner council decided to consult Lord Lyons, Her Majesty's ambassador, and Mr. Archibald, British Consul General in New York City.

Unfortunately, the gentlemen of the inner council underestimated the caution British diplomacy exercised in the U. S. A. One could never be sure how American public opinion would react to advice concerning the white waistcoat. The question was so much the more delicate as already the first voices from this side of the Atlantic had protested against the wearing of knee breeches by the American ambassador at Court functions in England.

Thus thrown on their own, the inner council sought aid from an undisputed society leader. Leonard Jerome found a formula making the white waistcoat compulsory and yet excusing those who were without it. At the family dinner table, he rather prided himself on this satisfactory way out of the impasse. Clarissa duly admired her husband's wisdom. Jennie asked: "And what am I going to wear to the ball?"

It was terribly hard to have to disappoint Jennie. For days she had been choosing among her fancy dress costumes. She had decided in favor of the costume of a vivandière. It fell to her father's lot to explain that little girls could not attend balls. "Don't be sad," concluded Leonard to comfort her. "We will have some dancing in a few days."

"I am not sad," Jennie replied courageously. Her brown little face was flooded with tears. Obediently she went to bed.

A few days later the vivandière costume came into its own. To make up to Jennie for the Prince's ball, Mrs. August Belmont gave an elaborate children's party. Jennie, everyone agreed, looked perfectly sweet in her costume. However a photograph, taken on this occasion, tells a rather different story. She did not smile into the lens. Her dark, black eyes look serious and searching. Their expression of early thoughtfulness belies her theatrical get-up: the high fur helmet, the white officer's dress uniform coat, covered with gold braid and tassels, and the ballooning hoop skirt of the period. Already in her tenth year a certain incongruity between her glamorous appearance and the deep earnestness of her nature was becoming apparent—even to the young girl herself. In the carriage, on the way to Mrs. Belmont's, she shed a few tears.

"For heaven's sake, why are you crying?" her perturbed mother asked.

"I . . . do . . . not . . . look at all . . . as I thought I . . . was going to . . ." was the only explanation the child could give. Many years later a worldly-wise woman, recollecting this scene from her early days, added philosophically: "A situation, which, alas! has often repeated itself."

CHAPTER II *Newport and the Civil War*

Into the days, chronicled in society annals as the days of a mass invasion of French chefs, the substitution of the art of dining for the old-fashioned gluttoning, the wholesale importation of European manners and mannerisms, and the ladies' new habit of sending to Paris for their hats, since they were now no longer satisfied with their old modistes—into these days of plenty, and particularly of snobbism aplenty, burst the opening shots of the Civil War. More than six hundred thousand men sacrificed themselves in the cause of freedom, for four years America was torn from top to bottom. Only Newport remained neutral ground.

In the words of Mr. McAllister, himself the son of a Southern gentleman and a Northern mother, Newport was a Southern colony. Indeed, in 1834 a few gentlefolk from South Carolina had been the first summer guests to come. After a time, a sprinkling of New Yorkers followed them. The first resort hotels came into being. The outbreak of the Civil War affected peaceful conditions in Newport only so far as the Southern guests had now to confine themselves to the "Touro," whereas "The Ocean House," "The Atlantic" and "The Bellevue" discriminated against them.

Conditions remained, on the whole, unchanged until the gusty Leonard Jerome swept the place. He first antagonized accepted tastes and customs by building what Lady Randolph later called "a charming villa more in accordance with one's idea of a seaside residence than the gorgeous white marble palaces." Victorian fussiness was banned from the structure. The beauty of Jerome's new building was its cleanliness and simplicity.

This American home teemed with European visitors. English guests and friends prevailed. One of them caused, unwittingly, an incident which showed Leonard at the height of his power and combativeness. His house guest, a colonel in the British army, rode his polo pony to the Newport Reading Room, where all the veterans of society were chatting and gossiping. Somehow, it appeared, they were annoyed by the stranger on horseback. They dared him to ride the pony into the hall of the revered old club. The English horseman did not hesitate. Egged on to do it, he actually did ride his pony across the narrow piazza, right into the hall of the club itself.

Newport was agog at the incident. What sacrilege! They sent a delegation to Jerome, withdrawing the guest card previously given to the colonel—whereupon, aroused by this slur on his friend, Leonard Jerome himself canceled his membership. He did not let it go at that. Aggravated, he retaliated in his customary lordly fashion. Opposite his own residence he built a superb casino for Newport, a building with clubrooms, a large ballroom, and a restaurant. The casino was ceremoniously opened with a masked ball. All the rooms in the first floor were converted into a series of charming supper niches. A huge tent was spread covering the whole park. The grounds were illuminated in a blaze of electric light.

Proudly Jerome surveyed his magnificent casino. He had scored another victory!

He had various reasons to be a proud man. The Civil War, a national catastrophe, gave him his great opportunity to exercise his two outstanding qualities: his patriotism and his uncanny business instinct. He immediately took a leading part in various national movements for the preservation of the Union. Lincoln had no more ardent follower than Leonard Jerome, who poured out his money with both hands for the cause. He bore the entire costs of the first great Union meeting in the Academy of Music, which started the war on the propaganda front. He was made Treasurer of the Union Defense Committee, and contributed largely to the expenses of that body. In directing the committee he was assisted by his friend Mr. August Belmont. Jerome's name usually headed the subscription lists. Frequently he sent $10,000 checks as his own contribution to the committee. A check of $35,000 went for the construction of the vessel "Meteor," built by private enterprise for the sole purpose of hunting and capturing the "Alabama," the pride of the Southern navy. With his brother Addison he donated $75,000 to war charities.

By the same token he practiced enormous private charity. War conditions made for tough going on the Street. Not all his fellow brokers had Leonard Jerome's skill in tightrope-walking. But every halfway decent friend who failed could borrow enough money from the tall, straight, spare king of the Street to start over again. There were no checks to be signed, and no obligations to be entered into. The handsome, witty, courtly man, always surrounded by crowds of business and social acquaintances, seemingly engrossed in amusement and affairs, remained a keen observer, ever on the lookout for those who deserved help. Sometimes, it is true, his keen insight failed him. Two or three times he was cheated out of considerable sums. In 1862, the agent of the State of Indiana swindled him out of $600,000 by selling him bonds of an unauthorized issue. Evidently the gentleman had banked successfully on Mr. Jerome's well-known inflammable imagination and spirit of enterprise. "If Leonard were only as judicious in his choice of men as he is in his choice of plans, he would die as one of the richest men in the world," Mr. August Belmont commented. Such deception and disappointment might well have disillusioned another man. But Jerome took the bad with the good. He never lost his composure. Unabashed, he admitted that most of his sweeping successes came from what he modestly termed his "first-hand information."

He did not receive this "information" in his capacity as the principal owner of the *New York Times*. His reporters were not expected to supply the boss with private tips of possible value in his stock exchange speculations. This purpose was served by a small army of personal confidence-men with and among the Northern as well as the Southern armies. Their code messages were simple enough. "The boy is badly hurt" meant that the Unionists had suffered a grave setback. News of this kind arriving a few hours before business on the Street opened was a bad shock for Leonard Jerome, but it paid dividends. When the message read: "The boy is getting worse," Leonard was despondent. So was Wall Street, after hearing the adverse reports in due time later on. The short interval, however, sufficed Jerome to carry out the boldest operations.

Oddly enough he saw not the slightest inconsistency in his double role as a fierce war leader on the home front and a war profiteer on a gigantic scale. Why, with the exception of the amazing Mr. Lincoln, Leonard's idol, everyone did his best to make the best of this best of all worlds. This, at least, was Jerome's explanation. In the era of push and plush this moral was generally accepted. Whether Leonard accepted it for himself, remains an open question. The fact is that immediately after the Civil War, he dropped out of politics for good.

His ups and downs in these years in which tremendous battles raged, not only at Chancellorsville and Bull Run, but in Wall Street as well, are best illustrated by two of his most memorable speculations. In the first year of the Civil War, the Pacific Mail Line, after innumerable, and sometimes dangerous fluctuations, was greatly depressed. Its stock fell to 69. A new ring of shareholders had to be formed. Twenty-six thousand of the forty thousand shares went to a group of operators for whom Brown Brothers acted as trustees for five years. In fact, Jerome was the head man and ringleader of the anonymous group. But as he was well known as an impetuous operator whose successes and reverses almost canceled one another out, he did not wish to assume public responsibility for maneuvers which seemed more promising as long as no one could guess the power behind them. His own family had not the slightest idea that he was engaged in a life or death gamble. It was only after Jerome's death that Lady Randolph learned the carefully kept secret. Understanding almost nothing of financial affairs, she thereafter liked to explain that her father had been the sole owner of the Pacific Mail Line for a couple of years.

Pacific Mail shares profited immediately from Jerome's financial witchcraft. Although not a great deal in the management or the volume of business changed, the value of the stock trebled. Finally they were rated at 180 despite the fact that in the meantime the capital had been doubled and the company paid 20% a year in dividends.

In the month of July, 1863, New York City was about to become one of the liveliest theaters of the Civil War. When the troops had all gone to stop General Lee in Pennsylvania, draft riots broke out in the City. Encouraged by Tammany Hall and its press, the mob attacked the buildings of the patriotic newspapers. They had already tried to storm the building of the *Tribune,* which had been saved only by the timely arrival of a strong detachment of police. Jerome did not grieve much over his competitor's troubles. He was equally unafraid of what might happen to his own paper. The *New York Times* lashed out sharply against the mob. To be on the safe side, however, the *Times* obtained two specimens of the recently invented Gatling gun. Under the personal command of the "consulting director," they were mounted inside the business offices. The entire staff of the *New York Times* was armed with rifles. After a few days a third Gatling was installed on the roof so that it could, if necessary, sweep the streets in any direction. This third gun, however, was kept trained, it was said, on the window of competitor Horace Greeley's office in the *Tribune* building near by. But this was probably a malicious invention. When the excitement died down ingloriously, Leonard Jerome celebrated victory by creating a fund for the benefit of the families of those killed and wounded in the riots.

No sooner was the mob-revolution broken than Jerome engaged himself in another ferocious contest. This time the fight was over the Hudson shares. A clique of bears sold them short. Jerome, who had himself scored his first successes on the short side, had by now reached the age and dignity in which a respectable financier despises the bears. Moreover, the bears had acted in a highly unpatriotic fashion in disrupting the market at a time the war demanded stable business conditions. Jerome had made sure that Hudson shares were fundamentally a good and sound proposition. He bought them up. As the struggle continued the bears ran out of money. Before the time for settlement came, Hudson stocks had risen from 112 to 180, while the bears, having lost their shirts, had to borrow money at the uncharitable, but then customary rate of 5% a day. They finally bought at 170 to 175, thus covering their short sales at 107 and 112. They were completely washed up. Leonard Jerome's profits were immense. Now he led the Street to the exclusion of everyone else. Even the Vanderbilts had not Jerome's power. King Leonard triumphed. But his triumph was short-lived.

The five years during which the Brown Brothers were to hold the Pacific Mail shares in trusteeship were up. The capital of the Line had in the meantime increased to twenty million dollars. Jerome had taken up over 50,000 shares at $200. Immediately the stock rose to 243. But a reduction in the next quarterly dividend, resolved by a majority of one voice in the board of directors against Jerome's eloquent pleading, brought the crushing avalanche. At this most unfavorable junction the Brown Brothers threw enormous quantities of Pacific Mail stock on to the market. There was no money to buy them. Within a few hours Jerome had lost eight hundred thousand dollars. In the end Pacific Mail was stabilized at 115. A crown rolled into the dust of the Street.

Feverishly, the unbreakable Jerome embarked upon other

speculations. But now reverses came as quickly as success had previously. His "magic" had gone from him. He proved vulnerable like other men. He was not ruined for good—in fact, two years before his death he made a last modest fortune with New Jersey stocks—but his wings were broken.

His family knew nothing of the tremendous fight he was carrying on. No one told them about it. Society was polite. Papa's personal bearing was unchanged. He still walked with the gait of an officer in mufti. With an iron will be controlled his strong features. His military mustache was never fiercer. Indeed, during the hectic years of his gigantic struggle he squeezed life to the last drop of what passed for pleasure. And he was obsessed by one idea: Jennie would soon be coming out. New York society must receive her as a princess.

At home, the only indication of the fatigue Leonard suffered behind his devil-may-care mask found expression in a certain slackening of the discipline the pater familias had thus far rigidly enforced. Now his daughters were, at least during the summers in Newport, "allowed to run wild, and be as grubby and happy as children ought to be," Lady Randolph recalled later.

This wider latitude given to half-grown girls was entirely in tune with the times. The period immediately following the war ushered in an unbridled era. Large classes of society had made enormous profits, and the post-war reconstruction further promised fabulous gains. People were tired of penny-pinching. Newport learned to forget the term "expenses." There were elaborate picnics and innumerable dinners, breakfasts and open-air balls. The merrymakers rarely missed the drive along Bellevue Avenue, prescribed for the afternoon hour from five to six.

Jennie became known as the "driving angel." Mrs. Ronalds, then the reigning beauty of Newport, presented her little friend with a small dog-cart, driven by two donkeys named "Willie" and "Wooshey." Now nothing else counted for Jennie but the daily drive along Bellevue Avenue, with the cart more often

than not filled with half a dozen laughing girls. As they tore
up and down, Willie and Wooshey were in frequent contact
with what Jennie termed "the business end of a tin-tack," a
stick she had christened the "Persuader." Leonard was amused
as he watched his daughter's antics. She would one day become
a perfect horsewoman. But the smart set who drove majestically
by were outraged by the holy terror. Their complaints increased
which only added to the fun. "These were delightful days,"
Lady Randolph recollected.

The fame of Newport spread over the fashionable world.
London society thrilled to the saga of the millionaire's beach.
But the general opinion in Belgravia was that it was certainly
no place for a man without a considerable fortune. Mr. Ward
McAllister was disappointed. He would have loved to see a few
younger sons of the peerage spending their summers in Newport. True, most of them were penniless. But they were good
fellows and excellent advertisements into the bargain. Their
presence would add a new glamour to Bellevue Avenue, and
furthermore it would serve to promote Anglo-American relations. Mr. McAllister was devoted to both. "Related nations
must understand one another," he argued. "It is the same with
nations as with the members of a family. Small differences of
opinion, I fear, are inevitable. But why magnify them? Why
shall two great and kindred peoples continue this unending
struggle over—venison? All right, we in America serve the
saddle, whereas in England they eat the haunch. But there is a
good reason for this difference of habit. In England dinners,
as a rule, are attended by more guests than in America. Hence
there is not enough meat on a saddle for an English dinner.
You see, there is an explanation for everything. Take, for instance, this nauseating feud about steaks. The U. S. A. eats
tenderloin steaks, England eats rumpsteak which, in this country, is only given to the servants. Are we a better people for that
reason? Let us be frank: The English used to kill their cattle
younger than Americans do; moreover, in the British Isles
cattle intended for beef has not been worked previously. I re-

gret to say," McAllister summed up, "but justice demands it, English rumpsteak is more tender than American."

Jennie Jerome listened attentively. She made careful mental notes of every winged word of wisdom. Somehow the thought flashed through her alert young mind that all the nonsense Uncle Ward was babbling would prove most precious to her.

"When you will play an important role in England..." McAllister addressed her suddenly.

What on earth made him think of such a thing? she asked herself.

"... you will also be free to disregard another American tradition. You will be able to serve our good old turkey not only on Thanksgiving Day but as a delicious summer treat.... I have long planned," he confessed confidentially, "to introduce turkey in summer. But Newport is not yet far enough advanced to accept this innovation." Mr. McAllister sighed. "Turkey except on Thanksgiving Day would still be considered a national sacrilege. This is a young country, yet deeply steeped in its short past. And we can be proud of it," he compromised, as always, with convention.

In her next season, her last in New York, as it turned out, the time had come for Jennie's debut. The great event was preceded by months of hectic preparation.

Jerome assumed a heavy duty. In spite of the fact that his business problems were becoming more and more complicated and that he had to devote every moment, except occasional evening hours spent in the company of La Patti, to his multiple enterprises, he embarked on the new venture, the last one in which he completely succeeded: introducing his daughter to society.

He gave theater party after theater party, followed by delightful little suppers, inviting to them most of the city's jeunesse dorée. And now Jennie, after a rigidly guarded childhood, had always to be surrounded by admirers. It became overworked and worried Leonard Jerome's new job to secure for his daughter a prominent place in every cotillion, and to see to it that she was never without a suitable dancing partner.

Still regarded as a portentous society leader, he discharged his task with ease. But in the end the business of smoothing his daughter's path took too much of his time. As ever a man of rapid decisions, he decided to give one party which would substitute for innumerable smaller entertainments. He would give New York a sensation: a banquet which should exceed in luxury and expense anything before seen in this country.

The setting for the feast was, of course, Delmonico's, then at the corner of Fifth Avenue and 14th Street. Leonard had Signor Charles Delmonico come, and told him: "The U. S. government has just refunded me $10,000 overpaid on duties." (Perhaps he knew that his credit was already the subject of some head-shaking, and so wanted to explain his largesse which otherwise might have aroused suspicion in Signor Delmonico's Italian brain.) "I am resolved to devote this whole sum to a banquet that will always be remembered. . . . I am aware it's a folly, a piece of unheard-of extravagance."

"We never expected anything from you, Signor Jerome, but greatness," Signor Delmonico made a profound reverence. If he could redress himself, in case of emergency, with the U. S. government, the credit was good enough. "But it will be difficult to spend ten thousand on a single banquet," he pondered.

This is how they spent it: The large ballroom at Delmonico's was taken up by a table for seventy-two guests, leaving only a narrow passageway for the waiters. Every inch of the long oval table was covered with flowers, but for a space in the center, left for an artificial lake, an ingenious device. It was a pond, thirty feet in length, and nearly the width of the table, enclosed by a delicate golden wire network, reaching from table to ceiling and making of the whole installation a tremendous cage. Four superb swans, brought from Prospect Park, floated on the pond, surrounded by high banks of flowers which prevented the birds from splashing the water on to the table. Around this enclosure, above the entire table, hung little golden cages with fine songsters which filled the room with their melody; the

RESIDENCE OF LEONARD JEROME

(This building, at Madison Avenue and 26th Street, New York City, was later the Jockey Club, and is now the Manhattan Club)

only dissonance being a fierce combat between the graceful, stately swans, which disturbed the guests for a time, but which caused much amusement. Around this table sat the most beautiful flowers of American womanhood, interspersed with the most eligible young men.

One place, at the right of the host, was left empty until the company had assembled. Their glasses were filled with the incomparable '48 Claret. But the guests had been discreetly asked not to lift their glasses until the party was "complete."

Exactly timing her appearance, Jennie entered. She wore a white lace dress without any jewels. Her black eyes and her dark hair contrasted strikingly with her white gown. Her eager young face with its slightly amused smile was so radiant that many of the guests felt the candles on the table were dimmed.

Jennie was launched into the sea of society. Immediately, she floated on her own power. Possessing the three requirements for social success—beauty, brains, and infinite tact—there was no need for her struggle for recognition. She let people seek her. Invitations to the house in Madison Square were more coveted than ever, now Jennie assisted her mother at receptions. Mr. McAllister's four hundred were delighted with the debutante. Soon on pleasant terms with everyone, she played no favorites. She thoroughly enjoyed the gaiety of her first season. There were innumerable dances from simple hops to magnificent balls. The most memorable of these was the fancy-dress ball given by the Schermerhorns in their palatial mansion at the corner of Great Jones Street and Lafayette Place. The guests were asked to appear in the fashions of Louis XV's court. Even the servants were dressed in period costumes. Bankers' wives and brokers' daughters blazed with jewels. Jennie wore a simple costume of pale blue silk. She was very "different," a word that from then on pursued her persistently.

She scored a popular triumph at the opening of Jerome Park, the race course her father established in Westchester county. This course, and the American Jockey Club, which he simultaneously organized to "improve the breeding of horses and to

elevate the public taste in the sport of the turf," made Leonard
Jerome known and preserved his name to posterity as the father
of the American turf in the north. The day of the opening of
Jerome Park brought the climax of his career as a leader of
society. It was, alas, the last great day in his life. But even on
this eventful day he yielded the laurels to his daughter.

Again Jennie sat in the place of honor at her father's right,
when his four-in-hand arrived for the first race at Jerome Park.

The grandstand, accommodating eight thousand spectators,
was jammed. All Murray Hill and Gramercy Park attended.
General Grant was an interested onlooker. The sale of liquor
was banned. The crowd behaved admirably.

Fascinated, Jennie watched the field. She could see the blue
and white of her father's racing colors coming nearer and
nearer. Jerome's famous horse "Kentucky," whose sire "Lexing-
ton" was of the best blood in England, came in first.

Leonard smiled. So the $40,000 he had spent on the animal
was not an entire loss. It was a good omen. Now everything
would turn for the better. The distinguished gathering cheered.
Jerome took his daughter by the hand, led her across the track,
and hoisted her on to the back of the winner. The grandstand
enjoyed it hugely. General Grant is reported to have thrown
his cap into the air like the youngest recruit.

The aftermath was less pleasant. Adelina Patti, infuriated
that Leonard had not hoisted her on to Kentucky, made a terrible scene when he visited her next day. Did he want to hide
her from the world? Was he ashamed of their friendship? Certainly not, he insisted. He was in no mood to quarrel with her.
The after-taste of the previous day's success should not be
spoiled by a struggle. Besides, he had struggled long enough.
To reconcile her, he promised to give an official party in her
honor.

The party, to which a group of theatrical folk was invited,
turned into a drunken affair. Signor Delmonico remembered it
as the "silver, gold, and diamond dinner." Years later he was still

describing the gold bracelets with the monogram of the newly founded Jerome Park that every lady had found under her serviette.

Toward dawn Leonard in his cups suggested to some of his lady friends a drive in the cool, early morning air. On the road to Westchester they stopped at a village inn, where Leonard slept deeply and soundly throughout the whole day and the following night. As he drove home, he was met at every street-corner by knowing grins. The story of his escapade, wildly exaggerated, had already made the rounds of New York.

When he reached Madison Square Clarissa's eyes were swollen with weeping. "Is there anything the matter?" he asked. "Nothing bad, I hope!"

"I don't suppose you would consider it so," Clarissa parried.

"Tell me what it is!" Jerome said anxiously.

"It's my health. . . . I feel that I should consult Dr. Sims."

Stunned, Leonard Jerome looked at his wife in amazement. Dr. Sims, once their family physician, was now practicing in Paris.

"Besides," she went on relentlessly, "the educational opportunities for the girls are so much better in Paris. There is nothing to equal the French finishing touch. What is more, expenses in Paris will be much less. You would not object, I suppose, if I, for one, helped you to save a little money."

She turned away.

Dr. Sims found his unforgotten patient in the best of health, when she sent for him to come to her Paris hotel.

CHAPTER III *Second Empire*

Like a stately vessel, with sails again swelling, Clarissa Jerome steered through the flood tide of her new life in Paris. She no longer stood in the shadow of her dazzling husband. Nor was she forced to listen quietly to the foreign songbird, La Patti. Now the belle of Palmyra was herself the beautiful foreigner. One of the first *belles Americaines* to settle down in Paris, her grave sweetness and her complete self-assurance enchanted the capital of fashion.

During the Second Empire Paris was indeed a women's city. Every beauty was welcome. Few questions were asked. No one inquired where Madame came from. Why, except for her harsh Castilian accent to which she determinedly clung no one could guess where Mademoiselle de Montijo herself had come from. Her deceased father, it was rumored, had been Spanish, perhaps even a Spanish count. Her clever, matchmaking mother was undoubtedly English. Nothing was certain about the daughter but the fact that she had been married in Notre Dame to become Empress Eugénie of France. Her age? No one was indiscreet enough to discuss a secret of state.

In this enchanting city of ageless women Clarissa Jerome enjoyed a second youth. No doubt, she fully deserved it. She was in the prime of life. Her beauty was ripening. The Grecian bend she had affected in New York was forgotten. Now she walked with the graceful dignity of a woman who is aware that she is

40

the center of constant attention, and who does not find this in the least embarrassing. Moreover, she belonged to the select few mothers whose charm is only increased when they appear in the company of their budding daughters.

During the first months in Paris Clarissa kept her eldest daughter, who was subsequently to become Mrs. Moreton Frewen, constantly at her side. The slight young girl, the only blonde in the family, with her gaily sparkling blue eyes set in a delicate oval face, made an effective contrast to her *maman*, a brunette with a figure of classic proportions.

Jennie, much to her regret, was still considered too young to take part in fashionable life. Paris, after all, was stressing dignity, overstressing it, indeed, under the rule of an upstart Emperor of a distinctly charlatanesque quality. The impromptu amusements, young people's cotillions, the innocent and noisy gaiety of cheerfully expanding New York would have been entirely out of place.

Mr. Washburn, the American Ambassador, was delighted to introduce his beautiful compatriot at court. Napoleon III liked American visitors, and assiduously tried to make them his friends. To his speculative spirit the mighty new country was a fairyland, where money was being produced by some strange alchemy. Perhaps he wanted to steal the formula, perhaps his sympathy was based on the restless and serious curiosity of his mind, much given to those scientific experiments and innovations in which America excelled. Under this regime Clarissa found success easy. She took up her residence on the Champs Elysées (already the pulsating heart of Paris) where the rents were still only a third of those on Fifth Avenue. With true Jerome speed she made her house one of the leading salons. Due to Mr. Washburn's amiable assistance, it became first a center of the diplomatic set, and soon a much coveted rendezvous of court society. Only poor Jennie felt that she was being relegated to a second childhood. She complained that only the faint echoes of the Tuileries fêtes reached her. "They were eagerly listened to by my curious and greedy ears," she reminisced.

Her life in Paris seemed definitely a decline from the early triumphs at home. Where was the day when she had been hoisted on to the winning "Kentucky"? Where was the night of the Louis-Quinze ball at the Schermerhorns? It all seemed so far away, only a memory, veiled in nostalgia.

But suddenly Paris became thrilling for her, too; it was more exciting than anything she had known before.

The Exhibition Universale, late in 1867 (the year of the Jerome ladies' debut in Paris), opened to Jennie the gates of the great world. Clarissa could not bear to leave the house on the Champs Elysées, and see Jennie pressing her dark face with the passionate black eyes against the window. The *belle Americaine* was at heart an American mother to whom her daughter was the most important thing in the world. With a faint shudder she felt that in Jennie the volcano, which she had always been forced to suppress in herself, slumbered. Then she smiled, and suggested lightly: "Do you want to come with me to the Exhibition? Mr. Washburn is giving a reception for American visitors."

For the first time Mrs. Jerome graced the American Ambassador's party with both her elder daughters. Subsequently they took part in all the festivities of the Exhibition. The Jerome ladies danced at the ball in honor of the Tsar of Russia. They sat at the table of honor at the gala for the German sovereigns, the assembled Kings of Prussia, Bavaria, Wuerttemberg. They had the privilege of exchanging a few pleasantries with King Leopold of Belgium, the old fox of Europe. They had a short conversation with an oversized gentleman, a man with the build and features of a giant, contrasting amazingly with his high-pitched voice. His name was Bismarck.

The memory of the Louis-Quinze ball at the Schermerhorns' no longer caused Jennie nostalgia. The merry-making bankers and brokers and their bejeweled ladies playing at being courtiers in elaborate uniforms and ball gowns carefully copied from old paintings were now replaced by the company of real crowned heads who, it is true, looked a good deal less royal. Uncle Ward McAllister would not have liked some of their table manners. Look at the way the old King of Prussia emptied whole mugs of wine in one gulp!

There was only one insurmountable obstacle on Jennie's way: the doors to Eugénie's receptions in the Tuileries were closed to her. Mrs. Jerome was a welcome guest. But the Empress firmly declined to have young girls in her entourage. She referred to some medieval court-order setting an age limit for admission to Her Majesty's presence. It came in handy to the woman *entre les deux ages*. Jennie felt deeply hurt by her exclusion. Yet she admired Eugénie, if only at a distance.

A short time before all France had hated their Spanish Empress for having driven her husband into the seduction and betrayal of Archduke Maximilian of Austria. The Mexican adventures seriously compromised Napoleon III, Maximilian's faithless sponsor. Actually Eugénie, as was generally known, had devised the plot. But her wit atoned for her political sins. Some of her quips became proverbial. At a *levée*, for example, the Empress sent to Princess Anna Murat, who had refused to marry the elderly Lord Granville, the following message: "Tell her, please, that after the first night it is all the same whether a man is handsome or ugly. After a week you won't even notice the difference." Such witticisms, spreading like wildfire through the capital, reconciled the Parisians with the beautiful perpetrator of the Mexican tragedy.

The crowds took their Empress again to their volatile hearts. Soon the pathways in the Bois de Boulogne were packed with cheering people most anxious to see Eugénie on her morning drive. The audience was largely feminine. Duchesses and *concierges* were alike eager to have a look at the most successful woman on earth. Perhaps a quick glance might divulge something of her secret.

An American girl, trotting on her pony through the Bois, beseeched her stern English governess: "Please let us stop until she passes. Perhaps she will notice us."

The Empress, however, as she drove past, stared straight ahead, creating around her a vacuum. She was ready to do her best for her occasionally loyal subjects. But a highly bred Spanish woman cannot easily forget all the mob hatred she had been exposed to. She was alone, and proud of her solitude. By coincidence her faraway glance fell upon a dark girl on a white pony. "*Vive l'Imperatrice!*" exclaimed the girl. Her peach-colored cheeks flushed. She blushed with shame at her impossibly conspicuous behavior.

But the Empress smiled. She lifted her white-gloved hand, and waved to the girl. Indeed, as her *aumont* proceeded, she turned around, a rare and entirely un-Imperial gesture, and her hand rose once more, like a fluttering bird.

When the Empress entered the *salon bleu* of her private apartment, the Spanish Order of the Golden Fleece across her left shoulder, and a high tiara of pearls and diamonds in her coiffure, she immediately recognized her young visitor. "It was good of your dear mother to bring you," she smiled. "She told me that you had seen me in the Bois."

This first meeting between Eugénie and Jennie did not take place at an official reception. It was at a *petit lundi*, a party for the Prince Imperial, who was generally called Loulou. These informal affairs in the late afternoon, sometimes lasting into the evening, were more sought after than the magnificent state balls, in the hurly-burly of which the individual guest was apt to be submerged.

Ladies, gentlemen, and young people stood at attention, ready to curtsy when Her Majesty passed. Only a little gentleman in his 'teens, stoutish, broad-nosed, with brown locks and curled lips somewhat too tightly pressed against each other, and with a questioning look in his earnest blue eyes, did not interrupt his game of *Bagatelle*. Loulou's mother seemed not to mind his rude behavior. Napoleon, otherwise indulgent and deferential toward his wife, could be very angry when she tried to apply rigid methods of education to his son. The father was helpless in his blind partiality for the boy. But in the Empress' place an elderly spinster whispered menacingly to Loulou: "Hadn't you better get up, Monseigneur?" Her whisper had a marked English accent. Miss Shaw, the Prince Imperial's governess, was a disciplinarian; she was not afraid of Napoleon's wrath. The little Monseigneur jumped up, his middle fingers pressed against the seam of the trousers of his white dress uniform. He exaggerated the obeisance. Toward his mother he was often sullen.

Eugénie had to be diplomatic, even with her only child. She overlooked his unsuitable behavior. Smilingly, she turned her full attention to Jennie, the newcomer. She stretched out her beautiful right hand with its long slim fingers. It was a rare honor.

Jennie kissed the tips of the Imperial fingers. In her embarrassment she asked the childish question: "Isn't that tiara frightfully heavy?"

"Frightfully!" Eugénie admitted. She looked at her Imperial tiara in the mirror. "Frightfully heavy!" she repeated.

Jennie sensed an inexplicable tension. She attributed it to her *gaffe!* "Heavens!" she exclaimed. "One does not ask a crowned head questions! Forgive me, Your Majesty!"

Loulou giggled.

"I think I shall forgive you!" Eugénie said playfully. She was amused by Jennie's embarrassment. She felt a little touched by the *ingénue's* innocence.

Once more she stretched out her hand. She drew the young girl nearer to her. But as Jennie advanced a step or two, her black eyes fixed on the beautiful Empress, admiring yet gauging her at the same time, both ready and reluctant to offer her own small hand, Eugénie, a wise woman, sensed: This is no ingénue. This is a child without childhood. She is as ageless as I. "Shall we be friends?" she asked. Resolutely, Jennie stretched out her brown hand. Their clasp was at once tender and firm.

The friendship between the Empress and the young girl from Brooklyn lasted until Eugénie's death half a century later, when she was ninety-four.

"Have you a governess, too?" Loulou entered the conversation. He was entirely oblivious of court ceremonial.

"She left me yesterday," Jennie regretted. "My mother said the first time I was received in the Tuileries"—deep curtsy before the Empress—"I could consider myself grown up."

"Miss Shaw will leave me too, very soon," Loulou replied hopefully. Then he straightened himself, stood at attention, like a real soldier, and mimicked with the hint of a smile on his curly lips, "The Prince Imperial needs military guidance, papa insists. *Le brave général Frossard assuméra mon éducation.*" He dropped into French. "The general has already presented himself to me. 'Now, Monseigneur,' he said, 'you will have to be obedient and to work hard at your lessons.' Funny words, aren't they?" Loulou chuckled. "'That is not so sure,' I answered. *Maman* always says No to whatever I want. But *papa* always says Yes, and besides I have my own will. That makes two to one. Of course, I must inspect the army if I shall once be Emperor of France. But why learn lessons? A soldier must learn shooting! ... However," he added, becoming a bit more modest, "if I make good in my lessons, I am getting some money for the poor. And one can't let the poor go without money, can one? Moreover, they say the honor of my uniform is affected if I refuse studying..."

When military questions were at stake, Loulou could only speak French. Here his boyish heart was involved. He was not really interested in anything but in soldiers, tin ones or real ones, in military bands, flags and drums. He had cherished his uniforms, already when he was so small that the tarboosh he wore was almost bigger than himself. He was a real soldier by nature. After watching a puppet play, glorifying his father's deeds in the Austrian war, he summed up his impressions: "But this show was not at all amusing." Conversely, he was deeply impressed when, one day, an immensely tall grenadier mounted

guard in front of his door. This was the real thing. "You must
have eaten a great quantity of soup," he said admiringly.

Loulou made his own strict rules of conduct. He had been
brought up to speak both English and French. He used English
with Anglo-Saxon guests, but never, when French people were
present. Yet when he met Jennie, he broke this rule. To make
things easier for her, he chatted in English an hour or so, until
his governess, Miss Shaw, interrupted him. "*Monseigneur, vôtre
chapeau!*" This was the signal to retire. With military precision
the boy obeyed. He whispered to Jennie in a hurry "Next Monday, Mademoiselle, is Monday again. *Petit lundi....* I mean."
And he rushed out of the room.

Now every Monday was *petit lundi*. Jennie became, in a way,
the second child in the house, in this immense, uncomfortable,
glorious and historic building, the Tuileries. It puzzled her that
in the midst of all this splendor there was no bathroom and that
there was a distinct smell of drains.

Assiduously, Loulou guided her through the old castle, introducing her to the ghosts who had haunted it since the days of
its builder, Catherine de Medici. To prove his perfect familiarity with ghosts, the young soldier challenged the apparitions
to games of hide and seek. He was a high-strung boy, this son
of a brilliant make-shift Emperor and the obscure Spanish
woman sharing the Most Christian Throne of France. He had
to shout because he could not express himself. Only once did
he try. He was confined to bed with measles, acquired from a
dancing partner at a children's festival in Compiègne, the Imperial summer residence. From his sick-bed he addressed a
letter to Mademoiselle Jeannette Jerome. The letter was pen-
ciled, written by an awkward hand, but in perfectly correct
English: "My dear Mademoiselle: Will you, please, forgive my
negligence in the last days? I am suffering from a slight indis-
position, I got the measles from a young lady with whom I unfortunately danced a mazurka. I should really not dance with
any other girl." No signature was attached.

The Prince Imperial recovered within a few weeks. His
parents celebrated the event with a banquet. "Has Mrs. Jerome
been invited?" the Prince Imperial inquired. "With . . . her
daughters? . . ."

"They will be invited . . . immediately," the Emperor promised.

To express the high good humor and the anxiety with which
Loulou looked forward to the banquet, he thrashed his best
friend, little Conneau, the son of the Emperor's personal physician. By way of reconciliation the Prince Imperial presented
his comrade with a gold dagger. But when the evening came he
refused to change into dress uniform. Instead the boy threw
himself on to his bed. Not even *le brave général Frossard* could
extract Loulou from behind the barricade of quilts and pillows.
He did not want to see any girls, the Prince Imperial shouted.

For Jennie it was a memorable evening. She had now outgrown the *petit lundi's* and was officially admitted to the Imperial Court. Besides, she wore her first evening gown with a
train. This unaccustomed addition had embarrassed her a little
as she mounted the grand staircase. The guests did not form a
procession, as was the custom at other courts. They elbowed
their way to the *salle de réception,* where they were supposed
to gather in a semi-circle. They did not, however, observe the
prescribed geometrical form. They hastened back and forth,
forming small groups, whispering furtively, and laughing much
too innocently.

"These French cannot possibly keep in line! They simply
cannot!" Count Hatzfeld, then a dashing young attaché at the
Prussian legation in Paris, approached the ladies Jerome with
this Prussian pleasantry. He was a faithful visitor at their salon,
never presenting himself without a too large bunch of roses.
"*Bei uns* . . . We line up in serried ranks when we are commanded to court functions," he addressed Jennie, and took the
liberty of expressing his delight in seeing Mademoiselle for the
first time at an official reception.

CLARA JEROME   JENNIE JEROME

Jennie nodded sweetly, and decided henceforth to call Count Hatzfeld "Monsieur *Bei Uns.*" The nickname survived throughout the decades. Its origin should not be forgotten.

The conversation stopped as the doors were flung open. "*Sa Majesté, l'Empereur!*" was announced. Napoleon III walked slowly down the stairs. His carefully staged entrance was the only moment where one saw His Majesty without the eternal cigarette between his lips. He had first taken up this truly French habit for reasons of democratic appeal. Now he was so consumed by chain smoking, his last passion, that his lips ached, he sometimes complained, if he could not burn them a little with the last puff of a *ciggi.* In spite of the constant pain caused by his progressive disease, he held himself erect. His private conversation was a mixture of affected bonhomie and genuine kindliness. He looked like a great actor, impersonating the Emperor of France.

A few minutes after his entry the court-marshal announced: "*Sa Majesté, l'Imperatrice!*" Silence fell upon the whispering groups. A grave question lay unspoken on everyone's lips. How would Eugénie be dressed? On this particular evening, Jennie recollected, Her Majesty, a resplendent figure, appeared in a green velvet gown, with a crown of emeralds and diamonds, spiked with pearls, on her "small and beautifully shaped head." Napoleon and Eugénie passed slowly along the circle of curtsying and deeply bowing guests, and then proceeded to the dining room.

The dinner was consumed at top speed. After precisely three-quarters of an hour the Emperor rose, and everyone had to follow him into the ball room, where their Majesties held *cercle.* Napoleon III preferred to address the savants, some of whom were his frequent guests. On this evening he enjoyed animated conversation with Pasteur, Sainte-Beuve and Theophile Gautier. At ten o'clock he retired. The lamps in the Emperor's study burned on until dawn. In these last years of his rule, crouched over a desk littered with maps, plans, memoirs and documents, he dreamed the dream of the French Empire, the supreme power on the Continent. But the stone in his bladder drove him crazy with pain, and so he made a mess of his dreams.

Whereas Napoleon was as reticent in society as was possible without impairing his scrupulous politeness, Eugénie was loquacious and talkative. His amiable and unpretentious attitude in private contrasted with her hot-tempered often whimsical impulsiveness. This outwardly incongruous antithesis held them together in an iron grip. They were so directly opposed to one another that they could not do without each other. After almost twenty years of marital struggle, they had become inseparable. Where their tastes and necessities clashed, they found compromises. If he had to transact business until dawn, she was in the habit of keeping some of her friends with her until the small hours.

"It is impossible to get the Emperor to go to bed," she smiled to Mrs. Jerome. "Won't you stay with me a little longer? For an informal chat."

Clarissa understood very well that the Empress had taken a fancy to her daughter Jennie. She herself was only asked to remain as chaperon, she realized. It did not hurt a bit. She was proud that Jennie's time was beginning.

The Empress led the way to her private apartments on the first floor. To be admitted there was a great distinction for her American friends. Jennie's excitement mounted. At the same time she had a curious feeling of calm satisfaction. Eugénie led her guests by a small private staircase to her personal quarters. She guided them through the ten exquisitely furnished rooms. On the walls hung portraits of her most intimate women friends. "The Duchesse de Cadore. . . ." she explained. "The Duchesse de Persignan. . . . La Princesse Malakoff. . . . Madame du Morny. . . . I need not introduce La Princesse Anna Murat. . . . And you do know my Comtesse Anna Walewska. . . ."

"Beautiful!" said Clarissa to each portrait.

Jennie devoured every single picture. Would she be a Princess Murat one day? Or a Madame de Morny? Or a Duchess?

Tea was served in Eugénie's mauve salon. A plebeian looking

small, dark, bony, elderly maid, obviously a peasant woman, put down each cup most unceremoniously on the jewel-studded little tea table. Everything about this woman—with the exception of her white cotton gloves—was dirty. Her voice was repulsive. She spoke a vulgar Castilian, a coarse exaggeration of Her Majesty's own accent.

"You may go to bed now, Pepita," the Empress said with a touch of timidity.

The answer was a flood of Spanish noises. A little embarrassed, Eugénie translated for Mrs. Jerome's benefit: "Pepita says she does not go to bed before having tucked me up. Why should she? she says. Her husband has been snoring for hours."

"Her husband. . . ?" Clarissa answered, to say something.

"Yes, her husband," the Empress replied indulgently. "He was a famous bullfighter in his day. In Barcelona. Then he married my Pepita. Thus he became a colonel in the French army. Now he wants to be a general. Since the Emperor refuses this promotion . . . for the moment, anyway . . . the dissatisfied husband is taking his revenge by snoring. He knows that my good old Pepita has some influence with me. But he does not know how little influence I have with the Emperor." Eugénie smiled. At that time of night she had to keep on talking, no matter about what, as long as she could pour out a hundred words a minute.

"So you are the Empress' treasurer!" Jennie watched the uncouth figure closely. Everyone in Paris knew Pepita by this nickname. She had earned it by the adroitness with which she extracted astronomic bribes and tips.

Ugly old Pepita did not bat an eyelash under Jennie's scrutiny. She herself appraised her mistress' young guest with unabashed curiosity. Then she burst out once more. It was again a rush of coarse sounding words. Again the Empress translated: "Pepita says that you are beautiful, very beautiful, Jennie, and the people will believe that you are still much more beautiful than you really are, because you have a beautiful soul, too, and an exquisitely beautiful brain. You will be a great Queen if you don't bother about the crown. The crown is only an empty symbol, my gracious chambermaid believes. But you shall never marry a *torero*. They die so soon, and if they do not die, they go crazy, Pepita says!"

The Empress' treasurer left the room. Probably she would waylay the ladies downstairs, as they were leaving. A quarter of an hour later, however, when the Jeromes departed, Pepita did not show herself.

No sooner was the peasant woman gone than Eugénie turned to Jennie: "Would you like to see my bedroom?"

Jennie expected Cleopatra's glittering workshop. What she actually saw was an enormous, almost empty white-painted room. A simple white bed stood against the wall. Above it hung a colossal oil painting of the Prince Imperial. Jennie suddenly realized that Loulou had not attended the banquet. She had not missed him.

The Empress put her fingers to her lips. "Loulou sleeps in the next room." She breathed the words. It was less than a whisper.

"Why don't you leave me in peace? Don't you see that I am asleep?" a voice, just breaking, shouted through the closed door.

"Be quiet, Loulou!" his mother answered. She tried to sound determined, but she could not. Loulou with his shocking manners and his torn and tortured heart must have been anxiously listening all the time. Perhaps he could hear Jennie speaking.

The Empress accompanied her guest as far as the staircase. Apologetically she said, as Jennie curtsied deeply: "He is confused. You are his first love. He does not know what it is all about. Poor boy!"

Jennie curtsied a second time and a third. Then she repeated politely: "Poor boy!"

She did not know what it was all about, either. Love? Certainly that was the affection one felt for father, the deep, if a little superior tenderness for her mother, the pleasure she had in her sisters' company. Love meant fidelity to the family. Throughout these years in Paris, Jennie knew no more of love than that.

Her dark, passionate looks were deceiving. Her only passion was to become one of those celebrated beauties with whom the Empress chose to surround herself, and whose portraits adorned the walls of Eugénie's boudoir. Subsequently, Jennie made friends with every single one of them. As if they were descending from their frames, the Duchesse de Cadore and Madame de Morny, Princess Malakoff and Anna Walewska stretched out their arms to take the enchanting American new-comer to their hearts.

She found a great friend in *la belle Mélanie,* the Countess de Pourtalès, of whom no one in Paris could speak without adding: *"Elle est étonnante."* In this woman "whose bewitching face and fascinating manner won all hearts," Jennie afterwards re-called, she encountered, perhaps, her last formative influence. *La belle Mélanie* was a leading lady in politics. The society of the Second Empire was torn by the conflict between Legiti-mists, the die-hards faithful to the House of Bourbon, and Bona-partists, the adherents to the new dynasty, who preferred to call themselves Imperialists. Countess Pourtalès achieved the miracle of becoming the social link between both camps. Her husband, being of Swiss origin and not too deeply concerned with the rivalries between French traditionalists, had come to Paris as a follower of the Lilac banner. But under his wife's in-fluence he did not mind accepting Napoleon's cause into the bargain. Their friends were in both camps. "From the charm of Mélanie's beauty and personality," Jennie recalled, "and due to the vivacity of her conversation, one could easily understand the sway she held over the whole society." Mélanie reigned su-preme over the fashionable set for so many years that envious rivals finally christened her *"la veille garde."* Nevertheless, as a grandmother she was still charming and much beloved. Her example taught Jennie how little years matter.

Also there was the amazing Princess Mathilde, "that woman" to Eugénie, the second lady of Paris to the rest of the world. Jennie called her "undoubtedly the most brilliant and intelli-gent woman of the Second Empire." She was the cousin of

Napoleon, and had done the honors for him in the Elysée, in 1848, when he was President of the Republic. Her mother was a Princess of Wuerttemberg, the King of Italy a relative. Her marriage to Count Anatol Demidoff, Prince of San Donato, had ended in a world scandal. After suffering countless indignities and cruelties on his part, she separated from him, supported by her uncle, Tsar Nicholas I, who forced his subject, Count Demidoff, to give her a large income, amounting, it was said, in the course of sixty years to twelve million francs.

Hence Princess Mathilde could easily maintain her own private court in her palace in the Rue de Courçelles, to which the *collet-monté* society and the entire Faubourg (St. Germain) flocked in greater numbers and with more avidity than to the Tuileries itself. The reason was that Princess Mathilde's palatial salon was much less rigidly ruled than the court was of necessity. Her house was the only one that upheld the traditions of the great eighteenth-century salons, in which wit and art mingled with royalty and power. The reputation of her salon was world-wide. Ranking foreigners were generously admitted. Some young and pretty Americans in Paris, with Jennie as their leader, met in the Rue de Courçelles such men as Dumas, Sardou, and Theophile Gautier.

Eugénie, tolerating no other deity, hated the competition. But at the pinnacle of her fame and glory, she had, from a distance, to watch the Princess Mathilde steal her thunder. In November 1869, the Empress ventured upon her journey to Egypt to open the Suez Canal. She was received as the fairy-queen, the new Cleopatra. The opera *Aida* which Verdi had composed in Her Majesty's honor, had its première in Cairo. The event had originally been planned for a Sunday. But the performance had to be put off until the following day since the Most Catholic Empress was a rigid sabbatarian.

On this same Monday, however, when Eugénie heard from all sides that *Aida* was but a shadowy imitation of her own splendor, on probably the happiest day of her life, in Paris the *petit lundi's* were resumed, but in the Rue de Courçelles, no longer in the Tuileries. Mathilde, recalling previous days in which she acted as Napoleon's hostess, found that one could not let Loulou mope along without a little social pleasure. Moreover, the Empress' nieces, Mesdemoiselles d'Albe, had implored Princess Mélanie to resume the dear old custom.

Jennie met Loulou again. He bowed very politely, but only at a distance. His personal guard of honor, now always in his wake, clicked heels in almost Prussian fashion. The young man was no longer Loulou. From head to toe he was the Prince Imperial. He only danced with his cousins, the Demoiselles d'Albe. When during the cotillion, Jennie happened—by an unfortunate coincidence, of course—to lose her left shoe, he picked it up and returned it to her with a bow. He did not speak. But he did not dance again that evening. He retired much earlier than had been expected. He excused himself. But he had to train with his regiment on the Champs de Mars early in the next morning.

The two met again at what was fated to be the last of the Emperor's famous parties (or "*séries*" as they were called) at Compiègne. On account of the Emperor's ever worsening state of health, and due to his increasing political worries, the party was on a much smaller scale than usual. However, among those invited were the ladies Jerome, now intimates of the court. The fête extended over three days. The first day was spent in hunting, shooting and dancing. There was a *grande chasse*.

On the second day an expedition was organized to see the Château de Pierrefonds, Napoleon's favorite castle. M. Viollet-le-Duc, the celebrated architect, showed the party around. Dinner was served in the ancient armory of the castle. The Emperor presented each lady with a souvenir in the form of a small dagger. In spite of the terrible strain, both physical and mental, he tried to seem in high spirits. Indeed, he achieved a semblance of his imperturbable bonhomie. The evening ended with a concert. Princess Metternich, the wife of the Austrian ambassador, sang risqué Viennese music-hall songs; no one, she was confident, would understand the words. The Prince Imperial followed her on the improvised stage. His berçeuses and bergeries disclosed a pleasant and cultivated voice. Jennie listened attentively.

But on the third day the guests were exhorted to be discreet in their amusements, and not to disturb His Majesty. A Cabinet Council was taking place in Napoleon's private apartments. The Prince Imperial participated for the first time. He was entitled to this privilege. Now, it was common opinion, he would soon undergo his baptism of fire. After the council, the general farewells ensued. Napoleon, very exhausted, but holding himself erect, and even managing to smile, had still a last surprise for his guests. There was a grand lottery in which all the tickets won prizes. The Emperor stood upright near two great urns from which the prizes were drawn, and as each guest received one, he wished him *bonne chance.* Shrewdly Jennie observed that the numbers could not be blind. A little juggling must have been going on, since her mother and Mr. Washburn drew valuable pieces of Sèvres china, whereas the presents for the younger people were less costly. She herself won an inkstand shaped like a handkerchief, filled with gold *napoléons.* Handing her the prize, the Emperor remarked: *"J'éspère, Mademoiselle, vouz n'oubliez pas les Napoléons!"*

A few days later the dashing Count Hatzfeld visited, as usual, Mrs. Jerome's Sunday reception. "I never saw His Majesty in better spirits than he was at Compiègne," he snarled. "And God knows where he will be next year at this time!" he added, chuckling venomously.

Jennie jumped up from her chair. She felt like shouting something frightful to the insolent Prussian face. But all she said was: "Let me get you another cup of tea." She smiled at the clean-shaven, monocled monster. What a pity there was not a single drop of poison in the house!

CHAPTER IV *Escape from Paris*

She hated *ces sales Prussiens* as much as did any-one in Paris; she admitted it candidly in her memoirs. But the alert young girl did not share the blind cocksureness that pre-vailed among the French during the crucial days when a fatal conflict seemed inevitable. Her intuition was not blunted by her strong sympathies. Her ambitions aimed high, her predi-lections were definite, but she was not swept away by her emotions. She was enchanted with brilliant Paris. Yet she re-alized that a dark future was impending, when Lucien Paradol, the well-known journalist and writer—incidentally the father of her favorite companion—made the casual remark: "Since France and Prussia are running on the same lines, collision is inevit-able."

This observation was made one Sunday afternoon in the salon of Mrs. Jerome. Lord Albemarle, an English friend, who had just been shooting in Norfolk, joined the conversation: "I met the Prussian General Blumenthal at the shoot," he related. "I told him I would like to see the Prussian maneuvers. 'It is not necessary to come to Prussia for that purpose,' he grinned. 'We will stage a review for you on the Champs de Mars.'"

Jennie listened without showing her burning interest. She regretted that Eugénie was not yet back from Egypt. This bit of gossip might have interested her. In fact, the Empress was already on her way back. She was flushed with her triumph in

Cairo, and outraged at what became known as the Hohenzollern incident. Prince Leopold of Hohenzollern (a tool of Bismarck, Jennie termed him accurately) was presented as a candidate for the throne of Spain. The Paris press called this claim *une sanglante injure pour l'Empereur Napoléon.* In fact it was a well calculated injury to Empress Eugénie. Should her adored Spain become a Prussian vassal? Eugénie was furious. She had always remained a Spanish lady of high degree, retaining Spanish interests above French ones. She had never quite understood the duty of reticence, imposed upon her as the very active co-ruler of France. Now she embarked upon her second, her fatal adventure.

After years of steering an enforced middle course Eugénie, surrounded by flatterers, fawned upon as a political genius resembling Catherine of Medici, dominant at the court councils, had become a violent woman. She reacted to the Prussian provocation in a typically feminine fashion. She hastened to Biarritz to attend a bullfight (dressed in a Spanish mantilla with pomegranate flowers in her hair), where she comported herself in an entirely Spanish manner. She observed the horrid scenes with visible relish and uttered loud battle cries in Spanish, encouraging both the *torero* and the resistance against Prussian insolence.

France, smarting under Bismarck's insult, again idolized the bellicose Empress for a few months. The whole country demanded war. Amazingly, Jennie, the young observer, was one of the few people who did not lose her head in these days of mass hysteria. She deplored the "rashness and violence" of the Duc de Gramont, the Minister for Foreign Affairs, and what she called the ineptitude and blunders of M. Emile Ollivier, the new liberal Premier who had just introduced some tolerant and necessary domestic reforms, but who "took upon himself and his colleagues the responsibility for the war *d'un coeur léger.*" Jennie could not forgive him this unfortunate sentence. Already in her early youth she had an uncanny instinct for the art, and the fatal importance, of the spoken word.

Napoleon did his best to avert the conflict, but his ever worsening disease sapped his powers of resistance. He was on the eve of a serious operation. Moreover, Herr von Bismarck was hell bent on bloodshed. He had already made his private dispositions on the stock exchange, faithfully carried out by Herr von Bleichroeder, the Jewish banker who wielded full power of attorney in the Iron Chancellor's complicated business affairs. There was no more room for retreat on either side. On the nineteenth of July, 1870, the Franco-Prussian War was declared.

Deeply perturbed, Jennie found herself in a city on fire with war hysteria. The citizens of Paris, as well as the army, had not the slightest doubt that the war would be but one long, straight march to Berlin. The only man who dared to dissent was General Comte de Tascher. Jennie had been a frequent guest at the house of his sister-in-law, Princess Tascher, whose weekly receptions were famous for their music, with gifted amateurs and artists playing and singing. The outbreak of the war was no reason to abandon these informal and amusing evenings. One of them, however, was disturbed by the General's prophecy: "Everything depends on the first encounter. If our men are then victorious, the campaign will be successful to the last. But the French cannot stand defeat. Once they are disheartened, nothing more can be done with them."

Whatever the outlook, the ladies Jerome decided to stick it out in Paris. It was folly. In New York Leonard burned the new Trans-Atlantic cable to urge his wife and children to escape to England. He had to be content with the answer that an injury to Clarissa's ankle prevented her from traveling. Her ankle was, indeed, badly inflamed. Dr. Sims prescribed absolute quiet and rest in bed. To prescribe absolute quiet to a member of the Jerome tribe was, of course, ridiculous. Bravely, Clarissa limped with her daughters along the teeming streets. In the first month of the war, the people's outbursts were still patriotic and monarchistic. "Exciting incidents crowded on us," Jennie later recalled. One day she saw Capoul, the Caruso of his period, and Marie Sass, the famous soprano, being recognized in an omnibus. The masses stopped the bus. Capoul and La Sass knew what was expected of them. They climbed on top of the vehicle, and began the first bars of the Marseillaise. In a moment the singing crowd drowned out their voices.

Society still went to the Opera, but no longer in evening dress. It was certain that the singers would be constantly interrupted by the gallery and made to chant patriotic songs. Frequently trouble ensued; stalls and boxes were quickly vacated, leaving the Opera to the excited masses who were shouting for an anti-Prussian demonstration. The streets were black with people. Carriages could not move. The Jerome ladies learned to get about on shank's mare. Clarissa limped painfully. "We found the greatest difficulties in getting home," Jennie remembered, "owing to the streets being filled with huge crowds marching to the cry of *'Des chassepots, donnez-nous des chassepots!'* " And she commented: "Poor fellows, they soon had them, and all the fighting they wanted!"

July and August 1870 were "hot months." This was not New York City during the Civil War, a comparatively quiet sector of the hinterland, only occasionally disturbed by hunger riots and mob outbursts which the police could control. Although much smaller in space than New York, Paris in 1870 had more than double the population of New York (2,000,000 inhabitants against somewhat over 800,000). The frightened and bewildered people literally trod on one another's toes. The continuous flow of bad news from the front—which Jennie followed by constantly changing the positions of the flags on her map—strained the nerves of the civil population to the utmost. Eugénie assumed the regency, while the Emperor left for Metz to join his army. He was told that 380,000 excellently prepared soldiers were awaiting him. Instead he was received by a poorly equipped soldiery of only 220,000.

This, at least, was the report the Duc de Persigny conveyed to the Jerome ladies. The duke was one of the most conspicuous characters of the extraordinary Second Empire. Born to the

humble name of Victor Fialin, he had been the oldest bosom
friend of Prince Louis Napoleon. He had shared the latter's
meteoric career, and had even been imprisoned for his cause.
But he reaped the benefits of his devotion. When Louis Napoleon became Emperor, his faithful friend was created a duke,
made ambassador in London, and finally became a cabinet
minister. Yet to Jennie he remained nothing but a "dapper
little man with a piercing eye and a pleasant manner."

Like the few others among their French friends who had not
gone to the front, Persigny frequently sought refuge and relaxation in the hospitable American house on the Champs
Elysées. Once he conveyed regards from the Prince Imperial,
who had just gone through his baptism of fire in the skirmish of
Saarbruecken. More often he brought less agreeable news. A
few days before it was published in the press, Jennie read the
copy of a telegram in which Eugénie bluntly informed Napoleon that Paris and its garrison were losing all confidence.
Eugénie demanded that the Emperor dismiss Maréchal Le-
boeuf from the supreme command, himself resign from active
direction of the war, and make Maréchal Bazaine Generalis-
simo. Jennie recognized that it would be a fatal appointment for
Bazaine. "Are they looking for a scape-goat?" she asked. The
Duc de Persigny was stunned. "You are the most amazing girl
I ever met!" he exclaimed.

On one or two occasions, great victories were bruited about.
The gloomy, doomed city of Paris rapidly seized on them with
elation. Flags flew from every window, everyone rejoiced, and
passersby on the street embraced one another. But the jubila-
tion lasted only a few hours. The streets emptied rapidly and
the blinds were drawn when the glorious victories proved to be
the defeats of Weissemburg, Woerth, or Gravelotte. A sinister
murmur rose through Paris: *"Nous sommes trahi!"*

On August 16th, MacMahon persuaded the Emperor to concentrate the whole army upon Paris, in order to defend the
capital to the last. But an imperative telegram from Eugénie
insisted that neither the cabinet nor the populace would toler-

ate such a retirement. She urged her husband to join his deci-
mated forces with Bazaine's troops. Napoleon, now a pale and
haggard figure, doubled up with pain, crouched in the corner
of his carriage, no longer asserting authority, ignored by his
generals and officers, jeered at by his own men, a shade of what
had once been an Emperor, submitted to his still flamboyant
wife's pressure. He embarked on the disastrous road to Sedan.

On the battlefield, in the evening after the encounter, he
wrote his letter of surrender to Wilhelm I. To Eugénie he telegraphed: "The army of Châlons has surrendered. I am a prisoner. Napoleon."

Paris proclaimed the republic. This was the moment for the
last foreigners to hasten their departure. Persigny proved his
friendship for the Jeromes in calling upon them immediately
after his last audience with Eugénie at St. Cloud, where the
Empress Regent had retired. The usually imperturbable Duke
burst into tears: *"Tout est perdu,"* he stammered. *"Les Prussiens sont a nos portes!"*

Another visitor was announced. Mr. Malet, secretary of the
British Embassy, had come to pay his respects and to relate
his latest experience. He had been delegated to German
headquarters to negotiate the evacuation of the English from
Paris.

At Versailles, the German headquarters, Bismarck had received him with wine and cigars. The Chancellor obviously
relished the trouble his Prussians were making in occupied
France. Certainly, he obliged, if the English wanted to get
away from Paris, he did not wish to make difficulties, although neither he—"I am not really all powerful, you understand, I am simply the obedient servant of my king, whatever
the world says"—nor anyone else could be of much help. But
every passport signed and sealed by His Excellency, the ambassador of Her Majesty, the Queen, would be honored.

After the fourth glass of wine the Iron Chancellor unbosomed himself. He offered his personal advice to Malet.
"Your people will be lucky if they get away," he said con-

fidentially. "The French will hate us with an undying hate, and we must take care to render this hate powerless. Paris will have to surrender, or the inhabitants will be cut off from the rest of the world, and left to stew in their own juice." He smiled while he spoke. But his high-pitched voice rose immediately as he continued: "If the Parisians continue to hold out, their city will be bombarded and, if necessary, burned down." Bismarck seemed displeased that no riots had broken out in Paris. He considered the declaration of the Republic and its acceptance by the whole of France as "definitely unpleasant." Why, he argued, if the French Republican government proved to be moderate and virtuous, it might become a danger to the monarchical principle in Germany. "What the King and I fear most," the Iron Chancellor had said, "is the influence of a French Republic upon Germans. We are well aware what a nefarious influence the Republic in America had upon our people. If the French should now fight us with republican propaganda, they would do us more damage than by their arms. . . ."

"And so," Mr. Malet ended his report, "I have the honor of conveying to you, ladies, the Chancellor's advice. Go while the going is good."

"We will not go!" Jennie answered briskly. She was not a quitter. She belonged in Paris. No home-grown son or daughter can be as fiery a patriot as the American expatriate is to his adopted land. This by no means implies desertion of one's own country. Throughout her life Jennie dreamed the American dream. But when Paris was in danger, it was there she wanted to be. The three hundred thousand Prussian soldiers with their Bavarian, Wuerttemberg, and Rhenanian vassals, looting the country and closing in on Paris, did not frighten her at all.

Moreover, Jennie rejected the idea of escape on account of her mother's health. "You could not leave, mamma," she argued persuasively. "Why, with this pain in your ankle. . . . You cannot even walk!"

"I could be carried," Clarissa replied, no less resolute. "And we do not have to leave the country entirely," she added. "There must be a sort of Newport in France, too." She must get Jennie away from the danger of a possible encounter with the Prussians, the anxious mother thought. Jennie would get into trouble. She could never control her temper, if such a meeting took place.

"Deauville!" Mr. Malet suggested.

"And how are we to get there?" Jennie persisted. "We are not British subjects. Your ambassador, Mr. Malet, could not do a thing for us. And whether Mr. Washburn can be helpful . . ." She indicated a slight doubt in the efficiency of the U. S. diplomacy. It was entirely unfounded doubt. Mr. Washburn sat out the whole long and terrible siege of Paris that ensued, a pillar of help to his countrymen and friends, and became a classic American witness of German atrocities.

"Let me take care of that!" Malet replied.

The British Embassy was jammed with English people who wanted to get out of Paris. The ambassador would have needed a dozen hands to sign and seal all the requested passports. But Mr. Malet had his way with the chief.

Still the question of departure seemed insoluble. In the hour of despair the confusion in Paris was worse than ever. *"Qui sait?"* was the only answer to the question whether and when a train would go to Rouen. The French did not refuse to do their duty. The drivers of the post-coaches sat on the boxes of their vehicles although there were no horses to pull them. The horses had been requisitioned for the army. But the drivers were *au service*.

Finally in the courtyard of the Grand Hotel a traveling carriage with a mountain of provisions and luggage was drawn up. Jennie and Mr. Malet helped Clarissa into the carriage. The sisters followed. Jennie, the driving spirit, was in charge of the passports. Here they were, duly signed and sealed and equipped with British visas through the courtesy of the British ambassador.

They were in a hurry to catch the train to Rouen, the last

one to leave the occupied zone. To avoid difficulties on the way, their car was protected by the crossed English and American flags. To Jennie this was still a mere matter of expedience, not yet the symbol of her life's endeavor.

Deauville proved very different from Newport. The high tide of war did not flood the fashionable resort, but every sort of flotsam drifted by. Deauville was crowded with refugees from what had been the Imperial Court. They did not dare to show themselves in daylight. One could not be sure how the new republican authorities would feel about the dispossessed courtiers. Moreover, even unoccupied France was teeming with Herr von Bismarck's bloodhounds.

The Jeromes established themselves in the Palace Hotel. They found their suite a little expensive, but, after all, it was only for a few weeks. Paris would successfully stave off the siege, and one would soon be able to return to the only city where life was worth living. In this hope they spent a quiet time at the resort until a remarkable incident occurred. One morning late in September, the door to Jennie's hotel room was flung open, and a stranger made his unceremonious appearance. Hastily he closed the door behind him. "Don't tell anyone a word, Mademoiselle Jennie!" said the strange man. "For God's sake don't let anyone know that I am here!'

Jennie looked up. Was it possible? This pale, haggard, unshaved creature—yes, of course, at second glance she recognized the shadow of M. de Gardonne. Not much was left of the court-chamberlain's immaculate appearance. He looked as if he were on the run. His imperturbable composure had given way to an expression of despair. "I so often enjoyed your hospitality in the Champs Elysées," he tried to smile, "that I feel encourged once more to prey on your good nature. I am aware that I do not look very presentable. But, you see, Mademoiselle, that is how one gets if one has had to spend two days and two nights hidden in the dunes...," the aging court-chamberlain blushed, "....as little visible as possible."

"Whom are you speaking to, Jennie?" came Clarissa's voice from the next room.

Jennie's dark eyes flashed a question to M. de Gardonne. Already she was his accomplice.

"To an old friend, mamma!" she called back. "Come in ... if you are dressed...."

Clarissa did not swoon when she opened the door. But she could not suppress a faint exclamation of surprise.

"Quiet, quiet, please," M. de Gardonne whispered urgently. "No one is to know that ... that you have such an early guest, Madame!"

"I should say so!" Clarissa answered emphatically.

"If my life alone were at stake," the old courtier said, and it was evident that he meant every word, "I would certainly not disturb ladies at this untimely hour. Nor would I present myself in ..." his fine blue-veined hand pointed to his torn and stained clothes "....this attire. But another, a very precious life is entrusted to me. It might, indeed, be a matter of life or death for a much beloved lady, if I should be caught ... before tomorrow morning."

Clarissa was still suspicious. But Jennie said: "What you need most, I guess, is a cup of tea. I'll call for breakfast."

"For God's sake, no waiter!" he interrupted her move toward the bell. "No one must see me. No one must know that I am here. I must preserve my liberty, at least until late tonight. You understand? I must! Please don't ask questions, ladies! Please," the poor fellow, until a few weeks ago a very mighty and somewhat haughty man, beseeched. "Let me spend the day in your rooms. After dark I will leave, and ..." he added quietly, "I believe, I will never have an opportunity of disturbing you again."

"Jennie!" Clarissa's voice sounded shaken. "Come into my room!" When she had closed the door, she asked almost breathlessly: "Do you believe he has committed murder?"

"You read too many of those yellow *romans policiers*,

mamma," Jennie replied. "Don't you see he is *preventing murder?*"

"Whose?"

"A much beloved lady's!" Jennie quoted de Gardonne.

Clarissa looked startled. "I . . . understand . . ." she said slowly. "Do you think the Prussians would shoot her?"

"No. Herr von Bismarck does not shoot women. He would behead her. Ceremoniously, of course! Probably on the same block where Marie Antoinette was decapitated as a courteous gesture. In front of a hundred thousand hand-picked spectators!"

M. de Gardonne was permitted to stay all day in the Jerome suite. The chambermaid was not allowed in to make the beds. Mme. Jerome's ankle was worse. She intended to spend the day resting, and did not wish to be disturbed.

The courtly intruder retired into a corner. He did not speak a single word during the whole day. When darkness fell, he very modestly cleared his throat to attract Jennie's attention. It so happened that she was alone in the room with him. He bowed deeply, tip-toed to the door, listened for a moment, opened the door, glanced rapidly at the empty corridor, and slipped out of the room, forgetting to close the door behind his back. Perhaps it would have made a noise. The hinges of French hotel doors were always poorly oiled.

Looking out of the window, Jennie saw him, a shade, as it were, slowly walking down the street. Suddenly "Spanish Ladies," the old English chanty, was whistled. The whistling man walked toward the hotel, running straight into de Gardonne. As far as Jennie could make out in the darkness, the man wore a dark, probably blue, coat, and light, certainly white, trousers, the English yachtsman's uniform. He had the rolling gait of a sea-faring man. Gardonne, the human shadow, almost disappeared at his side. Both walked noiselessly with enormous strides down to the pier.

Two days later a significant epilogue followed. Dr. Evans, the famous American dentist, practicing in Paris, and Dr. Crane, once medical practitioner at the Imperial Court, called on the ladies Jerome. It was only for a minute. Their carriage was waiting. Clarissa gladly received the old friends. They asked her to come downstairs with them. Perhaps she would like to shake hands with another old acquaintance. Jennie was to come, too. The old acquaintance insisted on seeing her.

A heavily veiled lady sat in the back of the carriage. She shook hands with Clarissa. Then her voice, ever with its harsh Castilian accent, addressed Jennie: "I want to thank you quite particularly, my dear child. Without your help and hospitality our friend in common could not have spent his perilous day so comfortably. Perhaps he could not have made the arrangements for my excursion at all. Good-by, my dear. I shall see you soon—in England!"

The coachman lashed the horses. A quarter of an hour later an English yacht weighed anchor. The crossing was rough, but Sir John Burgoyne, the famous yachtsman, was undaunted; he had taken his craft through heavier seas. Confidently, he expected to make Ryde, the little port on the Isle of Wight, in two days.

He stood at the wheel. The September gale swept the ocean. It swept over France. The man in the blue coat and white trousers whistled "Spanish Ladies" into the roaring storm.

CHAPTER V

The Refugees
and Herr von Bismarck

Now the Empress had escaped, there was little
hope that France would return to her old glory. Should they
remain in Deauville? Winter at the seacoast was not inviting.
Moreover, the hotel was about to close for the season. It had
to be farewell to France. The ladies Jerome crossed the Channel. But Jennie's heart remained in immortal Paris. In England she only hoped to find a temporary exile.

Her first impressions of London were disappointing beyond
her worst expectations. "A winter spent in the gloom and fog
of London did not tend to dispel the melancholy we felt,"
she reminisced. "Our friends scattered, fighting, or killed at the
front; debarred as we were from our bright little house and
all our household goods, it was indeed a sad time."

There was only one escape for the refugees: to build a
shadow-Paris on the Thames. London was teeming with French
refugees. Most of them led miserable lives. The Duc de Persigny was a sorry remnant of his old, proud self. Broken-hearted,
ill, and penniless, he was, Jennie observed, "put to many straits
to eke out a living." He had to sell some gold plates and other
precious belongings he had managed to take with him on his
escape. The once "dapper little man with a pleasant manner,"
always carefully groomed in his high-buttoned black morning
coat with gray trousers, never appearing without a silk hat,

white gloves, and a cane with a gold knob, was now reduced to destitution. Yet his spirit was unbroken. He dabbled in high affairs of state as if he were still His Majesty's cabinet minister and ambassador. Difficult as it was to scratch together the pennies for luxurious stationery and stamps, he flooded the world with letters, offering his advice on how to solve difficulties in international affairs. Having had his own experience with war, the old saber-rattler was now a confirmed pacifist. He even wrote to Herr von Bismarck, suggesting, as a guarantee of eternal Franco-Prussian peace, the enthroning of the Prince Imperial in Paris, with Eugénie to act as a regent. This was a proof of his utter unselfishness. He no longer liked the Empress, whose most devoted servant and vocal admirer he had once been. The life of a refugee does not tend to strengthen old ties. Indeed, it disrupts them. The other fellow, who has escaped as well, is always guilty of the whole calamity. Eugénie had visited her husband in his Prussian prison, the fortress Wilhelmshoehe. On this visit, it filtered out, she had treated her despondent mate rather haughtily. Whether such rumors were true or not, the Duc de Persigny, now an old man beyond his years, preferred even the restoration of the haughty lady to a continuation of life in foggy exile.

Herr von Bismarck, supervising the war that dragged on with the siege of Paris, had no time for correspondence with a ghost. Instead, the Duc de Persigny received an answer to his suggestion from Wilhelmshoehe. Toward the middle of January 1871 he visited Jennie (in whose mother's London house, a faint copy of the home in the Champs Elysées, he was now a persistent guest), waved a piece of paper, and asked: "Do you want an autograph for your collection, Mademoiselle? Read this letter from the Emperor, and keep it, if you care to. I'll have little use for it in the future."

The letter, dated Wilhelmshoehe, 7. January 1871, was a warning from Napoleon, begging the Duke not to meddle in the dynasty's affairs. Even benevolent interference could only make trouble with Bismarck. Evidently Napoleon had had to refute Persigny's plan as wholly unauthorized when the *Chancellier du Reich* asked him whether the Emperor was behind Persigny's scheming. *"Croyez, mon cher Persigny, à mon amitié,"* the angry epistle from Wilhelmshoehe closed. This sentence sufficed to convince Persigny that he had lost a life-long friend and master.

Jennie kept the letter in her collection, and Persigny retained his perfect composure—until life with his wife became unbearable. The Duchess had always been an exuberant Anglo-maniac. Chamarande, her château near Paris, had been entirely furnished after the English fashion, with an unfailing taste for what Jennie called "the least attractive stuffing of the early Victorian period." Several rooms at Chamarande had been strictly copied from Balmoral; they were decorated with tartan curtains and carpets which, again according to Jennie, had always made art-loving French visitors "rub their eyes."

The Duchess, having funds of her own, was determined to copy the copy of Balmoral somewhere on English soil. "In Rome behave as the Romans do, and in England like the English," she tutored her husband.

Somewhat incoherently the little duke replied: "I do not like the English weather." Then he took a Bible, one of the few presents from Napoleon he had preserved, and went to bed. For many years he had not thumbed through the Book. In the morning Bastien, his old valet, found His Highness's body with the Bible still clutched in the stiff hands. The Duc de Presigny, né Victor Fialin, had made his exit unassumingly.

Not all the fugitives from the defunct Imperial court who had gathered in London suffered similar sad fates. "Two pretty and lively refugees from Paris," Jennie recollected, "much entertained, and scandalized a little, London society during that winter, 1870-71. The Duchesse de Carraciolo and the Comtesse de Béchevet, with their respective husbands and a few Frenchmen who preferred shooting birds in England to being shot at in France, took a country house." At a party there, some French refugees amused themselves with a rather tasteless practical joke. One of them, professing to be a distinguished doctor from abroad, all of a sudden stared at the Comte de Béchevet, and uttered, with every sign of horror: "My dear comte, you are a dying man!"

Refugees are rarely shock-proof. M. de Béchevet was no exception. Immediately he felt his heart failing. He lay down on a sofa, and asked for a priest. Mysteriously, a "father" appeared. He was, of course, another of the French merrymakers, a partner to the jocose conspiracy. He received the dying man's last confession. Many of the tender and intimate secrets of the court in the Tuileries came to light. "They were eagerly listened to by the rest of the party," Jennie recorded, "who had hidden behind curtains. Their peals of laughter resuscitated the dying man." Personally, she was disgusted. To her it was a sorry show; the dead playing death.

All London was infuriated as the story made the rounds. The clergy protested formally against the blasphemous behavior of certain unwelcome intruders from France. Queen Victoria was not amused. Yet she betook herself to Eugénie, who had established her modest home at Camden House, Chislehurst. It was a gracious and courageous gesture to visit Eugénie at the very moment in which her subjects had challenged English taste. Victoria, obviously, did not wish to leave her good friend in the lurch. "My dear Empress," she said, entering the country cottage.

"The Empress is dead," replied Eugénie, curtsying like a commoner. Two ladies chatted. But it was no longer quite the same as in the days when their Majesties had exchanged state visits. Queen Victoria was merely charitable.

It was humiliating. Jennie felt ashamed to belong, in a way, among this macabre crowd of refugees from a shattered court. But they were her only friends. England was not yet her country. All she heard about the island were the eternal complaints about the fog. Her French surrounding harped incessantly on the disagreeable climate. England, the asylum, Eng-

land, having given the Imperial flotsam a new lease on life,—
England remained distant and impenetrable.

One day in February, 1871, Leonard Jerome crossed the
ocean for a short visit. He wanted to have a look at his loved
ones before proceeding to besieged Paris where he had an
appointment with the American General William Tecumseh
Sherman, who was just about to complete his European tour.

Paris, agonizing during the last weeks of the siege, was,
of course, the most difficult place on earth to be admitted to.
This difficulty had probably inspired both General Sherman
and Leonard Jerome to lay a large wager as to which of the
two would be the first to break through the Prussian cordon
around the besieged city. The great General Sherman spent
many months touring Europe at his leisure, until, relying on
his name and fame, he turned his steps toward Paris. He was
received with high honors both by the German jailers around
the town, and by the prisoners, the denizens of Paris.

However, he lost his bet. Already installed in the Metropole,
Jerome received him with a delighted chuckle. The Paris adventure was not very important; it was probably just one
more proof of Jerome's insatiable curiosity. But it had been
planned with scrupulous care. First Jerome claimed, and got
permission to visit Mr. Washburn, the American Minister. To
be on the safe side, he there attached himself to the U. S. General Duff, who entered Paris on February 7, 1871. The latter's
entrée was considerably less solemn than Sherman's arrival.
Prussian sentries searched General Duff before allowing him to
cross the lines, and confiscated a leg of mutton which the
general, well informed about the starvation in Paris, had cautiously stuffed into his pocket. Jerome, for his part, was taken
through the Prussian lines blindfolded. The third American
General in Paris, Mr. Burnside, was not molested at all. He
carried a Prussian *laissez-passer*, describing him as the "most
prominent general, next to Grant and Sherman, in the Civil
War," and he enjoyed Bismarck's personal benevolence. He

had the run of the fighting front. He was, people rumored, the most promising of the innumerable neutral peacemakers trafficking between Paris and Versailles.

Versailles was a German town during the occupation. Prussian soldiers replaced the local police. They tramped the streets in goose-step. The principal promenade resembled an avenue in Potsdam. The whole town had the appearance of a vast Prussian barracks. German artillery occupied the courtyard of the Royal Castle. German sentries paced at its gates. But for the silent, obviously uneasy patrols the broad streets were empty. The inhabitants of Versailles held strictly aloof from the invader's garrison. Intercourse was solely of a business nature. Only the waitresses in the restaurants smiled. They charged *méssieurs les cuirassiers* thrice the normal price for a glass of beer. At that, the *cuirassiers* did not get any further with them. Their gallant attacks were invariably repulsed. When the disappointed German heroes finally left the place, they could frequently hear the barmaids whispering behind them: "Jean, rinse out those glasses. The Fritz have drunk out of them."

German dignitaries, officials and officers were cold-shouldered in the houses in which they were billeted. German wounded filled the halls and corridors of Louis XIV's palace. The cellars of the *Hotel des Reservoirs* and *Vatel's,* the world-famous eating place, were depleted by the bibulous members of the *Zweite Staffel—*second squadron—composed exclusively of German princelings and dukes in the King of Prussia's personal service. But in one aspect Versailles was curiously cosmopolitan. All sorts of amazing people from the four corners of the globe swarmed there, engaged in a multiplicity of errands. Mere sightseers rubbed shoulders with adventurers, inventors of brand-new super-rifles, diplomats, go-betweens and intriguers from every country. Versailles under the Prussian jack-boot focused the attention of the whole world. Life was gay. Merrily they plotted and conspired. Banquets, gala receptions, even innocent skating parties were the order of the day—all to the accompaniment of cannon-thunder.

Leonard Jerome was immediately at home in this super-charged atmosphere. Although he had sold out his interests in the *New York Times* shortly before his journey to Europe, he fraternized with the large corps of correspondents covering the *Hotel des Reservoirs*, King Wilhelm I's temporary residence, and the most important beat in the contemporary world. His feelings were in no way involved in the Franco-Prussian conflict. The veteran newspaperman wanted only to ascertain the facts of the situation. Could business with the continent be resumed at an early date? This question alone expressed his emotional share in the great wrestling-match over European supremacy. If that man Bismarck stated that self-interest should be the guiding star in politics, why, Leonard Jerome had long applied this maxim both for the benefit of his beloved country and for his own. He felt no compunction in accompanying General Burnside on a visit to Herr von Bismarck. He overcame a slight pique because he had not been invited to dinner. After all, important affairs of state were to be discussed at table. Perhaps Burnside would spill the beans on the way home.

At the appointed hour Mr. Jerome appeared at 14 Rue de Province, the house of Mme. Jessé, the widow of a once prosperous textile manufacturer. Her mansion was now requisitioned as Herr von Bismarck's residence. Leonard was kept waiting for longer than an hour, an insult which he would never have stomached in New York, but to which he resigned himself good-naturedly as a sample of German manners. Besides, the time of waiting passed most pleasantly chatting with the widow Jessé, who crept out of the tiny attic room, all that was left to her, as soon as she heard that there was an American gentleman in the antechamber. Americans were tremendously popular with the oppressed French who hoped the unofficial meddling of the various American generals between Paris and Versailles would secure an acceptable peace.

Mme. Jessé could not conceal that she was, in a way, awe-stricken by the great man who had appropriated her house. Although herself on the brink of starvation, she relished the smells that rose from Herr von Bismarck's kitchen, and reached her attic room. Sniffing the rich aroma of the daily gala dinners was a sort of substitute for her own nourishment.

"He is certainly a strange man," she said, wavering between horror and respect. "When I complained to him that his servants had packed up all my plates and table linen, and carried them off, he replied: 'But they left behind a lot of nice things, didn't they? Let's have a look at this clock, for example.' Bismarck," Mme. Jessé continued, "grasped the old family time-piece, topped by a goblin-like figure, appraised it and asked: 'How much?' Well," the old lady recollected, "I replied just as crisply: 'Five thousand!' He put the chronometer back on the mantelpiece. Chivalrously he clicked his heels and said he did not want to deprive me of the goblin with its grimaces. It might be valuable to me as a family portrait."

"Mr. Jerome," a little Jewish-looking man interrupted the conversation, opening the door. "His Excellency expects you." (Dr. Moritz Busch noted in his diary: Received an elderly American gentleman in a red shirt with white paper cuffs.)

Bismarck, obviously in high spirits, offered the newcomer wine and cigars. "I was just confessing to the general," he said with a glance at Burnside which unmistakably drew the limit of how much was to be disclosed of the previous conversation, "that in my youth I was myself inclined toward the republican idea. But the German nation is not yet ripe for it. That is why I admire the Americans. Do you know Motley? The best man, I dare say, I have met in my life."

Leonard Jerome had no time to affirm that he was indeed, on excellent terms with the great American scholar-diplomat. Bismarck was already off on another tack. Well knowing that he was speaking to a renowned Wall Street broker, he complained about Baron Rothschild, who, until the war, had been Prussian Consul General in Paris, and yet had had the insolence to have his wine cellar emptied before the Prussian staff took over his château at Ferrière. "The Jews," he said, while his press-chief was listening the other way, talking eagerly to General Burnside, "the Jews have still really no true home; they are cosmopolitan nomads. Their fatherland is Jerusalem. Otherwise they belong to the whole world. But there are good and honest people among them, too. Perhaps there are not many such Jews now. However, they have virtues of their own: respect for their parents, fidelity in marriage, and charitableness. . . . Incidentally," he interrupted himself, "have you met Prince Radziwill?"

A tall, square-faced gentleman bowed from the waistline. He approached Jerome with three carefully calculated steps, and sat down next to him without the slightest movement of the upper part of his body. He had evidently been assigned to entertain the new guest, whereupon Bismarck turned around to resume his conversation with General Burnside. "We do not wish that the fortresses Metz and Strasbourg should be dismantled. We wish to take them over intact so as to turn the guns the other way round."

Not without difficulty Prince Radziwill embarked upon his task of polite entertainment. "Yes . . ." he said, and cleared his throat, "Yes . . . really. . . ."

He did not have to exert himself for long. Bismarck did not wait for General Burnside to answer. The Chancellor had had his say, and that was final. Jerome was a most welcome lightning-conductor. "The wine is more important than the Jews," Bismarck addressed him suddenly. In Prussia such a *mot* passed for a witticism. "Have a glass of Médoc. God forgive me the unpatriotic sin, but I even prefer it to our German Deidesheimer." It was *I* all the time. Bismarck was omniscient. He knew all about hunting, traveling, cuisine, and wines. His opinion on mushroom with the fish, his innovation of spicing the roast with a few slices of sausage, were almost as authoritarian as what he thought about horses. His egocentric conversation, however, was the megalomaniac's, not the braggart's talk. He admitted that he had been thrown from his horse at least fifty times in his life. "No harm is done," he said, "as long as you fall clear. But if you crash to the ground with your mare, and have her on top of you, gentlemen, that's too bad. Once upon a time it happened to me that I ..." He never ended the story. He was already insisting that a statesman should not gamble on the stock-exchange. There was usually not much money in it. Advance knowledge gives only very limited advantage. Political events are too insecure. They have their effect on the exchange only later, no one knows when. One can of course produce a bear market by manipulating political events. Many French Ministers are doing that. But in Berlin, where everything is so precise, state telegrams have only twenty to thirty minutes' precedence over bourse telegrams. Then one must have a Jew who can run fast enough to take advantage of the short intervals. Thus one could earn from five hundred to five thousand *thalers* (dollars) daily, which in a couple of years in office would amount to a good deal. Some do it. But it is a disgraceful business. Besides, in a constitutional state one is never sure of what turn things might take."

Bismarck recalled what had happened to him a few years earlier. On his way to Paris, to negotiate the Neuchâtel business with Napoleon in the spring of 1857, he had stopped at Frankfurt to order Rothschild to sell short, because a Prussian war with Switzerland was in the making. Rothschild warned him, but he, Bismarck, had answered, "If you knew what I know...." Rothschild shrugged and sold. Then the King of Prussia changed his mind. The war with Switzerland was called off. The stock market boomed. "And I lost my shirt with this accursed Jew Rothschild...."

Leonard Jerome was fascinated. Was Bismarck's story not his own? Why had he himself suffered so many reverses in the last years? Simply because he, too, was too much of a statesman. Friend Bismarck, he felt like saying, recollecting with relish the innumerable horse stories, dinner recipes, and travels through the wine card the Iron Chancellor had crammed into his hour-long soliloquy.

It was all wrong to call Bismarck a barbarian. Why, he dismissed his American guests in a most cordial manner, stuffing their pockets with excellent, full-flavored cigars, joking, "Pass around the bottles." In the same breath he addressed General Burnside: "Remember, in July neither the King nor I nor our people felt the slightest inclination for war. The declaration came as a perfect surprise to us, but still it raised no wish of conquest. Our army is excellent for a war of defense, but not easy to use for plans of conquest, for the army is the people, and nowhere are the people desirous of glory. They wish and need peace. That is the explanation why our press, the voice of the people, now demands a better frontier. In the presence of the ambitious French nation, greedy for conquest, we must, for the sake of peace, think of our future security, which we can only find in a better defense position than we have at present."

General Burnside uttered no opinion. Bidding farewell, he confined himself to praising the excellent organization of the Prussian army and the heroism of the troops. Jerome was enthusiastic. This man Bismarck was a man of peace, a man of great affairs, and a true connoisseur of life.

Probably Leonard Jerome, to whom horses, the stock exchange, and the wine card were essential elements of life, did not grasp immediately that to friend Bismarck they were nothing but an escape mechanism. During the long months of the siege of Paris the Chancellor was a restless, depressed man. The days passed slowly. He had to spend them mostly in detail work which was strange to his cosmic interests. His nights were sleepless, interrupted by lonely walks in the gardens of Versailles, which he had surrounded by high walls since he well realized that everyone in France hated him. He was sick of being exposed to constant attempts on his life. (Not that any individual incident had ever frightened him. But he complained that he could never go out without a pistol. The bodyguard was unreliable. His two great Danes were his only real protection.) Frequently he had to stop his stroll after a short time. This mass of nerves was an overgrown, overweight man; his feet ached persistently. When he returned in the middle of the night, secret documents, flowing in twenty-four hours a day, awaited him on his desk. They were mostly reports about the dissatisfaction of the generals who furtively plotted against the civilian dictatorship. Once Moltke, the commander-in-chief, had openly spoken out. In the name of the army he demanded an immediate attack on Paris. Idling in their winter-quarters the troops were getting restive. Paris could and should be cracked like a nut.

This old fool, Moltke, understood nothing of a bloodless victory. What would Europe say to the destruction of Paris? The Iron Chancellor despised Europe. But at this time the continent was still a reality. "Perhaps a later generation of Prussians will be able to send Europe to hell!" he confided to Dr. Moritz Busch. "But not we in our lifetime!" Moreover, if Paris had not to be cracked like a nut, the city would decay like a rotten apple. He had his spies inside Paris. Every half hour one of them was caught and shot, but thousands of others returned with the most encouraging news.

General Burnside, again in Jerome's company, visited Bismarck a second time, beseeching him not to destroy Paris. But on their second mission the American good-will ambassadors were not so well received. Abruptly the Chancellor replied: "Why shall Paris not be bombarded? Why should it be a crime against civilians to destroy collections, splendid buildings and ancient monuments? Paris is a fortress. Its treasures of art and its historic palaces don't alter the fact. If the Parisians wish to keep their monuments and their collections of books and pictures, they should not surround them with fortifications! ... I have only one message to convey to the Parisians. I will say: You two millions are answerable to me with your lives. I shall leave you to starve for twenty-four hours until we get everything we want from you. And twenty-four hours on top of that. What happens during that time is all the same to me. The delay will not harm me, but you!"

Silently, the Americans turned away. Bismarck stopped them for another moment: "And I have an excellent idea for the time when peace is concluded. We will establish a tribunal to try those who instigated this war, newspaper writers, deputies, senators, ministers."

"And you can bet this bloody beast will do it, too!" Jerome said after leaving. He was through with friend Bismarck. But again he misunderstood the Prussian enigma. Bismarck's bullying was bluff. He was firmly determined to stick to his strangulating policy of patience—the gift with which he was endowed least of all—even if it should choke not only Paris, but himself. A bloodless victory was falling into his lap. He had only to keep his army quiet for another few days. The confidential looting order he issued was to bridge this delay.

"And so this devilish brain devised the idea of distracting his men by pillaging and looting. Open season was declared," Leonard Jerome, back in London, sick of the European continent, concluded his report.

He ended his narrative, Jennie recollected, with what she called "a graphic description of the triumphal entry of the victorious army in Paris, rolling down the Champs Elysées. Masses of infantry, most of them wearing spectacles, marched by the Arc de Triomphe, which was barricaded, and through the deserted streets of the once gay city, singing *Die Wacht am Rhein*. Many were the stories of individual suffering and despair, of hair-breadth escapes and brave deeds, told him by the besieged." And many were the stories of General Sherman barking at the German victors whose outrageous cruelty made him positively sick.

Jennie never forgot a single one of these stories. The duties of her subsequent career forced her to mingle with the court of the Hohenzollerns, once or twice to visit Bismarck, and to entertain many aristocratic Prussians. The Germans always behaved in a cordial and polite fashion to her. Yet she could hardly breathe in their company.

CHAPTER VI *The Way to England*

The fog lifted, and the sun broke through the clouds. The ladies Jerome arrived in Cowes, on the Isle of Wight, to spend their first English summer—the summer of 1871—in a second attempt to find another European counterpart to Newport. They were searching for glittering copper, and struck gold. In Cowes, Jennie found her way to England.

In Cowes she did not feel a stranger. She was no longer a refugee in a hospitable, but impenetrable land. No insurmountable, if invisible walls encircled her foreign beauty. There were no barriers in Cowes. "People all seemed to know one another," she recalled. "The Prince and Princess of Wales and many foreign royalties could walk about and amuse themselves without being photographed or mobbed. There were no glorified villas, no esplanade or pier, no bands or nigger minstrels, no motors or crowded tourist steamers—no nothing, as children say. The lawns of the Royal Yacht Squadron did not resemble a perpetual garden party, nor the roadstead a perpetual regatta. Yachts sailed in and out without fear of losing their moorings, and most of them belonged to the Squadron.

The cheerful dignity prevailing in Cowes and the unenforced gentleness uniting a select group were in marked contrast to what Jennie had thus far seen: the mushroom growth of American millionaire society, and the operatic scene of a decaying

83

Imperial court. In the new atmosphere everyone was at ease. Peace replaced push.

"Ever since those early days Cowes had always so great an attraction for me, notwithstanding its gradual deterioration, that I have rarely missed my yearly visit. It had been so delightfully small and peaceful," she remembered in the autumn of her life, when spring appears to have been a serene time of the year. But while you live through it, spring is a violent season. Her spring in Cowes was not peace, but passion.

In her detached bearing, for the first time observing the show, rather than acting in the cast, she seemed unprepared for passion. Indeed, her first two summers at the English watering-place were notable only for their tranquillity. One could, of course, not conquer Cowes like Newport with a pair of galloping white donkeys. It was impossible to intrude vehemently into this gentle and cheerful, but patently self-satisfied circle. Lightheartedly, Jennie forsook the rousing triumphs of her American childhood and her Parisian debutante years. She no longer rushed. She was in no hurry. She displayed a calm detachment that attracted most flattering attention.

Pictures taken about that time show a young girl of rarely harmonious beauty. It was not then customary to be photographed with sparkling rows of teeth and an expressionless poster smile. From her yellowed snapshots Miss Jennie Jerome looks reflective and thoughtful. The playful ringlets in which she wears her rich, dark hair are the only attempt at coquetry that a young lady allows herself. Below a conspicuous high, regular forehead arch strong, almost masculine eyebrows. The eyes are large, dark, full of mute interrogation. The face is slim, the nose Grecian, except for a funny little tip that abruptly jumps out. The young lady keeps her lips firmly closed. The short, prominent chin she must have inherited from her very energetic father. The figure, of medium stature and light as a feather, is clad in the evening gown of the time—black silk, high-necked, long sleeves flowing with folds, ruches, and ribbons, bell-shaped, trailing. A heavy black silk dress such as this betrays no secrets. It asks riddles. Of such stuff was the young American made who was to be for decades one of the most courted women of royal London.

But she did not hasten her assumption of the invisible crown. It took her six seasons—three years, in common parlance—to be presented to Their Royal Highness of Wales, although Clarissa was sure that she could have arranged her daughters' presentation within five minutes. In the meantime, Jennie still cultivated faithfully the company of the scattered remnants of the defunct French court.

Eugénie, retired to a friend's country house in Chicester, lived in dire financial straits. She never spoke a word about her worries. Jennie, a steady visitor at Camden House, was the only person in whose company the Empress dropped her mask occasionally, and disclosed for fleeting moments the weary face of a silently struggling great lady, beset by debt, harassed by creditors, yet ever smiling. Such moments were infrequent. But once Eugénie made the remark: "Today, for the first time, I do regret the loss of the Crown. It would do no harm to have the precious piece—in the pawnshop."

It sounded like one more of the sardonic jokes in which she used to couch her nostalgia for power. But Jennie, to whom this pathetic witticism was addressed, felt the bitter pain below the bit of self-teasing. She already had sharp ears, a genius for friendship, the urge for activity, and, above all, perfect command of the high art of wire-pulling. She wrote a letter to the Comtesse de Pourtalès. In consequence, the countess came to Camden House on a visit. It was a surprise visit, indeed. Comtesse de Pourtalès had been the only lady-in-waiting at Napoleon III's court who did not escape, but decided to sit out the Republic. Already a grandmother, but still one of the most impressive women of Paris, she established the same close relations to M. Thiers, the President of the Republic, as had tied her to the last Bourbon, then to Napoleon III as president and pretender, and even to Herr von Bismarck during the occupation. Whether Paris was royalist, republican, Imperial,

German dominated, or republican again—to her Paris remained Paris, the object of her never-ending care. She had acted as hostess to Prince Louis Napoleon before his marriage, and now she was engaged in making M. Thiers and his republican set-up parlorbroken. Her brooch glittered in the colors of the tricolor.

Yet she curtsied in the old court manner in front of her Empress when she came to Chislehurst at Jennie's behest, to survey Eugénie's sad situation. A hostess of her sovereign perfection observed at first glance that things at Camden House were not going well. She did not make the slightest remark, but Eugénie, understanding her silence, explained apologetically: "A rather poor scenery, isn't it? I tried to save a few personal belongings when we were forced to leave the Tuileries. But the Prussians disturbed me. I had to escape as I was: in my black apron, without even coat, hat, or gloves. I nearly fell from the ladder, as I was trying to collect, and take away with us, a few antiques. They are missing here, don't you think?"

Countess de Pourtalès gave her Empress a long look of faithful allegiance. "The *sales Prussiens* behaved atrociously. It was really difficult to receive Herr von Bismarck after his soldiery wrought such havoc on the Tuileries."

"They destroyed my private apartment with particular relish, I was told," Eugénie remarked lightly.

Tea was served in brand-new cups, bought for a pittance in some cheap bazaar. Silently, Mme. de Pourtalès inspected the cups. Then she departed. Immediately upon her return to Paris, the countess called upon Thiers. Emphatically she called him "Mon Président!," gave him the long look of allegiance which she had developed to perfection in decades spent at Royal and Imperial courts, and exacted from him the promise that a part of the ex-Emperor's fortune should be restored to poor Napoleon in exile.

It was high time. Napoleon was just returning from the Prussian prison, and took up residence in Camden House. His room on the first floor, the best in the house, but unfortunately the only one that could be spared, was crammed with a large desk and with the remnants of his library. The heavy tomes filled all the available space, and covered the floor.

M. Thiers' decision to restore a small part of the Imperial savings came as a godsend. The turn of fortune had to be celebrated. Napoleon and Eugénie invited their last followers to a sailing expedition around the Isle of Wight. The ladies Jerome were the only foreigners asked. For the rest, the party consisted, as Jennie (endowed with an uncanny memory for invitation lists and menus) remembered, of the Prince Imperial, the Empress's nieces the Mademoiselles d'Albe, Prince Joachim Murat, the Duke Carlos d'Alba, a few other Spaniards, and two "faithful followers from the people," the valets.

Owing to the roughness of the sea most of the party sought "the seclusion that the cabin grants" before the little yacht had reached Shanklin Bay. But Freshwater and Beaulieu were still to be negotiated, and Eugénie was not the woman to give in. While les Demoiselles d'Albe, desperately ill, lay on the deck in a state of coma, and while the Prince Imperial chaffed the Spanish guests, who, in their utter extremity of seasickness, seemed to have entirely forgotten the glorious days of the armada, Eugénie stood near the mast, her hair blowing in the wind. Amazingly she did not try to protect it, although she usually wore a hat. But this day of rewon financial independence, of release from the shackles of poverty, was a day of exuberance. She enjoyed the sensation of the gale tugging at her curls.

When Jennie approached her, walking firmly along the deck of the tossing nutshell, the Empress received her with a laugh. As if she were torn out of thoughts persistently hounding her, she cried: "They have also utterly destroyed St. Cloud, where I held court during the Austrian war. Not one stone remained on the other, I was told." Perhaps she had to outcry the gale. Perhaps the past.

Napoleon, tottering, steered toward the mast. When his hands finally clutched it, he breathed deeply. But he remained silent. He looked old, ill, and sad, Jennie observed. His thought, she pondered, "could not have been other than sorrowful—and even in my young eyes he seemed to have nothing to live for."

This time her shrewd judgment was wrong. Shipwrecked Napoleon III still lived for his return to power. On the surface a dying invalid, he spent his last twenty-two months of English exile walking, as long as his legs would carry him, reading, and writing a never completed book on the organization of the French army. Besides, he indefatigably wrote long letters to a few faithful partisans in France. The epistles had but one theme: the comeback Napoleon would stage. To be sure, there was one difficulty, and it was not the languishing Third Republic. The obstacle was of a more serious nature. As a soldier l'Empereur had, of course, to enter Paris on horseback. Could he still ride horseback in his physical condition? Certainly he could. He invited General Rouher, the head of his conspiracy in France, to come to Chislehurst to see for himself. The brave general came. He was helpful at the rehearsal. So was Mr. Pietri. So was the friendly neighing horse. But when Napoleon III made his fourth and desperate attempt to mount, he collapsed, and fell into the arms of Eugénie.

For a few weeks he was bedridden. When he resumed his walks, he paid a few farewell visits to his friends. He was embarking upon a long journey, he explained enigmatically. Sorrowful, the last followers shook their gray heads. For God's sake, the adventure could but end in disaster. All Paris would yell: "Badinguet!"

Courteously, Napoleon also visited the salon of the ladies Jerome. Jennie was at home, and received him. A gentleman sat opposite her, a man perhaps ten years Napoleon's junior, showing the first signs of age, but still a tower of strength in comparison with the shadow of an Emperor.

"Papa," said Jennie. She tarried a moment. "I want to present you to the ... Comte de Pierrefonds."

"Your daughter is a born diplomat!" Napoleon smiled; even

this slight motion seemed an exertion. "I am very fond of her. So is the Empress. And, if I am not gravely wrong, the Prince Imperial, too."

The conversation lasted five minutes. Then the two black-clothed, elderly gentlemen accompanying the invalid, cleared their throats, which was the signal for departure. Sir Henry Thompson, the famous surgeon, had not liked the visit at all. It would only sap his patient's last strength. But Dr. Conneau, the Emperor's personal practitioner of long standing, had wrested his great colleague's consent with a simple shrug. It no longer made much difference.

A few days later Sir Henry performed two apparently successful operations on the Emperor. But a third became necessary, and after that agony set in. When the doctors called Eugénie into the room, Napoleon at first did not recognize her. It took a few painful minutes until her presence penetrated his failing consciousness. But then his very last moments were illuminated. With a faint gesture he indicated his wish to kiss once more the woman who, even if her misguided meddling had largely contributed to his downfall, had yet been his faithful companion in glory and defeat for exactly twenty years. Finally, he still tried desperately to turn his head around to old Dr. Conneau. *"Etiez-vous à Sedan?"* his last breath died away. The memories of love and combat, the twins, engulfed him, and led him mercifully through the doors of death.

Napoleon III was laid to rest in St. Mary's Church, Chislehurst. Jennie was among the small group of mourners. The Empress kept her young friend, when the others left. Perhaps she sought a refuge with youth. In a level tone of voice, heavier than usual with its harsh Castilian accents, she said, "He has bequeathed to me all his possessions, 125,000 francs." The corners of her mouth trembled. "That's what remains. And the priests say: united in this life and in the next one. . . . Well, one must go on . . . !" The last words were almost inaudible. Throughout the fifty years Eugénie survived her husband, she carefully kept his tomb in St. Mary's decorated with the pomegranate blossoms he had always admired in her hair.

The death of the Emperor entirely disbanded the small group of French refugees. Then, in the spring of 1873, Jennie grew completely into English society. Although her "singular beauty and gifted vivacity had excited general attention," if one may trust a sentence written years later by her most devoted admirer, her son, Winston, she had hesitated for three seasons before attending a ball in Cowes. The ice was broken during regatta week. The officers of the cruiser "Ariadne," then lying as guard-ship in the Roads, gave a ball in the Royal Yacht Squadron Castle in honor of the arrival of the Tsarevitch and his exalted consort. The Prince and Princess of Wales headed the large number of distinguished guests attending the ball. Had Jennie as a child not dreamed that the Prince would dance with her? Would the dream come true—thirteen years later?

The Jerome ladies entered the Castle in state. The next minutes were frightfully exciting. Standing on the left of the Russian guest of honor, the Prince greeted the procession that formed before them. Jennie curtsied. Edward and Alexandra, it was generally remarked, involved her in an unusually long conversation.

With a crashing chord the orchestra announced the first quadrille. The Prince bowed slightly. "My dear Miss Jerome," he said, suddenly serious, "certain people are bound to come to the front, and stay there. You belong to them." Then he nodded gracefully and opened the quadrille with Her Imperial Highness, the Tsarevna.

His place, opposite Jennie, did not remain free for a split second. Colonel Edgecumbe, an old friend of the Jeromes in London, seized it immediately. He was in a hurry to say: "I want to present Lord Randolph Churchill. . . ." There was no time for further introduction. The two young people had already joined the quadrille.

Lord Randolph was, to tell the truth, a poor dancer. Immediately she had, as if it were a premonition of fate, a great deal of trouble with him. His sense of rhythm was not overly developed, he was not endowed with harmony. The lack of both these qualities proved, later in life, a terrific handicap. During the first quadrille it was only a minor nuisance. He tried to laugh it away. His laugh was harsh, not melodious, but in its very weirdness and discordance, merriment itself. Against her custom—Jennie herself did not know why—she was forbearing with her partner. She liked his looks, although at that time they were more intriguing than impressive. By stature he was on the short side. His figure was slim and boyish. His brown hair was carefully combed, and parted on the left. His high forehead topped a well-cut face without, it was true, any remarkable features except for his large, searching eyes. A thin mustache—not yet the terrific walrus mustachios which, even exceeding Leonard Jerome's pride, were soon to become Lord Randolph's trademark—covered a thin upper lip and a slightly protruding, as if sensual, underlip. Already in his twenty-fourth year, his chin was thrust out sharply. He looked young and innocent, yet with a veil of early fatigue shrouding his countenance.

He was terribly excited dancing the quadrille. He stumbled occasionally. The figures confused him. His innate poise seemed badly shaken. It was, he insisted stubbornly, all due to the dance. When the inevitable waltz followed the quadrille, he confessed that waltzing made him giddy. To be frank, he detested all kinds of dancing. "But don't go!" he added hastily.

Jennie was not accustomed to sitting out a ball in the company of a young man. Yet she nodded; they sat and talked. Their conversation proceeded slowly. It was a well-bred conversation. So the ladies were staying at Rosetta Cottage? Indeed, it was a charming small house the family had rented for the summer. The tiny garden facing the sea was most attractive. Every insignificant word she uttered sounded like a revelation to him. When she invited him to come to dinner next evening—

"and don't forget to bring Colonel Edgecumbe along"—the orchestra played as if the violins were fiddling in heaven.

The dinner at Rosetta Cottage was excellent. After the meal the Jerome girls played the piano. Everyone chatted pleasantly. It was late at night when the two gentlemen went home. "Charming girls!" said Randolph. "Did you observe the dark one?"

"Not quite as intensely as you, I am afraid," the colonel chuckled.

"If she consents, I will make her my wife."

At the same moment, Jennie told her laughing and incredulous sisters that she had a strange presentiment: their new friend was the man she would marry.

Thanks to a lucky accident—one of those whims of fate that seem unfortunately to have gone out of fashion since the Victorian era—the two young people met next morning on a stroll along the beach. That same evening Randolph was once more a guest at Rosetta Cottage. Colonel Edgecumbe was otherwise engaged. This was his whist night. It was a beautiful night, warm and still. The lights of the yachts shone on the water. The sky was bright with stars. After dinner, the pair found themselves alone in the garden. Love's golden moment, Montaigne had called such a situation. Thus far, Randolph had always feared love. Suddenly his fear was gone. He proposed, and was accepted. They had seen each other on three evenings. In fact, he was still a stranger to her. Who was Lord Randolph Churchill?

His early youth had been more spectacular than remarkable. The son of His Grace George Charles, Seventh Duke of Marlborough, and Her Grace, the Duchess, née the Lady Frances Anne Emily Vane, eldest daughter of the third Marquess of Londonderry, he was born in London on February 13th, 1849. In tune with early Victorian custom the ducal couple had five sons and six daughters. Due to the frightfully high child mortality, three of the boys died in their infancy. The older of the two surviving sons subsequently succeeded to the title. The younger one, Randolph, had every expectation of the struggle for life to which a cadet of a great English house was fated.

The boy grew up with his brother and sisters. At eight he was sent to Mr. Tabor's preparatory school at Cheam. The space and happiness at home was now exchanged for the narrow life of school; yet, it appears, Randolph was treated with kindliness. He did not prove exceptionally clever at his letters, but he soon loved to read books on history, biography, and adventure. His imagination was early kindled, and not by books alone. His passion for horses and hunting, which became one of the dominant traits of his character, awoke during his boyhood. At the age of nine he rode so perfectly that, after having pestered his father for a long time, a pony was bought for him. The wiry, ragged little quadruped had been aptly called The Mouse. Randolph changed its name to The Hunter. To do justice to this name, Colonel Thomas, an old acquaintance of the ducal family, later to become Randolph's lifelong friend, introduced, on a solemn autumn day in 1859, the boy, then a little over ten, to the great fraternity of English hunters. "The day was fortunate," Winston reports in his father's biography. "Lord Randolph, carried to the front by The Mouse, was in at the death in King's Wood, was presented with brush and pad, went through the ceremony of being "blooded," and returned home in great delight, with glowing cheeks, well besmeared with fox's blood. From that day he became passionately fond not merely of riding to hounds, but of hunting as an art."

A letter is preserved from a school-fellow recollecting his impressions of Randolph as a lad. "I was a little more than eight, and I never saw him after he left Cheam. But I will never forget the large magnificence about his Cheam days, impressing me with the idea that, no matter how well another boy might acquit himself, Randolph Churchill would always go one better. I can never open the book of Ecclesiastes without recalling the breathless astonishment with which I heard him recite, with the vehemence he always showed in speech, those eight verses which tell us that "to every thing there is a season, and a time to every purpose under the heaven." For me Churchill achieved a wonder. . . . But his vehemence of speech did not mean violence of language. At that time he always spoke openmouthed, with a full voice and great rapidity of utterance, as if his thoughts came faster than his words could follow; the impression conveyed being that he was determined to overbear all opposition, and gain the mastery of argument."

Already before Randolph, at fourteen, went on to Eton, he was, it appears from this description, the stuff of which parliamentary leaders are made. His public-school career, to quote a word of Winston's, was "chequered." He cut his name on the new table in the classroom, and was punished severely by his preceptor, whom he called a "horrid man." The preceptor, in turn, called his pupil a "little blackguard" because the boy had been sitting "with his legs on the form." "I shall never do any good with him," Randolph complained. "He is so unjust."

Undoubtedly, Randolph was a difficult boy. A photograph from his Eton days shows that bulldog tenacity, which he, to humanity's great good luck, later bequeathed to his son. His thick hair tumbled about his forehead. His young face had a queerly determined expression. His short black Eton jacket was shamefully unpressed.

The youthful rebel was "agin" everything. When smallpox was rampant in Eton, he declined to be vaccinated. He termed the Queen's visit to the school "rather eccentric," because Her Majesty had come on a Thursday night, only to rush off again on Friday morning. He derided the enlistment in the rifle corps, at which the boys "had to take a sort of oath and sign their names to a lot of nonsense." He wrote home an account entirely lacking in respect of the visit to Eton of the Prince of Wales and his bride, Princess Alexandra. The Princess Royal's neck must have been stiff, young Randolph observed, for she sat with the boys "and bowed away as hard as she could go." The cheering of the boys gave him a headache. "I never heard such an awful noise in all my life." (Subsequently, he himself made the most awful noise in poised Victorian England.) His greatest pride was his participation in the schoolboy attack when the Prince and Princess of Wales wanted to get silently away in an open carriage after the ordeal of their visit.

"We all rushed after the carriage," Randolph reported to his parents. "It was a second Balaclava. The policemen charged in a body, but they were knocked down. There was a chain put across the road, but we broke it. Several genteel old ladies tried to stop me, but I snapped my fingers in their faces, and cried: 'Hurrah!' and 'What larks!' I frightened some of them horribly. There was a wooden palisade put up at the Great Western Station, but we broke it down, too. I got right down to the door of the carriage of the Prince of Wales who wildly shouted 'Hurrah!' He bowed to me, I am perfectly certain. But I shrieked louder. I am sure, if the Princess did not possess very strong nerves, she would have been frightened; but all she did was to smile blandly. I wonder, were there no accidents when the train at last moved off. We were all so close to the carriage." Finally he reported that in the free-for-all somebody had knocked off his hat. He never saw it again. And he signed himself: "Believe me ever to remain, Your affectionate son Randolph Churchill."

Was not this excess of royalistic exuberance, dangerously approaching open revolt, a clear indication that he was destined by fate to become the leader of the conservative revolution? The ducal father, however, did not recognize Randolph's prospective development at that early time. He sternly rebuked his schoolboy son's misdemeanors, such as pert speeches to masters, an overbearing manner, the unwarranted fagging of small companions, or the breaking of other people's windows. But these stern paternal letters were at the same time affectionate and pleasant. The Duke's rebukes were never founded merely upon authority, but always upon reason, arguing the matter quite fairly with his son, pointing out to him the consequences of his actions, and appealing to his good sense, his self-respect, and the love and honor in which he held his parents. The letters intermingled good advice with family news and accounts of doings at home, reports on the health of the domestic animals, and frequent allusions to public events. Wisely, old Marlborough educated his son under the guise of informing him. He often wrote about Disraeli, whose enthusiastic follower he was. He was a devout, yet not intolerant man. A written remark about an aunt of Randolph's was characteristic of the spirit of the times, which the seventh Duke represented to perfection. "Your aunt," he wrote, "who is with us now is most unhappy. For I fear she is a Roman Catholic at heart, and does not like to say so. If this be true, it would be much better for her to declare her mind; and then, of course, however we might be grieved, the matter would never be alluded to in conversation."

Randolph was deeply impressed by his father's epistles. Usually he answered, after some reluctance and discussion, with frank letters of submission. His father was the only man on earth to whom he ever submitted.

Randolph left Eton, where, as Winston put it, "he seems to have dreamed no dreams." He failed in his first attempt to pass the entrance examination to Oxford. He could only matriculate after having roamed through Switzerland and Italy for two or three months of recovery from the shock. For three successive years in Oxford, with unimportant intervals occasionally filled by study, he hunted down the rabbits of Blenheim, and became a past-master in chess. His father still asserted a slight disciplinary control, but Randolph, undoubtedly, had become the family pet. "He was," his mother wrote, "the soul of wit and fun and cheerfulness in these happy days." Suddenly, after almost three years of rather fitful study, he began to work in earnest. He passed his final examinations, narrowly missing getting a first. As recompense he was once more sent to the European continent, this time on the grand tour, which he thoroughly enjoyed. Returning, he went to Cowes. There was not the smallest cloud in the Marlborough family skies, when a letter to his father, dated August 20, 1873, exploded like a bomb.

"I must not any longer keep you in ignorance of a very important step I have taken," Randolph wrote. "A step which will undoubtedly influence very strongly all my future life.

"I met, soon after my arrival in Cowes, a Miss Jeanette Jerome the daughter of an American lady who has lived for some years in Paris and whose husband lives in New York. I passed most of my time at Cowes in her (Jeanette's) society, and before leaving asked her if she loved me well enough to marry me; and she told me she did. I do not think that if I were to write pages I could give you any idea of the strength of my feelings and affection and love for her; all I can say is that I love her better than life itself, and that my one hope and dream now is that matters may be so arranged that soon I may be united to her by ties that nothing but death itself could have the power to sever.

"I know, of course, that you will be very much surprised, and find it difficult to understand how an attachment so strong could have arisen in so short a space of time; and really I feel it quite impossible for me to give any explanation of it that could appear reasonable to anyone practical and dispassionate. I must, however, ask you to believe it as you could the truest and most real statement that could possibly be made to you, and to believe also that upon a subject so important, and I may say so solemn, I could not write one word that was in the smallest degree exaggerated, or that might not be taken at its fullest meaning."

Page after page the explanation went on, its racing letters and words, the crisp sentences and the involved, endless paragraphs, a son's desperate plea for paternal understanding. The worst of it was that he had to put down on paper the request: "I ask you whether you will be able to increase my allowance to some extent to put me in the position to ask Mrs. Jerome to let me become her daughter's future husband. I enclose Jeanette's photograph," was his last and strongest argument, "and will only say about her that she is as nice, as lovable, and amiable and charming in every way, as she is beautiful, and that by her education and bringing-up she is perfectly qualified to fill any position."

After a reference to the Jerome family, about whom Randolph knew next to nothing except the fact that Mr. Jerome was "obliged to live in New York to look after his business" (it is doubtful whether the seventh Duke of Marlborough would have understood any other explanation), love-struck Randolph concluded with the assertion that without Jeanette life would become to him dreary and uninteresting, and that his energies and hopes would become blunted and dead. Besides, he added, "she loves me as fully, and as strongly, if possible, as I love her."

Every word was true. Jennie and Randolph, born under different stars, molded by widely varying influences, she a cosmopolitan society-girl with a true American background, he an English country squire, revolting against conventions; she strong young blood, he the heir to centuries, which left their mark on him, both of frailty and tenacity; she having acquired laboriously the most refined polish, he imbued with aristocratic habits which he publicly attacked and privately cultivated—this pair of opposites was attracted by a polar magic. They were as far away, and yet as similar, as the north pole and the south pole.

How, indeed, could the wise old Duke of Marlborough have understood the unintelligible—the mystery of love at first sight? It did not fit at all into the pattern set by seven generations of Marlboroughs and countless Churchills before them. Everything about his son's decision was disturbing. Above all, its precipitancy was suspicious. The choice of an American bride-to-be was, to say the least, a problem. It was a bold innovation. Not even the Duke's profound judgment could foresee that Jennie's and Randolph's union would herald an avalanche of Anglo-American marriages in high society. Above all, he felt he must inquire into the standing and circumstances of the Jerome family. It took him ten days of pondering to arrive at this delaying decision. On August 31 he answered his son with a few Olympic lines: "It is not likely that at present you can look at anything except from your own point of view."

Then the Olympian thundered: "But persons from the outside cannot but be struck by the unwisdom of your proceedings, and the uncontrolled state of your feelings, which completely paralyzes your judgment."

The Duchess, for her part, wrote a few affectionate counsels of caution, patience, and self-restraint. The Marquess of Blandford, Randolph's elder brother, did his bit by contributing a few witty and satirical verses on marrying in haste and repenting at leisure.

Across the ocean Leonard Jerome learned of the attitude of the ducal family. He immediately withdrew his first somewhat grudgingly wired consent to the marriage. His American pride, it appeared, was offended. Actually, Mr. Jerome had a particular reason for his ban. This critical moment found him at a low ebb in his fluctuating fortunes, and he did not wish his favorite daughter, for whom he could not provide much of a dowry, to share the perils of the insecure life of a younger son of the peerage. Randolph's threat that he was determined to "make a living inside England or outside, an attitude which Jeanette, I may say, entirely shares with me" did nothing to mitigate Mr. Jerome's anxiety. He ordered his family to retreat to Paris immediately. Many American expatriates had returned there after the end of hostilities. American newcomers, too, for whom life at home, in the booming era of reconstruction, had become too expensive, were joining them.

Although not in concerted action, the Duke of Marlborough heartily agreed with Mr. Jerome's decision. For his part, he even forbade his son to make flying trips to Paris to see his beloved. All interviews, and even communication, were rigidly forbidden. These were the days in which the parents' control even over their grownup children was undisputed. Neither Jennie nor Randolph remonstrated. But they exchanged letters in an unending stream, and he came every four or five weeks for a day or two, just to breathe the air of the boulevards, not to say the Champs Elysées.

His vehement pursuit of his courtship, even at a distance,

was so intense, that the Duke began to fear for Randolph's balance of mind. Perhaps the father also understood that he was exposing his paternal authority to a deadly blow. After a few months His Grace had to acquiesce to a provisional, but formal engagement. Unbending, however, he insisted on delaying the wedding. Nothing but time, he declared, could prove the real strength of what seemed to him an obsession. "The longer the delay, the better," Mr. Jerome grumbled across the Atlantic. And so, after an absence of two years, Jennie was tucked away once more in Paris.

The Jeromes found their home in the Champs Elysées exactly as they had left it. Their goods and chattels were intact. Only the cellar had been destroyed by a shell from Mont Valérien, and no one had thought of repairing it. Paris lay in ruins. The first sight of the half-wrecked Tuileries and of the entirely destroyed Hotel de Ville gave Jennie a shock that made her cry, an emotional escape which she had not permitted herself since her tenth year. St. Cloud, where she had attended so many informal, gay court-fêtes, was razed to the ground. The Germans had gone, but their odor still heavily permeated the perfume of Paris.

The people of Paris could not forget. The statues around the Place de la Concorde, representing the most important French towns—Strasbourg, Lille, Nancy, Orléans—were draped in black. The social fabric, Jennie recognized, was just as badly torn as the city itself. In vain Clarissa Jerome tried to renew contact with her old friends. Many of them were dead, others ruined or in mourning, all were broken-hearted and miserable. The survivors among the aristocracy hid in their houses. The Faubourg St. Germain, the home of the old nobility who had, in later years, reluctantly come to accept the upstart Emperor, was now entirely disorganized. Its denizens drifted as if in a ship without rudder, Jennie observed. What little entertainment was still carried on was by the embassies and a small group of foreigners, mostly Americans. The Jerome girls made friends with the Misses King (one of them subsequently married Mr. Waddington, American ambassador to England), and with Mrs. John Munroe, the wife of the American banker. Their most intimate friends at that time were the Forbes of New York. Two of their daughters eventually married Frenchmen, one M. Odilon Barrot, the son of Louis Philippe's Minister, the other the young Duc de Praslin.

What little was left of French society was split up into innumerable cliques and côteries, each vilifying the others, and all engaged in a battle royal. Paris certainly remained Paris. Politics again raised its ugly head. A general hunt for scapegoats was on. Maréchal Bazaine was singled out as the chief culprit for the disaster that had befallen France.

Jennie went to his trial at Versailles in the Autumn of 1873. Here the heartbroken man, whom in all his glittering glory she had met repeatedly at Compiègne, three years earlier, sat in the prisoners' dock, looking impassively, and only smiling once, when his advocate argued in his defense. With a dramatic gesture, Maître Lachau exclaimed: *"Mais regardez-le donc! Ce n'est pas un traitre, c'est un imbécile!"*

Women stood on their chairs to have a better look at the *imbécile*. The long, low room, over which the Duc d'Aumale presided, was jammed to suffocation by a curious, mischievous, plebeian crowd. It was largely due to the hostility of this audience that Bazaine was condemned to death. His punishment, however, was commuted to a twenty-year term, and after a few months—on the ninth of August, 1874, to be precise— Bazaine was permitted to escape from the Ile St. Marguerite.

"If he was a martyr, I doubt if posterity will place a halo round his head," Jennie, having followed the whole trial with unconcealed interest, commented in a letter to Randolph.

Her political instinct was already wide awake, while his was still soundly asleep. "Public life has no great charms for me," Randolph wrote to his fiancée, "as I am naturally very quiet and hate bother and publicity, which, after all, is full of vanity and vexation of spirit. Still, it will have greater attraction for me,

if I think it will please you." With these words—every one of
them self-deceptive—he conveyed to her good news. It was his
father's fervent wish that Randolph should enter Parliament,
not so much for his own benefit as to hold the constituency of
Woodstock for the Conservatives. A general election was approaching, and since the Duke's own younger brother, Lord
Alfred Churchill, the veteran Member for Woodstock, was
showing dangerous Whig inclinations, the next in line had to
replace him. Woodstock was hereditarily a family constituency.
Hence, the next in line was obviously Lord Randolph.

Randolph saw his great opportunity. He suggested a bargain:
although politically disinterested, he would fulfill his father's
wish, if, on the other hand, the duke would grant him his own
heart's desire. First wedding, then elections. The Duke had to
suppress a smile in his old cavalier's face. His educational principles, still applied to a son who was about to become an M. P.,
forbade him to take the lad in his arms and bless him. Touched
and amused by Randolph's ruse, he was now definitely satisfied
that his son's passion was not a passing caprice, but sincere and
profound affection. "First elections, then wedding!" he coun-
tered. But that condition was only the feint of a last ditch stand.

Randolph, showing a surprising trading sense, agreed, provided that he was permitted to visit the Jeromes in the middle
of December. On these terms the deal was closed, and sealed
with a handshake. Randolph seemed a little absent-minded
during this short, but solemn scene. He was already counting
the days until December 15th. But on the eve of his departure
for Paris, his aunt, Lady Portarlington, fell dangerously ill.
The whole family gathered in her Irish castle at Emo. Randolph
could not absent himself. For a whole month he watched the
old lady's heroic, but hopeless death struggle. He was deeply
shocked when she died, and struck with emotion when she
was buried with much Catholic pomp. (Lady Portarlington
had been the aunt with secret Catholic inclinations referred to
by the Duke.) Randolph tore himself away the very night of

MISS JEANETTE JEROME

the burial. He crossed the Irish Channel intending to proceed to France at daybreak. But the morning papers carried the news that Parliament was dissolved. Of course the campaign for the next election must start immediately.

Randolph's indifference toward politics turned to acute hatred. He would not be kept from visiting his fiancée by the wretched business. But actually he was. The best he could do was to add telegrams to his daily letters which mostly dealt with his love, with hunting and shooting, and family gossip. Jennie's voluminous replies described the Bazaine trial and reported the political temperatures in France, while lamenting the cruel necessity that kept them apart.

For a short time his first political campaign interrupted his letters. During this interval he wired her every day. It was not enough. He resumed his long epistles. But the theme had changed. Within a single week four letters reached Mademoiselle Jeanette Jerome, all of them elaborately describing the joys and worries of campaigning. The joys were much the more plentiful. His election seemed assured. Indeed, he won the seat. In his last report to his fiancée, he boasted: "Ever since I met you everything goes well with me—too well. I am getting afraid of Nemesis. I always hoped I should win the election, but that under the ballot and against a man like Brodrick I should have that crushing, overwhelming majority (of 165 out of 937 voters) never entered into my wildest dreams. It was a great victory—we shall never have a contest again, in Woodstock. You never heard such cheering in all your life." The bug of politics had bitten Lord Randolph.

The Duke accompanied his son to Paris to meet his prospective daughter-in-law. He returned completely won over, withdrawing all his remaining stipulations for the delay of the wedding. The wise old gentleman was entirely carried away by his new, and now welcome, American daughter.

The last difficulty to be solved was the rather obstinate detachment of transatlantic Mr. Jerome toward the plan for an immediate wedding. Again the question of settlements cropped up. "Mr. Jerome," Winston narrates, "had strong, and, it would seem, not unreasonable views, suggested by American usage, about married women's property, and made some propositions which Lord Randolph considered derogatory to him. After an embarrassing discussion Lord Randolph decided to make good his threat of 'earning a living in England or out of it.' Face to face with this ultimatum, Mr. Jerome, who, after all, only wished to make a proper and prudent arrangement, capitulated after twenty-four hours' consideration."

One may be permitted to supplement this authentic report: In point of fact, Leonard Jerome had little money at that time. Practically all he possessed was his splendid manor on Madison Square, with the elaborate stables opposite and the theater above them. This property went to Jennie as a dowry. Leonard Jerome had never been a miser. And when his daughter's happiness was at stake, he gave all he had.

There was no longer any obstacle in the way. On April 15, 1874, a select little party celebrated the Churchill-Jerome wedding at the British Embassy in Paris. As a symbol of perfect family harmony, the Duchess's birthday was chosen as the date of the marriage. The newly-weds went on what was intended to be a continental tour. But Randolph was so impatient to show his bride Blenheim Castle, with its famous collection of old masters, its horses and hounds, and the faithful tenants who were a part of the place, that the young couple decided to see the European continent another time.

Their entry into the borough of Woodstock was triumphal. Now the happiness of life began every day anew. On the third of December, 1874, the *Times* of London printed among its birth notices the following:

"On the 30th November at Blenheim Palace, the Lady Randolph Churchill, prematurely, of a son."

"A young man in a hurry" from the very beginning, Winston was a seven months child. The fat and pink baby raised a terrific din. Her Grace, Frances Anne, Duchess of Marlborough, famed for her salty *mots*, shook her head and observed: "After all, I have myself given life to quite a number of infants. They were all pretty vocal when they arrived. But such an earth-shaking noise as this newborn baby made I have never heard."

Part Two: LADY RANDOLPH

CHAPTER VII *Conquest of London*

"Before the century is out, these clever and pretty women from New York will pull the strings in half the chanceries of Europe," Lord Palmerston, the British Prime Minister, had predicted upon the Prince of Wales' return from his American journey. A little more than two years later the scene was set for the invasion of England by American belles. The scene was Sandringham, the 7,000 acre estate which the Prince-Consort purchased for his son in 1862—the year of Edward's coming of age—and Marlborough House, the palace built by Wren, which was now set aside for the Prince. Both establishments were soon to become the centers of social leadership, which Edward exercised with a vengeance, probably to offset the fact that he was strictly kept out of state affairs by the Queen. His liberal and tolerant inclination, combined with an exuberant zest for living and insatiable curiosity for new faces and things, above all the friendly welcome he bade American visitors of either sex (with a slight preference for the fair one) made the Prince the strongest single influence in turning Victorian London into Cosmopolis.

The time was propitious for the change. After the fall of Imperial Paris the international set felt homeless. They were in search of a new capital of glamour and fashion. Continentals and colonials—the *nouveaux riches* from booming South Africa and rapidly expanding Australia, the China merchants and the retiring Empire builders from all over the world—found a friendly welcome on the shores of the Thames. Thanks to a very high influence they were no longer considered outsiders. The age of mercantilism broke into the quiet, aristocratic mid-Victorian era. Its strongest, and most remarkable exponents were, of course, the well-to-do Americans. By the score they transferred their European patronage and expenditure from Paris to London. When the sporting world of both countries came into closer contact, the heyday of Anglo-American social friendship approached. The earliest Anglo-American boat-race, between Oxford and Harvard, led to enthusiastic demonstrations of fraternity. Old, white-haired Dickens, presiding over the dinner at the Crystal Palace, warned in his most charming manner: "Beware of those Harvard fellows; they are very dangerous men," and supported his warning with a glowing account of examples of heroism in American history. On the other side of the big pond Lord Hartington, later the Duke of Devonshire, and Lord Rosebery, who was to become Prime Minister, made themselves extremely popular on repeated visits to outstanding American hosts.

Benevolently, the Prince of Wales smiled at the new transatlantic friendships. He was an ardent theater fan, and he found a new interest in the American spirit when, in the late Sixties, the theater from the other side swept London, and scored a number of hits. In 1866 Charles Farrar Browne triumphed as Artemus Ward. London had expected to meet a professional joker, thriving on slang. Instead it discovered a highly cultivated, decidedly intellectual, painfully sensitive gentleman quite without any nasal twang. Soon Colonel Bateman, the American impresario, rented the Lyceum Theater and produced a smash hit with Henry Irving as Mathias in "The Bells." Charles Albert Fechter became as popular in London as he was in the United States. Joseph Jefferson, in the part of Rip Van Winkle, created outright enthusiasm for the American scene among London theater-goers.

The shock-troop of the American conquerors of fashionable

London, however, were *"les belles Americaines."* They made good Lord Houghton's prophecy at the time when Jerome Bonaparte had established himself in the U. S. A., to wed Elizabeth Patterson, a Baltimore merchant's daughter: "In the next century," His Lordship had predicted, "this wedding will be looked back upon as the foundation of the American cult on the European side of the Atlantic." He had only erred in his timing. Already during the last quarter of the nineteenth century London society was largely influenced, and partly dominated, by American women. During the seasons of 1883 and 1885 the two most fashionable and outstanding concerts showed, "by Royal desire," exclusively performers selected among the London circle of American ladies.

Eagerly American debutantes sought to be presented at court. The rise of their great fortunes made it easier, but it was still a rare prize, since only three or four American ladies were presented every summer. The competition for this highest honor was murderous. It was, however, well worth while. Presentation was the open sesame to English society. Once a name was inscribed on the Royal List, invitations to the Buckingham Palace garden parties and balls followed automatically.

The Prince of Wales, generally fond of Americans—because, he said, they could tell a good story and were born card players —lavished his praises on the young, unmarried American women. "They are not as squeamish as their English sisters," he opined, "and they are more able to take care of themselves. They are livelier, better educated, and less hampered by etiquette." Few were the young American girls in London who could resist such flattery. Most decided to remain for life. The example of a much-proposed-to American heiress, who wrote: "I am writing my declensions. This London is a good enough sort of place for flirtations, but I mean to conjugate at home," found little following. Miss Minnie Stevens and Miss Beckwith became Lady Paget and Lady Leigh, respectively. Their pattern was eagerly copied by many an American bride who "conjugated" with the scion of a great English family, grafting the vigor of her race and wealth upon the old aristocratic stock. Anglo-American weddings became the great fashion. But when Lord Randolph Churchill brought home his American bride, it was not a fashionable event alone. A page in contemporary British history was turned.

The young couple first visited Blenheim, which, under the patriarchal rule of His Grace George Charles, Seventh Duke of Marlborough, and under the considerably more rigid regime of Her Grace, the Duchess Frances Anne, was a silent and rather secluded monument of British tradition and history; its gates were not yet open to streams of sight-seers.

Blenheim Palace is an Italian castle, surrounded by an English park. It embodies in stone all the remembrances of Woodstock, Oxfordshire, the soil of the oldest English culture. Here the Roman generals built their winter villas two thousand years ago. For a thousand years and more Woodstock had been a focal point of English life; it was noted before the Norman conquest. Here Saxon, Norman, Plantagenet kings held court. Blenheim was already a borough when the Domesday Book was being compiled. The park housed the wild beasts of Henry I. In the Civil War Woodstock House was held for King Charles until at last it was ravaged by the roundheads. Queen Anne presented John Churchill, the greatest of England's soldiers, with Blenheim Palace, the estate of Woodstock (the town was later to become the Oxfordshire capital of glove making), and a dukedom. Thus the House of Marlborough was created.

On a beautiful spring day in May, 1874, Lord Randolph and his lady arrived in his ancestral home. They came in a hand-drawn car. Some of the Duke's tenants, who were, by the same token, Randolph's constituents, had welcomed the couple at the railroad station and had insisted on taking the horses out of the shafts and dragging the newly-weds through the town to the castle.

To Randolph it was home-coming, indeed. He was back where he belonged. Again he would be, as his mother had expressed it, "the soul of wit and fun and cheerfulness" at home, again the "young autocrat," as he was called for the intense interest he took in all the affairs of the family, particularly in such questions as what balls his sisters had been to, and with whom they had danced. Now the three elder ones were already "out" —married—and the elder brother, the Marquess of Blandford, was serving with the Blues, the Royal House Guards. Blenheim appeared a little empty. But Randolph would bring his friends over to the castle again, and Mr. Disraeli, who loved young people, would come once more to talk and joke with them, and impart unobtrusively a bit of his wisdom.

Even the family could not give Randolph and his bride a heartier reception than did the farmers and peasants. Truly, they loved him. For years he had mingled with them, always courteously and considerately. He had frequently enjoyed the hospitality of their cottages, and shared both their merriment and their struggles. Indeed, the man who was to become England's stormy petrel was in his early youth the best-known and best-liked figure in his county.

Blenheim Castle lay basking in sunshine. Its magnificent aspect, probably combined with heart-warming memories, induced Randolph to the proud statement: "This is the finest view in England."

The couple was passing through the entrance archway. The lake, the bridge, the miles of magnificent park, studded with old oaks, "burst" as she later expressed it, upon the new Lady Randolph. She was awe-stricken. Of course, she would not admit to being awed. Her American pride, she explained smiling, when she recalled the incident, forbade such a feeling. Just in time Pope's lines about Blenheim flashed through her mind, and not without a touch of malice she quoted to Randolph:

> "See, sir, here's the grand approach;
> This way is for his grace's coach:
> There lies the bridge, and here's the clock
> Observe the lion and the cock,
> The spacious court, the colonnade,
> And mark how wide the hall is made.

The chimneys are so well design'd
They never smoke in any wind.
This gallery contrived for walking,
The windows to retire and talk in;
The council chamber for debate,
And all the rest are rooms of state."
"Thanks, sir," cried I, "'tis very fine,
But where d'ye sleep, or where d'ye dine?
I find by all you have been telling,
That 'tis a house, but not a dwelling."

She recited the satiric verses without the slightest ill will. It was the inevitable response of a progressive American girl to the impact, centuries in marble and stone must necessarily make on her. But the impact proved stronger than the first hesitation. Young Lady Randolph soon found that Blenheim was very much of a house; indeed, for long years it remained the refuge to which she ever returned, and her anchorage.

At first, life in a palatial country-house seemed strange to a young woman, until then accustomed to the hurly-burly of the world's two or three biggest cities. However, she adapted herself rapidly to the dignified and somewhat formal style, in which the Duke and Duchess of Marlborough lived. The rules were set by the Duchess; they were carried out with a firm hand. "At the rustle of her silk dress the household trembled," Lady Randolph reminisced. This silk dress, perpetuated in her portrait, was in the great stately fashion; it was covered with lace and adorned with an endless train. The Duchess did not follow slavishly the changing trends of Victorian modes. Faithfully she clung to the crinoline, even when hoop and bustle became *de rigueur*. Her hair retained its chestnut color well into her later years. Two ringlets fell on either shoulder. A pendant, dropping from a diamond necklace, pearl earrings, and a single ring on the fourth finger of her right hand, with a few bracelets were all the jewels she displayed. Her most precious jewel remained concealed. This was, Lady Randolph soon discovered, a warm heart, disguised behind a certain "over-masterfulness" of bearing, of which the Duchess was occasionally accused. But in case of need everyone among her circle, her children and even her distant relatives, sought comfort and advice from her. Fate, it later developed, had burdened her with heavy and painful tasks. She discharged them unflinchingly, without complaint, and with great determination. It was she, a high-placed observer noticed, who kept the "somewhat erratic Churchills" together.

Lord Randolph, both in his youth and still more in his mature years, did much to justify the attribute "erratic" that was pinned on his family. But he was hopelessly bested by his elder brother, who was thirty years of age when Lord and Lady Randolph came to Blenheim. Unwittingly this man played a decisive role in his brother's and sister-in-law's fate. George Charles Spencer Churchill (the Christian names were hereditary among the first sons of the family), Marquess of Blandford, later the eighth Duke of Marlborough, Prince of the Holy Roman Empire and Prince of Mindelheim in Suabia, was, it appears, an eccentric genius. Many people believed that he was much more brilliant than his brother Randolph. But, unlike him, he was not destined to temporary fame, although his name was rarely missing from the contemporary gossip columns.

The Marquess of Blandford, who had not studied at a university, was nevertheless much more seriously studious and scholastic minded than his younger brother. He was a French scholar far above the average. Lord Granville, British ambassador in Paris, was said to be the only man in England whose command of the Paris argot rivaled Blandford's, whose knowledge of the intimacies and intricacies of the Parisian scene, however, was unparalleled. Frequent journeys took him all over the Continent. As "unofficial gentleman" he maintained a voluminous correspondence with nearly every European chancery. Diplomats, cabinet ministers, ranking civil servants were his frequent guests at Blenheim, the palace famous for the lavish hospitality displayed by both the ducal father and his elder son. Not only statesmen, but men of letters, science, and affairs as well enjoyed the friendly atmosphere of the castle.

Blandford was a member of London's foremost diplomatic club, the St. James's, Piccadilly, where he met, and made friends with, Lord Palmerston. At times, he was the Prime Minister's most intimate and most important informer. But Lord Palmerston could never induce his young friend to don official harness. Blandford was anxious to retain his freedom, particularly his freedom to travel. His favorite country was India, which he explored repeatedly and leisurely.

But playing with great ideas, he never developed sufficient tenacity to carry them out. In his early youth he dabbled in politics, frightening his father with liberal inclinations; for a few years he even admired the unspeakable Mr. Gladstone. He wished to come forward as a parliamentary candidate for Westminster. Why he never actually stood, but confined himself to writing some thoughtful articles on contemporary questions for newspapers and magazines (and later some impressive speeches in the House of Lords displaying expert knowledge of foreign affairs) was never explained, least of all by himself. Since a gentleman had to have at least a semblance of a profession, he obtained a commission in the Blues, without showing great inclination for the military calling. His interests were rather on the artistic and scientific side. He was a recognized connoisseur of paintings. Higher mathematics, in which he was thoroughly versed, and physics, chemistry, and mechanics were his main interests for many years. He had established a chemical laboratory on the ground floor of one of the wings of the palace, and there he spent several hours a day. He was wont to interrupt his experiments all of a sudden for a drive through the estate in his favorite dog-cart with a very high-stepping horse. Then he returned again to practical experiments with the turning lathe, or to another of his hobbies: manufacturing with his own hands cigarette holders in meerschaum or amber, boxes in ebony, caskets of ivory, as presents for his friends. Without envy he admitted, however, that his younger brother Randolph was more skillful in manipulating the works of clocks and watches, as he was in the game of chess.

At the age of twenty-five Blandford had married the Lady Alberta Frances Anne Hamilton, a daughter of the Duke of Abercorn, related to half the greatest houses of the peerage. The marriage, later terminated by divorce, was martyrdom for both. More than once the Marquess was named co-respondent in a divorce suit. After such incidents he preferred to breathe the air of America for a while, where he and two of his friends, both English dukes—the Dukes of Sunderland and Manchester, enjoyed great social popularity: popularity with the profligates, as some grumblers at home termed it.

No one, however, could dispute the fact that Blandford, in his youth, shared with Lord Francis Knollys the honor of being the Prince of Wales' inseparable boon companions. He imparted to his royal friend some of his own intellectual interests. Although Blandford generally passed as an unconcerned, selfish epicurean, the Prince, knowing his friend better, realized that here was a man with deep interest in the underlying problems of the times. This made their ensuing clash and separation all the more tragic.

Towering *au dessus de la mêlée* was His Grace, the seventh Duke, one of the last born grand seigneurs in appearance and manner. He rarely left his home except to attend, as Lord President of the Council in Disraeli's first government, the Cabinet sessions. Even in his mature years he had preserved his youthful looks, a blessing on a life spent in dignity and righteousness, in kindliness and duty. His last pictures show a man who bears the weight of his years lightly. His smooth face, framed in white hair parted in the middle and covering his ears and reaching as far as the Dundreary whiskers, is unmarked by wrinkles. Below his high forehead arch strong eyebrows, still black, and overshadowing the inscrutable Churchill eyes. A straight nose, tight lips and a pugnaciously protruding chin convey the impression of controlled and tempered energy. His erect deportment makes him appear taller than middle-sized.

He is clad in the uniform of the Victorian gentleman: the black morning-coat with the silk facings reaching down to the knees, and the black and gray checked trousers. His style is formal, and it clearly appears that this mundane pilgrimage was spent in eminence and distinction.

Young Lady Randolph enjoyed her new home tremendously. She soon discovered her two favorite places. One was the flower garden outside the gates, laid out around a long, low building, the riding school, occasionally used for picnics and informal parties. This predilection was innocent. But people gravely shook their heads at the other place, where the American lady spent so much of her time. About a mile down the park there was a piece of boggy soil, haunted by snipe and moorfowl, fringing a stagnant, dull-looking sheet of water in which some of the biggest eels in England vegetated. The eels, of course, are miniature monsters. They are still terrible when they expire, after capture with rod and line, or with a net. Dying, and even after skinning, the eel still wriggles in a horrible fashion. Lady Randolph was a passionate eel-fisherwoman. No one understood this strange proclivity. She actually laughed at the eels' ferocious fight to the end. But since she soon proved to be an infallible snipe hunter, too (and the snipe is the most difficult bird to hit), and since she hunted her harriers in a genuinely professional manner, the delighted Blenheim tenancy and the whole countryside accepted her as a great sport.

For her part she felt, at first, the atmosphere of dignified Blenheim somewhat burdensome. Everything, she observed, was conducted in a very old-fashioned manner. The Duke and Duchess, for instance, would never have allowed anyone to help himself to a dish at the ceremonial luncheon table. The joints beneath massive silver covers were placed within reach of host and hostess, and together they carved for the whole company, for the guests, the grown-up members of the family and the children, as well as for the tutors and governesses who were included at the table. This work of carving seemed "no sinecure" to Lady Randolph. In her own house the service would not be quite as ducal as that. But she was impressed with the habit of equipping the children, before they left the dining-room, with food baskets for distribution among the poor or sick people in the neighborhood.

When Blenheim was full of guests, mostly gathering for shooting parties, breakfast was a ceremonious meal. No one could sit down to his cup of tea before the whole company was assembled. Already in the morning the ladies appeared in long velvet or silk trains. Lightly, with becoming modesty, they would admit: "It's a Stratton." (Yesterday it would have been a Patou, today a Norman Hartnell.) But to the amused ducal daughter-in-law from New York it sounded as if one of these pompous ladies were saying: "It's a Rubens."

Luncheon at a shooting party was, on the other hand, not the glorified affair into which it developed largely under the Prince of Wales' influence. At Blenheim the guests were quite content with a few cold bites, swallowed in a hurry, somewhere in the open air, to save time for the serious business of shooting. Mid-Victorian days and ways were dignified, but matter of fact. No one foresaw the time, very soon to come, in which the pheasants would get away, while His Royal Highness, surrounded by his friends, was relishing an elaborate eight-course lunch in a carpeted tent.

Dinner at Blenheim, even if restricted to the family, was a solemn full-dress affair. Afterwards everyone had the free choice between reading a book or banding together for a mild game of whist, for love, of course. Bedtime came when the clock struck eleven, which occurred at half-past ten if Lady Randolph had surreptitiously advanced the hands of the clock, very much to the delight of her sleepy in-laws. The eleven strokes ended the day in style. The family rose at the eleventh stroke, trooped into a small anteroom where each lit his candle, kissed the Duke and Duchess, and retired to his own bedroom.

On the surface such a life appeared very much like dull routine. But there was nothing of it. The Churchills were an explosive, if ever dignified little group. Their temperaments and affections, their humors, moods and proclivities, their quarrels and their laughter kept the kettle constantly boiling. The bubbles burst without doing much harm. Unpleasant things were not talked about. Lord Randolph's constant physical afflictions and ailments were not a topic of conversation. That the family fortunes of the House of Marlborough were dwindling was a sorry fact, never alluded to, nor expressed in any restriction of the ducal expenditure. For fourteen years after the day of her wedding (on November 11, 1869) the Marchioness of Blandford did not open her tightly-closed lips to utter a single word about her husband's escapades.

Jennie, indeed, was back in school. She had a good deal to learn, and to admire. The palace was truly a museum. It still housed the world-famous Sunderland Library, with its beautiful old leather bindings filling the immense long gallery with its white, carved bookcases and vaulted ceilings. Cabinets of Limoges enamels carried the visitor back through the centuries. The Duchess's sitting room was a show piece of genuine Renaissance. In a separate chamber the priceless Marlborough jewels were kept in gold cases. Other rooms were full of unique Oriental, Sèvres, and Dresden china. Centuries had contributed to the picture collection of four hundred and fifty old masters, among them Rubens, Van Dykes, Raphaels, presented to the Dukes of Marlborough by kings and crowned heads. The famous tapestries, representing the victorious battles of the First Duke, had been given him by the various towns that were the scenes of his triumphs. Once upon a time, four generations earlier, a French ambassador, visiting the Fifth Duke, kept asking unnecessary and almost insolent questions: "The house, the pictures, the tapestries—were they all given? This Raphael—a gift from the King of Prussia, I understand? Is there anything here that has not been given?" "I'll show you something," the Duke replied with a chuckle. Leading his guest outside, he pointed out the stone trophies and the effigy of Louis XIV which adorned the south front of the house. "These," he said,

"were not given. They were taken by John, Duke of Marlborough, from the gates of Tournai."

Most deeply impressed by Blenheim seemed the then Prussian Crown Prince, later the short-lived Emperor Frederick,
who was for a few days a house-guest in the palace. English life
seemed rather luxurious to his Spartan Prussianism. "Ach, much
too good, much too good!" he kept saying, as breakfast was
served him in a gold tea-service, got out in his honor.

Members of royalty were not infrequent visitors. Lady Randolph became quickly accustomed to execute the formal curtsy
combined with a most informal smile. It was her great good luck
to learn this refinement from an intimate friend of the Duchess,
another Duchess, the widow of the third Duke of Cleveland.
Her Grace was one of the last survivors, still going strong,
of the early Victorian generation. She was the grandmother of
Lord Rosebery, already at that time a budding statesman of
great promise. Among other qualities, her unapproachability
was famous. To her family doctor, the story went, who had written her "My dear Duchess" the old lady answered promptly:
"Sir, I am not your dear Duchess." When Lady Randolph
was introduced to her, no handshake, the rapidly spreading new
form of greeting, was permitted. Instead, the aged Duchess
acknowledged the young woman's low bow (the Duchess of
Cleveland was at least three times Jennie's age) with an equally
deep curtsy. Thus a friendship was established, which soon included Lord Randolph, always an old ladies' pet. Then Her
Grace wished to see the baby. Aged seven or eight months,
Winston was, of course, the leading man of Blenheim.

The young Churchills' first home in London was a modest
house in Curzon Street. Their means were limited, but their capacity for enjoying themselves was unbounded. London was an
enormous playground. Those days of 1874 were the heydays of
Victorian serenity. Profound peace reigned in politics after
Disraeli had won the elections which had brought Randolph

into the house. The unassuming back-bencher did not attract much attention. Throughout the first three years of this Parliament he did not speak longer than an hour and a half all told, mainly about the local affairs of his constituency, Woodstock, and on one occasion protesting the proposed establishment of a military camp in the vicinity of Oxford. Although he had spoken against the government to whose majority he belonged, Disraeli wrote the Duchess of Marlborough a friendly account of her son's performance: "He said some imprudent things, which was of no consequence in the maiden speech of the young man," the old statesman's letter read, "but he spoke with fire and fluency; and showed energy of thought and character, with evidence of resource. With self-control and assiduity he may obtain a position worthy of his name, and mount."

But at this moment Lord Randolph did not yet care to mount. He was exclusively occupied with being married to the most beautiful bride and in assisting her conquest of London. Lady Randolph was hungry for the world. After her comparatively quiet second sojourn in Paris, and after the rigorous happiness in Blenheim, she plunged headlong into the pulsating turbulence of her first London season, enjoying it with all the vigor and unjaded appetite of her youth.

The London season at that time was a whirlwind of balls and parties, of gaieties and excitement. Excursions to Paris, where her mother and sisters still lived and where Lord Randolph improved his taste for the French cuisine and culture, were frequent. In winter the young couple returned for a short visit to Blenheim, to hunt with the Heythrop Hounds. A night without a ball—which invariably lasted until five o'clock in the morning —was simply a wasted night. Many of the great houses threw their gates open to the fashionable throng. Masked balls were the great vogue. They climaxed in the entertainments in Holland House with its venerable historical associations and its beautiful gardens, the perfect setting for unforgettable nights.

Merrymaking had lost the touch of coarseness which had still permeated entertainment during the early Victorian days. The times, in which ladies and gentlemen found it great fun when young Lord Hamilton unloosed a sack of rats upon a crowded ballroom, were definitely gone. But the English predilections for practical jokes persisted. Now they were of a more innocent sort. At one of her first balls, Lady Randolph remembered, a lady who dabbled in hypnotism, then the latest craze, told Randolph she would experiment with him. He might try to do what he wished, *her* will would direct him. He threw his arms around his fair challenger, and kissed her. "I was just doing what I wished," he explained. Everyone was highly amused. Another time—this happened in Holland House—Lady Randolph herself, disguised in a painted mask and a blond wig, cornered a most eligible bachelor who had just returned from a moon-lit walk through the park with her younger sister, a guest from Paris. Lady Randolph, presenting herself as her sister's mother, uttered the fateful words: "I see, you just proposed to my daughter." Vehemently, the entirely innocent sinner denied this. But she persisted in threatening him that her husband would call on him the next day, reveal the family's identity, and ask for an explanation. In the meantime, Lady Randolph concluded, she would consider him engaged to her charming daughter. "Deficient in humor and not overburdened with brains, he could not take the joke, and left the house a miserable man," she concluded her recollection of this little incident.

But the gaiety on which she thrived could not dim her critical instincts. She soon decided that English people were dull-witted at masked balls. They neither understood nor entered into the spirit of intrigue. Perhaps, she concluded in all fairness, the reason for this dullness was that according to the English custom both sexes were masked, which would have been impossible abroad. The license a man in New York or Paris might have taken if his identity were to remain unknown would not have been tolerated. On the other hand, the respectability of English excesses of cheerfulness, the seasoned American belle observed, could easily become tiresome. "You don't know me! You don't know me!" was the happy parrot cry with which many a masked lady was perfectly satisfied to exhaust her animated conversation.

Lady Randolph had immediately fallen for the spell of London, and the capital had received her triumphantly, yet she felt occasionally hurt in her American pride. The predilections for the *belle Americaine* was still the privilege of the new society, under the Prince of Wales' leadership, but the sentiment was by no means shared by popular opinion. Perhaps the explanation was that at the time of Lady Randolph's entry in Belgravia only a handful of American women had already entrenched themselves in recognized positions, despite the constant influx of debutantes seeking presentation at court. There were, to be exact, three leading ladies from across the seas: Miss Consuelo Ysnaga, a Cuban heiress, afterwards the Duchess of Manchester, Miss Stevens, later Lady Paget, and Mrs. William Carrington. These beautiful pioneers were perfectly satisfied with their personal successes. Not so Lady Randolph. In all her joyful devotion to her new homeland, she remained a faithful daughter of the old country, which, reversing the usual conception, was America. Already in her early youth a strictly private life was not enough for her. An outstanding individuality, she was nevertheless endowed with a strong collective conscience.

Some notions about Americans, and particularly about American women, almost equally wide-spread in mid-Victorian England as on the Continent, offended her. "The American woman," she observed, "was looked upon as a strange and abnormal creature, with habits and manners something between a Red Indian and a Gaiety Girl. Anything of an outlandish nature might be expected of her. If she talked, dressed and conducted herself as any well-bred woman would, much astonishment was invariably evinced, and she was usually saluted with the tactful remark 'I should never have thought you were an American.' This was intended as a compliment. As a rule, people looked upon her as a disagreeable and even dangerous person, to be viewed with suspicion, if not avoided altogether. Her dollars were her only recommendation, and each was credited with the possession of them, otherwise what was her *raison d'être?* No distinction was ever made among Americans; they were all supposed to be of one uniform type. The wife and daughters of the newly enriched Californian miner, swathed in silks and satins, and blazing with diamonds on the smallest provocation; the cultured, retired, and refined Bostonian; the aristocratic Virginian, as full of tradition and family pride as a Percy of Northumberland, or a La Rochefoucauld; the cosmopolitan and up-to-date New Yorker: all were grouped in the same category, all were tarred with the same brush.

"The innumerable caricatures supposed to represent the typical American girl depicted her always of one type: beautiful and refined in appearance, but dressed in exaggerated style, and speaking—with a nasal twang—the most impossible language. The young lady who, in refusing to eat, said: 'I'm pretty crowded just now,' or in explaining why she was traveling alone remarked that 'Poppa don't voyage, he's too fleshy,' was thought to be representative of the national type and manners.

"American men are myths, few being idle enough to have leisure to travel. But they were all supposed to be as loud and vulgar as the mothers were unpresentable, and the daughters undesirable—unless worth their weight in gold."

Undoubtedly some personal incidents had contributed to forming Lady Randolph's harsh opinion. It was thought astonishing, even in society, if an American from New York knew nothing of one in San Francisco, as though they came from neighboring counties. On the continent this ignorance was even worse. A high-placed Frenchman once asked her whether she knew a certain Chilean lady. As she replied in the negative, he exclaimed: "*Mais n'êtes vous pas toutes les deux Americaines?*"

After much water had flowed under London Bridge, and as the busy and crowded years were passing, Lady Randolph's aroused opinions mellowed considerably. At the summit of her life she could proudly proclaim the great progress American women had made in Europe. Their position had become unassailable. Many of them were sharing the seats of the mighty.

The most jealous and carping critic could not find fault with the ingenuity with which they filled them. They were holding their own, and more than their own, in the worlds of politics, diplomacy, literature, and the arts. The old ignorant prejudices against them had been entirely removed, and for good. All this Lady Randolph recognized as a fact. She never boasted that she had been the principal single factor in promoting this happy development. Perhaps she was unaware that she lived her gay life constantly in the service of causes. The meteoric career of her husband, her son Winston's access to influence and importance, the intimacy of Anglo-American relations were the most important of these causes. She never forgot that she was born Jennie Jerome, of Brooklyn. The first cause she served was the recognition of the American woman in Europe.

The small house in Curzon Street did not provide a large enough frame. In the spring of 1875 Lord and Lady Randolph moved into a bigger house in Charles Street, which offered better opportunities to continue their pleasant yet purposeful life on a somewhat wider scale. Neither of them cared about the sorry fact that their income did not quite suffice, and that they were venturing into unending money worries. Nor did Lord Randolph, whose appetite for success was constantly whetted by his enterprising, beautiful, and loving wife, pay much attention to his prematurely failing physical strength. To Lady Randolph, a red-blooded American, illness was simply hypochondria. She remembered Ward McAllister's fretfulness. In the prime of his life he liked to surround himself with an army of doctors and quacks. Life was so sweet to him that he probably wanted to prolong its span to a hundred years, and then start out once again.

The case of Lord Randolph was considerably more serious. But only frail, aged Disraeli, himself already tottering to the grave, seemed to notice anything. In his novel "Vivian Grey" he prophetically drew the main lines of Randolph's character. Vivian, like Randolph, went in for politics for the excitement of the thing, and proceeded on the assumption that every man who seemed dull was necessarily an idiot. Vivian fooled and abused the stupid Marquess of Carabas, and smashed the house of cards the latter had established. But after his collapse, the fictitious—or not so fictitious, since many believed they recognized Olympic Mr. Gladstone in the figure—Marquess could go back to his park, his stable and cellars, whereas Vivian, when, in turn, his own hour struck, hardly knew where to hide. Since an early age Vivian had had a feeling of depression. He sensed that he had not long to live, and could not wait. Unless things he wanted came quickly, they were useless to him.

All these elements were only in the making when Lord Randolph, an indefatigable host and brilliant conversationalist, presided at the table of his new and a trifle too ambitious establishment in Charles Street. It took the old Jew's shrewd insight into human nature to recognize the warning beacons. Perhaps he wanted to impart a delicate lesson in moderation, when, dining for the first time in Charles Street, he refused to allow his glass to be refilled with the words: "My dear Randolph, I have sipped your excellent champagne. I have drunk your good claret. I have tasted your delicious port—I will have no more."

"I think Dizzy must have enjoyed himself," said Lord Randolph after the departure of the guest of honor. "But how flowery and exaggerated his language is."

"You are quite right," Lady Randolph agreed. "He sat next to me, and I particularly remarked that he drank nothing but a little weak brandy and water."

Both laughed, because the party had been a great success, because their days were rich and promising—never mind the creditors!—and because they loved one another very deeply.

It had been the first official party in Charles Street. True, the French chef, newly imported from Paris, had got rather excited at his London debut. The entrée, in the shape of patties, floated in the soup whereas the poached eggs, intended for the *potage*, appeared in lonely magnificence. Lady Randolph had excused herself for being a very poor housewife, but old Dizzy had come to her rescue: "A young one, a very young one."

He became a frequent visitor. He enjoyed Lady Randolph's company with the relish of a collector of beautiful times and memories long gone. Above all, he enjoyed her classic French, a language in which he himself was somewhat deficient. Yet, the old *bon vivant* did his best to drag French words into his own conversation. He pronounced them atrociously. Lady Randolph could not help laughing when the great Lord Beaconsfield on one occasion called a man whom he disliked "very gross, like an episeer." *Epicier* was the word he had in mind. The aged Prime Minister relished a pretty young woman's laugh, even if the laugh was on him. Whenever they met at balls or receptions the Prime Minister engaged her in conversation. This caused much chaff among her friends. Silly rumors cropped up. Only the Prince of Wales saw the friendship developing between the unequal pair in its true proportions. One day, at an evening party in Carlton House Terrace, he asked Lady Randolph, who had just finished another chat with the great old man: "Tell me, my dear, what office did you get for Randolph?"

For two years Lord and Lady Randolph lived strictly according to the peculiar London calendar. Their year began early in February, when the members of Parliament with their families came to town for a six weeks' session. Another six weeks of respite followed. May brought the "season." There were the classic races—the Derby, Ascot week, and finally Goodwood. The serious followers of racing looked forward to their week in Newmarket. Parties were arranged for the pigeon-shooting at Hurlingham, or to watch the shooting for the Elcho shield at Wimbledon. There were, too, the flower-shows at the Botanical Gardens. Religiously, Belgravia opened the doors of its freshly-painted and flower-bedecked mansions on the first of May to celebrate the most breath-taking, frolicking, ravishing and exhausting climax of the year: the London season, which lasted, with a short recess at Whitsuntide, until the end of July. On the first of August Belgravia closed its doors. Society fled. From October to early February the world's largest city was a desert.

Belgravia is, of course, a social, and not strictly a geographical location. In the Seventies the fashionable world reached out toward Bayswater—"Tyburnia" to the initiated—to the North, and to the South as far as South Kensington, with Piccadilly as its center. Mayfair, once notorious as one of the most disreputable and dangerous quarters of London, was its heart.

The denizens of Belgravia, whom Lord Beaconsfield had portrayed in innumerable novels, were coroneted, or hoped to become so. Most of them belonged to families long titled. No one was welcomed whose ancestors had been in trade or in the "city." People in commerce, as well as in certain professions, remained untouchables for a long time. A country squire, whose income from his estates permitted him to keep up an elaborate town house, would occasionally invite his doctor or lawyer to a formal reception, but rarely, if ever, to a dinner party. This exclusivism, it is true, deteriorated gradually during Lady Randolph's first years in London. Some of the new dwellers in Mayfair or Tyburnia had migrated from the old Russell Square district. A few of them wisely kept silent as to their ancestral origins, which were perhaps not quite unconnected with trade, though, if admitted, only with a trade having a romantic touch. It became permitted to have had a grandfather who had dealt in Arabian coffee, Indian rice and shawls, China teas and other exotic goods brought into the London docks by the famous clippers, then making sailing history.

Talk about money was taboo. It was supposed to be so plentiful that it was not worth mentioning. This fiction was still adhered to, when feudalism gradually declined through the constant decrease in the prices of agricultural products, which greatly diminished the income from big estates. Step by step feudalism was submerged by the rising finance. Speculation in railway stocks, a prospering industry, shares in the newly discovered diamond fields in South Africa or in the gold-rush in

California and Australia, the rapid progress of science and invention, the development of trade and traffic—all these elements made for the great transformation of English wealth and, consequently, society. A generation earlier *Punch* had divided the English social strata into three distinct groups: High Life, Middle Life, and Low Life. This separation was waning in the years Lady Randolph was about to impress her personal mark on English society. She herself belonged in both camps. By descent she represented the up-and-coming finance, whose drive and push she charmingly embodied, by taste and choice she clung to the old style, assuming it with incomparable adaptability.

In her second year in London she was already equally at home in the Strand, the shopping center and, by the same token, the core of theaterland, as in the aristocratic mansions in Bloomsbury or Bayswater. She knew the secrets of these houses: the enormous costs of upkeep and the eternal servant problem; but she joined in the convention that forbade conversing about them. She developed entertaining to a fine art. Her parties were a matter of careful deliberation in the selection of guests, food, wine, and, above all, in the consideration of private or political interests which could be tactfully pursued around the dinner table.

The arrangement of young Lady Randolph's day conformed strictly with the customs of her circle. The chief event was the daily drive between twelve and two in Hyde Park. During these hours the park offered the most brilliant and animated scene in the world. From the Queen down, everyone congregated to ride, drive, or walk. Young mothers were in the habit of displaying their children, who set off their beauty even better than their pet dogs. But Lady Randolph took exception to this rule. To her, little Winston was not a show piece.

For two hours the park was filled with a smartly dressed crowd, jostling one another to have a look at the four-in-hands, the pony-carriages, the stately barouches with their high-stepping horses, driven by bewigged coachmen next to whom

LADY RANDOLPH CHURCHILL SHORTLY AFTER
HER MARRIAGE

powdered footmen in gorgeous livery were seated. Rotten Row was kept entirely for riders. (Only the Duke of St. Albans, Hereditary Grand Falconer, had the privilege of driving through the Row, if he so chose.) Mingling with them, Lady Randolph recognized that the English had been rightly called the finest horsemen in the world. Invariably, the men were attired in frock-coats, pearl-gray trousers and varnished boots; they wore the irreproachable top hat and had not yet abandoned all elegance in favor of comfort. English women looked their best in riding clothes; they wore tight-fitting braided habits, stressing the slender figure.

Lady Randolph herself looked as if she had been born on horseback. Her strong masculine attributes, permeating her character as well as her appearance, asserted themselves to the greatest advantage in the side-saddle. Her outfit was as mannish as possible. A tall silk hat, low over her forehead, covered her rich black hair. Her expression was motionless; it made her profile appear statuesque. Around her neck she wore a snow-white Ascot tie. Her black riding coat was close-fitting. A row of twelve buttons trimmed it. Her stiff white cuffs, like a man's, and heavy leather gloves completed the picture of the beautiful woman who was also the perfect equestrienne.

Originally, reasons of health had been the purpose of the ride or drive in Hyde Park. One aim was reducing, since people lived and dined and wined too well. Both the men, most of whom worked hard, and the women, exhausted by unending social duties, needed an hour or two of exercise or, at least, fresh air. What began as exercise developed into a cavalcade. Finally, all the leaders of London's social life were to be seen in the great parade. In the Seventies publicists complained about the demimonde intruding into the Park drive. But their carriages were frequently the most gorgeous ones, and their public acclaim the loudest.

This public, incidentally, played an important part in the magnificent display on London's common meeting ground. The great show's allure to those who were then called the lower orders contributed a good deal to bridging the gap between classes. True, the original strict suppression of smoking in Rotten Row and similar polite rules could not be maintained in view of the increasing popular audience. In the Seventies smoking was not yet entirely accepted. It was banned from Bond Street, and of course from the drawing-room; even in clubs the "immoral, unclean habit" was confined to the smoking rooms. The smell of tobacco clinging to one's clothes or permeating the drawing-room draperies would be offensive to the ladies. If a gentleman wished to retire for a pipe or a "weed"—cigar—after the meal, he must change his coat, lest he return in a malodorous state to the ladies' company. Thus what America calls the tuxedo and non-English speaking people all over the world the *smoking* was born. The pipe-smoking masses thoroughly enjoyed the glamorous aspect. "To lean o'er the railings and inspect the Drive," observed Thackeray, "is a pleasure for everyone, Cockney or foreigner." Since class jealousy is unknown in England, the intimacy between the people of London and their social leaders, the habitués of Rotten Row, was only intensified by the parade in the Park, which developed into an important contribution to the formation of English democracy.

To show herself in the Park was only a small part of a lady's social obligations. Her mornings were spent in writing ceremonious notes and letters (Victorians being the most indefatigable letter writers and diarists of all time). Most afternoons were taken up by receiving *visites de digèstion*, which every guest was supposed to make after a formal party. At that, social intercourse was negotiated in the most leisurely fashion. Conversations were elaborate. The crowded hours of the day were always too short.

Only on Sunday life was entirely different. Sunday was reserved for strict privacy, as soon as the service in Church and the following church-parade in Hyde Park had been negotiated. A family luncheon ensued, to which only relatives were invited. Gathered around a huge mahogany table, laden with silver, cut-glass, flowers and food, the family respectfully watched the head of the house carve, while mother, opposite him, discreetly directed the tall, liveried menservants.

The afternoon was spent in silent digestion. Whist or music were forbidden. Children were not allowed to play with their toys. Women had to interrupt their novels. Singing or laughing were strictly banned. Tennis and that new game, golf, were prohibited. "It's Sunday!" was the reason given.

It was impossible to visit a restaurant. Dancing would positively have been a sin. In the Casino, the Argyll Rooms (later the Trocadero), Adelaide Gallery, Mott's and Caldwell's, then the fashionable nightclubs, the lights were dimmed, and the doors closed. Even the smart places like the Crillon and Gaiety, where young men about town "saw life" (in a cleaner way than years before in the Coal Holes and the Cyder Cellars), as well as the "bohemian" abodes, the Savage and the Eccentric—where bohemianism meant good food and good wine and modest entertainment—rigidly observed the Sabbath. Week-end parties were unknown in the days of stately barouches. It was good taste to put up one's equipage over Sunday.

Despite all his intellectual modernism, Lord Randolph, in his manners, determinedly observed the old fashions. On Sunday his brougham was kept in the stable. When the Prince of Wales, towering above accepted conventions, invited him and his lady to an intimate Sunday dinner at Marlborough House, Randolph insisted on taking a cab. This stubbornness had an amusing epilogue. It was a very hot night, and the Prince accompanied his departing guests to the door to get a breath of air himself. At that moment a footman announced in stentorian tones: "Lady Randolph Churchill's carriage stops the way." It was the cab. A descrepit Rosinante crawled up, dragging the most dilapidated of four-wheelers, well filled with straw. As Lady Randolph prepared to get in—which was not an easy venture in the days of enormous bustles—the Prince chaffed her. He hoped her conscience was better than her carriage. "Isn't this vehicle still better than the Queen's carriage, sir?" the repartee came immediately. It was no *lèse majesté*. Public conveyances were dubbed the "Queen's carriage."

The strict observance of Sunday, Lady Randolph recalled many years later, filled her with awe and amazement. She had lived most of her grown life in Paris, where every gay and bright event was reserved for that day, and could not understand the voluntary, nay, deliberate gloom and depression in which everyone in London indulged. Why, she asked, was it even forbidden to while away a wet Sunday afternoon (most of them were wet) with listening to good music? These were the objections she advanced. The real reason for her dissatisfaction, it appears, lay deeper. Lady Randolph was the personification of perpetual motion. She could not remain still one day out of every seven.

With her habitual determination she plunged into a campaign for reform. She promoted the incipient week-end movement under the slogan: Why waste days, when not obliged to, in a hot, evil-smelling, and noisy metropolis, as long as the beautiful English countryside is accessible to all sensible people? Why not enliven the country-house parties with golf, lawn-tennis, and bathing? With a twinkle in her eye to the mothers of marriageable daughters, she insisted that this kind of entertainment was certainly a better market to take the young hopefuls to than the heated atmosphere of the ballroom which the desirable *partis*—eligible bachelors—shunned for the greater attraction of air and exercise. Gardening became her personal predilection. Many of the proverbially beautiful gardens around English country-houses owe their existence and their meticulous care to the example set by Lady Randolph Churchill.

Her main concern in those busy days in which, under the veil of preoccupation with more or less nonsensical trifles, an influential woman was growing to full stature, was the reform of ladies' fashions. Upon her arrival in London Lady Randolph had found them "terrible." The *dernier cri* of Parisian fashions, she observed, appeared two years after it had been the mode in Paris. True, she had come to England not without a slight bias in that matter. The rumor had been spread in the Faubourg that English women were in the habit of wearing a muslin crinoline and a sealskin jacket at the same time, in order to be prepared for any sudden change of the notoriously unpredictable London weather.

Actually, the exaggerated crinoline had already vanished almost a decade earlier, when Lady Randolph started her fashionable reform. Many women regretted the departure of the dress that had swayed the feminine world of two continents for more than twenty years. The crinoline, it was generally agreed, imparted a suggestion of queenly dignity, and of a certain aloofness. When it disappeared, it was succeeded by enormously full skirts, which produced a different effect. The skirt was elongated into a long and sumptuous train of drapery that swept the floor behind. Slowly the overskirt grew narrower around feet and knees. The hidden hierarchy, which shaped the mysterious deeper undercurrent in the change of fashion, spoke of "contracting the knees." The new outlines, which gradually drew attention to the posterior, created a new word. For many years it was only whispered in polite society: sex-appeal.

Throughout the period the costume of women was heavy in cut and style; it was uncomfortable, stuffy and overloaded. Grand tenue, later only suitable for formal dinners, was worn at Ascot. Lady Randolph herself appeared on Cup Day in her wedding dress of white satin and point lace, with roses in her bonnet. At the theater, on the other hand, colors were banned. When Lady Randolph once dressed in pale blue for attending a play, her husband implored her to change her gown. Pale blue for the theater was too conspicuous for his taste.

A thousand differences of taste were to be observed, the intimate knowledge of which made the perfect society lady. Lady Randolph ought not to have appeared in dark blue, trimmed with crimson roses, at a ball at Dudley House, although she found it a particularly attractive dress. But Lord Dudley, her host, known as the "peer with the longest purse," asked her bluntly why she had come to his ball in such a "monstrous dress." His Lordship hated black and all dark colors. He referred to Napoleon I, who had never permitted dark dresses among the ladies of his court. Afflicted with a Napoleonic complex, his Lordship observed strict rules of dress at Witley Court, his famous place in Worcestershire. He himself appeared at breakfast in a velvet coat, but he insisted on his guests wearing morning coats. He recalled the memory of the unforgotten Prince Consort who had even gone deer-stalking in a cutaway coat and tight-fitting trousers. Poor Lady Randolph was taken for exhausting walks in the country in a long gown, plumed hat, and thin paper-soled shoes with Louis XV heels.

It was at this point that she revolted. She embarked upon a campaign for suitable country clothes, in which, she later recognized, English women came to set the fashion for the whole world. The country-dress revolution disrupted whole families. When Sir Hugh Hume Campbell, the rugged Scotsman, for the first time saw his granddaughter wearing an ulster, he dubbed it "fast and mannish, only one remove from the American bloomers"; no grandchild of his, nor any other lady in an ulster should even enter his house.

Punch, the conservative conscience of England, poured oil on to the fire with cartoons connecting women in short tailor-made country dresses with the girl that smoked and thus shocked society for many years of hard battle until her cigarette was generally accepted. The battle which had begun over the "fast and mannish" dress and led to the problem of the smoking lady finally became a fight for female emancipation. Superfluous to say that Lady Randolph was among the progressives. As a married woman, she believed, she should no longer be subject to all the restrictions and chaperonage to which she had submitted as a young girl in France. But London appeared much more strict and conventional than Paris had been, particularly in matters of propriety. A lady could only travel alone if she took her maid with her in the railway compartment. She was only permitted to walk in the most quiet streets and squares, otherwise she had to drive, but never alone, in a hansom, lest she might be taken for "fast." Fastness was permitted up to a point. It rarely exceeded a certain slanginess of speech, a pose of masculinity, and it could, at worst, deteriorate into a women's club discussing the inconveniences of matrimony. Fastness beyond that line would have invited ostracism. Mr. Punch could sleep in peace. His talk about the "loudness, fastness, and slang of the girl of the period" was a caricaturist's overstatement.

The "period girl" of the late Victorian era was the forerunner of the "new woman" who fully developed during the early Edwardian days. Lady Randolph belonged to neither of these groups.

Methodically, she made her way alone, or only in the chosen company. Soon the beauteous Princess of Wales was to become her intimate friend. Alexandra liked to surround herself with young women, which, incidentally, was a predilection of Queen Victoria's, too. The Princess and Lady Randolph had two particular interests in common. Four-handed, they played the piano, preferably serious music, Beethoven and Bach. Furthermore, both were eager to reform Victorian fashions and to eliminate the modish subservience to Paris. They found pleasure and understanding in one another. Prince Edward, for his part, lavished his graciousness on the Churchills.

CHAPTER VIII *Adventures in Ireland*

Exhausted from the business of pleasure, with its perpetual round of balls, dinners, musical parties and "kettle-drums"—afternoon teas—in London, and the incessant gaiety of archery, croquet, tennis, picnics, river and hunting parties in the countryside, the Churchills sought a little relaxation from the full-time job of two London seasons.

Lord Randolph was badly in need of rest. His physical frailty, affecting him already in this early period, was aggravated by the necessity of choosing from an embarrassing wealth of amusements, which were unduly draining his failing strength. Yet the advice of his numerous doctors to relax a little only spurred him on to plunge into renewed gaieties. Throughout his life Lord Randolph could only escape forward. True to style, Philadelphia, in the year of the Exhibition the most turbulent city on earth, was chosen as the place for a rest cure from the London turmoil.

Lady Randolph's nostalgia for America was a further motive for the flying visit. She had not been home since her early girlhood; moreover, she was worried about her father. His letters came ever less frequently; now sometimes they sounded less determined. Mr. Jerome still continued his activities on the Street, but he was no longer the "king." At a distance it appeared as if his blazing lights were dimmed.

His pride had suffered a terrible blow when Mr. McAllister

established the Patriarchs' Association, a tight little group of twenty-five social lions, now the self-styled leaders of the four hundred. Among the Patriarchs were Messrs. John Jacob and William Astor, De Lancy Kane, Alexander van Rensselaer, and William R. Travers. Leonard Jerome was omitted, perhaps on account of his vagaries of former years, or perhaps for the one sin that is not forgiven: to be out of luck.

Lady Randolph was anxious to see her father as quickly as possible. But at that time representative British travelers crossing the ocean had first to visit Her Majesty's Canadian Dominion. Canada sweltered under an August heat-wave. Eating nothing but melons and taking several cold baths a day proved only a slight palliative against the unbearable climate. This was an excellent reason to cut short the journey through the Dominion and to hurry to meet Leonard. There was only one last detour. The young Churchills, belated honeymooners as they were, could not miss Niagara Falls. From there they hastened to Newport.

Lady Randolph's childhood paradise had considerably changed during the years of her absence. Perhaps she had changed, too. She could not help comparing the old place with Cowes, and she decided that the new Newport savored more of town than of country. Yet the hospitality and kindness shown by the old friends of the Jerome family was most gratifying. As ever, Lord Randolph scored in society. He was generally accepted as a "bright fellow," and, indeed, endeared himself to many a substantial American citizen. The only objection occasionally raised against him was his "terribly English accent." He and Leonard Jerome became friends from the first. A passion in common for horses is a strong tie, offsetting whatever natural jealousy might exist between the father and the husband of the same beloved woman. The party proceeded to Saratoga for the races; they found a super-Newport. The English gentlemen—Lord Ilchester and Mr. Trafford accompanied the Churchills—were struck by the beauty of the ladies, the gorgeousness of their dresses, and by the exorbitant hotel prices.

Lady Randolph asked her father to remonstrate with the proprietor. Mr. Jerome agreed to do so. Once he would have bought the hotel on the spot to make his daughter more comfortable. Now he could only try to haggle with the owner, who, for his part, remained unmoved. "The lord and his wife insisted on two rooms, hence the expense!" he replied, shrugging. Obviously, Saratoga was not the place for a couple to occupy separate rooms.

And so to Philadelphia. The exhibition, Lady Randolph recalled, was the source of great interest and amusement. The most amusing aspect was the ladies' dresses. The bustle had just arrived in America, an outgrowth of the accentuated hoops. What was known as a "black panier" bunched the skirt over the rear of the hoops. Overloaded with ruffles, sashes, braid and fringe, at least twenty-five yards of material went into the making, and that was still considered meager.

It was an era of great extravagance. American society was turning over a new leaf. Up to the early Seventies a man worth a million dollars had been regarded as the possessor of a most respectable fortune. Now there was nothing remarkable about it. New York ideas of great fortunes leaped to ten, fifty, and even a hundred millions; lavish expenditure followed. Society no longer contented itself with the old-fashioned dinners for twelve to fourteen guests. Now it was no uncommon event for a rich man to give a dinner at Delmonico's for eight hundred people. Instead of the moderate staff of servants who had so far sufficed, the guests in the great brownstone mansions were now received in marble halls by five or six liveried footmen, and served at the table by others under the direction of the butler. Leonard Jerome's silver plate, which had once created a sensation, was now overshadowed by gold service. Soft strains of music accompanied the noisy entertainment. Every dinner party was an elaborate affair intended to show off the host's wealth.

Such entertainments surpassed themselves when given in honor of titled English guests. When the Churchills arrived,

Mr. McAllister's four hundred were still under the spell of the fancy-dress ball in honor of Lady Mandeville, a visitor from London. Every fashion artist in the city had set to work to design novel costumes, fancy dresses that would make their wearers live on in history. Each lady was adorned with orchids, the most costly of all flowers, just coming into the market in profusion.

A similar masked ball was given for Lady Randolph. Its climax was a cotillion in which six groups in various period costumes danced the quadrille. "The Hobby Horse" Quadrille embodied the Louis XIV era, with the gentlemen in pink silk, and the ladies wearing red hunting coats and white satin skirts. The "Mother Goose" Quadrille featured Jack and Jill. After the "Dresden Porcelain," the "Opera Bouffe," and the "Mary, Mary Quite Contrary" quadrilles, the final "Star Quadrille" outdid them all. The ladies who took part were arrayed as twin stars in four colors—yellow, blue, mauve, and white. Each wore an electric light in her hair, supposed to give her a fairy-like appearance.

Lady Randolph, the guest of honor, seemed mildly to enjoy the fun. But the extravagance involved was no longer to her taste. She had, she could herself not exactly explain how, outgrown all that. She had developed into a thinking and fighting woman. The lack of purpose of this excessive gaiety had become repugnant to her. When she recalled this first short stay after her marriage in New York, the "alert intellects of some compatriots" had "invigorated and refreshed" her. The fancy balls were rapidly forgotten.

The flying visit to America had not brought the expected relaxation. London, where the ladies were not in the habit of illuminating their coiffures with electric bulbs, seemed, after all, the better place to recoup one's strength. But after their return to England, the Churchills had only a few months of comparative calm.

Early in 1876 the Prince of Wales fell out with the Marquess of Blandford. The cause of the breach was of course a woman.

The gay Marquess had paid court to a married lady who stood high in Edward's favor. Although her husband had never objected to the Prince's attentions to his wife, he was considerably less tolerant when Blandford approached her. He threatened to sue the Marquess for alienation of his wife's affections. The Prince of Wales, it was rumored, although never proved, stood behind this threat; it was his revenge on the poacher Blandford. A divorce-suit with himself as co-respondent would have definitely ruined the Marquess's already tottering reputation. He felt his very existence menaced by social ostracism.

At this moment of peril and distress, when everyone avoided Blandford, only one man came to his support: his younger brother. Lord Randolph plunged headlong into Blandford's quarrels. He would, he announced, produce the Prince's own letters to the much sought after lady at the divorce trial. Under the pressure of this threat the husband, not wishing to expose the Prince of Wales, abstained from legal action. But the heir to the throne, who was already the uncrowned king of society, imposed a ban on the two refractory brothers. Blandford, a lone wolf without clear aims or strong ambitions, appeared not to care. To Randolph, however, the interdict came as a stunning blow. He was well aware that his house in Charles Street would be shunned by most of his friends. Indeed, society stayed away. Only Consuelo, Duchess of Manchester—the American Duchess, as she was generally called—made an exception. Frankly she told the Prince that she "held friendship higher than snobbery" and that she would remain true to her friends, the Churchills, ban or no ban.

By his action, which Winston in his father's biography called "fierce and reckless partisanship" Lord Randolph gravely impaired his social standing and his chances of making a respectable political career. But he was not a man of compromises. Overnight the young aristocrat, then aged twenty-seven, who, according to his wife, had been addicted to a rather frivolous society, became the fire-eater in public life. The Blandford case, though close to Randolph's heart, was not in itself important

enough to bring about such a complete volte-face. Nor could
his love for his brother fully explain it. The affair, it appears,
was simply the drop that made the boiling caldron overflow.
The volcano must have smoldered for many silent years before
erupting.

Lord Randolph Churchill retired into self-chosen isolation.
The fashionable world no longer smiled on him. He felt himself
humiliated by powerful enemies. He began to see ghosts. The
slightest constraint he sensed in those about him, seemed to him
a studied affront. London became hateful to him. Although
"genial and gay by nature, he contracted," to quote his son's
biography, a "stern and bitter quality, a harsh contempt for
what is called Society, and an abiding antagonism to rank and
authority." Perhaps, Winston Churchill, in recalling his father's
image, concludes, this misfortune, although hindering and in-
juring his following work, also spurred him on. He was prevented from wasting another dozen years in the frivolous and
expensive pursuits of the silly world of fashion. He developed
sympathies for the common people, and the courage to champion democratic causes.

Lady Randolph saw her world lying in pieces. But she did
not show the slightest emotion. Her place was at her husband's
side, there could be no doubt about that. She fought his battles,
but she fought them with her own weapons. On the surface,
she remained calm and smiling. She was still a gay young
woman of the great world. But a deep observer of human nature, Lord D'Abernoon, the British statesman-philosopher
(then still Sir Edgar Vincent), could recognize that a strange
power was developing in her. In his memoirs he described her
with the words: "No eyes were turned on the Viceroy and on
his consort, but all on a dark, lithe figure, standing somewhat
apart, and appearing to be of another texture to those around
her, ardent, translucent, intent, more of the panther than of the
woman in her look, but with a cultivated intelligence unknown
to the jungle."

Lord D'Abernoon had met her in the Viceregal Lodge in

Dublin where her father-in-law now held court. Mr. Disraeli had first offered this high honor upon forming his government, but the Duke had begged to be excused. With his shrinking income he could ill afford the expense involved. Moreover, he did not want to be parted from Blenheim.

Two years later, after his son's affair, he was more amenable to Mr. Disraeli's second approach, which was supported by the old Premier's frank suggestion that the resentment "in London" against Lord Randolph would blow over sooner in his absence. (The Marquess of Blandford was given up as a hopeless case.) Undoubtedly, the Duke of Marlborough accepted the Vice-royalty only as a heavy burden. But he was willing to bear it in order to remove his erratic son from the scene of his conflict. Randolph accompanied his father to Dublin as an unpaid private secretary. The Lord Chancellor had taken the view that the post was unofficial. It was an arbitrary opinion, but it reflected the general mood prevailing in high circles toward Randolph Churchill.

The State entry of the new Viceroy into Dublin, on December 11, 1876, was conducted with traditional ceremony. The Duke in dress-uniform rode at the head of the cavalcade, surrounded by a glittering staff. The ducal family drove in carriages with postilions and outriders through the crowded streets to the black and grimy old Castle. The clamor of the masses did not visibly disturb Winston's sleep. The baby, aged two years and a scant fortnight, was comfortably installed in the back seat of the stately victoria. Nor did the Irish cheering frighten Lady Randolph, although she was well aware that it was only a cheer of curiosity which could at any moment herald upheaval. Her mind was occupied with other things. Would she, relegated to Dublin, be able to carry on the struggle for her husband's rehabilitation? She did not delude herself. This struggle might last a season or two. Little did she foresee that it would take eight terrible years until she could bring about the reconciliation with the Prince of Wales, and that she would have to fight single-handed, since her flamboyant husband, it soon proved, persistently did his best to render her task on his behalf more difficult.

Lord Randolph and his family settled down in the Little Lodge, a long, low, white building with green shutters and verandas, set among trees, and surrounded by a green lawn, about five minutes' walk from the Viceregal Lodge. It was a friendly country house, and Lady Randolph found life there very pleasant. Yet it took her only a few weeks to pierce the fallacy of the Irish idyll. She found it strange that the magnificent Viceroyalty still existed and, apparently, flourished. To her progressive mind the institution was a relic from old times, when a letter from Dublin to London had taken a week, and when all urgent business had to be decided on the spot. In her days, the British and the Irish capitals were only a few hours apart, all political questions were decided in London, and the functions of the Lord-Lieutenant—the Viceroy's official title— were only formal. However intelligent and ambitious he might be, he was a mere figurehead, not even a member of the Cabinet, nothing more to Lady Randolph's realism than "a purveyor of amusements for the Irish officials and for the Dublin tradespeople, on whom he is obliged to lavish his hospitality and his money, with no returns and no thanks."

At that, the new Lord-Lieutenant, the Duke of Marlborough, stood under the shade of a most popular predecessor. He was following "Old Magnificent," as the Duke of Abercorn, incidentally the father of the Marquess of Blandford's wife, was widely called. The Duke of Abercorn's delightful personality and extraordinary good looks remained unforgotten when he was replaced. He was remembered both as a showman and a ladies' man. He required the ladies of his family to wear long, flowing veils that streamed out behind them as they were pompously driven through the streets. At the "drawing-rooms" (the court-receptions in the Viceregal castle), the Irish counterpart of Queen Victoria's receptions, pretty debutantes were made to pass the dais twice. The Duke of Abercorn was in the habit of rewarding their deep curtsies with an affectionate kiss. Sometimes he interrupted the parade to retire into his private suite, and comb and scent his beard, disarranged by his salutes, before the drawing-room was resumed.

Such showy nonsense had appealed to the Irish sense of humor. At first, people were disappointed when the immaculate Duke of Marlborough stepped into Abercorn's shoes. Now court life was more severe. Even the St. Patrick's Day Ball at the castle, taking place annually on the seventeenth of March and marking the end of the season, deteriorated, according to public opinion. True, everyone was still welcome to this ball. People appeared in the oddest clothes. A woman in a black gown with a white train, dancing in shoes one white and one black, was no rarity. The guests picnicked sitting on the floor of the historic halls. But now their best fun was spoiled. Sentries were placed between the merrymakers to prevent them from appropriating not only the food, but the plate, dishes and china.

The tension in Ireland grew. It did not yet look like revolution, only like dissatisfaction. Hence Lord Randolph felt no qualms about fraternizing with the malcontents. This association offered him a welcome opportunity to display his contempt for the stanch Conservatives of his own class, the big landowners in the Irish counties who had ostracized him in London. He mingled with the Dublin intellectuals, whose wit and wisdom he enjoyed, and frequently invited them to his house, although they would never have been received at the castle.

Lady Randolph, too, enjoyed the Irish esprit. "I have been three years in this country and never found a dull man," she acknowledged later. Her most assiduous admirer was Mr. Butt, for many years the leader of the Irish Nationalists. He was known as one of the foremost lawyers and one of the greatest orators of his time, and he was, despite his Irish isolationism, a true British patriot. The term Home Rule, later to become a sanguinary battle-cry, was his invention. He had coined it because he thought the old slogan Repeal would frighten the English—the last thing Isaac Butt would ever have wished to do. Patient himself, and ever counseling patience to his followers, he opposed the policy of extremism. To him, violence was repulsive. Parliamentary obstruction, the novelty introduced by the Irish Nationalist in the House, seemed to him striking democracy in its heart. He was proud of being a gentleman first, and a nationalist afterward. But his nationalistic enthusiasm was no weaker for his good manners. In his Protestant confidence in God—strange enough for the leader of a fiery Catholic nation—the old-fashioned Liberal did not mind that his annual Home Rule speech was not taken seriously by anyone. He was the first to laugh heartily when *Punch* called him: "A Butt without a button, a Butt that won't hold water..." He believed that he had found an ally in Lady Randolph, the American woman. He took her personal sympathy for political consent, which was gravely underrating her allegiance to England. Many were the evenings in the Little Lodge in which he tried to convert her to his Home Rule views. He did not succeed in this point, but he established a firm friendship with the son and daughter-in-law of the Viceroy, who, for his part, referred to this association half-seriously as "heresy."

Behind a very thin veil imposed upon him by his position, Lord Randolph, however, sided with the Irish frondeurs. He made many friends among them, joined their clubs, and academic societies, and was soon regarded a member of their circle. Indeed, he saw a good deal more of nationalist, anti-English politicians than his elders thought prudent or proper. Both in the House of Commons, where he only occasionally occupied his seat, as well as in John Bull's other island, he delivered a few speeches which aroused even Disraeli's displeasure, and were vehemently rebuked by the London Press. In his own constituency, at a dinner of the Woodstock Agricultural and Horticultural Show, on September 18, 1877, he defended the Irish obstruction in Westminster with the argument that their affairs had been constantly neglected. Their claim to Home Rule he opposed solely with the flattery that a House of Commons, composed only of Englishmen and Scotsmen, would sink to the level of a vestry meeting. Without the Irish members the life and soul of the House would be lost.

"This is the language of Mr. Parnell!" commented the *Morning Post,* the mouthpiece of the ruling Conservative Party. It was a dangerous comparison. Parnell, just in the making, was the embodiment of bloody Irish revolution.

The Duke of Marlborough was forced to disassociate himself in the strongest terms from his erring son. Another open scandal, about Randolph, was a grave embarrassment. But his own reputation was involved, and so he wrote to Sir Michael Hicks-Beach a letter for publication. "The only excuse I can find for Randolph," this letter began, "it that he must either be mad or have been singularly affected with local champagne or claret. ... Randolph is not in any way officially connected with me, and the assumption therefore that he represented my opinions would be both unwarranted and unfair. ..."

Lady Randolph found it high time to interfere. They would never regain their position in London, if her husband allowed himself to run riot. She did not argue with him. The young Churchills never argued with one another. At home both stormy-petrels were united in perfect domestic happiness. Actually, only a single controversy flared up during their marriage. It came at the moment of supreme tragedy. It lasted two minutes, to be subdued by her deep understanding and sacrificial love. But this incident was still far away.

In Ireland, she lured her husband into being good. She kindled his innate passion for horses, until he again found the attractions of hunting and riding greater and more irresistible than the mere diversion which Irish politics still were to him at this time. The most irresistible attraction, of course, was Lady Randolph herself, on horseback. She was well aware that she looked her best in the saddle. Randolph could not quite give up his habit of mingling with "the boys"—(his own expression for the jolly band of Irish nationalists he had made friends with). Occasionally in their company he still explored Donegal in pursuit of snipe, fished the lakes and streams of Ireland, caught lobsters, and cooked and ate them at the foot of the wave-beaten cliffs of Howth. He played half-crown whist in Trinity College or at the Dublin University Club, and delivered good-natured addresses, partly to sing the praises of the only philosophy he accepted: the epicurean philosophy; partly to apologize for his initial ignorance of Ireland. "I once called Dublin a seditious capital," he admitted, "but I have since learned to know Ireland better." It was time, indeed, he concluded, that other Englishmen should follow suit. Actually, it was the time when below a smooth surface forces were gathering to introduce violence into Irish politics. Wildly combative Parnell was about to dethrone the wise and gentle Dr. Butt.

Yet, in the end, his enchanting wife in the saddle at his side, became more important. The Londonderrys and the Portarlingtons, his rich, landowning English relatives in Ireland, still shook their heads over Randolph's political unorthodoxy, but everyone agreed that the young Churchills on horseback were the most striking couple in the land. Both light-weights, they rode hunters "indiscriminately," to use Lady Randolph's word. She admitted that she "begged, borrowed, or stole" any horse she could lay hand on. Some of her best days were spent in winter with the Meath and Kildare Hunts. They negotiated the "trappy" fences of the Kildare country, and the banks of Meath as though they had been born to it.

Country editors revelled in detailed accounts of the "tosses" Lady Randolph had taken. Such incidents happened frequently, yet to the tireless horsewoman hunting was a glorious sport. Even hunting in Leicestershire could not compare with it, she said. "With the exception of the Ward Union Stag Hounds and the Galway Blazers," she recalled exuberantly, "I think we hunted with nearly every pack of hounds in Ireland."

That this glorious sport reconciled her husband with his own kind, that he returned to the fold and no longer insisted on being one of the "bhoys," was more than a happy coincidence. It had been Lady Randolph's intention. Always, there was much in her heart that she disclosed to no one. She lived, although eternally beloved, much of her life alone.

Her little boy missed his beautiful mother. Winston must have been a supersensitive and impressionable child, already endowed with his fine sense for the melody of words. He remembers to this day the first sentence that impressed him: "and with a withering volley he shattered the enemy's line." His grandfather spoke these words as he unveiled Lord Gough's statue, in 1878. Winston, standing near the Viceroy, was not yet four years old. Yet he understood perfectly that his grandfather was speaking of war and fighting, and that a volley meant what the black-coated soldiers used to do with loud bangs so often in the Phoenix Park, where the little boy was taken on his morning walk. It was a perfect mental awakening for the war lord to be.

His first memories of his beautiful mother were a strange mixture of her distance and her radiance. "She shone for me like the Evening Star. I loved her dearly—but at a distance. My nurse was my confidante," Mr. Churchill recalls. Lady Randolph in riding costume, Lady Randolph with a diamond star in her black hair, Lady Randolph kissing her little boy (more a funny-looking than a beautiful baby with slightly bat ears), kissing him in a tender hurry because the horses were already neighing impatiently, and her tempestuous husband could not be kept waiting even for a split-second without suffering from his nerves—Lady Randolph in the confusion of a too much beloved woman must, indeed, have illuminated the eager boy's imagination like a dream. Dream-like, she faded. She must hurry away. She was to meet Elizabeth of Austria.

Lady Randolph's unique gift of making royal women her life-long friends misled many observers. Actually, it was not she who sought these friendships. They came to her inevitably attracted by the strength, vivacity, and an inexplicable magnetism she radiated. But she rewarded those who came, because they felt they needed her, with abiding loyalty, and she delighted them with the multitude of her enchanting qualities shared, to the same degree, by no other woman of her time.

Queen Victoria had no use for an enchantress. Her emotional imagination was entirely devoted to the memory of the Prince Consort. For more mundane sensations the adulation of the gnome-like Lord Beaconsfield for his "faery" was satisfactory enough. The ruler not only of an Empire, but of her century, felt not the slightest desire to be bewitched. Lady Randolph found only a modest place on the fringe of the Victorian court.

Empress Eugénie, however, clung to the American girl— whom she had first seen as almost a child, perhaps a soothing influence on the Prince Imperial in his critical boyhood years— with a determined faithfulness lasting to the end. Princess Alexandra, later Queen, continued writing letters to Lady Randolph, despite the breach between their husbands, asking when they might play the piano together again. The beautiful Princess had grown increasingly hard of hearing. Lady Randolph had conjured up Bach and Beethoven, played four-handed, to give her royal friend the illusion that all was not yet lost, and that music sounded just as beautiful to the inner ear. Now the Empress Elizabeth entered Lady Randolph's life.

When the two women first met, the Empress of Austria was a fugitive. At first, she only seemed to be horse-crazy. Before her arrival at Summerhill after an uninterrupted and exhausting journey from Vienna, she changed in the train into her riding costume. The moment she arrived she mounted a horse, and rode for a little exercise, over a small course which had been specially prepared by her orders. Crowds from all over the country had gathered to see the most spectacular guest ever to visit their island. But the Empress, in a hurry to be on horseback again, did not pay the slightest attention to the people. Even her official hostess, the daughter-in-law of the Viceroy, who used to substitute for the Duchess and was awaiting the Empress at the railroad station, had to content herself with a short nod and a passing smile from Her Majesty. Elizabeth was already spurring on her horse. "Rather haughty!" the station-master ventured to remark. "Very unhappy!" Lady Randolph replied, unmindful of the snub she had received.

After an hour or two the Empress returned from her solitary ride, dismounted, and entered the house in Summerhill she had rented. Lord Langford, the owner of the place, had with much care and at considerable expense furnished a luxurious boudoir for Her Majesty. It was hung in blue damask, and crammed, in the approved Victorian manner, with pictures, china, and all manner of ornaments. "Terrible!" was Elizabeth's only comment. Twenty-four hours later the overstuffed room had become a gymnasium in which the Empress exercised daily before hunting.

Ireland, the riders' and hunters' paradise, had never seen such an indefatigable horsewoman. The whole country was agog with amazement and admiration. Elizabeth rode gallantly and knew no fear, although Lady Randolph, herself an expert on horseback, observed that the Empress rode in the *haute école* manner, as taught to perfection in the celebrated Spanish Court Riding School at Vienna; hence Elizabeth was awkward at the gallop. Yet the Empress tried it incessantly. A frantic gallop gave her an unrivaled feeling of intense activity. Deliberately she took risks that were a constant source of worry to her pilot, Captain Bay Middleton. His principal task was to help Elizabeth out of many a ditch. This task was aggravated by the fact that the Empress' tightest of riding habits was buttoned down and strapped in every direction, which made it impossible for her to get up from a fall until the buttons and straps had been unfastened.

Riding out, Elizabeth invariably protected her face with a large fan, allegedly against the rays of the sun, in fact against the gaze of the people. She was an undisguised misanthrope, with only one longing: for solitude. But another curious habit of hers marred the fulfillment of her desire. In the Japanese fashion she used small squares of rice paper instead of pocket-handkerchiefs. She dropped them frequently, crumpled with a nervous gesture, and so she left a trace which Irish people were not loath to follow to catch a glimpse of the mysterious stranger.

Much to the regret of the Viceregal Court the Empress of Austria persistently refused to visit the castle. She hated official dinners; indeed, she hated the coarseness of the traditional cuisine. Terrified of losing her bodily elasticity and her slim figure, she was probably the first woman to live on a strict diet of half-raw beefsteak and oranges. Milk she liked so much that she took her favorite cows with her on her travels. But on some days she drank only a carafe of ox-blood. Of course these strange habits were kept secret. She did not visit the Viceroy because she was staying incognito in Ireland, she insisted. She did not wish to miss one single day's sport while in the country. The fact that she was a fugitive from her own court, where the ceremonious atmosphere almost choked her, the fact that after years of desperate flapping of wings she had just escaped her golden cage, was no one's business.

But the truth was as clear as daylight to Lady Randolph, when the two women on horseback chanced to meet somewhere in the narrow doubles of Meath. The effort to establish official relations had miscarried. But in the scenery of the Irish streams and deep ravines Elizabeth lost her arrogant shyness. Perhaps this was not due to the streams and ravines alone. Perhaps Elizabeth was attracted by the sudden appearance of the woman with the darkest eyes and the brightest smile, or her chivalrous gesture with her crop, in offering to the solitary figure she happened to encounter the right of the narrow, hardly passable way. It might have been the strangely foreign appearance that always made Lady Randolph seem a guest from a distant land, or the perfect self-assurance she displayed in any surrounding. Lady Randolph's spell remained inscrutable. But one could be sure that she would do the right thing at the right moment.

Elizabeth, for her part, did a most extraordinary thing. Indeed, she stopped and talked—reluctantly at first, and visibly embarrassed, then more rapidly, and finally halting again, and thoughtfully. The Empress was thirty-six at that time, some ten years older than Lady Randolph. But while the latter was just starting her career, Elizabeth had already lived her life. She did not look it, except to the experienced eyes of her young observer. The world saw a tall, slender, beautiful woman, her pale face framed by brown curls hanging in rich ringlets, her forehead slightly arched, with small, delicately molded mouth and nose. Her famed predilection for Hellas had obviously marked her. The graciousness and harmony of her movements were those of a dancer. Her taste in dresses challenged the fashion of her time. Elizabeth preferred simple white blouses and tight black skirts to the then prescribed bustle, the object of her particular contempt. The only ornament she wore was a black or green ribbon around the collar of her blouse. Her eyes had changed from an early blue to hazel. They were not quite as glowing as Lady Randolph's, and certainly not as questioning: they were wide, deep, and full of melancholy.

There could be no more distinct contrast than between Elizabeth, the Empress of Europe's oldest monarchy, the fugitive from the world, the restless seeker for solitude, the woman whose life dissolved in dreams, and Lady Randolph, the Brooklyn girl, the realist, endowed with an insatiable zest for combat and joy alike, appearing the life of the party, and being, in fact, the pillar of strength to those around her. This contrast did not separate them. Its magnetism was irresistible. As if by a magic touch, they found one another.

They soon had their heart-to-heart talks, a unique occurrence in Elizabeth's life. One day, in one of their now frequent rides together, the Empress smiled, recalling a truly happy event: "One hundred guns pounded. My boy was born. On August 22nd, exactly fifteen years ago. . . . He is a nice boy," she added, "perhaps a little too full-blooded and excitable. You will meet him. I'll bring him next summer. . . . You see, he is not quite the product of my education. I was allowed to give him life, but he

LADY RANDOLPH IN HER RIDING HABIT

has never belonged to me. He grew up under the care of "Wowo"... his nurse, Baroness Welden, I mean. ..."

Suddenly the picture of Winston, also a full-blooded and excitable baby, and also under the care of his nurse, as if he did not belong to his mother, flashed through Lady Randolph's mind. Against all rules of royal etiquette, it was she who ended the conversation with the Empress. "Excuse me, Madame, I must beg to be permitted to return home. I should," she added hastily, "look after my boy."

"How fortunate you are," Elizabeth sighed. "I was never permitted to look after my boy. ..." Then she gave her mare the spurs, and was gone.

In the summer following his mother's spectacular stay at Summerhill, Crown Prince Rudolph, Archduke of Austria, came for a short visit to Ireland. Not having inherited Elizabeth's shyness, he presented himself immediately at the Viceregal court. The handsome lad, then sixteen, received a hearty welcome. A ball in his honor was given in St. Patrick's Hall, Dublin. But it was already dangerous to entertain foreign royalty visiting the British Lord-Lieutenant in restless Ireland. The Mayor of Dublin being, he emphasized, in his own province, insisted on sitting in the armchair next to the Viceroy, whereas no place of honor on the dais had been reserved for the Heir Apparent of Austria. This might have been simply an oversight. But it was certainly a deliberate offense that the Mayor scrambled for the place immediately after the Viceroy, when the guests proceeded to the supper room. He claimed, and obtained, precedence over the Archduke. The Crown Prince Rudolph, refusing to be reconciled by profuse excuses on the part of the Duke of Marlborough, departed the next morning.

After this incident the Duke confined his and his family's social contacts primarily to the landed gentry in Ireland. Lord and Lady Randolph had a good time in the castles and estates in which they were guests. At Knockdrin Castle in Westmeath, where they stayed for a few months, they particularly enjoyed the hunting. "The foxes were as wild as the people were untamed," Lady Randolph observed. But she recognized that the people's condition had been caused by poverty and lack of education. Lord Sligo's place at Westport, County Mayo, offered excellent opportunities for snipe-shooting. But this time Lady Randolph did not enjoy herself. Her long walks in the neighborhood had dispirited her. Horror-stricken, she observed the heart-rending poverty of the peasants living in wretched mud hovels, more like animals, she said, than like human beings. If those surrounding her complained about the deplorable conditions prevailing in seething Ireland, her answer was that neglect and misery had rooted the people in their shiftless and improvident habits.

Except for politics and poverty, Ireland seemed delightful to her. She relished the beauty of the scenery of Galway and Connemara, enhanced, as it was, by the delights of trout-fishing. When her husband, whose political interest developed rapidly, went to London to occupy his seat in the house, Lady Randolph frequently stayed with Lord and Lady Wimborne at their castle, Muckross Abbey, famed alike for its shooting and its scenic beauty. But the magnificence she saw in so many places did not blind her to the peculiar Irish improvidence and extravagance. Sometimes she saw a splendid gateway on the roadside, but the stone pillars and wrought-iron gates led exactly nowhere, since all the money for the building of the planned house and been spent to erect the magnificent approach. In the summer of 1879 there was famine in Ireland. The wet weather had ruined the crops, which accounted for the starvation in the south and west of the island. The potatoes failed, grain would not ripen, the turf could not be dried. The government did its best in administering relief, but the best the government could do was not good enough. Spurred by her exceptional capacity, energy, and decision, the Duchess of Marlborough stepped in and appealed to the public for contributions to an Irish Relief Fund. Valiantly, Lady Randolph aided her mother-in-law. The Fund succeeded in collecting large sums. From Fair Head to Cock, and from Wexford to

Kilkee its help was felt as a blessing and deliverance. Never had gifts of charity been so widely and discreetly distributed. The Duchess and Lady Randolph lived, moved, and labored amid reports from poverty-stricken districts. They personally investigated the most pressing cases. They were undeterred by the nationalist Mayor of Dublin who diverted many subscriptions to a competitive fund of his own. However, his effort to steal the show miscarried. The Irish Relief Fund collected, and distributed with scrupulous care, £117,000, for these times a considerable sum. The Queen bestowed the Victoria-and-Albert Order on the Duchess. On the other side, even the Irish nationalist press was obliged to praise the Viceregal endeavors. Their success added to the popularity of the Marlboroughs in the country. Everyone was pleased. Only Lady Randolph observed the undercurrent. No philanthropic scheme, she realized, really touched the Irish people.

She loved Ireland, and returned frequently to the green island, maintaining many of her personal relations there. But she was not too disappointed when, at the elections of 1880, Mr. Gladstone, as expected, won an overwhelming majority. The Duke of Marlborough packed his bags and made free the Irish post for a Whig Peer. The young Churchills returned to London. Back in Belgravia, Lady Randolph felt it was all for the best.

CHAPTER IX *The Fourth Party*

"Having been married five years I begin to feel highly respectable," Lord Randolph wrote his mother on April 15, 1879, a few months before the family's departure from Ireland. Fundamentally, the man who was just on the point of becoming the challenger of many established institutions was by taste, by style, in his mold and texture firmly anchored in the early Victorian era. To him respectability, although he defied it every day, was still the highest virtue. His model marriage gave him the hold he sorely needed in the ventures of his life.

The marriage was blessed with another child. In February, 1880, shortly after their return to London, Jeanette bore her husband a second son. Master John Strange Spencer Churchill cannot by mere coincidence have been baptized with Strange among his numerous first names. He was a strange child, and turned out a strange man: the only invisible Churchill in a family conspicuous throughout the centuries. His childhood was overshadowed by his brilliant, naughty, and problematic brother, six years his elder. His mature life was lived in duty, but never in glory. Although he won distinction in both the Boer War and the World War, being wounded as a dispatch rider in the first and as a front officer in the second, and although he was rewarded with high English, French, and even

Portuguese decorations, he remained entirely un-Churchillian in his anonymity.

He cannot have inherited this modesty from his parents. Both were on the threshold of their years of fame, when the boy John was born. They had taken a little house in St. James's Place, which Lady Randolph herself called the hornet's nest. It became the center of political plotting and scheming.

After their Irish apprenticeship, both were now devoured by politics. The general elections of 1880 had overthrown Lord Beaconsfield and dealt the Conservatives a terrible blow.

It was very much a new decade that now began. The politics of the Seventies had ended with a bang. They had had the fascination of a duel. The combat between Disraeli and Gladstone had held all England spell-bound. It had been the greatest show in Parliamentary history. On one side stood the man of Midlothian with his terrific voltage, representing goodly, righteous, sober Liberalism. He was deferential to the person of the Queen, but not to her statecraft. He was the challenger, Mr. Disraeli was the champion: a frail little man, whose supposed black magic was actually incurable romanticism. He bewitched his "faery," the Queen. He was his own hero: the poor Jew boy who had become Peer of Great Britain, with belt and ermine, a mighty statesman, immortal as Earl Beaconsfield. But at the turn of the decade his party crumbled.

Lord Randolph was among the more fortunate Tories. By a small majority he had saved his constituency, Woodstock. But was his success really a Tory victory? He was out of sympathy with his own party's Irish and foreign policy. Disraeli, whose conversations in Blenheim had so often fascinated him, inspired him no longer. Conversely, the aging statesman did not take Lord Randolph very seriously. He shrugged at the young backbencher's occasional sarcasms and at his abstention from important decisions. Just another Oxford boy, was his opinion. But at the age of thirty-one, which he had now reached, in a most critical situation, regarded as a "queer customer" by his own Conservatives and as a gadfly by the ruling Liberals, Lord

Randolph proved his gift as a past master of parliamentary grand strategy.

His great opportunity came with the Bradlaugh incident. Charles Bradlaugh, a rabid athiest, had been elected as Liberal member for Northampton, in those days reputed the most radical town in England. When he presented himself on May 3, 1880, at the table of the House of Commons, he refused to take the oath, whereupon an overwhelming majority decided to reject him as a member. But Gladstone, whose record in religious matters was marred by his Act disestablishing the Irish Church, came, for reasons of parliamentary principles, to Bradlaugh's aid. The House was thrown into turmoil. The wildest pandemonium during the reign of Victoria ensued.

Lord Randolph scented a God-given chance for splitting the Liberals from top to bottom, since the Bradlaugh affair pitted the Whigs and the Radicals, both inside Gladstone's camp, furiously against one another. The conservative high councils, however, neglected the opportunity. Sir Stafford Northcote, their leader in the House, was much too kindly and well-bred an old gentleman to fish in troubled waters.

In his stead, Lord Randolph did the fishing with a vengeance. The fanaticism with which he flayed Bradlaugh the atheist, the heathen, the pagan, came as a surprise to Randolph's friends who had so far known him only as a polite and rather detached church-goer. Now he lost no opportunity to make God-fearing Gladstone responsible for the presence of the blasphemer in the House of Commons. But the Conservative leadership did not fare much better under Randolph's slashing attacks. Their inactivity, when Church and Altar were at stake, disgusted him.

The Bradlaugh scandal served to herald Lord Randolph's real debut in public life. An old and respected member of the Conservative Party, occupier of a corner seat on the Opposition Front Bench, got up with the words: "This is getting too hot for me!," and, with a courteous bow, exchanged his place with Randolph's modest seating accommodation somewhere on the back benches. Literally and figuratively, Lord Randolph Churchill had come to the forefront.

Attentively his wife watched him from the Ladies' Gallery. Her burning eyes were fixed upon him. Her lips were tightly pressed together, obviously to suppress her tendency to repeat or correct his phrases. As with most of his speeches, she had carefully rehearsed it with him beforehand. Nothing could excite her as much as listening to her husband's orations, she later admitted. "Next to speaking in public oneself," she said, "there is nothing which produces such feelings of nervousness and apprehension as to hear one's husband make a speech." She smiled in recollecting: "I, too, caught the fever!" But during Randolph's actual performance there was no smile on her face. The panther Lord D'Abernon had discovered in her was ready for the leap.

Lady Randolph introduced to England the type of the political woman, as opposed to the woman in politics which had prevailed before her arrival. Thus far, only few women had regularly visited the two galleries of the House reserved for them; the Ladies' Gallery, for which one balloted, and the Speaker's Gallery, to which one was invited by the speaker's wife. Only a handful of ultra-political ladies frequented them at that time. One was Mrs. Gladstone, picturesque and dignified, who was seldom absent from her habitual seat. Others were Mrs. Arthur Balfour, the wife of the "coming man," tall, handsome Mrs. Cavendish-Bentinck, whose flashing eyes and raven looks had gained for her the nickname Britannia, and Mrs. Chamberlain, the wife of the great Imperialist who, in 1880, still passed for a radical, tinged with the most fiery red.

A woman visiting the galleries underwent considerable discomfort. Female visitors, Lady Randolph observed sarcastically, were tucked away from masculine sight in true Oriental fashion. They were crowded in the small, dark cage to which the ungallant legislators had relegated them. The fortunate women in the first row were supposed to enjoy a great privilege. Actually, they sat in a cramped attitude, their knees against the grille, their necks craned forward, and their ears constantly on the alert if they wanted to catch a word now and then from their lofty perch. On the other hand, those in the second row depended entirely on the courtesy of the ladies in front of them for an occasional peep at the assembly below. Small wonder that the Ladies' Gallery resounded with strictly forbidden conversation. In vain the wife of the member who happened to be speaking tried to hush the noisy conversations. Defiantly, the chatter continued.

The more considerate female guests in the gallery retired to a small room in the rear where one could whisper without disturbing, and have a cup of tea. Many of the ladies availed themselves of the House of Commons stationery to polish off their correspondence, imparting, they hoped, a political flavor and a touch of their own importance, to those recipients who did not already know that the House of Commons stationery was available to every visitor.

In spite of the difficulties, however, the attendance of women audiences at interesting debates, or to hear a popular speaker or an important declaration from the government, grew incessantly. Largely under Lady Randolph's educational influence the growing generation of London hostesses were anxious to be —"or to appear to be," as Lady Randolph commented—serious. To be beautiful and wealthy was no longer sufficient. Those who aspired to be society leaders did not content themselves with mere accidents of birth and fortune. "Look at Jeanette!" was a frequently repeated slogan. Already she was Jeanette, not to her family alone, but to all London.

Out of the Bradlaugh incident grew the Fourth Party, a small group determined to satisfy the need for a more virile opposition. Sir Henry Wolff originated the idea. Randolph contributed both enthusiasm and leadership. Mr. Gorst added his political omniscience. Mr. Arthur Balfour, a nephew of Lord Salisbury, gravitated toward the group in vacillating allegiance. But the Fourth Party's wit, heart, dynamo, and hostess was Lady Randolph.

She openly assumed political powers which thus far had only been wielded behind the scenes by great ladies who were the embodiment of splendor and dignity; but at the outset of the Eighties their importance was fading. The total transformation of Victorian society was still twenty years off. Yet the general progress, the increasing neglect of accepted values, the acceleration of speed and the rise of new fortunes, commercial ones, no longer derived from large estates, tended to deprive the great lady of her stage.

Some of them endeavored to ignore the signs of the changing times. Born at the top, they were not engaged in the race for recognition. Persistently they refused to spend the autumn in London, even when autumn happened to be a critical time in British affairs. Unmindful of what might be happening elsewhere, they settled down in their country houses when the three months of the "season" were over. They did not budge until after Christmas. All of them loathed publicity. Birth and marriage had established them in their sphere. They had no need to lion-hunt for their parties. Their invitation lists had their "musts," and their only concern in arranging their dinners was whom to leave out for lack of room. Their photographs were not displayed in shop windows. People had to stand on chairs if they wanted to see a great lady riding or driving in the Park. They strictly forbade the use of their names in the gossip columns. They never divulged the decoration of their boudoirs, or the diet of their pets. What costume they intended to wear at Ascot was their personal business. Lists of dinner guests were guarded like state secrets. Indeed, many secrets of state were discussed at their tables.

Lady Randolph, embodying the coming type, was not content with pulling wires at her dinner parties. The part she played in public affairs was unconcealed. Both the venerable Victorian tradition, as well as the drive characteristics of the changing times, were perfectly blended in her. Haughty seclusion from the world by no means impressed her as a token of dignity. She did not court publicity, but as the wife of an assiduous politician and as a political woman herself, she perfectly understood its value. She did not belong to those who were constantly in a tearing hurry to see and be seen, but neither did she understand why she should not spend a few days in Paris, a week on the Riviera, or a fortnight in New York. An evening in a restaurant in the company of a few friends seemed not "emancipated" to her, as was then the common opinion. On the contrary, during her first year in London she complained that one could dine nowhere—particularly in summer when one's own house was closed—but at the St. James Hotel (now the Berkeley). When fashionable eating-places came into vogue, the Churchills were among the first to patronize them. They became habitués at the Bachelor's Club and the New Club at Covent Garden, where one could enjoy dancing with one's intimate friends, and were frequently seen in the Carlton Hotel.

Yet she accepted one of the most time-honored English traditions. Her house was her castle. It was, at that time, only the little House in St. James's Place, but she managed it with such perfect sovereignty that Thomas Escott, the great chronicler of the Victorian era, attested: "London possesses no more accomplished or charming hostess than the brilliant lady whom Randolph Churchill had made his wife." She never showed the strain which was increased by her awareness that her social functions were subservient to political aims. Perhaps the intimate gatherings in her house offered no real relaxation. Everyone was haunted by the fear that social amenities were a waste of precious time, if an evening did not fulfill its underlying aim. The temper and nerves of hosts and guests alike suffered from the wearing intensity of the gay parties. Yet the merriment in St. James's Place resounded in the neighboring house where Sir Stafford Northcote resided. Sir Stafford himself, the Conservative leader in the House, was a famous raconteur, noted for the raciest of Cockney stories. He did not mind that his nights were occasionally disturbed by the gaiety emanating from the Churchills' parties. Little did he realize that the aim of all this gaiety was to break his hold on the Conservatives and overthrow his rule.

Celebrities and insiders from all over the world were frequent visitors in St. James's Place. Lord Dufferin, British ambassador in Constantinople, and Lord Lytton, his colleague in Paris, rarely missed calling on the young Churchills when they were in London. There were many guests from the Orient, outstanding among them Valentine Baker, the English adviser to the Egyptian Khedive, Fred Buraby, the mystery man of India, and Condie Stephen, who knew all the secrets of the Far East. Their reports whetted the young Churchills' appetite for the Secretaryship for India. Indeed, this was the post reserved for Lord Randolph in the shadow-cabinet that so far was only a group of guests around Jeanette's table.

"Our house became the rendezvous of all shades of politicians," to quote Lady Randolph. "Many were the plots and plans hatched in my presence by the Fourth Party, who, notwithstanding the seriousness of their endeavors, found time to laugh heartily and often at their own frustrated machinations. How we used to chaff about the 'goats,' as we called the ultra-Tories and followers of Sir Stafford Northcote! Great was to be their fall and destruction!"

The Fourth Party, of course, was not only a conspiracy, but a serious effort to establish what Lord Randolph had baptized Tory Democracy. Although rebellious against the leadership, and rather uninhibited in its methods, the handful of members were true blue Tories at heart. Not the least of their ambitions was to break the radical rule of Gladstone which they considered a danger to the Empire, as well as to reconcile the millions of recently enfranchised voters from the poor and the working classes with a rejuvenated, progressive conservatism. Their influence over the English masses mounted rapidly, although their parliamentary group was confined to three or four who, incidentally, never left the official Conservative fold; each was a colorful personality.

The plan to make permanent the comradeship of the few

members who had joined Randolph in his fight against Brad-laugh (which had grown into a successful fight against both parties in the House) was devised by Sir Henry Drummond Wolff. He had known Lady Randolph already as Miss Jerome during her first summer in Cowes, and was proud of this priority. He divided his friendship fairly between Lord and Lady Randolph. "With his pink and white complexion that a girl might have envied, and a merry twinkle in his eyes, hiding behind a pair of spectacles, he was the best of company," Lady Randolph remembered him in his old age when cares and mis-fortunes had come heavily upon him. She was, however, afraid of his habit of treating the most serious questions in a flippant manner, and of turning everything into ridicule. Sometimes, to hear him and Randolph discussing the situation, the uninitiated might have thought the subject was a game of chess.

Randolph, for his part, was not frightened but fascinated by Sir Henry's studied superficiality. It was his own mannerism to sport a devil-may-care attitude. While he was consumed by worldly passions, he proclaimed, the whole world, as far as he was concerned, might go to the devil.

Sir Henry Wolff, who had entered public life in 1874 as M.P. for Christchurch, was the son of a distinguished traveler and scholar. Fifteen years Randolph's senior, he had already amassed a large and varied fund of experience and information, particularly on foreign affairs and international finance. But he concealed his wisdom behind a smoke screen of suavity, wit, and unperturbability, which made him Randolph's perfect partner. If he contributed notably to the strength of the Fourth Party, he added still more to the amusement of its secret councils.

The third Fourth Party member was of a very different mold. Sir John Gorst, a solemn-looking, bearded and bespectacled lawyer, King's Counsel at the London bar, was an old-timer. Sitting in Parliament since 1866, it seemed amazing that he associated himself with the little band of youthful heretics. The general surprise his association with Lord Randolph caused was further increased by the well-known fact that Sir John belonged to the few intimates of Mr. Disraeli. Actually, he had reorganized the Tory machine after the defeat of 1868, and the great Prime Minister credited him more than any other man with the victory of 1874, which had re-established Conservative supremacy. Hence Dizzy treated Sir John Gorst always with special regard and favor, although the latter now put all his political craft and adroitness to the service of the rebellious group. "Gorst is a pointer to find game for Lord Randolph Churchill to run down," an observer expressed it. On his old friend's insistence Lord Beaconsfield even visited the Fourth Party Council in January, 1881. But, in the words of his "faery," he was not amused. He departed without uttering a word of opinion, only with an admonition to his restive young friends never to forget the virtue of caution.

The fact that serious, distinguished, enormously industrious Sir John Gorst had openly adhered to the dangerous Fourth Party was decidedly a tribute to Lady Randolph's acquisitive talents. "His stern countenance belied him," she said. "He could make himself very pleasant. He had a music-loving soul."

Indeed, Sir John frequently accompanied Lady Randolph to the "Monday Pops" to listen to Joachim and Norman Neruda. Usually Mr. Arthur Balfour, the later Prime Minister, then the Fourth Party's problem child, accompanied them. Lady Randolph's friends often teased her about her "weird" companions at musical events. Indeed, the solemn, reticent Sir John Gorst and Arthur Balfour (according to Lady Randolph, "æsthetic-looking with long hair and huge spats") made a contradictory pair of escorts.

In 1880 Mr. Balfour was an affable young gentleman who had dabbled in philosophy and diplomacy, radiated an air of well-bred indifference, and seemed to take nothing but music seriously. He fought earnestly for popular concerts, his knowledge of the opera was remarkable, and he was an excellent performer on the piano. His evaluation of politics and music, respectively, was expressed in a letter he once wrote to Lady Randolph, to excuse himself from seeing her to the opera: "I am groaning and swearing on this beastly bench (in the House of Commons). While you are listening to Wagnerian discords, I am listening to Irish grumblings. There is a great deal of brass in both of them. Otherwise there is not much resemblance. I am sitting next to . . . , while I *might* be sitting next to you! I am an unhappy victim! However, there is no choice. Monday night is a most unlucky one for Richter (the famous Wagner conductor). The Irish have a talent for turning everything into an Irish debate. And I must answer. Your miserable servant, Arthur James Balfour."

The story went the rounds that Lady Randolph had converted Mr. Balfour to the Fourth Party by playing Beethoven and Schumann duets with him. She herself was not quite sure whether she had converted him at all. She was full of grievances against him. To her, it never seemed quite certain whether he belonged to the Party for which she was convassing among the most distinguished men of politics, or not. Lord Randolph shared her doubts as to Mr. Balfour's reliability. He used to call him "Postlethwaite," and made him the object of much friendly chaff. No one thought Mr. Balfour quite reliable in politics. He seemed but distantly attached to the calling, lacking in energy, void of ambition, simply sitting in the House as the representative of a family borough. It appeared to Lady Randolph that Mr. Balfour's allegiance depended on his uncle's, Lord Salisbury's moods. Her opinion was generally shared. She, however, understood better than anyone that Mr. Balfour was secretly hankering after the "wicked three," whose company had for him all the sweetness of forbidden fruit. Even when things were going badly for the Fourth Party, and Mr. Balfour repudiated indignantly that he was even a member, Lady Randolph persisted that, by taste and interest, he was. History, she said, would write him down as such. History, indeed, has written down Mr. Arthur Balfour as the untiring, tenacious minister who through many years controlled the House of Commons and shaped the policy of the British Empire.

Sometimes it was, indeed, hard going. The Tory-Democratic salon in St. James's Place received outstanding Liberals as welcome dinner guests. Sir William Harcourt and Sir Charles Dilke, two of the most prominent Liberal leaders, both descendants of great Whig families, were still acceptable in the Duke's judgment. But when Mr. Joseph Chamberlain came to dinner, the monocle in his eye, the orchid in his button-hole, and his imperturbable, provocative, radical smile around his thin lips, His Grace lost his patience with his son and daughter-in-law. He took Randolph seriously to task. He could not understand, he stated frankly, how a man like Joe Chamberlain, who was a socialist, or not far from one, who was in bad odor for having, as Mayor of Birmingham, refused to drink the Queen's health, could be admitted to a decent house. "Certainly the influence of such a man could not be anything but pernicious."

All London society pitied the aged duke who was cursed with a prodigal son. The Prince of Wales's wrath was widely quoted. Indeed, His Royal Highness did nothing to mitigate the impression that he was still displeased with the erring pair. He was quoted as saying that he heartily disagreed with the Liberals. Only their administration of the City Council of London and their fight against Lord Randolph Churchill he approved of.

This fight, incidentally, did not impair the most courteous and formal social relations between political antagonists. Nothing worse could occur than the following encounter. Lady Randolph, it was known, spent such time as her social and political activities left her with efforts at painting, a predilection her son Winston has inherited from her. Once a dinner guest in the hospitable house of Sir William and Lady Harcourt, her host and his two political associates, Mr. Chamberlain and Sir Charles Dilke, playfully begged her to preserve them for posterity by painting their portraits. "It is a chance to immortalize yourself and us," Sir William encouraged her. "Impossible," Lady Randolph replied. "I should fail. I could never paint you black enough." Whereupon Lady Harcourt embraced her. The daughter of Motley, the illustrious historian, was proud of the quick wit of her sister-American.

The Fourth Party developed rapidly into an important factor in the House. Its members were soon called the "watch-dogs," a grudging tribute to the unceasing censorship they assumed both toward the problem-ridden Liberal government and the feeble, ineffective Conservative opposition. Their favorite attitude was to present themselves as the guardians of the public purse. No item of expenditure was too small to escape their criticism, no economy too petty to be advocated. Such activities gave them a leftish touch. Indeed, in all social and financial questions Lord Randolph advocated the poor man's point of view.

The word *Bolshevik* was not yet invented at that time, but the ruling classes, whether Whig or Tory, were quick in anticipating it by expressions like "Pug! . . . Toady! . . . Sycophant! . . . Quack . . . !," which were constantly hurled at Randolph. His appearance, due to his small stature, his irritable expression, and the absurd, enormous walrus mustachios, was now depicted as Puck, hovering over grave party councils, or as a small dog, barking at the moon. *Punch* had him in a nutshell of a rowboat, blocking the way of the racing shells, and jubilating: "In the way again! 'Ooray!"

To all these attacks Lord Randolph had but one reply: he was executing Lord Beaconsfield's political heritage. "Dizzy" had brought the workers into the conservative fold, and he, Randolph Churchill, was determined not only to keep them there, but to cement the combination of Tory Democracy and labor's mounting power in politics.

Lord Beaconsfield, retired after the crushing defeat of 1880, but still maintaining a sort of invisible control over party matters for the last year of his life, remained sphinxlike. At first it appeared that the great man regarded the activities of the Fourth Party with approval. In the autumn of 1880 Sir Henry Wolff visited him at his house in Curzon Street to inform him of the Bradlaugh controversy, and to complain about Sir Stafford Northcote's over-caution. "I fully appreciate your feelings," Lord Beaconsfield replied, "but you must stick to Northcote. He represents the respectability of the party. Personally, I wholly sympathize with you, because I was never respectable myself.... But don't you, on any account, break with him. Whenever it becomes too difficult you can come to me, and I will try to arrange matters."

Far from censuring the spirit of independence, Lord Beaconsfield, indeed, encouraged it. Again he displayed his old interest in promising young men, in making one of his rare, and the last, visits to the Peer's Gallery to hear Lord Randolph speak. Asked by Sir Henry James, who himself praised the young member's parliamentary skill and attitude, what he thought about Randolph, the old sage replied: "Ah yes, you are quite right. When they come in, they will have to give him anything he chooses to ask for, and in a very short time they will have to take anything he chooses to give them."

Early in November, 1880, Beaconsfield invited Sir John Gorst, his old friend and party-whip, to Hughenden. "He generally expressed great confidence in us," Gorst reported to Lord Randolph. "He thought we had a brilliant future before us."

But the word future did not hold much promise for Randolph. A premonition of how short his future would be spurred him on relentlessly. He was, as usual, ahead of his time, and too hurried in his impetus. He had to overcome his hidden consciousness of nervous exhaustion. Once the confession escaped from his lips: "The ideal life would be to lie in bed all day, dozing over a book, to dine in one's dressing gown, and then with all convenient speed find one's way back to bed again." Instead, he plunged into the race for Beaconsfield's successorship, the moment the great man had breathed his last, on April 19, 1881.

This seemed excessive haste to Lady Randolph. She was her husband's faithful co-worker, accompanying him on his laborious campaigns throughout the country—incidentally, she endured the fatigue of such campaigning much better than he—sharing his convictions, and expressing his arguments in her own witty style. But she knew where to draw the line. In the summer of 1881 she felt an attack of irresistible nostalgia. Lord Randolph, ever a devoted husband and mostly helpless against his beloved wife's whims, had to interrupt his hectic activities for another short visit to New York.

The visit brought a bit of rest and quiet. Strangely, the peaceful atmosphere the Churchills found in Jeanette's dynamic home-town came from no less a veteran fire-eater than Leonard Jerome. Jennie's father, as he now proudly called himself, had, at last, made his peace with the world. Not with the Street. He had entirely dropped out of Wall Street and was disgusted with it. But he was by no means disgusted with life. He had scored his last, to him the crowning triumph.

An aging man with stooped shoulders, he was wont to stroll down Fifth Avenue, still swinging his inevitable cane with the golden knob, but with a careworn expression which he poorly concealed with remarks like: "It's healthy to walk. I do it for reducing." Besides, he did it because his splendid horses had, years before, been scattered under the hammer of the auctioneer. Much worse still, he had had to watch the Jockey Club decaying, and to give up Jerome Park.

Racing became vulgar. Bookies infested the courses. The old Liberal was against banning them by law, but he dreamed of rejuvenating the high art of racing by founding another course for exclusive society. His step became slow, his eyes were dull, his means strictly limited. But he clung to his dream.

All New York knew it. He could hardly venture upon his forenoon walks without being stopped by an acquaintance: "Have you found a few dollars to build your new track?" he was good-naturedly taunted.

One day he answered: "No, but I've found forty million." It was the custom of the time to identify a man by his fortune.

To have found forty million meant to have made the acquaintance of the lottery millionaire John A. Morris. This gentleman, who had amassed his millions from the pennies of the many, was fascinated by the idea of entering society as the backer of a fashionable race-course. And so the great race-course near the village of Westchester, known as Morris Park, was founded. The New York Jockey Club was instigated. Mr. Jerome became President. He resigned by his own choice when the Club was absorbed by the American Jockey Club, which proved a most fortunate amalgamation. Leonard Jerome's happiness was complete. He imparted some of it to his daughter and to his son-in-law, who, in his thirty-second year stood badly in need of some rest of spirit and soul.

The summer season of 1881 was over when the Churchills returned. Habitual autumnal calmness brooded over London. Smart society received or visited in country houses. Politicians mended fences in their own constituencies or sallied forward on piratical raids in the bigger towns, the importance of which was steadily increasing with the progress of industrialization. Since both Belgravia and Westminster were scattered all over the country, everyone wrote everyone those endless witty and erudite letters, tastefully spiced with French bon mots and classic quotations, intermingling gossip, report, and courtesy, which were the preferred pastimes of the Victorians, and at the same time their serious duty.

Randolph undoubtedly was one of the most prolific letter-writers of the time. Most of his epistles, although carefully preserved, were never published. They were, in the judgment of his literary executors, too spontaneous, too frank and self-revealing. Full of personal allusions, reflecting his changing moods, chatty and droll, interspersed with sharp judgments or—as his son Winston put it—often extravagant and reckless expressions, they mirrored accurately his self-contradictory nature. Even in these years of social gaiety and political promise there ran through them a recurring sense of weariness and of disgust with politics—of the early, deep fatigue that marked his life. Yet these missives delighted their recipients. "The only fault I find with them," Sir Henry Wolff, their chief recipient in these years, replied "is that they are too short; I should like several volumes. Your letters are to me like a glass of the best champagne—exhilarating and stimulating. It is only your versatile and brilliant genius which could produce such lively correspondence in the dull season."

Hand in hand with his assiduous letter writing went a systematic campaign into which Randolph plunged immediately upon his return from New York, with his wife indefatigably assisting him. He found a jubilant welcome in Oldham (later Winston's constituency), where he spoke to six hundred working men, sweeping them off their feet with his demands for Fair Trade and taxation of foreigners. His appearance in Hull was a triumph. There he had to repeat his speech to another cheering audience, and was immediately invited to repeat it in Glasgow, "preaching to a lot of Scotsmen on home politics, which they probably understood much better than I do," he commented with studied modesty.

Attacking both Gladstone and his own leaders, he was already the principal platform speaker in England. He no longer considered speaking a fine art. To him speaking in public was a function of citizenship to be discharged with energy and precision, in order to reflect the thoughts of an inarticulate multitude. Yet his popular appeal did not make him abandon his personal touch.

"His wit, sarcasm, his manner of piercing personalities, his elaborate irony and effective delivery gave an astonishing popularity to his speeches," Lord Rosebery, Randolph's school friend at Eton, admitted.

Not all the Liberals, however, were equally liberal in their judgment. The radical provincial press attacked Randolph incessantly. But, oh, wonder, the ultra-Conservative Carlton Club received the prodigal son with open arms when he returned from his triumphs, mostly scored in workers' meetings. It be-

longs to the many apparent paradoxes in Randolph's nature
that the man who was soon to attract larger audiences than
any other statesman of his time, including the miraculous spell-
binder Gladstone, was in his private life a clubman par excellence. He regarded the Carlton Club as his second home.
He was not less interested in its ménage than in that of his
own house. He made it his business to see that the earliest
plover eggs from East Anglia were regularly on the sideboard
and that the larder was duly replenished every spring by
Brobdignagian hams, whose succulent perfection was a secret
known only to Sir George Wombwell's tenants in the Easing-
wold district.

From the clubs, Lady Randolph was, of course, barred.
Otherwise, the couple shared every free minute and every
busy day. Jeanette never let him go alone when he toured
the country. Her presence was one of his greatest political
assets. The excitement his speeches created was climaxed by
the gorgeous aspect of the dark beauty, modestly seated in
the background, looking somewhat strange as long as she was
silent, but bewitching the people as soon as her conversation
revealed her unaffected manner. The smile around her lips
never faded, although "men," she reminisced, "fared better on
those occasions than their womenfolk, for on the plea of having
to prepare their speeches, they could seek the solitude of their
rooms." The guest speaker's lady, on the other hand, had to
sit out tenaciously all the gaiety her host—usually a local magnate who at the meeting would take the chair—had to offer.
This gaiety included unending hours of conversation, mostly
about platitudes, Lady Randolph remembered, with the wives
and daughters of supporters. But the charming naïveté of the
provincial ladies, their genuine human interest, and their hospitality, so elaborately extended, struck a responsive note with
Jeanette. Her smile that so fascinated the Midlands came
naturally. She was happy to be able to keep her husband,
whose frail health was her constant worry, under her unceasing,
affectionate control.

She was her real self in the great political salons. Not all of them opened their doors to the Churchills at that time. Conservative society largely followed the Prince of Wales' example in avoiding the "rebellious" pair. Only Lord Salisbury, Disraeli's political heir, made an exception. Destined to become Prime Minister as soon as the Tories would return to power, he obviously wanted to end the running feud between the orthodox group and Lord Randolph. He demonstrated his good will in betaking himself to a meeting at Blenheim, where he stood and spoke with Lord Randolph on the same platform.

Soon afterward he invited the Churchills to a reception at Hatfield House. The seat of honor, on Lord Salisbury's right, was occupied by Lady Randolph. She was charmed with her host's apparent interest in her conversation, "however frivolous" her subject. She had never had a more pleasant dinner companion, she reminisced many years later. But the next lady who had the privilege of talking to the great man received exactly the same courteous attention, Jeanette observed.

Next to Lord Salisbury she admired Mr. Gladstone, of all people. Randolph, who had christened him "Old man in a hurry" (a nickname later to be applied to Winston) attacked him so spitefully that even friends considered this hatred pathological. They regretted that Lord Randolph simply did not understand how to deal with Gladstone.

Lady Randolph, on the other hand, understood this art very well. Having met the old man in a hurry on many a social occasion, she discovered that all the craft required was to say an intelligent "Yes" or "No," once Mr. Gladstone had started on his subject. To venture an opinion of one's own was definitely dangerous. The man of Midlothian would listen in grave silence, but he had a disconcerting way of turning sharply around, his piercing eyes fixed inquiringly upon his conversation partner, and putting his hand to his ear, in a gesture of sheer incredulity.

On the other hand he could be extremely gentle. After a

furious clash he had had with Lord Randolph in the House, he met Lady Randolph at a dinner party in Spencer House. She had come unescorted, since her husband was exhausted from his parliamentary battle. Mr. Gladstone greeted her with the words: "Alone? I hope Lord Randolph is not too tired after his magnificent effort."

CHAPTER X *Shadows*

In the summer of 1882 Lord Randolph suffered his first physical collapse. His wife had seen it coming for some time. She did not falter under the blow. On the contrary, she displayed that air of cool, detached imperturbability with which she always concealed her strong feelings. She acted immediately. Randolph was transported to a pretty cottage with a delightful lawn and rose garden on Wimbledon Common. The Duchess of Marlborough joined the couple. Months of tender care by his devoted wife and matchless mother slowly restored his health.

But he remained a marked man, and he knew it. From his thirty-third year the thought of disease became his obsession. His case was progressive paralysis—unmentionable in Victorian times. Being himself afflicted by grave illness, he showed a wretched delight in attributing physical incapacity to his opponents. He criticized Sir Stafford Northcote, the "goat," but not for lack of character, talents, or experience. To ailing Lord Randolph, Sir Stafford was an aging man whose strength failed year by year and whose extraordinary physical disabilities oppressed him with increasing severity. Randolph attributed the last Conservative defeat to the "decay of Lord Beaconsfield's physical vigor." His ferocious attacks on old Gladstone went so far that someone warned him: "You will kill Mr. Gladstone one of these days." "Oh no," came the

178

rejoinder. "He will long survive me. I often tell my wife what a beautiful letter he will write her, proposing my burial in Westminster Abbey."

Slowly, the shades descended on the exuberant family Churchill. The sudden death of the Duke was the first stroke of fate. His Grace died in harness. On June 28, 1883, he had made in the House of Lords what was generally considered his greatest speech, on the Deceased Wife's Sister Bill. On the night of July 4th, after a pleasant dinner with Randolph at Blenheim, he went to bed, apparently in the best of health and spirits. Early the next morning he was found dead by his servant: struck down by a sudden affection of the heart.

To Lady Randolph it was almost as if she had lost her own father. The old Duke had always been most kind and gentle to her, and she, in turn, understood the affectionate nature under his rather chilly and reserved, ever dignified, attitude. Although she did not share his extreme Toryism, which held in abhorrence anything approaching change, she definitely felt that a piece of her own world was gone.

What upset her most was the terrific impact the Duke's death made on Randolph. He passed many hours reading over his father's letters, all of which he had carefully preserved since his boyhood. Many more hours he spent in Church. Now religion was not a political utility to him, as his opponents had accused him in the Bradlaugh case. He deeply longed for consolation, and was more regular in his devotional exercises than during any other period of his life. The game of politics had, at least temporarily, lost all its attraction. For the remainder of the year he did not visit Parliament He was badly missed by his friends in the House, and urged to return. But he wrote to Wolff: "I am not up to it physically or mentally, and I am longing to get away abroad. It is very melancholy here...."

Lady Randolph made a flying visit to St. James's School to bid her boy good-by. The condition in which she found the child horrified her. Winston had spent two years of anxiety in school, which, indeed, prepared for Eton mostly by adopting the Eton fashion of flogging with the birch. This chastisement was a great feature in the curriculum. Winston Churchill could never forget it. Not even in the reformatories, the state-controlled institutions for juvenile criminals, would the cruel flogging have been possible that the Headmaster of St. James's was wont to inflict upon the little boys under his care.

The mental torture the boy was exposed to was no less abominable. Stubbornly he refused to yield to what he—already in his ninth year—termed hateful servitude. The masters tried to break his resistance. But since they did not appeal to his reason, imagination, or interest, but only relied on their large resources of compulsion, they utterly failed. Not one of them, apparently, understood that their unruly disciple was a genius in the making. They only saw a poor pupil at the bottom of the form, yet precociously reading books beyond his years (his father had presented him with *Treasure Island*), making little progress at his lessons, and none at all at games. The treatment meted out to Winston at his first school affected his health. He fell seriously ill. His mother had not come an instant too early. She took him away. Still, she accused herself of having come too late.

Was it impossible to lead three lives at once? To be a devoted wife carrying the burden of a nurse on her shoulders, a watchful mother with a difficult child, and a great lady in her own right? Nothing was impossible to Lady Randolph. It seemed quite natural to her that a woman should have more duties and harder ones than a man. She felt sure of strength to fulfill all of them. Her sense of responsibility was united with her inexhaustible vitality. She decided that both her husband and her son needed some fresh, invigorating mountain air. Neither the customary trip to New York nor a visit in Monte Carlo, where the Churchills had spent a short sojourn a few months previously, would do. She did not want to run into people. She chose Gastein, the Austrian spa in the Alps, already a well-known watering-place, but not yet discovered by her English, American, or even French acquaintances.

Some persons, however, are fated to "run into people." The Churchills had scarcely established themselves in the villa they had rented, when walking the beautiful promenade from Bad Gastein to Hofgastein on a late July forenoon, they met Bismarck. Not knowing the Iron Chancellor personally, but knowing enough about him from her father's account of Versailles, Lady Randolph urged her husband to proceed quickly. She wanted to avoid a chance meeting. Bismarck, of course, overlooked passers-by. But his two inseparable companions, iron-gray and black great Danes, huge and highly strung, bold and dangerous, very much resembling their master, became suspicious at the Churchills passing close to them, and in a hurry. The beasts growled. Their tails stiffened. They were called back by the Chancellor's other two inseparable companions: heavy-set, square-jawed Prussians, the bodyguards, who, for their part, now assailed the strangers: "The promenade is reserved for His Excellency."

"They take us for anarchists," Lady Randolph smilingly remarked to her husband, audible enough for Bismarck to hear her irony.

Her English attracted Bismarck's attention. He was just about to woo London, but Liberal Mr. Gladstone was showing little understanding for the German monster's tenderness. Nevertheless, the tenacious Bismarck was in the habit of treating important English people with consideration. In perfect Prussian fashion he introduced himself, as if his likeness were not known all over the world. Perhaps he was aware that in his sixty-eighth year, in 1883, he looked very different from the pictures glorifying him. His walrus-mustache which had once even exceeded Lord Randolph's trade-mark was gone. Instead, a short white beard had grown. His lion's mane had vanished. Now Bismarck was quite bald; only a few hairs on the back of the head and on the temples remained. His eyebrows were still bushy toward the middle, but thinned toward the sides. The wrinkles below his eyes, and the lines that ran from his nose to the corners of his mouth, always deep, were now cavernous. His smile was frightening. But it turned into a broad and amiable grin when he learned that the man he was addressing was Lord Randolph Churchill, the famous Gladstone-baiter. Much to the surprise of his bodyguards and to the apparent misgivings of his yelping great Danes, the eternal cuirassier clicked his heels.

"Your Lordship, Your Ladyship," he said ceremoniously in correct, if halting English. "May I have the honor of your company at dinner tomorrow, or, say, tonight. . . ."

The evening with Bismarck was entertaining. Randolph and Bismarck were excellently met. The Iron Chancellor chatted incessantly of hunting, horseback riding, traveling, and cooking—all also Randolph's favorite interests. They perfectly agreed that mixing champagne with sweet wines was a barbaric fashion, because one would get intoxicated too soon, but they disagreed slightly on the quantity one should eat. Whereas Randolph, a gourmet, advocated moderate portions, Bismarck confessed to being an omnivorous glutton. This was, he said, his only trouble with his master. "We get lean fare at the Emperor's table," he chuckled. "When I note the number of cutlets I help myself to only one, being afraid that if I take two some guest will go hungry. Only one cutlet apiece is provided."

Lady Randolph recalled that the food at Napoleon III's court had been exquisite, but not so plentiful, either.

"Charlatan!" said Bismarck. It sounded spiteful and repulsive. The great man immediately noticed that he had made a *faux pas*. Turning closer to his beautiful guest and rapidly changing his topic, he asked her whether she had children. Without waiting for her answer, he insisted that watching his children grow up had been the only true joy of his life. He had, indeed, forgiven them all, and allowed them everything—except personal freedom, of course.

Winston would have personal freedom, it flashed through
her mind. Then she tried to speak about music and books.

Bismarck turned the other way. "I'll give you a precious
piece of advice, Lord Randolph. Try fish with mushrooms. Or
roast beef with *wurst*. . . . It goes perfectly with Deidesheimer.
Even with claret."

Emperor Wilhelm I slept peacefully and, being an early
riser, retired soon to bed. When Count Lehnsdorff, whose little
villa the Churchills had rented, invited his house guests to
visit *La Solitude* where His Majesty, the German Emperor,
would be pleased to receive them, he said in unmistakable
Prussian fashion: "Dinner at five, lights out at seven!"

The Emperor was eighty-six at that time, but still going
strong. His Spartan style of life, to which he attributed his
longevity, was only slightly relaxed in Gastein, his favorite
summer resort. There he bathed not only in the waters whose
healing powers were the best remedy against gout—His Majesty discussed no topic with such relish as gout—but also in
pleasant memories. Three years earlier Gastein had been the
place of his meeting with Emperor Franz Joseph of Austria.
Good old Bismarck had skillfully used the monarch's entrevue
to manufacture the Austro-German offensive and defensive
alliance, which, ratified in 1882, gave Germany the power of
attacking third nations, and sealed the doom of the Austro-
Hungarian Empire, now following helplessly in the big brother's
wake. The bloodless victory of Gastein, as Whilhelm I and
Bismarck, with a twinkle in their tired eyes, called it between
themselves, enhanced mightily the beauty of the mountainous
landscape around them. Nowhere else was the aged German
Emperor as accessible and easy-going.

He was, Lady Randolph observed, a fine-looking man, notwithstanding his great age, and he displayed that old-world
manner which she found as attractive as it was rare. His cheerfulness impressed her. It stunned the other guests. They had
never seen their senile Emperor in such an exuberant mood.

He chaffed the young people at the table and occasionally spoke of his own youth.

At dinner he discarded all the dietetic rules of the cure he was undergoing. Lady Randolph found it mysterious that one could eat so much and yet grow so old. Wilhelm I began his meal with poached eggs, and went on to potted meats and various old German dishes, drinking many cups of strong tea, and ending with strawberries, ices and sweets, washed down with tepid champagne.

Lady Randolph sat on his right. When dinner was over he drew her into a corner. At seven, remembering Count Lehnsdorff's warning, she wanted to rise. But the Emperor's gouty hands rose quickly in protest. He made her sit down again. Two more hours were spent in animated conversation. Randolph dozed in that accomplished manner which was generally taken for silent thinking.

"We talked banalities," she said when they were finally permitted to leave. "It was not very exciting."

Randolph smiled. "For the old man, not either?" He was amused by the electrifying effect his beautiful wife had had on the octogenarian. He had been watching them. The sleep of this restless mind was, at best, half sleep. In fact he had listened during their whole conversation. "The Emperor spoke scarcely a word to me," he wrote on August 8, 1883, to his brother. "My wife, however, sat by him and had much conversation, which, I ascertained, was confined to the most frivolous topics."

Probably it was the word frivolity that made the Marquess of Blandford, now the eighth Duke, join the Churchills in Gastein immediately. He was happy to find Randolph again in his old buoyant spirits. The baths in the healing waters had done the convalescent good, and it was the rare time in Randolph's life in which his system was not poisoned by politics. Toward the end of August the brothers returned slowly home together through Switzerland. Randolph had to show off his regained physical strength. He persuaded his brother to climb the Rigi Kulm with him. "We'll make it like the meanest and commonest of Tow Rows," he predicted cheerfully. Not to distress excitable Randolph, the Duke reluctantly gave in. The conquest of the glacier proved a little more difficult than expected. Blandford had frequently to help, occasionally to nurse his brother. "It is quite impossible to do justice to Blandford's more than womanly care and tenderness. . . ." Lord Randolph wrote to his mother from Pontresina on August 16th. The brothers were as near to each other as ever.

The old political divergencies between them lost their importance. The Duke even promised Randolph that he would show himself worthy of his new title by joining the Carlton Club. This step would not yet be formal adherence to the Conservative party, but at least a return to the Tories' social home. Lord Randolph, a mighty man in the Carlton, immediately wrote a letter. The answer was not encouraging. Even as the eighth Duke of Marlborough, the elder brother was still regarded as the unspeakable Marquess. He had better not apply for membership. Randolph was furious. He wrote his reply with a pen dipped in vitriol. He threatened that he would himself quit the club.

Deeply touched by this new proof of fraternal faithfulness, the Duke invited Lord and Lady Randolph to spend the autumn and winter with him in Blenheim. They would be a happy family as in the old days. The invitation was cheerfully accepted. In Blenheim the volcanic brothers clashed in the most fiery conflict of their lives.

In many great families, questions concerning the interpretation of ancestral documents on the subject of heirlooms provoke occasional controversies. At Blenheim such a controversy flared up when Randolph discovered that the priceless Sunderland library was gone, and most of the precious old masters had disappeared from the portrait gallery. Meekly, very much against his custom, the eighth Duke admitted that the usual circumstances—a discreet allusion to the fact that he was eternally debt-ridden, and hounded by his creditors—had forced him to part with much of the old stuff. Moreover, the Lord Cairns Act, one of the first measures introduced by the Liberal government, threatened grievously to affect the sale of heirlooms. It was good to sell while prices were soaring, and before the market became flooded with the art treasures of almost all the peerage.

The upward movement in the price of pictures had begun a few years previously. Blandford, it now proved, had followed the development with keen attention. Probably he had prepared his devious plan long before. Now he was in a position to defend his transaction with valid arguments: "Remember 1878 ..." he started his apology.

It was the year of the historic Berlin Congress. To Randolph, however, it was the memorable year when he had made friends with Joe Chamberlain. To Jeanette it was the year in which she had earned her first money by selling poems to a magazine. To Blandford it was the year in which *Enamoured Cavalier*, an oil portrait by an artist not of the highest distinction, netted, at the Bredel sales, the unprecedented, but since then frequently surpassed amount of 4,300 guineas, whereas a quarter of a century before famous portraits by classic Dutch masters were considered an extravagant buy at 330 guineas. Still, the Duke explained, this was but a beginning. A Gainsborough, which as late as 1876 had secured only a few shillings over 367 guineas, had lately changed hands at ten times the price. The Marquess of Hertford bought some ten or twenty pictures for fourteen thousand guineas. Lord Dudley bid ten thousand guineas for a portrait of the Duchess of Devonshire, who, by her kiss, had won the Westminster elections for Charles Fox.

Lady Randolph listened carefully. She was always highly amused by her brother-in-law's easy talk in serious moments. He reminded her of her father. It was the same mixture of enthusiasm for beautiful things, knack for business, and recklessness. "You should go to America," she said smiling.

"I've frequently been there. It's too expensive ... at the moment!"

"But one can make money over there!" she answered.

The idea that one could make money in America, where he had always wasted thousands, struck Blandford as a new one. He stored it away in his mind.

Randolph, for his part, knew his brother too well to let himself be put off by the famous Blandford loquaciousness. "What, exactly, has disappeared from our family treasures?" he asked sternly.

"Well, Rubens' *Progress of Silenus* is gone, and *Lot and His Daughters* ... and ... and a few other pictures from the dining room ..." the new duke admitted.

"Never mind," Lady Randolph came to his rescue, although with sadness in her heart. "What is missing from the dining room is not missing at all. It was never looked at, as it is. The governesses, sitting primly between their charges, would never have dared to raise their eyes to such paintings. And the members of the family were much too familiar with them to pay any attention."

Lord Randolph looked at his wife disapprovingly. He was smoking his thirtieth cigarette since the argument had begun. "Is that the lot?" he inquired severely.

"Then there still had to go ..." Blandford avowed.

Randolph was lighting his fiftieth cigarette when his brother finished his confession. The twenty-five best pictures in the collection, valued at a total of 400,000 guineas, had changed hands. Raphael's *Madonna Ansidei* had been purchased for seventy thousand guineas, and Van Dyke's *Charles I on Horseback* for 87,500, by the National Gallery. Baron Alphonse de Rothschild had bought two Rubens' at 50,000 each. The Berlin Museum had acquired a Sebastiano del Piombo. The Tsar of Russia was among the buyers. Several family portraits, notably the *Fortune Teller* by Sir Joshua Reynolds (depicting Lord Henry and Lady Charlotte Spencer) had been sold. And the entire Sunderland library had been bought up by Messrs. Puttick and Simpson, who netted an enormous profit when the books went at their sales.

All was finally scattered. Lady Randolph recalled what had happened to her father's priceless belongings. She mourned the losses, but she could not bear a grudge against her brother-in-law. She knew too well how millions can vanish. She had already been through all that.

The brothers engaged in a ferocious struggle. Lady Randolph took no part in it. She helped the Duke hang the remaining pictures in new positions and distributed them so carefully that only those familiar with the collection could see how badly it had been reduced. It was more difficult to reconcile the brothers. For a time they were not on speaking terms. Randolph wanted to leave Blenheim immediately.

Just now, at the start of the shooting season? Jeanette argued. The logic of this questioning was compelling. Randolph revived his harriers. His wife was given the proud post of whipper-in. But to her own discomfiture she could never remember the names of the hounds.

Lord Randolph had a new opportunity to show himself the better man. He spent many hours a day at the kennels. He knew not only every dog's name, but all their peculiarities and qualities. He forgot the old masters over horses and hounds. As usual, Jeanette had him where she wanted him to be. She arranged a full reconciliation between the quarreling brothers within less than two weeks.

CHAPTER XI *The Primrose League*

Blenheim entirely absorbed the Churchills. Local problems were the only ones that counted. Randolph struggled for an extension of the railway line from Oxford, then the terminus, to Woodstock. His interest in state affairs seemed waning. He longed to become what he had been destined by birth to be: a country gentleman, a little busy, a little lazy, and a little contemptuous of the world.

Another wife would have been happy to see her combative husband mellowing. Jeanette was frightened. There was no peace in him, she understood. He was simply physically exhausted. Otherwise a man of thirty-four, of Randolph's temperament and ambition, would not give up. He would not survive in retirement. Only in activity could he keep going. He was not an onlooker, else she could not have shared his life so completely. Strong and entirely healthy herself, she could not watch her husband abdicate. One gallops till one falls. Her father had always said so.

Randolph called her the fountain of his strength. Gratefully the lone wolf took her advice in both great and small things. When the Irish troubles flared up again, causing grave concern to the Churchills, she suggested he should visit Cardinal Manning in London. The Prince of the Catholic Church might well become the peacemaker.

But as Randolph stood in front of the white-haired, wise

189

priest, he felt helpless and humble. It was a unique experience. Instead of speaking politics, he felt an irresistible desire to open his heart.

On the same evening the Cardinal told a friend: "I had a long talk with Lord Randolph Churchill today. He spoke despondently about his physical resources. I am grieved to think he will never live long enough to make the mark he might have done on his country."

At that time even his most intimate friends knew nothing about Randolph's slow and painful duel with decay. They missed him in the House. One day Sir Henry Wolff appeared in Blenheim, where, as it happened, the whole family, including uncles, aunts, and cousins, was assembled. He brought along an idea. "It's just about a little flower," he said in that bantering tone that was habitual when the members of the Fourth Party devised important plans. Out of the idea of the little flower grew the most successful social-political organization ever known in England, and Lady Randolph emerged as the uncontested leading lady in British politics.

Sir Henry Wolff had nursed his idea for some months. It had come to him on April 19, when, after the unveiling of Lord Beaconsfield's statue, he entered the House and was received by Mr. Cove, the popular superintendent of the members' cloakroom, with a primrose. "Take it," the man said. "Everyone wears it today." Indeed, when Sir Henry entered the Chamber all the Conservatives had Beaconsfield's favorite flower in their buttonholes.

Sir Henry's shrewd political mind was impressed by this demonstration. As he walked home from the session with Lord Randolph, he ventured the casual remark: "Why not start a Primrose League?" Randolph was instantly interested: "Draw up a plan," he said.

After months the plan was drawn up. The central idea was to put the Conservative Party, or rather its ideology, on a popular basis. It was necessary to find new contact with the masses. Campaigning was becoming ever more difficult. The expenses, particularly in urban districts, mounted so rapidly that the need for voluntary helpers became urgent. Besides, the Electoral Corrupt Practices Act, just passed by the Liberal Government, made impossible the old measures of influencing the voters. The free distribution of "blue beer and beef" (blue being the Tory color) was now forbidden. The old manorial influence on rural voters was waning. The industrial voters showed a dangerous inclination to follow the radical slogans. Joe Chamberlain had just established the "600" in Birmingham, the first political caucus in which the people themselves decided what they wanted (or rather what Mr. Chamberlain wanted), whereas the Conservative organization adapted themselves only slowly to the social changes.

With Beaconsfield they had lost their magic. Lacking this, the best thing to replace it was a symbol. On the second anniversary of Disraeli's death all London had worn the Primrose. Business men wore them in their buttonholes, cab-drivers had stuck them behind their horses' ears, they filled the windows of the flower shops. Undoubtedly, the Primrose exercised a general appeal. Symbolically, it carried on the tradition of the great statesman, who in his youth had been the real prophet of Tory Democracy, and about whom two years after his death even the haughty *Times* of London wrote: "Lord Beaconsfield is still the object, we do not say of a cult, but at least of admiring and affectionate curiosity."

Moreover, Victorians loved symbols, badges, grades, and honorary distinctions. Their spell was particularly strong among the working class, which supported fraternal organizations like the Foresters, the Oddfellows, and the Good Templars, above all for the variety of their regalia and the magniloquence of their nonsensical titles. The new bourgeoisie, just coming into being, showed, too, a distinct desire for color. Living in the new residential suburb districts, life seemed rather drab to them. The women were left alone to kill time from Monday till Friday. A romantic fellowship would attract this middle class to the Conservative fold, particularly if the fact was brought home to them that there was only one party for ladies and gentlemen; Radicals were just outsiders.

All that had been discussed frequently between Sir Henry Wolff and Lord Randolph. But until October no third person was let into the plan. Jeanette did not show any disappointment over the fact that, for once, she had been omitted from a plot. When at last she was let into the secret, the idea of founding the Primrose League appealed strongly to her. It would open a wide field of work and of new chances for the women of England, who, of course, were to be admitted, although they were not yet enfranchised. Probably the dramatic side of the League added to its attraction for Lady Randolph. It would be great fun to be a member of a "Ladies' Grand Council," perhaps a "Dame President," and to rule her own "Habitation." She felt slightly ridiculous at this childish delight. But her histrionic instinct was aroused. Now the great rôle had come her way.

The very evening Sir Henry disclosed his long concealed idea, Lady Randolph enrolled all the female members of the assembled family as "dames," although the official formulation of the "Ladies' Grand Council" was still a few months off. The Duchess of Marlborough was evidently to become the leader of the female auxiliary troops. Lady Randolph modestly contented herself with being "Dame No. 11." But there was no doubt for her, nor for anyone else, that she would be the driving spirit in this corps of women.

True, the whole business with its highfalutin terms sounded a little naïve. At home, Lady Randolph herself laughed over the grandiloquent names she had now to incorporate with her otherwise precise and cultivated language. It was not easy to keep serious while using expressions like "Knight Harbingers," "Ruling Councilors," "Chancellors of the League" in pretended earnest. The Brummagem gaudy badges and "ye ancient" diplomas printed on vellum challenged her American sense of irony. But it was the very thing the fun-starved Victorian suburbanites wanted.

Moreover, there was nothing in the endeavors of the League to laugh about. It was, indeed, the legitimate spiritual heir to the "young England" school Disraeli had created at the outset of his career. By its constitution the Primrose League was to "embrace all classes and all creeds except atheists and enemies of the British Empire." Gentlemen, and soon also ladies, wishing to enroll, had to apply in writing to the Registrar of the League, care of Messrs. Lacy, Hartland & Co., London, E. C., whereupon the following declaration was to be subscribed: "I declare on my honor and faith that I will devote my best ability to the maintenance of Religion, of the Estates of the Realm, and of the Imperial Ascendancy of Great Britain...." Strangely, this strongly conservative formula had been worked out by the Ruling Council of Four, whose members—with the single exception of wavering Mr. Balfour, replaced by Sir Alfred Slade—were identical with the rebels of the Fourth Party.

Recruits joined, Lady Randolph expressed it, "slowly but surely." In the first months the wearers of the Primrose badge exposed themselves to general ridicule. But undoubtedly, it was the right thing. It materialized the dream Lord Beaconsfield had expressed in a great many novels, of entertaining Tory Democracy by large gatherings in which dukes should rub shoulders with their tenants, and industrialists with their own workers. Indeed, the gatherings of the Primrose League which soon flooded all England were a strange medley. The laborer and the local magnate, the provincial lady and the grocer's wife mingled freely. Some critics called it, quoting Disraeli's word, the mass in masquerade. But the meetings of the League were actually a vivid expression of the genuine article, English democracy.

Until the turn of the Seventies only the "Ten Pounders" had had the vote. They had been eligible for yearly invitation to the squire's house. Since the vote had increased by millions, the lower middle classes, the artisans, farmers and laborers held the political power. They would have felt embarrassed by receptions at Hatfield House or Devonshire House or Compton Lodge. The Churchills gave the masses what they wanted. One of the first "habitations" was founded in Woodstock. The parks of Blenheim were widely opened. One of Lord Randolph's retainers suggested opening the celebration with the old song "God bless the squire and all his rich relations, And keep us poor people in our proper stations."

Lady Randolph instantly discarded this foolish suggestion. She volunteered to convey the invitations personally. She visited the farmers and the glove-workers' houses, brought along food, lighted the stove personally, cooked savory stew from the best but—for educational reasons—simplest ingredients, even helped scrubbing the floor with brush and soap. English people had never seen anything like it.

They had never had such gatherings, either. Usually, a great lady presided—Lady Randolph herself scores of times—or some son of a noble house. People were proud of the company. The proceedings were never cumbersome. The political speech was short, and to the point. The people had the choice between adhering to the Conservative banner or being regarded as outcasts. As soon as they understood that, the amusement followed: climbing of greased poles for prize pigs, dancing in the moonlight, fireworks, distribution of little gifts such as blankets, flannel petticoats, toys for the children. It was impossible to resist the temptation to join a Primrose League meeting.

The triumphal success of such meetings, particularly in the Midlands and in the South, made it also soon dangerous to abstain. The local grocer and baker had to join, if he did not want to be accused by a whirlwind whisper campaign of adulterating his flour or selling inferior Australian mutton for English, and thus losing his lady customers. One branch of artisans certainly never missed the gathering. The tailors were sure to run into their customers who, according to a venerable English habit, never paid their bills, and could make an effort,

at least, to collect their debts. Every village park, an open green
or any available space was, once or twice a year, turned into
the meeting-place of the Primrose League's local habitation.
An avalanche was unloosed. The League's membership rose
rapidly. After twenty years—the Churchills had long retired—
it numbered one million eight hundred thousand members.
Today still the Primrose League is the very stronghold of the
Conservative Party.

Evidently there was a good deal of opposition to overcome.
Gladstone's uncanny political instinct told the great old man
that the slightly ridiculous Knight Harbingers and Dames were
shoveling his grave. He counterattacked methodically. Suddenly the entire Liberal press burst out with the accusation
that the Primrose was a fake symbol. It had not been Disraeli's
favorite flower. The answer was an overflow of primroses in all
Conservative circles. Processions marched with the symbol in
buttonholes, clubs decorated their houses with it. Working men
trimmed their caps with the primrose, cabbies wound them
around their whips, young girls sold bunches of them to passengers in trains. Lady Randolph used no other bouquets. The
Wars of the Roses had not been as furiously conducted as the
war of the Primrose.

The worst clashes occurred on the women's front. A hand-
book for Liberal Women Workers declared: "The existence of
the Primrose League cannot be overlooked, although we de-
spise and condemn its ridiculous paraphernalia and its appeal
to the ignorance and frivolous vanities of women." Dignified
Mrs. Gladstone told the Liberal Women's organization: "The
efforts of women should be open and clear, avoiding the
methods and manners of Primrose Dames." This was a clear
allusion to Lady Randolph. Henry Labouchere, once the famous *News* correspondent in besieged Paris, now the leftest of
the left, made it still clearer. Under the title "Mollitics" his
magazine *Truth* burst out: "Every Parliamentary candidate
must now have his Moll, to simper while he asks for a vote,
to grin and wave a handkerchief at the telling points in his

speech, and to be assaulted by the police, if the exigencies of the case render a little female battery expedient."

All England knew that by no means every Parliamentary candidate, but actually only one of them was constantly accompanied by his wife when campaigning. All England knew that there had been most disagreeable scenes when Lord Randolph had attacked Birmingham, the liberal stronghold, and in vain tried to wrest it from its traditional radical owners. All England knew that Lady Randolph had courageously sat out on the battered conservative platform the organized hoodlum assaults. She had, in fact, staved off the worst by her unsurpassable, haughty indifference toward the mob.

Again she proved her indifference toward political insult and attack. She addressed innumerable habitations of women, she became President of many of them. She officially opened the Grantham habitation in Croydon in double harness with the Duchess of Buckingham. She founded the stronghold in Knutsford. A sort of female bodyguard, she constantly accompanied her mother-in-law, when the Duchess of Marlborough made her appearance as President of the Ladies' Grand Council.

Her inborn tact taught her the right approach to every sort of gathering. She could smile at and chat with the right people. Occasionally she could visibly suppress a few tears, and in other instances move her audience to tears. She had her way with the men, but, which was more difficult, she did not antagonize the women. In fact, she mobilized hundreds of thousands of them. Her supreme political triumph came after three years of hard labor. In the first days of June, 1886, she went, in Mr. Balfour's company, to Manchester to open a large Habitation. Her hands trembling with excitement, her notes hidden behind her fan, she addressed the crowd in the city's biggest hall. Her fiery speech predicted Gladstone's immediate downfall. The *Manchester Guardian* reported this speech verbatim, and added: "Lady Randolph was ably supported by Mr. Balfour, M. P., Lord Salisbury's nephew."

A few days later, on June 7th, the great old man went down in the House. Apparently, he fell over the Home Rule Bill. Actually, the Churchills had slayed him: Randolph with his parliamentary tactics, Jeanette contributing her bit with a little tact.

CHAPTER XII

House Beautiful

How she managed to stand the strain imposed upon her by unceasing social activities combined with her political exertions is one of the many secrets Lady Randolph never disclosed. Actually, she thrived on a pace that would have been too much for any woman but a daughter of Leonard Jerome.

In her early thirties her beauty had lost some of the panther touch which Lord D'Abernon had attributed to her a decade before. Now a thin veil of thoughtfulness, as it were, lay on her smooth, untroubled face, in which the joys and trials, the ventures and adventures of the years had not left the slightest crease or wrinkle. She wore her rich black hair piled up; the tumbling ringlets covered most of the forehead. Full brows arched over the jet-black eyes, already proverbial for their lucid vivacity. Her skin still retained the warm, peach color of the Italian baby. But her expression was searching and serious, and there was nothing babyish about it.

She preferred to wear a high lace collar, probably to increase her stature, for she was not tall. She was one of the first ladies to do away with the modish tyranny of the past. In general, the costume of the early Eighties showed no great improvement over the styles of the previous decade. "Smart bustling" was still the vogue, although the more practical and worldly women diminished their bustles while lengthening train and skirt. The

198

aesthetic school, with which Lady Randolph sympathized without belonging to it, insisted on a shapeless, clinging garb. Both tendencies had a markedly beneficial effect on emancipating women from the heavy and uncomfortable lines that a few years before had almost immobilized them.

Lady Randolph's beauty demanded a beautiful frame. Upon their return from Blenheim the Churchills established themselves in a new house, at 2 Connaught Place. The careful choice of the site was remarkable. Although it belonged to the exclusive 350 houses in which alone "all London" could live, it was not in the center of what Thackeray had called: "The doubtful zigzags of Mayfair and Belgravia, that pale and polite district where all the inhabitants look prim and correct, and the mansions are painted a faint whitey-brown." No. 2 Connaught Place was among the squares and terraces beyond the new Bayswater and Tyburn border line. This line was invisible, but by no means without importance. It marked the residential quarter of the new society rather than that of the old nobility whom Mayfair and Belgravia sheltered. Those arch-Conservative districts gradually lost some of their importance since many Victorian magnates, their ambitions only embracing the turf and hunting, retired from noisy London. The young Churchills were passionately interested in both those sports. But for their home they chose the modern neighborhood whose dwellers were about to form circles of their own. It was just one step from the center of early Victorian respectability. But this slight aberration was generally remarked. Their friends christened 2 Connaught Place: House Tyburnia. The name was a program.

House Tyburnia's windows gave on to Hyde Park, commanding a beautiful unbroken view from Marble Arch to Knightsbridge Corner. Just opposite, affixed to the railings of the Park, there was a small tablet that marked the site of Tyburn Gate, where some forty years earlier thieves and criminals had been hanged in public. Lady Randolph sometimes wondered whether her new house would be full of the wailing ghosts of the poor wretches who had been executed there. She was disappointed when none appeared.

Next to attacking Mr. Gladstone in the woman's crusade of the Primrose League, her main preoccupation in the winter of 1883 was furnishing the new house. Her brother-in-law called her hard work "disposing her stage properties." She did not mind such banter, and he did not exaggerate it.

House Tyburnia should be, and actually became, entirely different from the early Victorian style of art and architecture. The Great Exhibition had imposed on the average British home an impossible standard of taste, prevailing for some forty years. Encouragement of trade and industry had been the Exhibition's first task, and in this way this large group of customers, the new middle class, was induced to become snobbish. They could not prove their subservience to current conventions any better than in the decoration of their homes. Solidity, the quality appreciated above all, found its full expression in heavy walnut or mahogany tables, broad leather chairs, dark and largely floral wallpapers, and red plush or "rep" curtains. The drawing-rooms were stuffed with glittering candelabras and huge gilt mirrors. Carved rosewood tables cluttered the bedrooms. Terra-cotta plaques, blue China plates, Japanese fans were perfect dust traps. A family album with father and mother in their wedding garments as the pièce de resistance could not be omitted from the table in the dining room, with its crimson and gold walls. The houses were similarly made up on the outside. The front door looked like bronze, and felt like wood. Frequently the walls were covered with paper imitating marble. Doors and woodwork were disguised as oak or walnut.

Lady Randolph laughed about such nonsense. The house in Charles Street which they had bought and furnished after their wedding had been pretty much according to the then accepted style. In her ignorance of the climate, as she excused it later, she had covered the walls with light silks, and she had nearly cried with dismay when she saw the havoc wrought upon them by the fogs of London. Her dearly bought experience stood her in good stead when she came to furnishing House Tyburnia. Plush curtains and embossed wallpaper were banned. In Connaught Place she set a new style, soon copied by many enlightened families. The rooms were paneled, the walls painted clean white. Her new abode was the first private house in England equipped with electric light, produced by a small dynamo that was placed in the cellar underneath the street. The only drawback was that its noise greatly excited all the horses approaching the house.

Proudly, Lady Randolph displayed her electric fireworks at the first dinner she gave in her new home. But in the middle of the feast the lights went out. The guests had to remain in utter darkness until the lamps and candles which had been high-handedly relegated to the cellars were again unearthed. Progress had its price, Lady Randolph found.

The short-circuit had another, rather unpleasant aftermath. Lord Randolph had just spoken enthusiastically in the House of Commons in favor of an Electric Lighting Bill. Now, since all London was laughing about the mishap, he felt no longer able to accept the gift of the installation which the company, by way of advertisement, had offered, free of charge. Stiffly, he asked for the bill, and was overcharged double or treble the real price.

It was not always easy to pay heavy bills. Once, in these days, Lady Randolph found in an old shop in the city some large painted panels. Although they were grimy and in a deplorable condition, her keen artistic eye, sharpened in the picture gallery of Blenheim, immediately saw their value. Their price was three hundred pounds. But this time Randolph, who usually indulged his wife's every whim and wish, simply could not afford them. Sadly, she looked at her walls which were to remain empty. Her regret was not mitigated when the panels were sold shortly afterward, and recognized as Morlands, worth seven or eight thousand pounds.

She had, however, many good pieces of old furniture picked up in her years in Dublin, where they came on to the market from the dismantled houses of impecunious Irish landlords. Things could be bought cheaply in those days, particularly by a purchaser endowed with hereditary Yankee trading sense. During the following years, millionaires bought up practically everything. What was left, Lady Randolph complained, was held at fabulous prices. But the house in Tyburnia was happily established. Soon all London called it House Beautiful.

Domestic happiness coincided with Lord Randolph's rapidly mounting influence in politics. True, he had to fight the hard way. Lord Salisbury had refused to come forward and head the Tory Democratic movement. He soon displayed the same marked coolness toward Randolph that permeated all the higher ranks of the Conservative Party. Sir Stafford Northcote, the senile leader on the Opposition Front Bench, had good reason to hate Randolph, the "gadfly." All the other old men who had sat in the last cabinet and hoped to get back their posts in the next one, were alarmed at Randolph's tremendous success with the masses.

They explained it with this alleged super-demagoguery. Actually Lord Randolph Churchill's platform rhetoric now reached the highest point of popular efficacy. On the rostrum he indulged in vehement, superabundant gestures and wildly melodramatic attitudes. One of his preferred gestures was to strike one clenched fist against the other open palm. Sometimes he raised both fists in an emotional climax. He showed readiness to follow Parnell's sentence: "I am willing to take off my coat for my country!" and appeared about to divest himself of his outer garment. This gesture was often contagious. Under his spell his enthused listeners threw off their own coats. "Lord Randolph Churchill's meetings produce a spectacular sight," the *Pall Mall Gazette* reported. "The audiences emancipate themselves into the deshabille of shirt sleeves." Lord Randolph was entirely unashamed of the impact he made. "Blue book speeches are not in my line," he explained without excusing himself. "If I tried them nobody would attend to them." But as if to offset such excesses he comported himself in private life with the most punctilious Victorian dignity. Except for occasional declamatory moments, in private conversation Randolph avoided vehement gestures or intense accents. He manifested the style of the club man. "At Westminster," Escott, the chronicler, observed, "he was apparently more concerned about his mustache than about invectives. He was solicitous rather for the fit of his boots than the effect of his words."

He dressed in the quiet cut, color and style that originated in Bond Street and Savile Row. In an unshowy manner, so utterly opposed to his habits in public, he developed into a masculine fashion-leader. He taught his colleagues and friends among the Irish Nationalists to don evening dress for dinner parties. He was among the first to replace the top hat—called "pot" hat —by the "gibus," the collapsible opera hat which could be taken into one's box at the opera or into the room at an evening reception. He never went out in the evening, or danced, without white gloves. When silk knee-breeches for ceremonious appearances were tentatively tried out, Lord Randolph was among the first to wear them. But the Prince of Wales did not like it. Silk knee-breeches for evening wear, he insisted, were his privilege.

Lord Rosebery attested to Randolph's wonderful manners. They were courtly, frank, and merry. True, Randolph sometimes enjoyed quarrels, but still more the inevitable reconciliations. He had all the qualities for success, the later Liberal Prime Minister added. He was brilliant, courageous, resourceful, unembarrassed by scruples. He oozed fascination, audacity, tact. He was ready in debate, unrivaled in his conversational skill, a rare combination of personal, popular, and parliamentary gifts.

In general and mixed society he was often silent. In a private dining room, in the Turf Club and even at the Carlton, where he was not surrounded only by friends, however, he excelled. He was at his best in his own well-appointed home. Intensely modern in his thoughts, he yet retained the flavor of old-world courtesy and inimitable personal restraint. Sometimes he liked to play the vanished grandseigneur. In such moods he called the Income Tax Commissioner invariably Sir Alfred, and a Yorkshire baronet who was London's biggest bacon-and-ham supplier Sir George. He could show artificial courtesy and friendly geniality as well as freezing remoteness. Living in the most progressive, modish and showy circle of London, and exposing the habits, caprices, and styles of a new era, yet the Conservative asserted himself, particularly when he visited the Dowager Duchess at 50 Grosvenor Square. Although insular-minded in politics, he was cosmopolitan by personal predilection. His and Jeanette's home was the natural anchorage for all distinguished American visitors. Only Lord Rosebery received overseas guests with the same hospitality.

Whatever Randolph's changing causes and interests, he remained devoted to his three life-long passions: racing, hunting, and chess. Besides, he took gastronomy as seriously as did Macaulay.

With such a unique pair of hosts, House Beautiful had necessarily to become a center of London's high life. By popular demand Lord Randolph had been elected chairman of the National Union of Conservative Associations, which represented the Tory electorate. Assiduously the Central Committee of the party, chiefly composed of members of the Carlton Club, and directing all party affairs as well as controlling the moneybags, tried to offset the influence of Randolph's National Union. But the people remained behind Churchill in his effort to reform and popularize the Tory cause. His rapidly growing prominence in the political world attracted considerable attention in the social set as well. The Churchills, Lady Randolph remembered, were bombarded with invitations. Few members of the fashionable world still held aloof because the Prince frowned on the most popular couple in London. Generally, society smiled again upon them.

A curious phase had come over society. Publicity intruded. Only at Queen Victoria's court the virtue of self-effacement was still rigidly maintained. But it was a shadow court, compared with the Prince of Wales' establishments in Sandringham and Marlborough House, where the prevailing idea was to live before the public. Privacy became a forbidden luxury. The man in the street was to become thoroughly familiar with the houses, the tastes, the habits of even third-rank social leaders. "Ladies of Quality," as the type had been called in the eighteenth century, now permitted their photographs to be published in magazines and displayed in shop windows. One day a picture of Lady Randolph found its way into a shop. Her best friends severely censured her, and advised her to prosecute the photographer. She herself felt confronted with a dilemma. For the sake of her husband's political popularity, she did not wish to appear exclusive or snobbish. But she did not relish the public exposure of her likeness. She was an American patrician by birth, and an English aristocrat by marriage. Her life was devoted to public activities. But her face still belonged to herself. She was well aware what an asset beauty was. But she was horrified at the thought of being mistaken for one of the Professional Beauties who now took London by storm. After all, Lady Randolph Churchill did not belong in the same category as that woman Lily Langtry.

There was nothing wrong with the expression "Professional Beauty," nor with the ladies embodying it. Artists extolled them. Duchesses added to their invitations the line: "Do come; some P.B.'s will be there."

Lily Langtry, the daughter of the handsome Dean of Jersey, was the leading Professional Beauty. But her head was not turned by her success. She knew that she was a passing fashion. While society lay at her feet, she laboriously tried to carve out for herself a career on the stage. She chose the opera. Her voice was not attractive. But her appearance on the stage, with her beautiful face and figure, was a vision of divinely fresh womanhood. She met the Prince at a supper party after her operatic debut. Her career was made.

In her second season she achieved presentation at court. She came to the "drawing-room" late, in the hope that Queen Victoria would already have retired and given her place to the Prince of Wales. So, indeed, it was. The princely couple sat on the dais. But Alexandra looked straight into the air when Lily Langtry kissed her hand; the Princess displayed not a flicker of a smile.

Lady Randolph used the opportunity to tell an interviewer that among beautiful ladies, no one could dispute it, the palm belonged to the Princess of Wales. Then she retired to Ireland, to visit her friends the Londonderrys.

Innocently, her husband wrote her. "I dined with Lord Wharncliffe last night and took in to dinner a Mrs. Langtry, a most beautiful creature, but very poor, it appears. They say she has but one black dress."

The visit with the Londonderrys was cut short. Lady Randolph returned instantly.

Society ladies banded together in a feline conspiracy. They bore the Professional Beauty no grudge. It occurred quite coincidentally that they all had their photographs removed from such shop windows as exposed Lily Langtry's likeness habitually in the center. They even extended such a degree of sympathy to the intruder that they applauded violently her poor performances in the opera. The more she became an actress, the less she would be a lady.

Yet this was the very time in which the theater became accepted. As the pit gave way to the stalls, society began to gather at the play. The Churchills were great patrons of the stage. They introduced to London the French habit of making a first night a social event. They did this not by theatrical enthusiasm alone. Everything they did had also a political reason. The theater, like the turf and the club, should develop into a center of ever-expanding society, now also embracing eager and ambitious suburbia—of course into a conservative center. Tory Democracy, the word made the rounds, was created by Disraeli. But it was decorated and disciplined by Lord Randolph Churchill and his amazing wife.

The natural center of conservative society remained the salon. For many years Lady Dorothy Nevill's house in Charles Street, Berkeley Square, had been the scene of the most important gatherings. Born in the middle Twenties, Lady Dorothy was, in the early Eighties, the living memory of the antique and aristocratic age of post horses and the grand tour, before the crinoline had come in, and when no lady would go to the theater or was allowed in the streets of London without a proper escort. Yet she kept in step with the changing times. She opened her salon to the first secret meetings of the Fourth Party, substituting for Jeanette who at that time was staying at Blenheim and had no London home. Invitations to the Sunday luncheon parties at Lady Dorothy Nevill's were much coveted. As the week-end fashion came in, however, they lost some of their attraction. The old lady felt that she would soon have to resign. With a *gamine's* smile she said to Jeanette: "When we get into our years, my dear, we mustn't be shocked at anything. You are not yet in your years, not by a long stretch. Yet you are already shock-proof. You will be my heir."

Lady Randolph, indeed, carried on the tradition of the great hostess. She discharged the difficult double task of captivating London society and at the same time taming the beloved fire-eater at her side. The second of these was the more difficult. The wider Randolph's popularity spread throughout the country, the more 2 Connaught Place was filled with important people, the more stubborn grew his determination to have all or nothing.

For a mere whim he once resigned the championship of his Conservative Union, perhaps above all for relishing the triumph of his re-election, which duly came to pass within a few days. On another occasion he threatened that he would retire definitely from English politics, to seek health and amusement abroad. He made good his threat by actually going to India for a few months. Aboard H.M.S. "Rohilla" he departed on December 3, 1884. To the initiated his journey did not look like resignation at all. Randolph, they agreed grinning, was preparing himself for the Secretaryship of India.

Much progress was made in the months of his absence, during which Lady Randolph carried the Churchill banner singlehanded. Precisely for that purpose she had stayed at home ... if not to receive once more some of his glowing love letters which she had now been missing for ten years. They came again regularly.

Upon his return in March, 1885, Lord Randolph found himself in a position of unusual importance. He had won no war, negotiated no peace, introduced no great reform, had never held public office ... yet England welcomed him with general acclaim. His membership in the coming Conservative government seemed assured. No one knew it better than his wife.

He could not believe it. He only felt fatigued. Still in the turbulent days preceding Gladstone's imminent fall, Lord Randolph told a friend in the Turf Club: "I am very near the end of my tether. In the last five years I have lived twenty. I fought Society. I fought Mr. Gladstone at the head of a great majority. I fought the Front Opposition Bench, my own party leadership. Now I am fighting Lord Salisbury. I told him I would not join his government unless Northcote leaves the House of Commons. But Salisbury will never sacrifice his old friend. I am done."

Sir Stafford Northcote, for his part, was asked: "What place will you give Lord Randolph when the government is formed?" "Ask rather," replied the leader of the House, "what place will he give me!"

He got, indeed, no place at all. On Randolph's insistence he was dropped from the Commons. Created Lord Iddesleigh, Sir Stafford was promoted to the House of Lords. The way was free for Lord Randolph Churchill. At thirty-six he belonged to the three or four indispensable men in British affairs. The Salisbury government was formed on June 23, 1885. On June 24, Randolph was appointed Secretary of State for India. Next to the Foreign Office, his was the most important post in the Cabinet.

Jeanette sighed with comfort. An "office of profit under the Crown"—the official term for cabinet-membership—would make it much easier to keep House Beautiful going.

CHAPTER XIII *Last Stretch Uphill*

Having joined the government, Lord Randolph's seat at Woodstock was now vacated. He had to submit himself for re-election. But his first days in office confronted him with so many new tasks that he decided not to lose time by entering the contest personally. He was no longer *Champagne Charlie*, the idol of the platform. Now he was one of the decisive factors in British politics. Moreover, the Liberals, on whose tolerance Lord Salisbury's interim government—"the cabinet of caretakers"—depended, had promised they would not contest the new minister's by-election.

So Lady Randolph was assigned to the job of campaigning alone. She was not alarmed at the prospect. But it proved to be touch and go. The seat of Woodstock, and with it Randolph's government office, were by no means secure. The constituency had entirely lost contact with its member. The people of Oxfordshire resented his preoccupation with Irish affairs. After all, they had elected him to fight for the local glove production. Jeanette had only a fortnight to make up for her husband's years of negligence. Energetically she went at it.

She was no longer the passionate but passive onlooker from the Ladies' Gallery. She had now a place of her own in English politics. If the occasion demanded it, she could speak in the Oxfordshire dialect, which was much more popular than Randolph's Oxford English. She did not exert her husband's spell

210

on the masses. She shunned his tricks. But she had the gift of
making every listener her personal friend. At that time polls in
a rural district were decided by some thousand-odd voters.
Hence she had only to win over some five hundred men. It
seemed not much of a task.

Yet she was up against heavy odds. The Liberals did not
keep their promise of non-interference. Mr. Corrie Grant hurried down from London, appealing to the electors upon a single
issue. It was not, he declared, a struggle of politics or even principles, but a fight to oust a single man: Lord Randolph
Churchill, whose violent statements against Mr. Gladstone and
the Liberal Party had disqualified him.

No challenge could have aroused Jeanette more strongly.
Although she may have disagreed with many of her husband's
rhetoric excesses, to her the stormy petrel was, above all, a very
beloved man of frail health who needed her protection. In her
early thirties she was already the lion mother. Menacingly she
shook her black mane. She had made up her mind to win, and
so victory was assured. Moreover, the Duke of Marlborough,
her brother-in-law, would help. The influence of Blenheim
Castle was still considerable upon the tenants.

The eighth Duke, however, displayed a puzzling attitude.
The clash with his brother about the picture sales had left a
bitter after-taste. He could not forgive the Conservatives that
the Carlton Club, their stronghold, had refused him. Above all,
Mr. Gladstone's personal magic attracted the Duke's vivid intellect. But incorrigible old Blandford was always more a man
of bold ideas than of perseverance. He finally avoided the dilemma of having to take a definite stand over the election by a
queer demonstration of his leftish inclinations. He invited three
thousand children from the London slums, from Whitechapel
and the wretched districts east of Temple Bar, to come to
Woodstock on a special train. There they were fed from tables
heaped high with cakes in pyramids and oranges in mountains.
After the young ragamuffins had duly wrought havoc on the
parks, he led them in a parade, singing the family hymn: *Marl-*

brouck-s'en-va-t-en-guerre. Whereupon the three thousand children were dispatched back to their slums before sunset.

All the world was now to know that His Grace's heart was beating on the left. This business negotiated, the Duke sent Lady Randolph, with his compliments, as soon as she arrived to campaign for the Conservatives, a superbly horsed new Victoria, the most beautiful equipage in his stables, to ease her canvassing in the widespread district. At the same time he invited her to stay at Blenheim, as usual. The invitation, however, did not include her political headquarters. These remained in the Bear Hotel, where Lady Randolph had also spent the first night in Woodstock.

She was surrounded by a select staff of faithful co-workers. Heading the committee was the Dowager Duchess, who again proved that she was not in vain a descendant of the Stewarts, one of the greatest political families in English history. Jeanette's constant companion was Lady Georgina Curzon, her sister-in-law, a famous driver, who had brought her tandem. The horses of this smart turnout were decorated with ribbons in pink and brown, Lord Randolph's racing colors. Lord Curzon, Lady Georgina's husband, played only a minor role in the campaign, whereas Sir Henry Wolff, whom Randolph had delegated as an official observer, reported to his friend and leader that he was feeling quite superfluous among the women strategists.

Lady Randolph presided over the daily confabulations at the Bear Hotel. Feeling, as she later recalled, that the eyes of the world were turned on her, she relished the hustle-bustle of the committee rooms. Normally, a by-election at Woodstock, Oxfordshire, would not have excited the attention of the political world. But the Churchills had a knack of dramatizing any event connected with them. In this sense Lady Randolph had become a true member of the tribe. Ever inclined to self-teasing, she was sometimes an amused observer at her own play, but she always remained a most violent performer. Hers was the gift of being at once actress and audience.

Well known to most, and with a smile for all, she canvassed indefatigably from morning until night. At first her Primrose Badge, prominently displayed on herself, on her carriage, and on the horses, provoked many a grin. So far there was no "Habitation" in Woodstock; the badge was unfamiliar and seemed ridiculous. In outlying districts, in which the farmers knew little of the late Lord Beaconsfield's favorite flower, opponents occasionally pursued the carriage, jeering and shouting at Lady Randolph. On such occasions she used to stop her horses, climb down from the carriage, and face the hostile crowd, who were immediately converted to respectful listeners first, and frequently into voters afterward.

In general, however, Lady Randolph relied less on mass-appeal than on the personal impression she made. Within a few days she had come to know the constituents of Woodstock as intimately as Belgravia, of whose society she had encyclopedic knowledge. A. was doubtful in his attitude, B. obdurate, while C.'s wife, a wicked radical, wanted her husband to vote the wrong way. Such potential enemies were the first to be tackled. She visited them in their homes or picked them up during their field work, and plunged immediately into her argument, which was twofold. If the man looked particularly shrewd, she accosted him: "If you want to be on the winning side, vote for us; of course we are going to win." Her eyes twinkled. Blue beer and beef were banned by the new law, but patronage could still express itself in many ways. If, on the other hand, she met a man who was just a plain man, she implored him: "Oh, please vote for my husband; I shall be so unhappy if he does not get in!" Her eyes displayed no artificial pyrotechnics. Their deep, long look was a gift of nature. Both arguments proved irresistible. When the Conservative agents started on their long speeches on the disgraceful failure of Mr. Gladstone or on the dangers inherent in arch-radical Mr. Chamberlain, they heard more than once the answer: "Don't bother. We've already heard the lady. . . ."

Jingling rhymes, the popular poetry of the times, celebrated her success.

"But just as I was talking
With neighbor Brown, and walking
To take a mug of beer at the Unicorn and Lion
(For there's somehow a connection
Between free beer and election)
Who should come but Lady Churchill, with a turnout that was
    fine.

"And before me stopped her horses,
As she marshalled all her forces,
And before I knew what happened I had promised her my vote.
And before I quite recovered
From the vision that hovered
'Twas much too late to rally, and I changed my coat.

"And over Woodstock darted
On their mission, brave, whole-hearted
The tandem and their driver and the ribbons pink and brown.
And a smile that twinkled over,
And that made a man must love her
Took the hearts and votes of all Liberals in town.

"Bless my soul! that Yankee lady,
Whether day was bright or shady,
Dashed about the district like an oriflamme of war.
When her voters saw her bonnet
With the bright pink roses on it,
They followed as the soldiers did the Helmet of Navarre."

Feeling that the tide was turning against them, the Liberals especially imported two of their prettiest lady speakers from Girton to offset the impression Lady Randolph made on the men of Woodstock. Now Lord Randolph's election was assured. The result was announced on the evening of July 3. Churchill's majority was doubled against the last election in 1880 which he had personally contested. Even the Duke had undergone a last-minute change of heart. On the morning of election day he announced that all his carriages were at the disposal of Conservative voters who cared for a free ride to the polls.

In the evening a large crowd gathered in front of the Bear Hotel. Slightly bored by Lord Curzon's and Sir Henry Wolff's short addresses, they cheered uproariously when Lady Randolph appeared on the balcony. The tears in her eyes contrasted most effectively with the happy smile that played around the corners of her mouth. "From the bottom of her heart" she thanked the good people for having elected Lord Randolph a third time. Not a single word was said about her own contribution. But the six hundred telegrams of congratulation which swamped the local post-office testified that the eyes of England had indeed been fixed upon her.

The more chilling was the fact that upon her return to London there were no street demonstrations and no enchanted crowds. Passers-by hurried along without so much as turning their heads after the female conqueror of Woodstock. The curtain had fallen. Randolph, however, raised it again. "Yours is all the glory!" he said, embracing her. His kiss meant far more to her than even Sir Henry James's, the Attorney General's, heart-warming letter of congratulation. But this letter later proved of greater consequence.

Randolph made a perfect minister: he handled power to the manner born. His dealing with Indian problems was very much to the point, and generally acclaimed. What important part Jeanette, his constant inspiration, played in blueprinting such difficult and bold projects as Indian railway construction, the first subject that commanded Lord Randolph's attention, was never generally known. She understood that railways were necessary to bring the crops from the fertile valleys into famine-stricken districts. Leonard Jerome's daughter even knew that a four per cent guarantee was essential to stimulate capital for the formation of the Indian Midland Railway Company, which, indeed, was one of the great achievements of Randolph's tenure of office. "He was, in fact" Sir Arthur Godley, the permanent Under-Secretary in the India Office, attested, "an excellent head of a great department." Not all the merit of his inspired administration can, of course, be attributed to his—except in her private dealings—money-wise and business-minded American wife. Lord Randolph himself developed a surprising sense for facts and measures as soon as responsibility was entrusted to him. But he acknowledged his indebtedness to Jeanette with the words: "You helped me more than all my other endowments."

She helped him out of the gravest confusion of his first ministerial period. Although professionally in care of India, he was still considered the natural liaison-man between the government and the Irish nationalists, among whom he numbered so many friends. The Irish leader was now the hotheaded Parnell; the Lord-Lieutenant in Dublin was Lord Carnarvon. The representative of the Crown and the Protestant squire who drove the poor Catholic peasants from restiveness to resistance could not come to terms. Sulking, they avoided one another. Lord Randolph tried his hand again and again as a mediator.

Jeanette found the formula. "Our house will be empty toward the end of July," she said, as if discussing a routine matter. "Even the hosts will be gone. They could meet in perfect secrecy in Connaught Place, couldn't they? If nothing comes of their meeting, no one need hear of it, and neither of the partners would have lost his face."

"The partners?" Randolph asked.

"Lord Carnarvon and Mr. Parnell," she answered.

The meeting took place. The conversation is not on record, since even the servants had been granted a sudden holiday. Peace between the British Empire and the Irish revolutionaries was not established. But the meeting in the empty House Beautiful, with the blinds drawn, led to the Parliamentary truce between the Irish Nationalists and the Tories, which offered the only hope of defeating Mr. Gladstone's Liberals at the impending general elections.

These were the busiest and thus the happiest days in Lord Randolph's life. Next to the anxious attention which his office constantly required, he had to watch the Irish turmoil, and even contested, in double harness with Colonel Fred Burnaby, Birmingham, the stronghold of Liberalism, the great Radical Joseph Chamberlain's own home.

This contest was of a very different order from the good-natured play at Woodstock. Lady Randolph could never forget its exertions and labors. Sandwiched in between her small, carefully dressed, fragile husband and Colonel Burnaby, a six-footer, weighing two hundred and twenty pounds, a master pugilist and the toughest soldier ever to serve under the Queen's colors, Lady Randolph's strange beauty attracted much attention in the Birmingham streets. The capital of hardware production had never seen such a dazzling woman. Yet it was not always friendly attention. One night as they were walking back to their hotel after a meeting, a crowd of opponents displayed their hostility in such an unmistakable manner, jostling the group of three, that Jeanette, for the first time in her life, became admittedly nervous. To Colonel Burnaby, in spite of his enormous frame and gigantic strength a gentle soul, the aspect of the trembling lady he adored was unbearable. He made a single gesture with his arm and the crowd scattered instantly.

This was the only time during the nine elections in which Lady Randolph took an active part (Woodstock twice, Birmingham three times, South Paddington twice, Oldham and Manchester once each) that she was frightened. For the rest, she attested to the lasting fame of English manners that she never encountered a disagreeable incident or any rudeness, although she, the wife of a politician whose beat and stronghold were the labor districts in the big cities, made it her habit to venture into the slums. The worst that could occur was the following scene in Birmingham. "Lady Churchill wants to see you," the wife of a slum-dweller cried into the cellar, into which her husband had retreated to inspect the beer bottles. "Well, tell Mrs. Churchill to go to..." the answer came in guttural tones from behind the barrels. Whereupon the fair lady beat a hasty retreat. But a butcher, whose shop was next door, stopped her. Expressing his indignation at his ill-bred and probably drunk neighbor, he gave her a hastily collected bunch of flowers, promised his vote, and sent, a few days later, half a sheep as token of his admiration.

It went without saying that the Dowager Duchess came to Birmingham to help her daughter-in-law in fulfilling her arduous duties. It took a good deal of the old lady's courage. This was the first time that women had canvassed in Birmingham, and both the Duchess and Lady Randolph engaged in it thoroughly. Every single house in the constituency was visited by one or the other of them. The Duchess went one way, Lady Randolph the other. They contributed the personal touch which Randolph, in his mostly riotous mass meetings, could not supply.

The constituency was a large one, and the work was exhausting. The voters of Birmingham were nowhere near as amenable as the good people in Woodstock had been. The men were highly argumentative, and even their wives were perfectly informed about contemporary affairs. More than once, Lady Randolph admitted, she emerged second-best from an argument. But such oratoric defeats only sharpened her crusading spirit. She made it her custom to invade factories during the dinner hour to address a few words to the personnel. Frequently she was received in sullen silence. On one occasion the spokesman of the men cleared his throat, scratched himself behind the ear, and having thus negotiated all amenities, burst out that, frankly, his comrades did not like to be asked for their vote. "Why not?" came her repartee. "You have something I want! How can I get it if I don't ask for it?" This bit of American common sense made the crowd laugh. The ice was broken. But how the men voted, Lady Randolph distrustfully remarked, she had no way of knowing.

Finally a majority voted for their traditional leaders, Messrs. Joe Chamberlain and John Bright. Randolph was defeated, but by such a narrow margin that he decided not to give up Birmingham. At the next opportunity he would again contest the radical stronghold. It was his firm decision, to which his wife heartily agreed.

The defeat had no serious consequences. On her cautious insistence her husband had established as a measure of precaution a second front at home. In South Paddington, their own London quarter, Randolph was invincible and Jeanette generally adored. Duly the district elected him a day or two after his failure in Birmingham, by a two-to-one majority.

Back at House Beautiful, Jeanette changed into a dark blue evening dress. As if to get rid of the sweat of Birmingham politics, the couple spent the first evening after their return at Romano's, the newest of the fashionable eating places for gourmets.

The cabinet of caretakers, lacking a majority in the House, had tough going. Its position depended entirely on the wavering attitude of the Irish Nationalists, whom Randolph made every effort to conciliate. Sir William Harcourt, a Whig leader, derided the Conservative party for "stewing in Parnellite juice," and Randolph retaliated with wild attacks on the Whigs although, in his heart of hearts, he wished to break their unnatural alliance with the Radicals inside the Liberal Party and to bring about their union with the Tories. To his wife he admitted that one of them, the Marquess of Hartington, had infallible judgment in political matters. Yet he constantly abused the Marquess, who still refused his invitation to come over and help the Conservatives. One day at a dinner party the Churchills met the Marquess, and Jeanette asked him frankly whether he intended to accept her husband's invitation. "I have not yet decided," Hartington answered, visibly embarrassed. "But when I do, I suppose I shall be thought either a man or a mouse." "Or a rat!" she replied rashly. The Marquess laughed, as the French say, *d'un rire jaune,* and was silent. But Randolph took his wife to task: "Those are the remarks that upset a coach," he said in grave earnest. But he continued criss-crossing the country, darting about Dorsetshire, Sheffield, Worcester, and Manchester, attacking the Liberals with a vigor of metaphor and a raciness of language that attracted universal attention.

Only the Prime Minister, who had become his younger colleague's paternal friend, seemed preoccupied: "The strain of doing two things together," he wrote on September 13, 1885, "is enormous. And if you once go a step too far, if you once break the spring, you may take years to get over it." The warning came just in time. A few days after having received Lord Salisbury's letter, a new attack of his disease forced Randolph to interrupt his man-killing work. He retired to his brother-in-law Lord Wimborne's house in Auchnashellach, Scotland, to do a little fishing in the Carron and to relax.

About his way of relaxing, his letter to his wife from his rest cure, dated September 27th, gives an impressive picture: "I have written twenty-one letters today, some of them long ones. ... I think your letter to Lady Dufferin admirable and all your plans with regard to her fund most excellent. I should advise you to get hold of Mr. Buckle (the editor of the *Times* of London) and fascinate him, and make him write you up. ..."

The reference was made to an action Lady Randolph and Lady Dufferin, the wife of the Viceroy of India, had started together. They were collecting a fund for the National Association for Supplying Female Medical Aid to the Women of India. This cumbersome title covered a most charitable enterprise. The Association, indeed, mitigated much suffering in India, it gave employment to a number of English female doctors, who had to make their way against heavy prejudices, and it opened a career for many native Indian women.

The Churchills stood in the focus of London's attention. Challenging Victorian habits, they were, according to a widespread bon mot, "the first of Her Majesty's subjects who did not take their pleasures sadly." All middle-class women took Lady Randolph as their great example. Once Marshall and Snelgrove, the department store, had the honor of exhibiting a piece of knitting she had done. Immediately suburban women plunged into fashionable needlework. Her dresses were assiduously copied. Her tiny cap-bonnet of crepe with a single large tea-rose at the side and strings of soft blue silk tied in a bow beneath the chin, while from the back a gauze veil hung to the waist, became the "baby-bonnet," the hat of the season. For a time mauve was her favorite color. Of course mauve became the color of the year. Gunter's, the confectioner's shop at Berkeley Square, was crowded in the afternoons, since everyone wanted to watch Lady Randolph having her peach ice.

The Churchills' patronage made the new restaurants just coming in fashionable and acceptable to society. Although Lord Randolph preferred to eat in his own well-appointed house, both he and his wife understood the necessity of showing themselves at the Café de l'Europe in Haymarket, at Epitaux in Pall Mall, Verrey's in Regent Street, the Blue Post in Cork Street, Cavour's in Leicester Square, not to forget Bertollini's and Rouget's. Thus they kept constantly in the limelight. The clubs vied for Randolph's membership. The Carlton was no longer his only second home. He joined the Athenaeum, the foremost club for diplomats and scholars, the Turf Club, and venerable White's. Publicity-wise, they did not shun the haunts of the busy Fleet Street men either. Many an evening was spent in the Rainbow, the Cheshire Cheese, the Cock. At Simpson's, on the Strand, they still show the table in the left corner on the first floor often reserved for Lord and Lady Randolph Churchill.

All this was in addition to Randolph's onerous duties in the government. One of his first acts in the India Office was to appoint Sir Frederick Roberts to be commander-in-chief in India, although powerful influences supported the claims of Lord Wolseley. Less than ever did he give way to powerful influences. He could now rely on Lord Salisbury's unwavering support. Both were prodigious letter-writers. During the seven months of his first Ministry the Prime Minister wrote no less than one hundred ten letters to his lieutenant, sometimes three or four a day, all in his beautiful handwriting. The letters were full of expressions of friendship. Only once a conflict occurred. Queen Victoria wished to appoint the Duke of Connaught to the Command in Bombay. Lord Randolph was against it. Lord Salisbury loyally supported Her Majesty's wish. But he had "no intention of taking any decision out of Lord Randolph Churchill's hand." The Duke of Connaught was not appointed; his brother's misfortune made the Prince of Wales laugh heartily.

For eight years Lady Randolph had been waiting for this laughter. Sir Henry James, both her friend and the Prince's, interpreted it to her. Edward, he assured her, was reconciled. His Royal Highness bowed to Randolph's success, and to Jeanette's charm and graces. He was ready to forget the Blandford incident. And he sent his kindest regards.

House Beautiful got a spring-cleaning with a vengeance. Immediately a new chef was imported from Paris. The Churchills' timetable was badly upset. They could not as usual arrange dinner invitations for weeks ahead. They could not tell when the great evening would come. "How about Friday next?" Sir Henry James suggested on one of his frequent calls. "Both their Royal Highnesses will come."

It was, indeed, a royal gesture. Instead of inviting the Churchills to his palace, the Prince of Wales insisted on coming himself.

No. 2 Connaught Place radiated the light of a thousand candles. There were no electric experiments on such an eventful evening. Against his habit, the Prince was on time. When Lady Randolph curtsied, Princess Alexandra took her into her arms and said: "We haven't played Bach for a long time!" The company was assembled. It was a select small group: Lord Rosebery, Mr. and Mrs. Chauncey Depew, Mr. Henry Chaplin, an important Tory M. P., and, of course, Sir Henry James. Above them towered the great old man of Midlothian, who had accepted even the invitation of his most bitter opponent, since he himself, in the autumn of his life, had set the rule that dining together turns foes into friends.

The dinner was in the best Ward McAllister style. Jeanette's New York education was not entirely wasted. The first choice was between clear turtle soup and potage printanière. The Prince helped himself to a spoonful of both. Mr. Gladstone recalled the Spartan blood soup, and lectured on its nutritious value. The fish was already served—again a choice, this time between turbot naturel with lobster sauce, or salmon with parsley butter—and the great old man was still in Sparta, although his sympathies were obviously with Athens. But when he slowly became aware that he was eating fish, he recalled the many happy hours he used to spend with the rod by the streams around Hawarden. Thirty or thirty-three years ago it once happened . . . This led, of course, to his parliamentary recollections which did not end before the guests went home.

"You are certainly not an American food-faddist, Lady Randolph!" the Prince said, highly pleased. It was the only objection Edward had to some Americans, or rather to their diet. A satisfied smile illuminated his benevolent face.

The eight terrible years were over.

CHAPTER XIV *Dinner with Victoria*

The tide rose, and the Churchills were rising with it. In spite of Lord Randolph's successful opposition to the Duke of Connaught's, her favorite son's, appointment to the command of Bombay—an opposition duly sugar-coated by Lord Salisbury—the Queen was attracted by her new India Secretary's deference as well as by his mounting fame. She relished his fight against Mr. Gladstone, whom she had always disliked. Indeed, the man of Midlothian's fall and Lord Salisbury's assumption of the power brought her back from the retirement in which the Queen had sought refuge during Gladstone's rule. Emerged from her self-imposed solitude, Victoria threw herself vigorously into public activities. It was but the last flicker of the evening sun. Yet she presided again over the "drawing-rooms," visited theaters and concerts, laid foundation stones, drove in her open car through the once more cheering streets, unmindful even of heavy rain, opened the International Exhibition in Edinburgh and the Coal and Industry Exhibition in London's South Kensington. She was reconciled with England. She liked every member of the government of caretakers, and Lord Randolph above all, for having so violently attacked Mr. Bradlaugh (who had coined the poisonous term "princely paupers"), and for the fact that he had been so instrumental in removing Mr. Gladstone.

In the summer of 1885 Randolph wrote extremely deferential

reports to keep Her Majesty posted on current Indian affairs, invariably beginning with the words: "Lord Randolph Churchill presents his humble duty to Her Majesty and begs to submit..." The Queen approved of his activities in office, and gracefully nodded consent when her new Secretary of State for India adopted a sharp tone toward Theebaw, King of Burma, who was a mass-murderer, and a traitor into the bargain.

The boy-king of Burma had slaughtered his thirty brothers, including their families on the same generous scale, when he succeeded his father to the throne. He insulted the British resident in Mandalay. No Englishman in Burma was sure of his life. Outrages upon British vessels on the Irrawaddy were frequent. Moreover, English banks, railways, mining and timber concessions were wrested from their owners, and handed over to the French, who, in turn, exported chorus-girls by the score to the Far Eastern Royal Palace.

Lord Randolph, although anti-Imperialist on account of his predominantly insular feelings, could not look on. The British-Indian army marched; the Burmese hordes were routed at Minhla on November 17, 1885, at the cost of one English officer and three men killed, and five officers and twenty-four men wounded. On November the 27th, Mandalay was occupied and King Theebaw a prisoner. Randolph had made his contribution, his only one, to the consolidation of the British Empire. On November 30th he received the following letter:

Windsor Castle, November 30, 1885.
Dear Lord Randolph:

The Queen wishes to personally confer the Insignia of the Order of the Crown of India on Lady Randolph Churchill on Friday next, the 4th of December at three o'clock.

Will she come here to luncheon?

The 1:10 train from Paddington is the most convenient one, and if Lady Randolph will let me hear

whether she comes by that or another train, I will send
the carriage to meet her here.

                         Yours very truly
                         Henry Ponsonby.

It was the greater a tribute, as it was unexplained. Randolph
had, indeed, deserved a high decoration, but Jeanette had
received it. Was it being generally assumed that all his merit
was actually her inspiration? On the surface it might have
looked that way; and a wave of smiles inundated Mayfair. But
as usual the professional insiders erred. The conquest of Burma
had been Lord Randolph's own scheme. It had occupied his
mind ever since, during his travels through India in the winter
two years before, an astrologer had told him that he "would return to India shortly in connection with a warlike expedition."
The Hindu astrologer, eager to earn his reward, had also assured Randolph, after casting his horoscope, that he had "never
seen so good a star since Lord Mayo's," the Viceroy who, at the
summit of his power, was assassinated in the Andaman Islands.
The ambiguous prediction had, of course, deeply impressed
Randolph, ever conscious of his short life expectation; his
thoughts constantly rotated around the prophecy. Like most
Victorians, he was a deep believer in horoscopes and the con-
stellation of the stars. Perhaps the Hindu astrologer had
spurred the Secretary of State for India unconsciously into
his Burmese venture. However that might have been—this
time Lord Randolph's action was definitely taken without
Jeanette's advice or support. Laboring under her early impressions of both the Civil War and the Franco-German bloodshed,
she was more inclined to encourage her husband's habitual
pacifism.

The truth about the Order of the Crown of India was that
Lady Randolph had longed for the pretty pearl and turquoise
cipher attached to a pale blue ribbon edged with white, which
the Duke of Albany had designed when the decoration was
instituted by Queen Victoria. She could have received it for

her splendid work on behalf of the Female Medical Aid for India. A few months earlier the Queen had indicated her willingness to bestow the decoration on her much admired, loyal American subject. But Randolph, as Secretary of State for India, would have had to recommend her, and he demurred at the idea of promoting a favor for his wife. Now the Queen acted over her Secretary's head. The gesture was extremely personal, but fortunately Mr. Gladstone was gone. No one would object.

On the morning of the appointed day Lady Randolph received her instructions from the lady-in-waiting. They read: "Bonnet and morning dress, gray gloves. To kiss the Queen's hand after receiving the decoration, like the gentlemen today. A room will be prepared for her."

The audience was strictly formal. The Queen, with one of her daughters and a lady-in-waiting, received Lady Randolph in a small room. Standing with her back to the window, the long white veil she wore appeared against the light like an aureole. Evidently her position was deliberately chosen, and the impression of the aureole artificially created. Queen Victoria was sixty-eight at that time, Lady Randolph half that age. The small, stoutish Queen, white-haired, with a pale complexion, and opposite her the dark young woman with the vibrant expression in her sharp-cut face made an amazing contrast. It was white in white, the Queen's sunlit veil, her hair, her dress, against black in black, Lady Randolph's piled-up curls, her famous eyes, her black velvet gown, heavily embroidered with jet. Once more, it was the attraction of opposites. The Queen, her lady-in-waiting later remarked, had for many years not smiled so graciously in a private audience as in addressing a few kinds words to Lady Randolph!

Jeanette felt her knees trembling. Her proverbial courage deserted her. Here she was confronted by the century incarnate. She murmured something, a sort of respectful answer, but she did not quite understand herself what she was saying.

Queen Victoria approached her with a few halting steps. Her hands, however, were still firm, and with a determined gesture she stuck the pin of the decoration right into Lady Randolph's flesh. The jet studding the black velvet dress had caused this misfortune. When she had recovered from the shock, tales of Spartan boys who did not flinch under the lash flashed through her mind. Yet she must have winced a trifle. The Queen, realizing what she had done, showed grave concern. Eventually the pin was put right. Lady Randolph curtsied herself out of the Royal Presence.

"Oh, you have forgotten your handbag," the Queen said. Smiling, she followed her visitor to the door. It was the first and last time in Lady Randolph's life that she did not find a reply. But as the Queen looked at her benevolently, Jeanette, almost Jennie again, felt that this little touch had relieved an otherwise somewhat formal ceremony. Outside the door she excused herself to the lady-in-waiting who accompanied her for having been awkward and nervous. "You need not be troubled," came the rejoinder. "I know Her Majesty felt more shy than you did."

But Queen Victoria was obviously amused. A few days later a Royal command invited Lord and Lady Churchill to dine and stay overnight at Windsor. It was an intimate reception. Dinner was served in a small room. Conversation was carried on in whispers. Lady Randolph found this enforced custom oppressive and conducive to shyness, although she personally did not yield to this inhibition on her second meeting with Her Majesty.

When the Queen spoke, even the whispers ceased. Victoria's own remarks had to be answered while the whole company listened. But one was not supposed to say much even in replying.

It was amusing, the Queen said, to talk to a Lady Churchill. She herself had once adopted this name. Oh, it was a great many years ago, in Scotland, on an excursion from Balmoral. She and the Prince Consort had decided to travel incognito.

So they adopted the names of Lord and Lady Churchill. The *real* Lady Churchill, a member of the party, was called Miss Spencer. General Grey went as Dr. G. The two ghillies, Grant and Brown, were instructed simply to say Your Lordship and Your Ladyship. But once "Your Royal Highness" slipped out of faithful Brown's mouth, as he addressed . . . Victoria interrupted herself. She mentioned the Prince Consort's name no more often than necessary. It was quite embarrassing, she concluded, for it happened in a crowded pub. But the loyal Highlanders feigned not to have heard the slip of Brown's tongue.

The company was astonished by the facility with which the Queen talked to her new friend. Would Lady Randolph miss dancing after dinner? she asked good-naturedly. Well, then she had better go to Sandringham. Life in Sandringham was a perpetual round of balls, she smiled without the slightest sign of disapproval. Oh, in her youth she herself would have loved to dance every night. She recalled the festivity at her eighteenth birthday, in honor of her coming of age. How she would have loved to join the waltzes and the *galop!* But in her exalted station she was only allowed to dance the quadrille. Faintly the unreal pictures of long faded dancing partners came to life again. The Hungarian cavaliers had been the best looking. Count Zichy and Count Waldstein, how handsome they were in their colorful Hungarian dress uniforms! Well, all that lay fifty years back . . . exactly half a century.

The aged Queen's restless spirit ranged through the past. How was the Empress Eugénie? Somehow Victoria knew that the ex-Empress and Lady Randolph maintained a regular correspondence. She was pleased to hear that Madame spent most of her time on the Riviera, well taken care of by the French Republic, for whose tourist business she was the greatest attraction. It was good to know that Eugénie had recovered from the shock. It must have been terrible to lose a beloved husband at such an early age. Suddenly Victoria was silent. "He loved primroses best," she began again. "The ambassadors

of spring, the gems and jewels of nature, he used to call them."
And she quoted the words with which Disraeli had obviously
impressed her, slowly, as if they were melting on her lips.
" 'They are so much better beloved for their being wild. An
offering from the Fauns and Dryads of Osborne, showing that
Her Majesty's scepter had touched the enchanted Isle.' . . . I
sent him some Osborne primroses while he was on his death-
bed," she recalled. "I wrote a line that I would have loved to
pay him a little visit, but I thought it better he should be
quite quiet and not speak. My note asked him to be very
good and obey the doctors."

Queen Victoria was strangely agitated on this evening. It
seemed almost as if Lady Randolph's presence had once more
worked a miracle. But there was another underlying reason.
Late that night, at an hour the Queen would, under normal
circumstances, long have retired, Mr. Henry Matthews arrived
in haste. The Home Secretary had been called to come in a
hurry from London to assist, as an ancient custom prescribed,
at the birth of a young Prince of Battenberg which was due
at any moment. The Queen had not spoken a word about
the event the Castle was anxiously awaiting. That was probably
why she had escaped into the past. Not until Mr. Matthews
had safely arrived did she turn to Lord Randolph with an
explanation: "I know you are a cabinet minister, too. Besides,
you are a married man . . . a happily married man," she repeated with an appreciative side-glance at Lady Randolph,
"and you have children yourself. And you were at hand. But,
forgive me, Lord Randolph, you are still a little too young
and inexperienced," she concluded, highly sovereign and fully
matter of fact, "to attend to such important business of state."

An hour or two later, after the guests had retired, they were
torn from sleep by an infant's sharp cry. The next Prince of the
House of Battenberg saluted life.

The Churchills sent a silver spoon as a birth present. Some
four weeks later the Queen received from Lord Randolph what
he termed a New Year's present, a Viceregal proclamation:

"By command of the Queen-Empress it is hereby notified that the territories formerly governed by King Theebaw will no longer be under his rule, but have become part of Her Majesty's Dominions, and will during Her Majesty's pleasure be administered by such officers as the Viceroy and Governor-General of India may from time to time appoint."

CHAPTER XV *I've Danced with the Prince*

The government of caretakers was turned out of office on the twenty-sixth of January, 1886. Lord Randolph lost his ministry, but neither he nor his wife lost their equanimity. Mr. Gladstone, they were aware, had won a pyrrhic victory. He could easily defeat the Conservative minority cabinet. But, stubbornly insisting on Home Rule for Ireland, he split his own Liberal Party from top to bottom. The Churchills had reached their goal: the great Whig leaders, most of them their personal friends, left the Liberal camp. Sir Henry James, the Prince of Wales' political adviser, once Attorney General in Gladstone's government, wrote to Lady Randolph: "From now on I will regard No. 2 Connaught Place as my lighthouse."

Parliament was dissolved on the twenty-seventh of June. A fierce campaign was starting. Randolph was at this time the country's foremost mass-speaker. His meetings were crowded. Everywhere the electorate's attention was focused on the strange looking, dark, fighting woman at his side. Their biggest and most important meeting was held in Manchester. The Drill Hall, then the largest in town, was crowded to suffocation by eighteen thousand people, most of whom had to queue up for hours for a place. Another twenty thousand less fortunate lined the streets and covered the roofs as the Churchills in their four-in-hand drove through the town. The police esti-

232

mated that, all told, two hundred thousand people had turned
out to see them. Randolph spoke two hours, his wife but a few
minutes. Yet she made a strong impression. As she and her
husband left the building in separate carriages, her equipage
was so jostled that two men were killed in the free-for-all to
have a near look at her.

Lord Randolph proceeded to Belfast. Ulster received him
with almost royal honors. Enthusiasm swept the land when he
coined the slogan: "Ulster will fight, and Ulster will be right!"
But at the peak of his popular triumph Lady Randolph had to
stop her husband. The strain of the initial campaign had so
exhausted him that she feared for his life. Most determinedly
she sent him off to Norway. The fire-eater was always obedient
to his wife. Indeed, he went to Torresdal. Immediately upon
his arrival, on July 10th, at eleven o'clock in the evening, he
wrote her how badly he missed her, now that he was 1,500
miles away from Connaught Place. But he was full of cheer.
"I expect the Tories will now come in, and remain in some
time. It seems to me we want the 5,000 pounds a year badly.
But really we must retrench. I cannot understand how we get
through so much money...."

He did not return before being safely elected in his home
constituency, South Paddington. His majority rose from 2 to 1
to 3 to 1. Once more Lady Randolph, to whom the campaigning had been entrusted, had scored; this time single-handed.

This success brought her again to Victoria's attention. Asking
Lord Salisbury, the leader of the victorious Conservatives, to
form a government, the Queen pointed out the desirability of
including Lord Randolph, the husband of that charming lady.
Upon his return from Norway he had the choice between the
Indian, the Irish, and the Foreign Secretaryships. At a meeting
at the Carlton, however, Sir Michael Hicks-Beach, Conservative leader of the House, insisted that Lord Randolph should
take over his own position, the leadership of the House, connected with the Chancellorship. "Lord Randolph is my superior in eloquence, ability, and influence," the old gentleman

said. "The position of a leader in name, but not in fact, would be intolerable for me. It is better for the party and the country that the leader in fact should also be leader in name...." Very much against his habit, but quite earnestly, Lord Randolph pleaded his youth and inexperience; he could not accept the position second only to the Prime Minister. Here the matter rested for a night.

During this night Lady Randolph found the solution. It was quite understandable to her that her husband did not want to displace his veteran friend, who had always honored the younger colleague with his advice and counsel. But what if Sir Michael chose to go to Ireland as Viceroy? This was at that critical moment the hardest job in England's government. Only a hero would sacrifice himself in taking it over.

The next morning Sir Michael made the heroic decision. Now his post in the government was free. At thirty-seven Lord Randolph Churchill was made leader of the House and Chancellor of the Exchequer. According to hallowed tradition, he was now heir apparent to the Prime Minister.

Congratulating him, a friend asked: "How long will your leadership last?" It was a clear allusion to his coming Premiership. "Six months!" replied Randolph gaily. "And after that?" "After that?" repeated Randolph, ever smiling: "Why, Westminster Abbey!"

After two general elections, succeeding one another in rapid sequence, England was deeply tired of political feud and fury. Everyone was longing for domestic peace. For a time, even Randolph was affected by the general desire for reconciliation. For a few months he made an excellent leader of the House and an admirable, competent Chancellor. Even the *Times* of London, not always his friendly critic, observed on September 17th: "The Chancellor of the Exchequer is making great progress in the art of so answering questions as to keep the House in good temper. This he does sometimes by making judicious concessions, sometimes by a sly turn of humor, sometimes by a touch of good-natured irony." That judicious concessions, turn of humor, and good-natured irony belonged to the favorite weapons in Lady Randolph's intellectual armory, and that she imparted them to her husband, was not necessarily known to Mr. Buckle, the editor of the *Times,* although he belonged to the vast crowd of her admirers and was a frequent guest in House Beautiful.

Above all, Victoria emphasized her sparingly accorded personal sympathy for Lord Randolph: "I am particularly commanded by the Queen," wrote Lord Iddesleigh, the Foreign Secretary (whom Randolph had kicked upstairs into the House of Lords), from Balmoral on the sixteenth of September, "to say that Her Majesty was greatly amused by the contents of your box last night. I suppose you won't understand this message without the gloss—there was a sprinkling of tobacco in it.... Her Majesty is very sympathetic over the sufferings of our friend in the House of Commons. You have indeed a very hard task, and it is not very clear how it is to be lightened." No other of the Queen's subjects, committing the *lèse majesté* of leaving some tobacco in the dispatch-box for Her Majesty's personal inspection, would have got away with less than permanent disgrace.

At the end of the session, on September 22, 1886, the Queen even sent him a handwritten letter: "Now that the session is over, the Queen wishes to write and thank Lord Randolph Churchill for his regular and full and interesting reports of the debates in the House of Commons, which must have been most trying. Lord Randolph has shown much skill and judgment in his leadership during this exceptional session of Parliament."

But his personal friends stressed another angle: "Don't worry yourself, and get knocked out!" wrote Joseph Chamberlain on September 1. "You must really take more care of yourself," Mr. Arthur Balfour warned. "I am afraid your work is getting intolerably hard," wrote Lord Salisbury in his fine longhand. "Don't sit up too much."

Jeanette used to read her husband's personal mail. Sometimes her heart was heavy.

The days of fight, it seemed, were over. Everyone was reconciled with Lord Randolph. Many were the endeavors of well-meaning friends to reconcile him in turn with the world. His ascent had been rapid. Now was the moment to take a deep breath, to mellow, and slowly to grow into the English harmony.

But Lord Randolph was both by inclination and by temperament unable to live in harmony. Despite his high rank in a Conservative cabinet, he adopted a radical outlook that soon outdid Gladstone's. His conduct of office stunned and alienated his best friends. Publicly he attacked Lord Salisbury, to whom he owed so much, and who, after all, was his chief, as an "Imperialist." He advocated a foreign policy of strictest isolationism. "Indeed, I think if he had lived," his great son wrote many years later, "he would have resisted the South-African War to an extent that would have exposed him to the odium of the very working class elements of whose good will he was so proud."

After delivering a speech at Dartford, which antagonized every one of his twenty thousand Tory listeners, the atmosphere around him grew so tense that Lady Randolph again decided her husband needed a change of air. Secretly and silently the Chancellor and Leader of the House crossed the Channel. The trouble was, however, that his meteoric career had already made for his outstanding European reputation. The whole continent had come to regard him the future master of British politics. From the moment he arrived in Calais his every step was watched, and his every harmless nonpolitical remark interpreted as having international importance. In vain he traveled as a simple Mr. Spencer, accompanied by his friend Mr. Trafford. It was rumored that he had been seen in Paris and Berlin; possibly he had also been on a secret mission to Bismarck at Varzin. In fact, Messrs. Spencer and Trafford had only made the rounds of museums and picture galleries in Prague and

Dresden. In Vienna he was trapped. Even Lady Randolph had to learn from the *Times* that "the two travelers whose every step is watched by the European press have been residing at the Hotel Imperial since yesterday."

The Viennese newspapers were full of the most intimate accounts. Mr. Spencer looked somewhat fatigued, yet he had visibly enjoyed Milloecker's operetta *The Vice-Admiral* at the Theater an der Wien, and bought quantities of the famous Viennese leather goods at Weidmann's. His only interview had been given to the manager of the Imperial whom Mr. Spencer had confidentially informed that he had come to Vienna to see not a single soul, and had decided to receive no one, without exception. What, then, could such a statement imply? The Viennese press oracled vaguely. But since no trace of a European plot could be found in Lord Randolph's words, the guesswork gave way to elaborate descriptions of his appearance, of the shape of his hat and the color of his coat.

On October 12, Randolph wrote his wife: "I am hopelessly discovered. At the station yesterday I found a whole army of reporters, at whom I scowled in my most effective manner. Really it is almost intolerable that one cannot travel about without this publicity. The reporters have been besieging the hotel this morning, but I have sent them all away without a word. I did not dine with Paget (the British ambassador in Vienna) either. I sent him word that as I saw no one in Berlin, I did not wish to see anyone here. This pottering about Europe suits me down to the ground, if it were not for the beastly newspapers." Thus the poor Viennese newspapers had to pay for the hostile attacks of the London press, and the British Ambassador to the Imperial Court of Vienna was snubbed on account of the growling in many conservative manors and cottages at home.

It cannot have been easy to be married to a man whose longing for escape was being frustrated by the whole European press, and whose whereabouts was only disclosed to his own wife by curious crowds, gathering at faraway continental railroad stations. But a rich and full life is never without its problems. Lady Randolph expressed this conviction frequently. The married state in itself is difficult, particularly if it is further complicated by deep and anxious love.

Randolph's vagaries in politics first amused, and then attracted irresistibly the Prince of Wales. Although Edward was to become the King of the middle classes, in his forties, a little belatedly, he still enjoyed nothing so much as the fine art of *épater le bourgeois* (stun the solid citizen). There was no better way to do this than by associating himself with the one man whose brilliance was as generally conceded as his demeanor was universally condemned. The eight terrible years were now entirely forgotten. The Churchills were preferred guests at the great reception in Sandringham in honor of His Royal Highness's forty-fifth birthday. The Prince and the Princess, Lady Randolph reminisced, displayed their hospitality with the simplicity of which English royalty alone has the secret.

She felt instantly at home in Sandringham. She had known the Prince ever since her first season in Cowes. For his part, Edward had maintained his respect for her, even at a distance, during the eight years. Her visit to Sandringham, however, brought the great change. In these easy, informal days the mutual sympathy grew into a real friendship that lasted to the very end.

Life on the Prince of Wales' seven-thousand-acre estate was not very different from life in any pleasant country house. The guests enjoyed a high degree of liberty. At any hour they chose from nine o'clock on, they could have breakfast at small round tables in a simple dining-room, yet, oddly, decorated with precious Spanish tapestries, a present from the King of Spain. The men were in shooting get-up, most of the ladies wore elaborate day gowns. Lady Randolph alone preferred short skirts and thick boots, a strange attire in this surrounding; but no one objected.

The Princess did not appear before midday. Like any English

housewife, she had plenty to do in running her house and looking after her children. The Prince, too, rarely showed himself before noon, when he joined the shooting parties.

The ladies whiled away the mornings with books and newspapers, at the piano, or at the writing tables in the large hall. Then they drove or walked to mingle with the gentlemen in the red-carpeted tent in which luncheon was served. Here the Princess with her daughters on their ponies made her appearance. Conversation at the luncheon parties was most animated. Even the young Princesses, notorious for their diffident manners in public, were full of fun and gaiety. Lady Randolph was the gayest of all. Everyone listened to her so fascinated that her husband had gently to remind the company of the birds waiting to be shot.

The sport was exceedingly good and well managed, owing to the Prince of Wales, who, himself an excellent shot, made all important arrangements personally, instead of leaving them to the keepers. The ladies formed an audience of most interested and expert spectators. First champion was Lord de Grey, who shot in one stand fifty-two birds out of fifty-four. To win a bet, he shot with only one hand.

Randolph's nervous hand constantly trembled a little. But the competition excited him. He took his stand, flanked by two loaders, equipped with three guns. His wife watched him with the ardent, translucent gaze that she had developed while listening to his speeches. The other onlookers pitied the man whose poor state of nerves was everyone's secret. As he raised his gun, everyone expected a cruel failure. Everyone was silent. Everyone felt embarrassed.

Crack ... crack ... crack ... not a single miss. With perfect calm Randolph turned to his wife. He did not speak. The man of many words was a silent lover. He wanted, she understood, to comfort her. His eyes were still keen, and his hand was steady. He was not really so ill.

The shooting-party applauded. Even Lord de Grey complimented the better man. Lord Randolph Churchill was the hero again. But only for a fleeting moment. Sporting triumphs were short-lived.

At five o'clock in the afternoon all was forgotten. The simplicity of the day attire was replaced by elaborate tea-gowns. After tea Signor Tosti, the Prince's favorite entertainer, sang a few melodramatic and witty songs. He had a beautiful voice, and was by the same token a sprightly master of ceremonies. In his delightful impromptu manner he could ramble on for hours.

Dinner was a ceremonious affair, with everyone in full dress and decorations. When the guests were assembled, Their Royal Highnesses were announced. The sitting order rotated. Each lady in turn had the privilege of being taken in by her royal host, who arranged the list himself. Dinner lasted exactly an hour. Conversation was fairly animated; there was none of the stiffness that pervaded Windsor and made one fear the sound of one's own voice.

After dinner the Prince had his rubber of whist. The rest of the company sat around and talked until the Princess made a move to retire. The other ladies trooped off together, stopping to laugh and chatter in the passages. And so to bed.

Only Lady Randolph's day was not yet over. Alexandra loved to ask her into her boudoir, when the formal part of the long and busy day was negotiated. There the two women sat among objects and souvenirs of every sort. The dressing-table was so littered with miniatures and photographs of children and friends that there was no room for brushes and toilet articles. They were not alone in their heart-to-heart talks. An old and, as Lady Randolph observed, somewhat ferocious white parrot did his best to disturb the conversation when it was getting most intimate. When the bird felt neglected, or objected to the talk that kept him from falling asleep, his pecks could become quite disconcerting. They reminded the ladies that it was really bedtime. But it happened repeatedly that Alexandra still came into Lady Randolph's room to ask whether she wanted anything. She soon needed the captivating, under-

LADY RANDOLPH CHURCHILL IN MIDDLE LIFE

standing, and resolute American friend. Alexandra had, it appeared, been very much alone.

The days at Sandringham were characteristic for Lady Randolph's life, filled to the brim with both joy and exhausting work. She had to cram into her crowded days that unending stream of letters she, like her husband, constantly wrote. She had to keep in touch with her home, with her sons, her political friends, and all her innumerable relations. She kept her watch half an hour fast, lest she be unpunctual at the formal gatherings which were in themselves a full-time occupation. Yet, much to her own embarrassment, she was always a little late. There was never a free moment. Even the most insignificant incident set her a task. Before the photographer made a snapshot of the crowd of guests, Lady Randolph inconspicuously directed her husband to the place next to Lord Salisbury. The picture would remove much public misunderstanding. Lady Randolph was no longer actress and audience alone. She was stage manager into the bargain.

Everyone wanted her help, or her advice. People chose the most inopportune moments to approach her. Just when the quadrille opened the ball, the grand finale of the feast at Sandringham, Isabella, Comtesse de Paris, heiress to the Lilac throne, a rather unattractive, mannish-looking, middle-aged lady with short-cropped hair and a sharply chiseled profile, pressed Lady Randolph into a corner and exacted from her a detailed account of how she had managed the Primrose League. The League having been so successful in England, the legitimist countess wanted to establish a copy, a League of Roses, in France. "The restoration in France is at stake. Is it not more important than the Quadrille?"

The Prince of Wales, although a monarchist by profession, begged to disagree, as he suddenly showed himself. He had been looking everywhere for Lady Randolph. It was his supreme compliment that he wished to open the ball with her.

Memories flashed through her mind. "I have been waiting for this dance . . ." she tried to explain. No other woman would have dared to count up the years. But she was sure of herself. She knew that time had not touched her. She was not afraid to look back. "Remember 1860?" she asked, "Your Royal Highness's visit in New York?"

For heaven's sake! He had been nineteen years old, and Prince Charming! Now he was a middle-aged man with slightly receding hair and an ever-expanding waistline. In a wondering voice he asked: "Did we dance together as far back as that? ... Yes, there was a ball in New York, I distinctly remember. Of course there was a ball. Rather noisy, too, if I am not mistaken!"

"No," she shook her head. "We did not dance. I only dreamed of dancing with you," she added softly. "Of course it was not possible. I was still in the nursery...."

Now her dream came true. Now, as the orchestra struck up a valse, she danced with the Prince. His breath came heavily. Occasionally he had to wipe his forehead with his handkerchief. Surely he was relieved when the music stopped. But she did not mind. She gloried in her dance. She had built a world, a world of realities, out of her childhood dreams.

Next morning, back in London, the habitual worries returned. Lady Randolph had to make the first preparations for a state reception. Due to the indefatigable chivalry of old Lord Iddesleigh (whom Randolph had just ferociously attacked for his stubborn stand toward Russia), the Foreign Office was at her disposal. The reception was still four weeks off. But it would be her great opportunity to be the official hostess of England. She had to proceed carefully. The smallest slip would be a catastrophe. There were many problems to be considered: the list of invitations, both the official list and her private one, the question of expenses, the multiple problems of the cuisine. It would be a terrible failure if, say, the Salisburys wouldn't come. Randolph's picture with the Prime Minister must be followed up by a new public display of their private friendship.

But inside the black, curly head, behind the high forehead

filled with thoughts and plans, the music played on and on. Lady Randolph had never in her life whistled. She was just listening to the tune her fantasy played. It was a popular ditty: "I've danced with the Prince, I've danced with the Prince, I've danced with the Prince of Wales...."

CHAPTER XVI *Hybris*

Lord Salisbury, the Prime Minister, much to his regret, could not say whether he would be available for the reception the Chancellor and Lady Randolph were to give in the Foreign Office. But some two weeks after Sandringham, on December 18th, he came to House Beautiful for an intimate dinner. Only a few guests were present. Unanimously they noticed underneath much personal courtesy an air of harsh political antagonism between host and guest of honor.

Lady Salisbury, who impressed her hostess as a woman of great strength of character and full of common sense, most likable in spite of a rather brusque manner, dominated the conversation. She disdained the ordinary social twaddle which she was so often called upon to listen to. The duties of a statesman's wife, she insisted, were earnest and arduous. They involved the necessity of making a thorough study of the problems of the day. Had dear Lady Randolph, for instance, paid proper attention to the plan of campaign or to the budget, the two foremost questions at the moment? A short but sharp cross-examination, conducted by Lady Salisbury, exposed Jeanette's deplorable ignorance of the details of the budget her husband was about to introduce. She vaguely knew that it fluctuated between eighty and ninety million pounds—"a distinct increase over the estimates of Lord Beaconsfield's administration," Lady Salisbury remarked, shaking her majestic

244

head—but about the details of the Sinking Fund, England's leading lady in politics was woefully uninformed. "There are perhaps other ways of helping one's husband," she suggested. Lady Salisbury violently denied this possibility.

Lord Salisbury softened the argument. He excelled in the art of managing individuals, including such difficult types as his wife, or, for that matter, his host. His experience, his patience, his fame, his subtle and illuminating mind secured for him an ascendancy quite apart from his paramount authority as Prime Minister. He did his best to keep his cabinet together. That was why he had come to this intimate dinner. The fact could no longer be concealed that his right-hand man, triumphant in Parliament and the uncontested favorite of the voters, often found himself isolated and alone in a cabinet, many of whose members owed their appointments to him. Between fish and roast, Lord Randolph admitted frankly that this disproportion perplexed him. Over brandy and cigars, he still insisted on the fact that it was he who had got the majority together, that he was responsible to the people for continued social reforms, and that retrenchment in "superfluous" expenses was his determined decision. The repast had been exquisite, like every meal at Lady Randolph's table. But even her favorite peach-pie left a bitter after-taste. It appeared even less likely than before that Lord Salisbury would be able to take time off to appear at the Churchills' official reception.

Lord Randolph was, as ever, in a hurry. His budget had to be presented in the middle of January; hence the estimates had to be considered in the cabinet before Christmas. Pledged to the hilt by his public promises in the cause of economy, the Chancellor of the Exchequer bluntly informed his two colleagues from the service departments, the Secretary of War and the First Lord of the Admiralty, that they would have to reduce their demands. Lord George Hamilton, the First Lord, was ready to cut out fifty thousand pounds. But he warned that this was all he could sacrifice. He beseeched Lord Randolph not to pursue the matter any further. Neither he nor the Prime Minister, he explained, could be pressed beyond that point. If a rupture took place, the common cause would be damaged irretrievably. Lord Randolph, however, had worked himself up to his habitual frenzy. He was impervious to arguments. Not only was his personal popularity at stake, but also the policy of demonstrative pacifism to which he was so strongly devoted. Seven outlying coaling stations of the Royal Navy should cease operations, he demanded, to emphasize the Empire's complete detachment from international strife.

With the same stubbornness, Lord Randolph insisted on cuts in the army expenditure. In vain Mr. W. H. Smith, the Secretary for War, pointed out that there was no hope whatever of any reduction in the army estimates, already curtailed by the loss of 100,000 pounds of Indian money. In vain he stressed that he, too, was committed to economy, though not able to neglect "the absolute minimum required for the safety of the country." In vain, he even offered his own resignation, to leave to Lord Randolph, the more important man, the responsibility of the decision.

Randolph was once more obsessed by his crusading spirit. Everyone felt it, and the word cropped up that was to follow him through the remainder of his life: Don Quixote.

Lord Salisbury, in a letter to his lieutenant, expressed how glad he was that not he, but the cabinet, would have to settle the dispute with Smith. "But it will be a serious responsibility to refuse the demands of a War Minister so little imaginative as Smith, especially at such a time," he added. "I am rather surprised at George Hamilton being able to reduce so much."

On December 20th, the Chancellor of the Exchequer was summoned to Windsor. Evidently Queen Victoria wanted to use her personal influence on her intractable favorite. It was rare that the old Queen descended into the regions of personal politics. By chance Lord George Hamilton, First Lord of the Admiralty, happened to travel by the same train. He found Lord Randolph in excellent spirits, which became almost exuberant when Randolph said briskly that he intended to retire that very day. Deeply shocked, Lord Hamilton urged him to be patient. Randolph remained, his colleague observed, "inscrutably gay."

The Queen received the stormy petrel with studied graciousness. It was an evening audience and lasted late into the night. Lord Randolph spoke of many things, yet not a word of his intention to resign escaped him. He stayed overnight in the castle and wrote, on Windsor stationery, the fateful letter to his Prime Minister. It read, in part: "The Navy votes show a decrease of nearly 300,000 pounds, but it is illusory, as there is a large increase in the demand made by the Admiralty upon the War Office for guns and ammunition. The Army estimates, thus swollen, show an increase of about 300,000 pounds. The total, thirty-one million for the two services, which in all probability will be exceeded, is very greatly in excess of what I can consent to. . . . I must request to be allowed to give up my office, and retire from the Government."

The signature under this fatal document was not yet dry when Lord Hamilton presented himself in Randolph's room to urge once more patience and moderation. In excellent humor Churchill read him what he had written, yawned, and thought it was high time to go to bed.

Next morning, when both ministers returned by train to London, a little interlude followed. Neither of them had change to pay for the morning papers at the station bookstall. The train was just leaving. The news-vendor said: "Never mind, my lord— you will pay when you come back next time."

Lord Randolph grinned all over his pale, fatigued face. He whispered to his companion, as if it were a joke: "He little knows I shall never come back."

He returned to his office in the Treasury and conducted business as usual. On the twenty-second of December, he paid, still in his capacity of Chancellor of the Exchequer, an official visit to the Master of the Mint. Sir Henry Wolff, his faithful friend, accompanied him. Returning on the underground, and pacing the platform while they were waiting for the train, Wolff asked some random questions about the Treasury plans. "Upon my word," the answer came abruptly, "I don't know now whether I am Chancellor of the Exchequer or not." Sir Henry was stunned. Throughout the inspection Randolph had not made the slightest allusion to his personal crisis.

He probably hoped that Lord Salisbury would not let him go. He had gambled on being irreplaceable on the strength of his unique popularity. But it proved to be a miscalculation. In these crucial days he certainly was neither physically nor mentally capable of cool consideration.

On the same December 22 on which he still made an official inspection, Lord Salisbury sent him by special messenger a letter from Hatfield House. It began: "I have your letter of the twentieth from Windsor . . . ," contained an unmistakable acceptance of the resignation, and ended with the words: "The issue is so serious that it thrusts aside all personal and party considerations. But I regret more than I can say the view you take of it, for no one knows better than you how injurious to the public interest at this juncture your withdrawal from the Government may be. In the presence of your very strong and determined language I can only express my very profound regret."

A short comment on this letter which ended Lord Randolph's career may be permitted: the issue was not serious, but, on the contrary, ridiculous. A few thousand pounds were at stake, less than a third of a thousandth part of the total budget, and immediately after Lord Randolph's resignation the matter was satisfactorily arranged. There was, indeed, no problem at all. There was a gravely sick, eccentric man. But was he, as Lord Salisbury accused, sub rosa, a quitter? Not necessarily. During the momentous Victorian times a lofty and disinterested political atmosphere prevailed, free from the selfish ambitions of a later age. Sir Michael Hicks-Beach, Lord Hartington, Sir Stafford Northcote, Sir Henry James, even Joe Chamberlain, all had voluntarily resigned from or refused high office or positions of greatest authority rather than compromise what they believed to be their cause. It is, on the other hand, true that all of them had more weighty reasons when they decided to go, and that none of them used his threat of resignation, as Lord Randolph did, in the most accomplished high-pressure manner. Personally, however, Lord Randolph Churchill was undoubtedly persuaded that he, too, had to make the sacrifice, though he must have felt that his sacrifice, in view of his controversial position and frail health, was not temporary resignation, but something irrevocable; political suicide, at least. Nothing else explains the fact that his dangerous and, as it proved, entirely helpless and hopeless gamble was the only secret he ever kept from his wife. Evidently he wished to go down alone.

Lord Randolph Churchill, half a hero, half an unbalanced, sick man, and very much of a gentleman, acknowledged Lord Salisbury's letter of parting the moment he received it. His answer was courteous. He affirmed that "not niggardly cheese-paring or Treasury crabbedness but only considerations of high state policy" compelled him to sever "ties in many ways most binding and pleasant." Then he left his office and went home.

Lady Randolph received him, preoccupied as usual, with social matters. The invitation cards for the impending reception in the Foreign Office, a new high-water mark in their career, were already engraved. Now the definite list of guests must be settled. "Oh, I shouldn't worry about it if I were you!" he answered with studied nonchalance. "The reception will probably never take place."

She was stunned.

"Shall we go to the play?" he suggested quickly, to relieve the situation. "Let's ask Henry to go with us!"

Sir Henry Wolff accepted the invitation with delight.

But the first act of *The School for Scandal* obviously bored Randolph. He excused himself. He would go to the club, he said. His hectic impulses were not new to his wife. She wished him luck at the baccarat table.

Lord Randolph left the theater. He betook himself directly to Mr. Buckle, gave him a copy of his letter of resignation, and authorized the editor of the *Times* to make it public, although he had not yet been released from office by the Queen. Perhaps she was even not yet informed about his resignation. He did not return home until dawn. Lady Randolph was already asleep.

She was awake long before her husband, always a late riser. While having breakfast, she read the *Times*. On page eight she dropped the paper. At this very moment he appeared. "Quite a surprise for you?" he said with his most boyish chuckle.

Lady Randolph remained silent. She felt too utterly crushed and miserable even to ask for an explanation or to remonstrate. She understood the finality of the decision he had taken without consulting her. The tragedy was made still clearer to her when eventually Mr. Moore rushed in. The permanent Under-Secretary of the Treasury was Randolph's most intimate assistant. A middle-aged man, modest in appearance, not given to many words, he was in fact his chief's faithful slave. Mr. Moore, who thus far had never allowed himself the slightest expression of criticism, looked into Randolph's smiling face; he stared into Lady Randolph's blank eyes, and quite forgetting his years of inhibition, he cried: "He has thrown himself from the top of the ladder, and will never reach it again!" Six weeks later Mr. Moore, until then in splendid health, died of a broken heart.

The work of her life was shattered. Randolph's expectation of life was up. For him there was no way back, and no life outside politics. Only a few days earlier, still believing himself firmly in the saddle, he had, in his playful melancholic manner, uttered the words: "I have tried all forms of excitement from tip-cat to tiger shooting, from 'beggar-my-neighbor' to Monte Carlo, but I have found no gambling like politics, and no excitement like a big division." Without this excitement, there would be no whip to urge on the tired horse.

Even the immediate future looked gloomy. Lady Randolph could rightly claim that it had been she, above all, who had made sure that Randolph would enjoy the fruits of office for years to come. Apart from honor and glory, it was a question of making a living. Without the "fruits" House Beautiful could not possibly be kept going. Should they retire to their little country house near Newmarket, and become a pair of provincial squires? How long would he stand the blissful quiet? Would they have to move into the Dowager Duchess' mansion in Grosvenor Square? How long could she put up with this sort of life?

Lord Randolph, his insight painfully sharpened by his fall, must have felt her pondering. Although she had not said a word, he shyly caressed her hair. But his voice sounded adamant, as he said: "Politics and money do not go together. Put that thought away!" Her father had taken blows of fate with the same imperturbability. But her father had never been ill, not a day in his life. And in her father's career, ups and downs were inevitable. He was, after all, not Her Majesty's Chancellor of the Exchequer. Randolph would not be much either, from now on. Now he was entirely dependent on her. It was bitter comfort. Yet she cared for him more than ever in these dark days.

They were surrounded by chaos. Somehow she had to rearrange thoughts and things. Happiness, she told herself, does not depend as much on outer circumstances as on one's inner self. In practice, alas, such theories offered little consolation. She was by temperament not given to meditation alone. Out of her despair the loving woman's fighting spirit rose, renewed and strengthened.

This time it was a desperate fight. The political world stood aghast. The Liberals rubbed their hands in sheer delight. The Conservatives called Lord Randolph a deserter. The masses were stunned. Friends fell away by the score, though many of them owed him their success, if not their political existence. Sir

John Gorst, his intimate of the Fourth Party, criticized the "slacker" in unmeasured terms. "Gall and wormwood!" Lady Randolph replied; then she felt terribly ashamed of herself. Randolph confined himself to quoting Zachariah: "I was wounded in the house of my friends." A day later, waking from his trance-like silence, he murmured: "No man is so entirely alone and solitary as I am."

Two days after Lord Randolph's fall general astonishment had become general anger. Westminster resounded with "I told you so." Very few declared themselves his friends. He was severely censored in the Conservative press, and vociferously abused in the clubs. Gossip-mongers imputed to him the worst and meanest motives, ranging from a diseased temper to calculated treachery. The public was informed through a thousand channels that Lord Randolph Churchill had aimed a deadly blow at the Tory-Whig Union, either through personal ambition, or by personal spite. The rupture with Lord Salisbury was complete and irrevocable. Worst of all, the Queen was grievously offended by the fact that her Chancellor had not deigned to ask her for his release, but had entertained her with political small talk on the very evening he abused the stationery of Windsor Castle to write his letter of resignation. And at that, this letter was prematurely published, perhaps the worst offense.

Randolph was unable to defend himself against the deluge of abuse engulfing him. He hoped that publication of his letter of resignation might clear up his motives, and vindicate his stand. But constitutional observance forbade a Minister to anticipate his declaration of resignation to the House, which by an unfortunate coincidence was not in session. Randolph requested Lord Salisbury's permission to make an exception from the Parliamentary rule. The Prime Minister answered by telegraph, a means of communication he rarely used: "I cannot agree. You clearly cannot do it without the Queen's leave." Victoria, of course, would never give her permission.

In this desperate crisis Lady Randolph played her last trump.

She asked the Prince of Wales to lunch. It was an absurd demand. It was almost preposterous to expect his Royal Highness to come to the house of the outcasts. But the Prince had not forgotten the enchanting, if somewhat laborious waltz they had danced some three weeks earlier. Precisely at the appointed hour he stood on the threshold of doomed House Beautiful. The three had a long confabulation. Randolph stated his case. He had by no means intended a lack of respect to his Queen. Indeed, when his letter appeared in the *Times*, two days had already passed since Lord Salisbury had received it. Randolph felt certain that Her Majesty had been informed. Edward murmured a few apologetic words about his own political impotence. Then he suggested that Randolph should explain the matter to Sir Henry Ponsonby, his mother's chief secretary. He kissed Lady Randolph's hand and left slowly and thoughtfully.

Randolph wrote many pages of respectful explanations. Two days later the mail brought three letters. Henry Labouchere, his Radical foe, sent him, most surprisingly, a cordial note of encouragement. Mr. L. J. Jennings, the well-known die-hard among the ultra-Tories, assured him of his unbreakable allegiance. But Mr. Jennings was always an eccentric. In 1871, he had, as editor of the *New York Times*, broken up the Tammany Ring in a merciless newspaper crusade, and hunted the notorious Boss Tweed into jail, where the latter died. The third letter was Sir Henry Ponsonby's reply. "Dear Lord Randolph: The Queen has read your letter relating to the announcement of your resignation before it had been accepted by Her Majesty, and commands me to thank you for your explanation. Yours very truly, Henry Ponsonby." Not one word more. It was the end.

An odd incident followed. After Randolph's resignation, the whole cabinet had to be reconstructed. At this opportunity Lord Salisbury himself took over the Foreign Office; its last holder, Lord Iddesleigh, had apparently been forgotten; in the strife and excitement of these harsh days his unwarlike figure had dropped out of men's minds. Philosophically Lord Iddesleigh, who as Sir Stafford Northcote had been overthrown from his position as a leader of the House by Randolph, murmured: "In his rise, Churchill has driven me from the House; in his fall, from the Cabinet." Mustering his last strength, Lord Iddesleigh went on the same afternoon to bid farewell to the Prime Minister. He did not get further than the anteroom. His old heart disease overtook him, and he expired in the presence of Lord Salisbury, his life-long friend.

Randolph was deeply grieved. He accused himself of having been the unwilling agent of this tragedy. Perhaps he saw his own fate in the mirror of death. He wrote a compassionate letter to Salisbury, mourning the passing away of an excellent man and a true gentleman. Then his own strength was definitely exhausted. Once more it was high time for him, his wife decided, to leave the country for a restful journey. Such escapes had saved him repeatedly. Perhaps he should go to North Africa this time. No, she could not come with him. She had to carry on, to repair, if possible, the broken links. But before departing—did he not want to see his son? They had not been to see Winston since the boy was at Harrow. Perhaps it was time to think about the next generation.

Harrow was as good as its name. It was a harrowing place of detention for Winston, now aged twelve. Due to his frail health, it had been impossible to send him to foggy and damp Eton. His father had grudgingly made this decision. A proud old Etonian himself, he resented the necessity of his elder son's break with the family's educational tradition.

Winston had not done well in the entrance examination to Harrow. He had been unable to answer a single question in the Latin paper. Fortunately, the headmaster, Dr. Welldon, showed discernment in judging the poor pupil's general ability. However, not even his insight could prevent Winston from being only two places from the bottom; and since his two rear-rank men disappeared almost immediately through illness or some other cause, Winston's position was revealed in all its humility when, at the roll call, he was the last boy to be called up. Since his father's name, immediately after his fall, was in everyone's mouth, visitors gathered in large crowds on the school steps in order to see Winston march by at the end of the boys' parade. Thus he became early accustomed to publicity, but mostly he heard the irreverent comment: "Why, he's last of all!"

When the parents came to see their long-missed son, Winston solemnly displayed his tin soldiers. They were all arranged in the correct formation for attack. With a keen eye and a captivating smile, Lord Randolph studied the array for twenty silent minutes. At the end he asked his boy if he would like to go into the army. "Yes!" Winston said at once. His father had discerned Winston's qualities of military genius. The boy's heart beat in exuberant pride. So much graver was the shock when he was told that his father had only suggested the army as a career because he had come to the conclusion that Winston was too much of a dunce to do well at the Bar, where Lord Randolph would have liked to see him.

He was a difficult boy, but a tenacious one. While still at the bottom of the school, he succeeded in passing the preliminary examination for the army, if only modestly and without honors. "He is certainly not possessed of *hybris*," said Dr. Welldon to his parents, perhaps alluding to Lord Randolph's fate.

Hybris is the Greek term for the excessive pride that invites the inevitable fall. Lord Randolph was strangely silent. Lady Randolph was very proud of her son. Now it was a little easier to let her husband go to Africa. She was left behind to keep the flag flying. But she was not alone. She had full confidence in her boy, the commander of fifteen hundred tin soldiers. Winston, too, would keep the flag flying.

CHAPTER XVII *Rain and Sunshine*

Randolph could have returned over a golden bridge. As early as on January 11, 1887, scarcely a fortnight after the scandal caused by the resignation, Lord Salisbury wrote to the perturbed Duchess of Marlborough: "When the House of Commons has decided on the subject on which Randolph parted from us, this decision must be accepted. After that it will be quite open to Randolph to rejoin this or any other Conservative Ministry as soon as opportunity occurs."

Two days later Mr. Smith, Randolph's opponent in the struggle for the army estimates and now his successor as leader in the House, wrote his predecessor with equal amiability: "All that has happened is an incident in the career of a young politician of quite temporary character. I look forward with confidence to a future—the sooner it comes, the better—when I shall be in the retirement I long for, and you will be leading a great party with prudence and firmness and courage."

For their part, the Unionists, the dissenters from Gladstone, opened their arms to him. Chamberlain made overtures, and Lord Hartington appeared not averse to forgetting old feuds. But Lord Randolph Churchill, embittered and unwilling to forgive those whom he accused of having brought about his downfall, rejected the reconciliation offered by both sides. Once more he spoke in the House, ostensibly to explain his resignation, in fact to deride the Unionists, whom, he admitted, he

256

had only regarded as a "useful kind of crutch," as well as his own party, to whom he reaffirmed his allegiance, but not without severely criticizing their leadership. Naturally both camps were alarmed and offended. Unanimously the London press adopted an attitude of solemn rebuke. Chamberlain wrote Randolph a letter: "My dear Churchill! Why will you insist on being an Ishmael—your hand against every man? Why did you go out of your way on Monday to attack me? You know that I am the mildest of men, but I have a strong inclination to hit out at those who strike me, and my experience teaches me that no private friendship can long resist the effect of political contest." The letter only conveyed a warning, but with a dangerous growl.

Lady Randolph understood the necessity of the moment. She had to get him away from the firing line. Under her persuasion, which, in a letter to his mother, Randolph described as: "after great reflection and balancing of everything," he decided to take the long envisaged holiday abroad. He left on February 3, 1887. His inevitable companion, the man who listened, was once more Mr. Harry Tyrwhitt.

A flood of letters to his wife followed from Algiers, Constantine, Tunis, Palermo, and finally from Naples. To his mother Randolph wrote from Biskra: "I was so glad to get your letter, long and interesting, from the Castle. I expect you must have found it pleasant there on the whole. If anything could remove any lingering doubts I may have had as to the prudence of leaving the Government, it would be the charm of this place, which I should not be experiencing except for that rather strong proceeding."

His first letter to Jeanette, dispatched on February 9th at the Hotel Regence, Algiers, contained the revealing words: "It is certainly very pleasant getting away from the cold and worry of London. I have hardly given two thoughts to politics since I left; but I wonder whether there is still much carping going on against me; or whether my flight has disarmed my enemies." From Biskra he sent a glowing account of the beauty of the

North African coast, ending with the sentence: "I confess I do not think much of politics and rejoice over my freedom and idleness—which, I hope, will not shock you." And again from Constantine: "I consider my position a very good one, and, though it may seem a strange thing to say, better than if I were in my old place in the Government. I am feeling very well, I am thankful to say, and keep blessing my stars that I am not in the House of Commons. If people only knew how little official life attracts me, they would judge one's actions differently." Yet he wrote to Jeanette from Palermo on March 2nd, with an audible sigh of relief: "I have today got hold of a whole week's file of the *Times*, down to the twenty-fifth, which has posted me up in political matters." Page after page he continued to his most patient listener and reader discussing every trifling bit of parliamentary gossip. Finally, before coming home, he sent her, enclosed in his last letter from Naples, a request to prepare for his overdue speech in Paddington. "I can quite understand the political situation, having read all you wrote," his message ended. "For me it is not unsatisfactory; but for the general Tory prospects it is little promising. What a fool was Lord S. to let me go so easily! Give Winston the enclosed Mexican stamp!"

Although Lord Randolph's letters to his wife were written in a cheerful and optimistic vein, Mr. Harry Tyrwhitt, his traveling companion, had no doubt that his friend felt very bitterly the sudden reversal of his fortunes and the crisis in his career. During the whole trip of which Randolph gave so gay an account, he reported, the poor man was afflicted by fits of profound depression; he would often sit by himself for hours, plunged in gloomy thought.

For Lady Randolph, on the other hand, there was much struggle and a good deal of sadness, but never more than, at worst, a fleeting instant of gloom. Assiduously she used her husband's well-timed absence to mend his fences. Queen Victoria's Golden Jubilee, in 1887, seemed a heaven-sent opportunity to reconcile the Queen, who, although Lord Randolph was in disgrace, felt no grudge against her charming American subject. Victoria herself saw to it that Lady Randolph should have a good place in Westminster Abbey, where the Jubilee celebrations climaxed. "As the wife of an ex-cabinet minister," the Queen decided graciously, "Lady Randolph Churchill is entitled to a preferred seat." It was a thoughtful excuse, everyone knew, to classify Lady Randolph merely as an ex-cabinet minister's wife.

She was deeply impressed by the magnificence of London during the days of the Jubilee. The capital was crowded to its utmost; people had come from all over the world to see the pageant. London looked more festive than ever. The days were blessed with the proverbial "Queen's weather." Below the blue skies, and in the bright sunshine, flags were waving everywhere. An excited, yet patient crowd filled the thoroughfares and the route of the procession. Deliberately the wife of the member for South Paddington mingled with the crowds. Her smile and her vivid countenance belied any foolish rumor that her husband's regrettable retirement had caused any difficulties whatsoever. Every voter was out on the streets, and everyone could see for himself that nothing was wrong with the Churchills. His good lady would otherwise hardly have looked so radiant.

In Westminster Abbey, however, she forgot about pretenses. The Cathedral was illuminated by dim lights, pierced here and there by the rays of the summer sun, as it streamed through the ancient stained-glass windows. The Queen, representing the glory and continuity of England's history, sat alone in the middle of the great nave, a small, pathetic figure, surrounded by the vast throng whose gaze was riveted upon her. A wave of emotion passed over the assembly as silent tears were seen dropping one by one upon the Queen's folded hands. Certainly the fact that the *Te Deum* being played had been composed by the Prince Consort added another note of deep affection and sadness to the burden of Her Majesty's memories. Unashamed,

Lady Randolph sobbed. The tension was too great. Her nerves gave way. Understandingly, her neighbors looked the other way.

So well was the ground prepared by Jeanette that Randolph, upon his return, did not, as he had feared he would, run up against misgivings and prejudices. On the contrary, both the Churchills were invited to all kinds of public and private functions in connection with the Jubilee. One of the most remarkable events was an invitation from the White Star Company to cruise for a few days aboard one of the company's ships, in order to witness the Naval review in the Solent. The invitation was most tempting. The cruise might possibly have important political consequences. As the outcome of a personal chat between Lady Randolph and the company's manager, Lord Hartington and Mr. Chamberlain were asked to join the excursion; so was the Duchess of Manchester, another American lady with her fingers in British politics. Like Lady Randolph, whom she had helped in the Primrose League, the American Duchess was bent on bringing together the Tory Democrats and the Whigs. This scheme of a "National Party" fitted right into Randolph's plans.

The cruise proved a propitious opportunity for furthering them. Lady Randolph lured Lord Hartington into the deck chair next to hers, and chatted with him. Their small talk was in Victorian parlance termed "frivolities." In the meantime Randolph, in his stateroom, tried desperately to recover from his sea-sickness, the price he had always to pay for his nautical pleasure. Jeanette feigned astonishment when Mr. Chamberlain suddenly disturbed her innocent idyll. Great Joe was never a man of many words and excuses. Drawing up a third chair, without preliminaries and with his usual directness, he instantly plunged into the matter of the "National Party." Lord Hartington, taken by surprise, looked uncomfortable, and answered in monosyllables. Undeterred, Joe Chamberlain pressed home his points. It took considerable time before the chilly attitude of

Lord Hartington began to take effect on him. The conversation languished and died. The subject was never re-opened. By his straightforwardness the great Chamberlain had disrupted Lady Randolph's fine spun net, just as it was closing around Hartington, who, she understood, was a difficult person, hard to persuade against his will, and most uncompromisingly definite in his likes and dislikes. He obviously liked her, and might have been convinced by her gentle and gradual approach. But there was a gulf of education, manners, tastes between him and the radical Chamberlain that not even political expediency could bridge. This, at least, Lady Randolph told her husband, was her personal opinion. Randolph abided by it. He entirely dropped the scheme of a National Party.

Yet his wife's interference, perhaps because it was not carried beyond the border of a discreet tryout, reconciled Hartington with both the Churchills. The later Duke of Devonshire was a most portentous man, slow, but infallible in his decisions. He decided that Lady Randolph was one of the most admirable women of the time. This conviction was strengthened when she sent him a "pot-hat" for his birthday. Although this gift was only part of a conspiracy (fifty friends sent the notoriously sloppy peer every sort of headgear from the ceremonious silk-hat to the flannel cricketing cap) Hartington considered it an excellent joke, and instantly invited the Churchills to Hardwick Hall. The clouds were receding.

In his own home Lord Hartington proved that his rather stern countenance belied a gentle soul. No one, Lady Randolph remarked, was more pleasant or more easy to get on with. He himself was full of practical jokes, the predilection of the Victorian age. He allotted to Randolph Queen Mary's Bedroom, a chamber of small dimensions with windows on all sides so that the occupant could be spied on day and night. This room had been constructed as a cell for Mary, Queen of Scots, but Mary was beheaded before she could occupy her jail at Hardwick. However, Randolph could not sleep. Whether the ghosts of the Queen of Scots hounded his nights, or recollections of a more recent date, remained undisclosed. He was, for the first time, not in a combative mood.

House Beautiful had, indeed, to be given up. There was no retreat to Blenheim, either. The eighth Duke reported from Newport, Rhode Island, where he was spending the summer as a guest of Mr. Paran Stevens, that he had been introduced to the widow Lillian Hammersley, one of the most beautiful women of New York society. As Miss Lillian Price of Troy, New York, she had been a famous belle, one of the eight beautiful girls entertained by Mr. Corcoran of Washington at his cottage at White Sulphur Springs. There had, of course, been nothing wrong about this entertainment. Lillian—he simply called her Lillian in his letter—was the daughter of Cicero Price, a Commodore in the U. S. Navy, a national hero. She had married Louis C. Hammersley, of New York, who a few years later had died childless, leaving her with the income from six million.

Never had a letter of the *bel esprit* Blandford been as accurately to the point. Lady Randolph understood his enthusiasm. His new acquaintance's beauty plus the income from six million made for a formidable combination. Blenheim stood bitterly in need of being freshly gilded. The century-old castle was badly in need of repair and modernization. She heartily welcomed the match she saw developing, and was honestly pleased that another New York woman should join the phalanx of fair Americans in England. But two American hostesses were definitely too much even for the most weather-beaten, historic castle. Quietly she took leave of the dream of returning to Blenheim, where her most pleasant time in England had been spent. The Churchills moved to their small house, Bemstead Manor, on the Chieveley estates, about three miles from the town of Newmarket. Its proximity was not mere coincidence. The choice was the outcome of a conversation Randolph had with Lord Dunraven, the only Fourth-Party man and minor member of the government—he had been Under-Secretary for Colonies—who had voluntarily decided to follow his leader into political exile. Both were fed up with Salisbury and Gladstone. They talked shop: the turf, of course. Until then Randolph, always a great horse-lover, had not yet had his own stable. Now, in the company of Lord Dunraven, and with his last pennies, he bought a number of racehorses. Robert Sherwood, the famous trainer, was hired to look after them.

It was Jennie's youth in New York, all over again. For a few months Randolph, like her father, talked nothing but horses. For hours every day he would study the racing calendar with Sherwood to decide upon the entries for his stable. He even got up early in the morning to watch the horses doing their gallop between six and seven o'clock. It was an invigorating life. He visibly recovered. His harshness faded as his stable did well.

Soon he was a shrewd judge of "form." In handicaps, especially, his forecasts were so often fulfilled that he acquired an almost prophetic reputation in the sporting world. On the morning before a race, he would for hours ponder over calculations which, with the aid of Ruff's Guide, often led to correct conclusions, and still more frequently to those which were "almost right." The stable became a paying proposition; for the next two years it stood high in the winning list.

The financial situation improved considerably. The Churchills had a little superfluous money to spend. Again it slipped out of their pockets. They decided to travel. Abroad, he still was the statesman with the international reputation. Abroad, he did not feel suffocated as he sometimes felt in the House which he now visited only rarely, once more seated on the old back bench below the gangway. Where would they go?

To Spain! they decided after a long and happy confabulation. Lord and Lady Randolph, the newspapers reported, were going to spend the winter in Spain. It sounded very convincing. The average reader, well informed about politics as well as personalities, knew that the ex-Chancellor was physically not very robust. The Spanish sun would do him good. And Spain was perhaps the only country where England had no political interests. It was the perfect holiday ground.

"We will bake in the sun on the beaches of the Guadalquivir!" Lord Randolph announced emphatically.

"It will be delightful to meet the Tsar again," Jeanette whispered in reply. "Wasn't it under his auspices, as Tsarevitch ..."

"In the Royal Yacht Club Squadron ..."

"Fourteen years ago," she laughed unabashed. Time was no menace to her.

Was it really fourteen years ... as long as that? It seemed a day to him. A day and a night. It would be a second honeymoon trip, a well-deserved one. "Jennie!" he said. In moments of great happiness one does not say Jeanette. It takes too long.

CHAPTER XVIII *Castles in Spain*

The railroad station was crammed with reporters. A barrage of questions received the Churchills. "What are you going to propose to M. de Giers?... Will you appear in audience with the Tsar?"...

The plot was discovered. The gentlemen of the press knew that Lord Randolph had deliberately encouraged the rumors about his forthcoming journey to Spain in order to hide the fact that he was on his way to St. Petersburg. That his ruse was only due to his desperate longing for a bit of privacy was completely unintelligible to the news-hounds. The hottest story of the winter 1888, they were sure, was within their grasp. But the mystery man in British politics—a position Randolph had reached by falling out with everybody—only showed his teeth, and shoved away Mr. *Times,* Mr. *Pall Mall Gazette,* and, with particular relish, Mr. *Standard,* representing the official conservative mouthpiece.

Fortunately, his wife was talkative. She predicted the coming spring fashions, she regretted that Mr. Oscar Wilde, a young poet, was so little recognized, indeed, almost unknown.

The station-master whistled. The train left. The rotary press, however, was faster than the Victorian railway. Screaming headlines received the Churchills in Paris where they were to change trains. *Le Lord Randolph,* the indefatigable boulevard-trotter and habitué of Paris shows and nightclubs, was always welcome, but now, as "officious" ambassador of Lord Salisbury, more than ever. Perhaps the welcome guest would stay a little longer on his return from his portentous negotiations in St. Petersburg.

At home the press was considerably less friendly. London newspapers dilated gravely on the tricky journey. The *Times* warned the Tsar not to be misled, as his predecessor had been by a certain Quaker deputation on the eve of the Crimean War, by any assurance of British friendship which might be offered by the "most versatile and volatile" of English politicians. Lesser papers showed less restraint in their language. Openly they charged Randolph with being on a secret mission. Every thinkable and unthinkable reason for his journey was given. He was gathering material for a campaign against his own government. No, he was traveling on the Prime Minister's personal behalf. If he was neither for nor against his cabinet, why did he go to St. Petersburg at all? Why should an ailing man exchange the Spanish sun for the Russian winter? Why, even a professional deserter would hardly desert the sun of Seville for the Russian snow. No one believed that he simply wished to have a good time going to Russia as a tourist, and meeting or making Russian friends. Even the Foreign Office displayed its suspicion. It published an official statement: "Lord Randolph Churchill has no mission from the government to M. de Giers. His presence in St. Petersburg is wholly without the knowledge of the Foreign Office, and he has no official status. His Lordship alone knows why he gave up a contemplated Spanish tour for a visit to the Northern latitude." That last sentence might have been written by Lord Salisbury himself.

It encouraged the popular press to abuse Lord Randolph without measure. The Tsar would refuse to see a vulgar globe-trotter. There was no person whom the Russians more heartily despised than the member for Paddington—"a boastful, rattling, noisy egotist with no principles, and, apparently, with no conception of duty or honor."

Finally there was one widely discussed argument that seemed

irresistible to prove the political character of the mysterious journey: Why, then, does Lady Randolph accompany her husband? She always lets him go alone on his fishing and hunting trips. But whenever she is present, things are about to happen.

It was a drab departure. Lady Randolph, always eager to comfort her husband, attributed the melancholy not to the ugly voices from London that still pursued them but to the scenery they were crossing. The vast and dreary expanse of snow-covered land between Berlin and St. Petersburg was flat and uninteresting. To live for long months every year buried in that cold, monotonous silence would sufficiently account for the vein of sadness which, she believed, was the basis of the Russian character, displayed in all Russian music, painting, and writing. Were they not themselves affected by the melancholy of the country they were traversing?

Sadly, he shook his head. As if things were as simple as that! In fact, he insisted, his limbs were cramped and tired from sitting day and night and night and day in the uncomfortable compartment of an uncomfortable train. Neither mentioned the chorus of vengeance from London whose echo still sounded in their ears.

The Russians did their best to welcome the Churchills. The visit of the prominent English couple had been anxiously awaited. Everything went smoothly. Railway officials and custom officers behaved like attentive servants. Special carriages were reserved in every train. Untouched, the luggage passed the customs. The only nuisance was the swarm of reporters at the St. Petersburg station. True to style, Lord Randolph briskly dismissed these "mischievous people" (an incident that, some years later, caused Winston, then himself a newspaper correspondent, to protest that, after all, the reporters must make a living like everybody else).

Jeanette arrived with a feeling of perfect comfort. While Randolph was still grumbling about the inevitable news-hacks, she stretched her limbs, breathed deeply, and consciously enjoyed again moving at will. In small things, as in big ones, she knew how to make the best of circumstances.

They arrived late in the evening, but Lady Randolph was never tired. At least she would never have admitted it. The broad streets through which they drove, full of life and animation, invigorated her. Flooded with electric light, St. Petersburg seemed much brighter than London. If this sparkling life and the modern appearance of the capital of mysterious Russia disappointed her romantic expectation a little, she kept it to herself. Randolph had to be cheered up. She pointed out the rather shabby exteriors of the houses, with their small double windows and tiny doors. Yet she observed a seemingly incongruous waste of space. Russia was certainly not England, and St. Petersburg not London with its narrow old streets, in which every inch counted. In the lavishness of its waste space, the Russian capital reminded her rather of the new, booming American cities. Strange how the memories of America recurred ever more frequently, as England became more and more her battlefield.

Soon, as the invitations flowed in, she saw the interior of Russian houses. The contrast between their poor outward appearance and their inside luxury amazed her. It was not the custom, as in London, to have a house of one's own. Rather on the Parisian model, several families lived under the same roof. The entrance and the staircases, however, were brilliantly decorated with rich carpets, with candles and flowers, which gave the abodes the appearance of private dwellings. Another Russian contrast not escaping her gift of discernment was the difference between the great number of pompous valets and the miserable lives they led. When they were not wearing their resplendent uniforms and lining the staircases, they were tucked away in the dark, damp cellars. Certainly, the housewife in her noted, these Russian noblemen who soon swarmed around the Churchills were indiscriminate in their expenditures. Most of them kept whole families of useless dependents simply in order to boast a great retinue. The Russian nobility of the day was becoming impoverished, she remarked. Yet all their social entertainments were extremely well done, perhaps a bit overdone. Already in the afternoon their homes were splendidly illuminated, with a profusion of electric light and scores of candles into the bargain. Flowers were expensive. They had to be imported from the faraway South. Notwithstanding this difficulty, some aristocratic houses were transformed into veritable hot-houses. They were smartly furnished with all that money could buy, and modern art suggest. To Jeanette, however, Parisian salons showed more artistic taste. On the other hand, the St. Petersburg drawing-room was superior to its London counterpart, overcrowded with entirely superfluous ornaments.

These were Lady Randolph's first impressions in the Russian capital. The London press, however, kept harping on the mystery behind the Churchills' journey. Special correspondents were sent after them. The *Pall Mall Gazette* reported that Lady Randolph scored "her habitual triumphs" as she went about sleighing and skating. A lurid description of the black-haired, brunette woman so perfectly contrasting with the snow-covered scenery around her followed. She drove through the heaviest city traffic in an ordinary Russian sleigh, smaller than the English and American cutter, tightly wrapped in a thick fur rug which not only protected her from the cold, but kept her from falling out, as she indulged in her favorite sport of making one horse gallop and the other one trot, although they were in double harness. Her ice-waltz on the frozen lake of the Palais de la Taurid was the talk of St. Petersburg. In comparison with her, the Russians were poor skaters, and she could never find a competer t partner for figure-skating. On the other hand, she rapidly learned the high art of tobogganing down the icy hills on enormous sleds carrying half a dozen or more people, the forerunner of the bobsleigh. Whether the *Pall Mall Gazette* correspondent understood it or not, this perilous sport gave her a thrill she had so far only experienced when, in hunting, she had to get, at a terrific pace, over a big fence, leaving the field behind. Undoubtedly there was a touch of wildness in the cultivated dilettante, the writing, painting, and piano-playing

woman, the music-lover, connoisseuse of old masters, the devoted wife and nurse, and the mother shining, as Winston expressed it, like the evening star.

Her picture taken in St. Petersburg explained something of
her new maturity. Now she wore her crown of black hair in a
loose profusion of ringlets. Her face had an expression of
sovereign determination. Her eyes seemed to have grown still
larger. They reflected her indomitable courage and will power.
At the court of St. Petersburg, polished and just a trifle savage
like herself, she dwelt in her castle in Spain.

The Churchills were well received at Court. True, Sir Robert
Morier, the British ambassador, much to his regret, left for
Moscow on official business the very day they arrived in St.
Petersburg. But on the next day, M. de Giers, the almighty
Foreign Secretary, sent for Randolph, and had a most pleasant
conversation with him, lasting an hour. Shortly afterward the
Tsar and Tsarina, not waiting, as was the custom, for the New
Year's Day reception, only a few days off, summoned Lord and
Lady Randolph Churchill to Gatschina.

Gatschina, the Windsor of Imperial Russia, was about an
hour by train from St. Petersburg. Innumerable stories circu-
lated about its secrets. It was, Lady Randolph had been told,
more closely guarded than any border-fortress, and visitors
were frequently stripped before being admitted to the palace.
She found exactly the contrary to be true. Gatschina was easily
reached by a public road leading through lovely gardens. Exactly one sentry stood at the door of the palace, in its curious
mixture of splendor and unpretentiousness, typically Russian.

The Castle exhibited its grandeur inside. Its six hundred
rooms and endless corridors were filled with priceless Oriental
porcelain. The walls were adorned with precious tapestries and
old masters. The Churchills felt a slight pain when they redis-
covered some of the most precious pictures from the Blenheim
collection, which Blandford had sold to the Tsar. Courtiers,
couriers, and lackeys in black-and-orange liveries, their caps

embellished by tossing black, white and orange ostrich feathers, gave a colorful and barbaric touch to the scene—which changed immediately when the guests were curtsied into an apartment that, Lady Randolph found, savored of the early Victorian style with mediocre pictures, undoubtedly furnished particularly for English visitors. There a luncheon was served, followed by innumerable cups of tea, while the audiences went on. None lasted longer than five minutes.

Lord Randolph, however, remained almost an hour with the Tsar, discussing the political questions of the day. He left a carefully written account of this conversation from which it transpires that the Tsar was sitting at a large writing table in a small cabinet, and asked his guest to seat himself on a low yellow bench on the opposite side of the table. The conversation began in French, which was a great disappointment to Lord Randolph, since he was well aware that the Tsar spoke perfect English. The first topic of discussion was the respective merits of Russian, English, and American cigarettes. But soon the talk shifted to the eternal theme of war and peace. The Tsar observed that the English newspapers were wildly attacking Russia, probably, he added with a smile, because they were bribed by Herr von Bismarck. Randolph defended Bismarck, who, at worst, might have subsidized one London journal, but he used the opportunity to let off steam about what he himself thought of English gazettes in general. Within five minutes perfect harmony had been established.

It did not take Lady Randolph as long as that to win over the Tsarina Maria. Her Majesty's first question was after her sister, Princess Alexandra, from whose letters, it filtered out, the Tsarina was already perfectly familiar with Jeanette. Lady Randolph duly eulogized the Princess of Wales. She closed her report with the words: "To sum up, the gracious and charming Princess is, indeed, your sister, Madame!"

Tsarina Maria asked endless questions about England and all that was going on in the social life of London. She regretted that being the little mother of all orthodox Russians, she could no longer spend her summers at Cowes. "I'll never forget the ball at the Royal Yacht Squadron," she said, as if she were again the little Danish Princess. She appeared somewhat lost in the labyrinth of Gatschina. "I distinctly remember your dress, when we first met. The people called you Little Jennie."

Suddenly they were very close. They smiled at one another. "Our husbands are still talking," the Tsarina said, to find an outlet for her slight embarrassment.

"About Mr. Gladstone, I am sure!" Jeanette answered with unfailing instinct.

Indeed, Lord Randolph was just elaborating on the advanced age and the visible decay of the great old man, and was assuring the Tsar, who, for his part, had no love for the Liberal reformer, that the present English Parliament would last another three or four years and that it was hardly conceivable that after that period Mr. Gladstone would still be physically capable of official duty, even if the next polls were favorable for him, a remote contingency. He spoke himself into that white heat the mention of Gladstone's name always produced, and had to stop, interrupted by an attack of coughing.

And Lord Hartington? inquired His Majesty. Was it not possible that he would make up his quarrel with Monsieur Gladstone?

It was impossible, Randolph assured him, after a whole year of differences had passed. Both men had become hopelessly embittered in their quarrel. After all, Lord Hartington could not blind himself to the truly anarchical domestic policy of Mr. Glad . . .

Perhaps it was too much even for the Tsar of Russia. He turned the conversation, asking about other British statesmen, about whose position and ideas he seemed astonishingly well informed. What was Lord Granville, *cet homme charmant*, doing? Did Lord Derby enjoy his well-deserved retirement after so many years of glorious labor? How did Mr. Goschen carry the burden of his new office?

Mr. Goschen, indeed, carried the burden of Randolph's office. But magnanimously his predecessor praised him.

In the meantime the Tsarina was showing Lady Randolph the palace. The most remarkable among many rooms was a large attic, recalling the hall of an old English country house, full of comfortable armchairs and writing-tables with games and toys on them. "Our private England," Maria explained. "We often dine here. After the meal the tables are removed, and we stay on until bedtime."

Strange, Lady Randolph thought. To stay on in the dining-room if one has a few hundred rooms to choose from. The tastes of the absolute monarchs were obviously extremely simple.

Soon their husbands joined them. Jeanette was deeply impressed by the Tsar's unpretentiousness, so much at variance with his towering frame and majestic bearing. His manner made an impression of sincerity and earnestness on her. He would be a most desirable ally for the British Empire.

This seemed exactly what the Tsar wanted to be. Before dismissing his guests, he assured Lord Randolph how much he would like to come to London to talk things over with Lord Salisbury *"jusqu' à présent l'ennemi acharné de la Russie."* Lord Randolph had just two minutes' time to explain that His Majesty was under a wrong impression. Lord Salisbury was a true friend of Russia. He himself knew from their collaboration in office that the Prime Minister did not care a hoot about Bulgaria, and that his concern for Constantinople was strictly limited. Provided that Russia respected England's preponderant interests in Afghanistan, he could not see a single cause of conflict in the world.

Then the Churchills left the palace. Lord Randolph was highly pleased with his statesmanship. He was no longer speaking for a single soul in England, but the Tsar of all the Russias had eagerly listened to him. Randolph's *aide mémoire* ended with the words: "His Majesty, who throughout the interview had been wonderfully kind, quiet, and simple, talking evidently with unreserve and allowing me without displeasure to do the same, brought to a close a conversation which had lasted about forty-five minutes."

The next day the Churchills had intended to go to Moscow. But they had scored a success again, a success, which, like most of their triumphs, turned out a little embarrassing. They received an invitation, amounting to a command, to re-appear at Gatschina, this time at an official dinner. All the carefully made arrangements for Moscow had to be cancelled. They boarded a special train that conveyed the hundred and fifty guests to Gatschina. On arriving, a long line of royal carriages took them to the palace, where they had to sit out an entertainment consisting first of a French one-act play, then a quartet from *Rigoletto*, then the duo from the *Huguenots*, then a whole Russian play, quite unintelligible, and finally another Parisian sketch, all before supper was served. During the entre-actes the Emperor and the Empress walked about and spoke to their guests. Everyone went to the large buffet for refreshment. Yet it was an ordeal. The show was too long and the supper too rich.

At dinner, Randolph sat at the Tsarina's table, between the beautiful Grand Duchess Elizabeth, the daughter of the Duke of Hesse, and the Grand Duchess Catharina. Lady Randolph had been allotted a seat in the third row of tables. But as soon as Maria noticed this *gaffe*, she asked her to sit at her own table. Changes in the seating order were extremely rare. The general attention caused by Lady Randolph's change of place was increased by the fact that Her Majesty chatted with her throughout the supper.

The Russian court etiquette became increasingly surprising to Lady Randolph. The Tsar got up from his chair, walked around between the small tables, and talked to the guests. Yet all the diners remained seated, even the officers. It was, Lady Randolph was told, due to a tradition introduced by Peter the Great, who disliked ceremony of any kind. His odd protocol was, like all Russian traditions, anxiously respected.

On the whole, the protocol at Gatschina seemed much less

rigid than that at Windsor. It was not the custom to treat the members of royalty with deference. The ladies did not dream of curtsying to a Grand Duke. They would rise only when the Tsarina did so, or at the entrance of the Tsar. Even then, making their obeisance, they bowed stiffly from the waist, more in the Prussian fashion and more ungraceful even than the English "bob," which, much to Lady Randolph's displeasure, was beginning to replace the formal curtsy.

A couple of days later, the Churchills received the third invitation—within less than a week—to appear at Court, this time to attend the New Year's reception at the Winter Palace in St. Petersburg. Never had foreigners been treated to so much Imperial attention, and never had two nervous wrecks been harassed by such an ordeal. But they enjoyed it immensely. It was just that sort of exertion that kept Randolph going, and inspired his wife to muster all her indefatigable social graces. She had only to think back to London to realize that she was dancing on a volcano. But such menacing thoughts accelerated her waltz-step and made her smile more radiantly than ever.

The whole Court gathered at eleven o'clock in the forenoon, an un-Christian hour, Randolph grumbled, to attend the New Year's reception. The Tsar greeted them with the hallowed phrase: "Good morning, my children!"

"We are happy to salute you, little father!" they answered in unison.

The mass in the palace-chapel was a trifle too theatrical even for Jeanette's—mostly suppressed—histrionic tastes. But the show was perfectly organized. On the right, the dresses of the women made a sea of warm colors, the soft red and green velvets of the ladies-in-waiting predominating, their long, white tulle veils like halos touched here and there by dancing rays from the midday sun that entered through the rich stained-glass windows. On the left, the men presented a scarcely less brilliant group. Although the service was orthodox, the Lutheran pastor in his dark velvet cassock stood next to the Catholic Cardinal in his purple robe, their presence adding a note of tolerance to the ceremony. The royal choir, composed entirely of male voices, was the most beautiful Lady Randolph had ever heard. There was a strange melancholy in their singing. Lady Randolph admitted that she would rather have heard one of Handel's grand oratorios on this solemn occasion. Nor would she have regretted the absence of the resplendent crimson surplices richly braided with gold, which looked to her more fitted for an operatic chorus than for a church choir. But on the whole, the ceremony deeply impressed her. And, what was more important, she observed how well and contented Randolph looked. Before leaving the strange church, she thanked God in a few plain English words for all her happiness and for her husband's apparent improvement.

The Mass negotiated, the procession reformed and returned to the Palace. The foreign ambassadors were asked into a reserved room where the Tsar addressed a few privileged ones among them. It was Their Excellencies' only occasion during the whole year to speak to the sovereign to whom they were accredited. For the rest the Tsar refrained from personal interference with the business of diplomacy, which was left strictly to M. de Giers. Randolph, although only an unofficial visitor, was particularly honored by being invited to join the diplomatic reception. Sir Robert Morier, Her Majesty's Ambassador, smiled wryly. The two British statesmen had found no opportunity to exchange more than a stiff "how do you do?" But this mutual reserve did not in the least impair Randolph's high good humor.

After the signal success the Churchills had scored at court, they were almost buried in the avalanche of invitations Petersburg society showered on them. Polostov, the President of the Council (tantamount to the Lord President in England), and high in the favor of the Tsar, endeavored to exercise almost a monopoly on his newly acquired English friends. M. Polostov had inherited from his father-in-law the Steiglitz School of Art, which the Churchills were eager to visit. They returned silently from their inspection. At last they had discovered where the famous Italian cabinet from Blenheim had gone. Blandford had stubbornly shrouded its whereabouts in mystery.

The same evening they went to the opera to hear *La vie pour le Tsar!* by Glinka. Lady Randolph found the music charming, expressing all the Russian national characteristics, both deep sadness and wild, boisterous gaiety. However, the orchestra seemed rather feeble to her ear, as she was accustomed to the intoxication of the Grande Opera in Paris. Moreover, she observed with slight misgivings that the ladies in the audience wore high dresses, whereas to her the low décolleté seemed *de rigueur* for the opera. Her own décolleté made her feel quite naked. Pretending that she was freezing, she wrapped herself in her fur coat. The Tsarina, in the Imperial box, saw her gesture, and followed suit. It was another mark of consideration. To emphasize this fact, Maria nodded across the stalls to her English friend. The Tsarina's wrap was of sable. It had cost £12,000, Lady Randolph was told, and was day and night protected by a special guard. With Queen Victoria, no woman was exposed to such unfair competition. Jeanette felt a little homesick in all the glamor that was St. Petersburg. Her taste for glamor was, by that time, more than satisfied.

Yet, she could never return to her hotel before the small hours. For the Russians the evening began at midnight, with the second supper, after the opera. They had, Lady Randolph noticed with a shudder, enormous appetites, and were fond of good living, eating often to excess, to say nothing of the quantities of vodka and champagne they could drink. To be dead-drunk was by no means considered a heinous offense. The night the Churchills had spent in Gatschina, the officer in charge, responsible for Their Majesties' lives, a colonel of the Preobrajensky Guards, the smartest cavalry regiment in Russia, was so drunk that he fell heavily on Lady Randolph's shoulder when he was presented to her. The guests near by propped him up. Everyone laughed, evidently thinking nothing of the incident.

The best meal, however, was served to Lady Randolph at the celebrated new restaurant Cubat. The host himself filled her plate with helpings of a size that would supply a regiment of starved soldiers. Cubat had just left the service of the Tsar, whose chef he had been, since the salary, equivalent to eight thousand pounds a year, did not satisfy him, and furthermore because he was sick of having secret police watching his every gesture, pouncing on every pinch of salt, lifting the cover from every pot, and forcing Cubat to taste every dish before it was served. Cubat loathed eating. So he had started his own restaurant.

Randolph, engrossed by his story, asked Cubat why he did not leave the land of tyranny and establish himself in Paris. Cubat found this an excellent idea. Indeed, he bought the Hotel Paiva in the Champs-Elysées, opened the Cubat restaurant, and flourished tropically for three weeks. After this short time he had to close shop, a broke and broken man. His prices had been so excessive that thrifty Parisians would not pay them. This was the only practical result of Lord Randolph Churchill's secret mission to Russia.

The splendid balls, receptions, dinners and parties with which Russian Court and society had lavishly entertained the Churchills ended with a real triumph. Lady Morier, the British ambassador's wife, opened the gates of the embassy to eight hundred guests to bid farewell to Lord and Lady Randolph. Sir Robert, the host, who danced the first waltz with Lady Randolph, whispered into her ear that he had postponed another official mission, this time to attend the maneuvers in the Crimea, in order to spend her last Russian evening with her . . . and, of course, with Lord Randolph. At the age of thirty-eight, which she had now reached, she had listened to a good many whispered confessions, but none that had amused her as much.

"I could simply not have let you go without having had you in my house," Lady Morier assured Randolph, giving him a long look. "You make me quite dizzy," Randolph replied, a little too bluntly. But he spoke the truth. Every polka-mazurka made him dizzy.

Grand Dukes and Princes, courtiers, ladies-in-waiting, all the beauty, wealth and power of Imperial St. Petersburg had gathered to honor the Churchills in the British Embassy. At the end of the great evening, the orchestra played the Tsar's anthem. Randolph murmured, "Do you think Salisbury has authorized this ball?" The orchestra ended up in the grand finale: *God save the Queen*. "How could it be otherwise?" he read from her lips.

Their Majesties, the Queen, the Tsar and the Tsarina, were toasted. Obeying the Russian custom, Lady Randolph smashed her glass against a mirror. Then she asked her hostess for a cup of tea.

In Berlin, on their first stop on the way home, it seemed already quite natural that Sir Edward Malet, the British ambassador, came to the station and invited the Churchills to his house. Lady Ermintrude, his wife, a daughter of the late Duke of Bedford, and an old friend of Jeanette's, showed undisguised curiosity about the ball in the St. Petersburg embassy, and regretted that the dinner party she would herself give in honor of the Churchills would have to be on a much more modest scale. But the court in Berlin was positively ascetic in comparison with all she heard about the doings in the Winter Palace. However, whereas the Moriers had only discovered the hospitable spot in their hearts after Lord and Lady Randolph had conquered the capital for themselves, Sir Edward and Lady Malet showed no hesitation in immediately sponsoring the distinguished English guests. Apparently Lord Salisbury was indeed reconciled with the entirely unofficial journey he had so sharply criticized in his Foreign Office release.

Everyone that counted came to the dinner, including Princess Karl Egon Fuerstenberg, the uncrowned Queen of Berlin. One of Lady Randolph's habitually rapid friendships with women developed across the dinner table. Next morning the

Princess took her new friend to the picture gallery to show her
the latest acquisitions all Berlin was raving about: two Rubens'
and a Raphael. Lady Randolph suppressed her tears. She had
seen the pictures every night in Blenheim; Rubens' *Andromeda*
and his gigantic *Bacchanalia,* as well as the *Fornarina* by
Raphael, had hung on the wall of the dining-room, just opposite
her seat at the table.

The Churchills were bidden to a gala performance in the
opera. They were the old Emperor's personal guests in his box.
Sembrich sang in *Les Noces de Figaro.* The cast was wonderful, the orchestra perfect, far surpassing anything one could
hear in London. The only slight disturbance was the aged
Emperor's rhythmic, but not very melodious snore.

On the third day of their stay in Berlin, the Churchills were
received in the Old Castle in Potsdam. The Emperor, although more than ninety, and, as it was, in the last weeks of
his life, looked upright in his smart uniform. He recalled
Gastein, he even remembered Winston and John, and the fun
everyone had had with the children.

Suddenly a door was opened, and the Empress Augusta was
wheeled in. The old lady was dressed in youthful blue satin,
bejeweled down to her waist, her venerable head crowned with
a magnificent tiara. She was a brave, if somewhat pathetic
figure. Tirelessly she inquired after the Tsarina, whom, she
understood, "Lady Churchill" had just visited, and she asked
many questions about Queen Victoria, with whom, she understood, Lady Churchill was in such intimate contact. It was a
misunderstanding. Empress Augusta mistook Lady Randolph
for Jane Lady Churchill, a lady-in-waiting in Queen Victoria's
early youth. When the difference was discreetly alluded to,
Augusta shook her tiara-laden head. Could there, indeed, be
two Ladies Churchill?

Dinner was taken at small tables. Lady Randolph was seated
next to Prince William, soon to become Wilhelm II. He spoke
about nothing but uniforms. Yet he must have been impressed
by the beautiful foreigner. The very next day he came to tea

with her in the British embassy. There he unbosomed himself. He sharply criticized the sloppiness prevailing at his grandfather's court. "Men have to come to court balls for discipline, and women for deportment!" he bellowed. Permission to dance should only be given by Imperial order, and the privileged should rehearse the intricate step of the stately minuets, the only decent dance, for many days beforehand. Woe to those who would dance out of time. Under his rule, the Prince insisted, dancing masters would sit aloft in a gallery, recording the *faux pas* they observed, and bringing the matter to the attention of the authorities. Prince William had spoken himself into a belligerent mood. He left abruptly, clicking his heels.

Much to Randolph's regret, Bismarck was absent from Berlin. His son, Count Herbert, however, replaced him, and invited the Churchills to luncheon. To Lady Randolph he seemed a little rough and uncouth, but he won Lord Randolph's heart by remarking: "As for Mr. Gladstone, my father always says he will drag England to the lowest depths of hell."

Randolph was perfectly happy. On British embassy stationery, as if to emphasize his success, he wrote to his mother: "Here we are very comfortable. I never traveled with so much circumstance before. The Malets are most kind, and anxious to make everything very pleasant. At luncheon with Herbert Bismarck. No one else present but Herr von Pothenberg, Prince Bismarck's *chef de cabinet*. We talked very freely for a long time, and drank a great deal of beer, champagne, claret, sherry, and brandy. Herbert Bismarck is delightful, so frank and honest. . . ." He really could not understand all the spiteful talk against Germany, and particularly against Bismarck, which was going on in England, above all in the houses the Prince of Wales honored with his visits. Now Randolph derided himself for having, in his Oxford years, planned to volunteer with the French in their war against the Prussians.

Finally the Churchills made their rounds in Paris. The Marquis de Breteuil, who had accompanied them on a part of their Russian journey, did the honors. He took them to meet General Boulanger, whom he adored, and who at that time was supposed to become either dictator or President, paving the way to a monarchy, Bourbon or Bonapartist, it did not make much difference. Lady Randolph was not very much interested in the scheme. She had had her fill of French politics in her early youth. She avoided, as far as possible, the château of the Duchesse d'Uzes, where Boulanger had established his shadow-court, and clung to her friend of yore, Mrs. Ferdinand Bischoffsheim, a clever and beautiful American lady, in whose drawing-room expatriate American artists and intellectuals mingled with their French brothers in letters. The uncontested center of this circle was Paul Bourget, already one of the Forty Immortals, wearing *les palmes académiques*, happily married to a most attractive and talented woman, and adored both in France and in England, where he had spent many years.

Yet this favorite of the gods wrote Jeanette a letter, ending with the sentence: "Turgenev is right. Life is a brutal affair."

Just returning from her castle in Spain, Lady Randolph disagreed. Life was wonderful!

CHAPTER XIX *Early Autumn*

Turgenev was right. The homecomers, flushed
with success, found a chilly reception in England. On the day
they disembarked in Southampton, the august *Times* thought
it worthwhile to fill three columns of its foreign news with
rumors about Lord Randolph Churchill. Immediately his combative mood was rekindled. His first speech in the House, on
April 25th, was an attack on his own party's administration,
which, in Lord Randolph's opinion, was going back on its
promise of local self-administration for Ireland. Joe Chamberlain supported his friend, though only on technical grounds.
At this time the two were not political allies but intimate
friends. Chamberlain had just returned from the United States.
He was in great spirits, not because he had so successfully
managed the Canadian Fishery Agreement, nor because the
Americans had honored him with a truly royal welcome, but
for a much more important reason: He had met Miss Mary
E. Endicott, a descendant of one of the oldest Massachusetts
families, connected by marriage with the Putnams, Winthrops,
Lawrences, Parkers, Gardners, in fact with the entire New
England patriarchy. She had deeply impressed him at their
first meeting, when she accompanied her father to the reception in the White House given in honor of the English envoy
extraordinary. Five years previously Judge Endicott had been
a most conciliatory member of the Round Table Conference in

London. His daughter was not only beautiful; what counted more, she proved to be informed on every single detail of this historic conference. Mr. Chamberlain was spellbound. Immediately he resolved to abandon his long and sad widowerhood. Next day he appeared in the Endicotts' house with quantities of red roses, instead of the famous orchid in his buttonhole. Mary accepted him. But the wedding had to be postponed for more than half a year. The Irish vote at the impending American elections must not be antagonized by an American politician's daughter marrying an English statesman. Judge Endicott held a key position in Washington. Hence Mary's engagement had to remain a secret.

No secrets, however, could be kept from Lady Randolph. The touch of the mother confessor she had acquired in years of marriage and family life, invited revelations. Mr. Chamberlain had scarcely been half an hour Lady Randolph's guest when, shyly and proudly, he took Mary's photograph out of his breast-pocket.

A pleasant luncheon followed, celebrating the next Anglo-American union. The trifling affair of Randolph's candidacy in Birmingham, casually mentioned by the hostess, did not disturb the harmony. To be sure, Birmingham was the happy fiancé's own territory. There he was the boss with absolute, dictatorial power. But if his friend Randolph was, indeed, hankering for a great industrial constituency, why, Birmingham, after all, had five boroughs. One of them, at least, should go to Tory Democracy. Lord and Lady Randolph, as it was, had done yeoman work at the last election in the much-contested city. Randolph's failure had only been a near miss.

The boss of Birmingham had no objections. He even promised his support across party lines. The matter was quickly settled. Conversation reverted to the multiple charms of Miss Mary Endicott.

Not all American marriages in Lady Randolph's intimate circle, however, were equally promising. A few weeks after the

Churchills' return from their continental trip, Randolph's elder
brother betook himself to New York to marry Lillian, the
widowed Mrs. Hammersley. In England the second marriage
of the divorced duke would have attracted unpleasant publicity.
The ceremony had to take place in America. Mayor Hewitt
performed the civil marriage in New York's City Hall. A
Baptist clergyman repeated the performance in church.

The English peerage and high society, however, refused to
recognize the union. Queen Victoria declined the lady an audience. Moreover, the well-connected and highly influential divorced wife of the Duke barred her "illegal successor" access
to all the great houses.

Lady Randolph was in a quandary. She could and would not
snub an American woman from a distinguished family the Jeromes had known so well. On the other hand she could not
expose herself and her husband to a second ostracism, again on
account of the incorrigible brother-in-law. The eight terrible
years still weighed too heavily on her mind. In the midst of
the general confusion she did once more the right thing. She
threw herself on Queen Victoria's mercy. First the aged Queen
seemed entirely deaf to pleading. Lady Randolph shed tears.
She rarely used this last, desperate weapon, but when she did
it never miscarried. "Very well," the Queen consented hesi-
tatingly. "Bring the lady to a drawing-room."

The Duchess of Marlborough was brought, and, after many
hours of waiting, presented. The Queen nodded silently. She
did not extend her hand. The newly imported Duchess suffered
a nervous collapse. She took the next boat to New York, and
spent most of the following years traveling, both in America
and on the European continent. In the meantime, Blenheim,
which she scarcely saw for four years to come, was repaired
from cellar to roof with the money the late Mr. Louis C. Hammersley had left her.

In November, 1888, trouble arose about Suaking. The
chronic skirmishing and raiding around that pestilential Red
Sea port developed into serious fighting. It was a welcome

opportunity for Randolph to get himself once more into hot water. As if he had completely forgotten his own conquest of Burma, he now vehemently assailed the Conservative government who felt obliged to restore peace in the troubled area. "The idea of risking the life of a single British soldier in that part of the world is inexpressibly repugnant to me!" he thundered in a voice that no longer carried so well. Perhaps he was far ahead of his time. But the Conservatives only heard the applause from the opposition benches for a man who was, at least formally, still aligned with the Tory camp. A new wave of disapproval was unloosed. Lord Randolph Churchill was talking his neck into the noose.

He was now entirely out of joint with his party. He stood almost alone in the House of Commons. All the orthodox and official forces were hostile to him. Twice within the last few months—in the matter of Irish Local Administration as well as in the Suaking affair—he had directly provoked Lord Salisbury. It really seemed as if his wife were his last supporter. Lady Randolph was not downhearted. She could not allow herself, or him, to yield. She was perfectly aware that her husband's political defeat would mean his physical end. Personally, she no longer cared much about politics. It was too thankless a task. There were, thank God, other things in life. But not for him. Women can adapt themselves to all conditions. Particularly women with such a wide range of interests as this cultivated American Englishwoman had developed. But men are singleminded. She must, she decided against her own inclination, but spurred by her unending devotion, keep him in the fight.

The great opportunity came on March 27, 1889. On that day Mr. Bright, long holder of a seat in Birmingham, who still at the last elections had beaten Lord Randolph, passed away. Now or never was the chance for Randolph to entrench himself once more with the masses of the English people and to exchange his safe seat in politically unimportant, traditionally conservative Paddington against a victory in Birmingham, the capital of hardware, one of the young, great industrial cities in which a new England was in the making. It could be but victory, since Chamberlain was to support the candidature.

To everyone in the Midlands Randolph's election was a foregone conclusion. The Conservatives in Birmingham, a strong group, heartily fed up with their constant exclusion from local power, welcomed him jubilantly when he came to contest the town. His first visit was, of course, to Joe, the old friend. But Randolph met a different Chamberlain. The great man, happily married for a few months and no longer putting aside his political interests for the pleasure of showing Mary's photograph, had no more use for a potentially dangerous competitor moving into his own stronghold. He would not have minded letting any insignificant Conservative back-bencher have a go at one of the boroughs. But Lord Randolph Churchill in Birmingham would not mean simply a Conservative seat; it would imply a sharing of power. Mr. Joseph Chamberlain shrugged. He did not remember any compact.

The conflict had to be fought out. A few days of high tension followed during which Randolph was encouraged from every side to plunge into the fight. A Conservative delegation from the district called upon him in the House of Commons to ask his permission to nominate him formally. He begged a friend to receive the gentlemen, and keep them waiting. He would be back in half an hour. Actually, he was back in ten minutes. "I just spoke once more with Chamberlain," he said. "We agreed to leave the decision to a three-man committee." The three men were Sir Michael Hicks-Beach, a Conservative cabinet member, Lord Hartington, who would not let himself get into trouble, and Chamberlain himself. Their decision was in the negative, as was to be expected. Surprising his followers, and, it appeared, letting them down a second time, Randolph yielded to the decision. He addressed a letter to the Conservative voters of Birmingham, excusing himself for not standing. This letter only increased the general wrath. Again he was the quitter and the deserter. No one understood that there was simply no more fight left in the ailing man.

At first, even Jeanette did not understand it. On the day Randolph returned from Westminster and informed her of the pressure brought to bear upon him by the three-man committee, and that he had given in, she accused him of showing the white feather for the first time in his life. The following five minutes were the only clash that ever threatened to disrupt their marriage. To her this was his second resignation. He had made a secret of his plans, just as when he had blundered in frivolously and petulantly throwing away his office. It was an entirely different case, he insisted. This time he was only abiding by the opinions of the leaders of both parties. "But not when those leaders are your political enemies!" she raged.

Slowly, his head sank. He was completely exhausted.

She threw herself into his arms. "Don't!" she cried. "Come, we'll go out to dinner! Come, we'll laugh about this fellow Chamberlain! He doesn't deserve anything better. Come with me!"

He came with her. That night she did most of the talking. After all, he still had Paddington, his safe seat. Perhaps it was a blessing in disguise that he would not have to exert himself in Birmingham. She shuddered, she admitted, when she thought of campaigning in these slums once more. "After all, we are no longer children."

No, they were no longer children. They were husband and wife, and many years of life in common, every minute spent in high tension, lay behind them. Indeed, the day before had been the fifteenth anniversary of their wedding. Both had forgotten it. These last days had been hectic, and they were just a little fatigued. They still loved one another. Yet for a while they felt something like a slight estrangement.

Paddington did not prove as amenable as had been taken for granted. Lord Randolph's aberration to Birmingham gave the local Radicals an excellent opportunity. Churchill's opponents, Alderman William Lawrence and J. E. Hilary Skinner, advertised on posters: "Citizens of Paddington! Don't allow your borough to become a refuge for a political traducer! Will you vote for a lord? Say no, and vote for Lawrence!"

But Paddington voted for a lady. Again she spoke at public meetings, visited every available voter in his house, attended faithfully the Working Men's Club, whose endless business proceedings and "smoking concerts" she had to sit out. She took part in the discussions in the Town Hall, and had to discard, for the duration of the campaign, all her new, pretty spring dresses. She had to be appealing to the plain people, not chic for the smart set. That was bad enough.

Worse was the support she once more got from her mother-in-law. The old Duchess could, of course, neither fail nor falter, but she could still less adapt herself to the new language and manners in the period of England's social transition. Her supreme argument still sounded: "His lordship would appreciate, indeed..." and "Personally, I would not withhold my sympathy from the faithful people who ..."

Jeanette tried desperately to induce Her Grace to accept the language of the new age. She failed completely. The overdue mother-in-law versus daughter-in-law conflict, which Jeanette had skillfully avoided thus far, seemed inevitable. "I know London better and longer than you, I dare say," the Duchess insisted pointedly. Jeanette ignored the allusion to her New York descent. Mr. Smith and Mr. Jones were all that counted for the moment. In her imperturbable determination she won an overwhelming victory for her husband, who had all but sat out the campaign. The influence of the Primrose League had helped considerably. The anniversary of Lord Beaconsfield's death occurred, fortunately, during the last days of Lady Randolph's campaigning. His memory was still lingering on in the English mind. No man could transform this asset more powerfully into political energy than Lady Randolph did in conjuring up the spirit of the fatherly friend. But her own play made her feel uneasy. She felt ashamed of having to drag a dead man into the game of vote-getting. It would be her last contribution of this sort, she firmly made up her mind.

When the election was over, Randolph wanted to leave immediately—anywhere. Once more he proved his astounding mixture of fiery fighter and congenital escapist. But a surprising invitation to one of the political gatherings at Arlington Street delayed his departure. What did Lord Salisbury intend by this invitation? Did it indicate his wish for reconciliation? The Churchills took the chance. They visited Arlington Street. Nothing happened. Lord Salisbury had simply made one of his polite gestures. Mr. Jenkins, Randolph's last faithful follower, who, during his years in America had learned to call a spade a spade, took up the matter with the Prime Minister. Salisbury seemed not quite to understand what Jenkins was talking about. He felt not the slightest rancor against Randolph. In a week, there would be a state dinner in his house, and he would ask the Churchills again. They came once more, and once more, except for a bare greeting, neither Lord nor Lady Salisbury exchanged a word with Randolph.

It was a mystery. But was it an intended slight? A few days later a third invitation arrived. This time the letter was addressed to Lady Randolph. It read: "My dear Lady Randolph: Will you and Lord Randolph come here to dine and sleep on Sunday the 22nd, and help us receive the Irish delegates on Monday? We shall be much pleased if you will come. No Sunday trains are good, but the best leaves King's Cross at 1 P.M. or 6:30 P.M. We will meet either. Yours very truly, G. Salisbury."

Randolph observed with a grin that his usefulness, evidently, was not quite exhausted. When the Irish were to be tackled, Her Majesty's government still needed him. Moreover, a public garden party at Hatfield House was announced for Monday, and Lord Randolph Churchill was to be after the Prime Minister, the principal speaker. He had a great chance to re-establish himself. Or an opportunity for mischiefmaking.

He chose the latter alternative. On Sunday at half-past twelve his wife reminded him that it was high time to change into traveling clothes. He wrapped himself tighter in his dressing-gown, and refused to go at all. "You go alone. You will represent us with more dignity."

In vain she pleaded with him. In vain she talked common sense. In vain she beseeched him not to leave her alone. He was simply not in the mood. He had twice been fooled into accepting Salisbury's nauseating invitations. Now the laugh would be on the old man. Jeanette took the train alone. She got into the carriage Lord Salisbury had sent to the station. She was shivering in the mellow spring sun. She felt no longer able to bear it. She would entirely abandon politics, she decided.

Slowly, with magnificent poise, radiating her most enchanting smile, she mounted the staircase of the Elizabethan castle as if she had not a care in the world. But her smile froze on her face when looks of blank dismay and a general ominous silence answered her feeble excuses for Randolph's absence.

It took Lord Salisbury a minute or two to recover from the shock. Nevertheless he invited Lady Randolph to sit at his side. He chatted with her throughout dinner. They talked about books, races, and the play. She had never a chance to switch the talk to Randolph. The versed old debater made it impossible to bring up the subject. Victorian society did not discuss awkward topics. Only domestics, the saying went, speak about people; gentlefolk discuss ideas.

The masses of people, however, brought on Monday morning in special trains from London, were not entirely composed of gentlefolk. Everywhere the cry for Randolph went up. Many people had traveled half over England to hear him. The large Irish delegation saw themselves deprived of the only English statesman they enjoyed listening to. They were disappointed to miss him. He had failed to come without any reasonable excuse. Was he really a quitter? Many people, it is true, had long called him a deserter. Lady Randolph wanted to excuse his conduct. But on second thought she suppressed the urge. It would only make the rift more noticeable if she gave any explanation whatsoever.

Unheeded, she slipped away. She had never felt as uncomfortable, she recalled many years later, or experienced anything more disagreeable.

Randolph, obviously conscience-stricken, did not even ask her how matters had gone. Plainly with the intention of reconciling her he surprised her with good news. He had made up his mind to buy the little black mare by "Trappist" out of "Festive" that had so impressed her at first sight. He would, by Jove, risk the investment, although it was not easy to part with three hundred pounds.

It was an excellent idea, she said, though the purchase of a horse could offer little solace in the grave crisis. But Lady Randolph, anxious about her husband, did not wish to discourage him. They went to the Doncaster sales, where the beautiful, if minute mare was purchased. Jeanette was just reading Renan's *Abesse de Jouarre*, so this became the animal's name. Looking at his acquisition, Randolph was still skeptical. His wife, imbued with the horse sense of the Jeromes, assured him that the gallant little thing's heart was bigger than her body.

Against the advice of the trainer, L'Abesse de Jouarre was a starter for the Manchester Cup. Her owners did not watch her. Randolph was off for another fishing expedition in Norway, Jeanette, nursing no grudge against England, was visiting friends at a country house along the Thames. Both were stunned by the news from Manchester. L'Abesse de Jouarre had won triumphantly. Her backers got twenty to one. Lord Randolph himself had won a considerable sum. Subsequently L'Abesse won the May Plate at Newmarket and the Two-year-old Plate at Pontefract. A year later she was victorious in the Prince of Wales handicap at Sandown, second for both the Liverpool Cup and the Gold Vase at Ascot, and winner of the Portland Plate at Doncaster. Finally she was sold for seven thousand pounds. The Jerome horse sense was brilliantly vindicated.

Other horses who carried off turf prizes for Randolph's colors —"chocolate, pink sleeves and cap"—were Abbé Morin, Blue Peter, Inverness, Trapezoid, Sea Urchin, and Larkaway. He was so successful that Colonel North, the Nitrate King, one of

the richest men of the day, entrusted him with the management
of his own stable. Randolph's management was unorthodox.
It depended on his wife's equestrian instinct, and on his own
dreams. He was, like most Victorians, rather superstitious. One
night in Doncaster, he had a pleasant, and, it proved, highly
profitable dream. He saw a number hoisted. On consulting his
card the next day he found that only one horse running had
such a high number. Inquiries led him to believe that this horse
had a much better chance than the odds against it suggested.
He backed it heavily, although his trainer again warned him,
and scored once more.

Such strokes of good luck reconciled Randolph a little with
the world in which there was no place for him because he
wanted too large a share. Since the gulf between him and Lord
Salisbury seemed unbridgable, he cultivated, under Jeanette's
soothing influence, pleasant relations with politicians of every
shade. In spite of violently attacking the great old man in the
House, he had always retained friendly personal intercourse
with Mr. Gladstone. Now Lord Randolph appeared frequently
in his sister's, Lady Tweedmouth's house—her husband had been
chief-secretary in Gladstone's cabinet—to meet the old giant
from Hawarden more often than he had ever done before. He
treated the grand old veteran with the utmost deference; each
appeared to derive much pleasure from the other's company.
"Randolph was the most courtly man I ever met," Gladstone said
in later years to his friend Mr. Morley. "And that is the man
you have left?" Lord Randolph, in turn, questioned a Union
Liberal dissenter, to whose apostasy he himself had actively
contributed. "How could you have done it?"

The Churchills, politically in retirement, were now frequent
guests in some of the most pleasant and distinguished English
country houses. Their favorite week end haunt was Waffeston
Manor, a Gallic château on the model of Fontainebleau, in
which Baron Ferdinand de Rothschild received the cream of
society. The Edwardian days of perfect tolerance were ap-

proaching. Racial or religious prejudice was considered vulgar. The Primrose League gladly accepted the support of great financial dynasties. Mr. Lionel Cohen was co-opted into the ruling body; Lady Randolph had introduced him and promoted his election. The Prince of Wales himself brought Baron Hirsch, the millionaire and philanthropist, to Waffeston Manor, where they formed a happy group with Sir William Harcourt and Sir William Gregory, both old Victorians of the deepest dye, scholars and men of the world, statesmen, diplomats and literati. Lady Randolph was in her element. When they moved for a short time to Brighton, where they took a suite of rooms in the Orleans Club, with windows on the sea, and the fresh air definitely invigorated Randolph, she found family life very much more pleasant than the life in politics she was about to abandon for good. And to make the happiness complete, Winston joined his parents.

He was still a worried and troubled boy, and he stood badly in need of a little parental care. He had twice failed to pass the examination into Sandhurst. The pedantry of the public school did not agree with him. When they told him that Mr. Gladstone used to read Homer for fun, the boy, whose taste for the man of Midlothian was entirely spoiled by his father's attacks on him, had only one answer: Serves him right. Lord Randolph shook his head. He had himself been anything but a promising pupil. "Neither a wet bob nor a dry bob," he had been called in Eton slang. And now, looking back ever more frequently on his youth, as he felt his premature end approaching, he confessed that the time and money expended on his school and college career could not strictly be called a remunerative investment. But in the autumn of his life he somehow discovered the attraction of Greek wisdom. He wanted to read Aristotle's *Politics* in the original, and in fact he sat down, in spite of turf and society, and hammered Greek grammar into his own head. Soon he could read Aristotle. His boy could not. Lord Randolph regretted it. A few years later, Winston himself regretted it, too. But then he had no time to think of the classics. He had been removed from Harrow, and was tucked away, a forlorn hope, in the school of a "crammer." Captain James kept an establishment in the Cromwell Road which specialized in preparing for Sandhurst. The Captain, Winston remarked, was like one of those people who have a sure system for breaking the bank at Monte Carlo, with the important difference that in a majority of cases his system produced success. Winston did better, and he was allowed into his parents' company. Now he was occasionally present at Lady Randolph's receptions. He had lunch with peers and ambassadors, and his interest in the world grew.

Lord Randolph, under his wife's unfaltering guidance, was a man of the world again. He was at his best when, on the twenty-sixth of July, he defended in the Commons the Prince of Wales' right to a civil list for his newborn son which was questioned by some radical M.P.'s. As if he had never suffered the eight terrible years, he eulogized the Prince, convincing the House that the costs of British royalty were much lower than the expenses of most other monarchies and some great republics and how much better were these things ordered in England! The House, irrespective of party divisions, cheered. More important to Jeanette, her husband was "respectable" again. But that was the very impression he hated to make. Her happiness lasted only two days. On July 28, 1889, Randolph delivered two speeches in the Midlands, tearing to pieces the Conservative government to whom he still owed formal allegiance, and developing for himself a progressive program that outdid Gladstone at his wildest. The political world was speechless. Only Chamberlain, the ex-arch-radical just discovering Imperialism, wrote Randolph a short letter: "If that is what you call Toryism . . ." it ended.

Was all this mischief her fault? Jeanette pondered. Was it a punishment for the quiet months she had just enjoyed? Why had Randolph again got so entirely out of control? Should she resume the daily work of supervising, discreetly, but determinedly, his every word? The Ladies' Gallery had no more much attraction for her, since her husband had lost the Leadership of the House. It was no pleasure to see him crouching on his modest bench below the gangway, still respected, but, indeed, avoided by most other members. Her remote control might do him good, she decided. It might give him a feeling of security. On March 11, 1890, in her fortieth year, looking barely thirty and feeling a hundred, Lady Randolph drove again to Westminster.

The House was packed. Lord Randolph was to speak on the Parnell case. The topic—the *Times* had published a Dublin report linking Parnell with the outrageous Phoenix Park murders—and the speaker—the fallen star emerging from his self-chosen retirement—were equally arresting. Lord Randolph was heard in a strained, unusual silence, which seemed to affect him, too. He began to speak with a strange slowness, deliberation, and absence of passion. Jeanette's heart was heavy with apprehension. It was the lull before the storm.

Continuing in the same even, passionless voice, yet tense with explosiveness, he examined the merits of the case. The House listened with undiminished attention, the ministerialists with growing but controlled resentment.

Parnell, a man guilty of many political acts of violence and uproar, had, nevertheless, no connection with the Phoenix Park murders. Slowly Randolph's voice rose. The accusation against the Irish leader was libel. Then came a pause. Lord Randolph appeared perfectly composed. Only one woman in the Ladies' Gallery could discern how he paled, and how hard his right fist was pressed into the palm of his left hand. Quietly he asked those about him for a glass of water. No one stirred. Believing that he had not been heard, he asked again. But the front-benchers hated him in this electricity-charged moment with such bitter partisan passion that even this small courtesy was refused him. How she managed to suppress her outcry, Lady Randolph never understood. She knew how his lips were burning. And there she sat, and could only look, and look, and look around. Whether young Mr. Baumann, the Conservative back-bencher, caught her despairing glance, or whether he understood the situation—he got up from his seat below the gangway and brought a glass of water. As he returned, the Irish members greeted the savior with a half-sympathetic, half-ironical cheer. Lord Randolph, grasping the glass, said solemnly: "I hope this will not compromise you with your party!"

Now he began to speak louder. He violently assailed the unconstitutional measures the government, in his opinion, had adopted in inquiring into the case. His voice dropped and, in a fierce whisper, he named the forger of the documents incriminating Parnell. "Pigott! ..." his words became unintelligible. Only the repeated cry: "The bloody, rotten, ghastly, foetus, the foetus Pigott, Pigott, Pigott..." was clearly audible. Each time he called the name, his trembling fingers pointed at the government bench. Honorable members had the impression that he was accusing the government of having called the forger Pigott into existence.

This was, of course, by no means so. Pigott, a lone wolf, committed suicide by shooting himself in the heart. The *Times*, which had published the forged documents, was gravely compromised. It filtered out that Mr. Buckle, the editor, had only printed them under pressure from general-manager Mr. MacDonald.

Randolph's speech, however, raised a furious outcry against him. The entire Conservative press denounced him as a traitor. The party's official mouthpiece, the *Standard*, declared he had no further right to be regarded as a party member. Even his own last followers deserted him now. On the next day he was to have addressed a meeting at Colchester. It was cancelled "owing to the sudden illness of Lord Brooke" who was to have taken the chair. The chairman of his own association in Paddington resigned; the various Conservative clubs in the borough passed strong resolutions condemning their member. Opinion in Birmingham was very hostile. The worst loss was Mr. Jennings, his last faithful friend in the House. In a sharp speech he entirely disassociated himself from Lord Randolph

Churchill, rightly fearing that he otherwise would be linked
with the outrageous behavior of the man, as whose lieutenant
he was known. But the very honorable Mr. Jenkins, who in
New York City had taken on all Tammany single-handed and
successfully, could not bear the breach with Randolph. Although only fifty-six years of age, and apparently in good
health, he died of heart failure a few months after the breach.

In the meantime, Lady Randolph had taken her husband
back to Newmarket, where he spent much of his time in the
Jockey Club. It was again the moment to leave. He stood badly
in need of fresh air, some leisure, and complete rest from politics. Mr. Harry Tyrwhitt, his old traveling companion, had leased
a *dahabeah,* "Ammon Rah," at Edfu, sixty miles south of Luxor,
on the Nile. Lord Randolph joined him after a preliminary
detour to Monte Carlo. His first lines from there to Jeanette,
dated November 25, 1890, read: "So today is the meeting of
Parliament. How thankful I am not to be going down to the
House!..." The rest of the Monte Carlo report was full of
speculations whether Parliament would be dissolved in the
spring, and reflected grim satisfaction that Lord S. would now
have to be guided by "a bird in the hand."

Lady Randolph kept him dutifully posted about Gladstone,
Parnell, and the possibilities of the dissolution of the Commons.
He replied that he was enjoying his desert domicile very much.
He thrived on good food, Hochheimer hock, champagne, Pil-
sener beer, Marquis chocolate, ripe bananas, fresh dates, and
literally hundreds of French novels. He played piquet at a
penny a point. Yet this scoundrel Harry had beggared him last
evening by beating him over ten thousand points. Under such
happy circumstances his interest in English news and newspapers was negligible.

In some ways, his stay in Egypt, short as it was, proved
really a blessing—the last blessing Lord Randolph Churchill
was to enjoy. His final letter from the *dahabeah,* dated January
3, 1891, reads as if he had already crossed the bridge. Eternal
Egypt, it appears, made him understand the pettiness and fu-

tility of the struggle in which he had already wasted most of his life.

Now he wrote home: "In such a frame of mind, embracing a period of ten thousand years, your home politics, your House of Commons interests, the eloquence of Smith, the courage of Balfour, the honesty of Hartington, the financial genius of Goschen and the adroitness of Joe, all acted upon, stimulated and developed by the lax morals of Parnell, present themselves to my mental optics in the same manner as fleas may attract the notice of an elephant. I am living with Rameses, Thotmes and Seti, and I have despised the Ptolemies as parvenus, and Cleopatra as a ——! Imagine therefore how infinitely little becomes of the struggle of the Kilkenny factions, the senile drivelings of Mr. Gladstone on Ravenswood, which you think worthy of mention, the remorse of the officeless Harcourt, or the doubting gloom of Morley. . . . This heavenly climate tames the most ferocious gout, and tranquillizes the most irritated nerves. I do not think I have ever experienced so pleasant a time as during the last three weeks. I have arrived at the condition of a true philosopher; nerves calm, health good, everything to please the eye and the mind. The past affords matter for agreeable reflection. The future appears without vexation. I please myself with the imagination that if I were to die tomorrow, I should have experienced and exhausted, prudently abandoning before satiation, every form of human excitement."

He returned, a quiet, thoughtful, resigned man, who, in reflecting on the origins of human kind, had discovered the meaninglessness of that short gallop through life, and was quite ready to go.

Strangely, or perhaps by providential dispensation, he met a man in exactly the same mood as himself, a man he had known for many years and had always admired, but whom he came fully to understand only now, as both stood on the threshold of eternity. Leonard Jerome had come to England. For good, he affirmed with an engaging, slightly conscious smile. The Coney Island Jockey Club was now firmly established. His last job was done. He would, incidentally, remain the Club's president, even as an absentee. The doctors had advised him that the temperate English climate would be better for his gout and rheumatism than the changeable American temperatures. Also his old heart wanted a little rest and care. Above all, why shouldn't he be where his family was? Hadn't he a right to see his grandchildren?

Winston was fascinated by his American grandfather. Many years later he recalled him as a magnificent-looking man with long, flowing mustachios, a rather aquiline nose, and still very bright eyes. The fact that Grandfather's back was bent and his shoulders stooped escaped, it appears, the boy's admiration. So strong was the spell of the eternal clubman and horse-lover even in his last months.

The whole family assembled around him. Clarissa came from Paris. "Now we will never part," she said. She had matured into a perfect French grandmère, whose salon, although only open to old friends, was still much coveted. Jennie's two married sisters kept their father constant company: Mrs. Moreton Frewen, the wife of an English Parliamentarian whose ancestors had for centuries played distinguished roles on British politics. She had a baby. Mr. Jerome delighted in rocking little Clare, later to become sculptress Clare Sheridan, on his knees. His third daughter was happily married to Sir John Leslie. Her son became the poet, novelist, and scholar Shane Leslie. Lady Leslie, residing at Glaslough, County Monaghan, Ireland, is the only one of the three beautiful Jerome girls still alive. She is Winston Churchill's favorite aunt.

Lady Randolph was Jennie again. She found deep satisfaction in watching the two men, her father and her husband. Both spoke about politics as a matter of the complete past. Yet they outdid one another in expressing strong opinions on contemporary events. Both were agreed that chess was the only intelligent pastime. Their love of horses was another bond between them. The question whether Kentucky or L'Abesse de Jouarre had been the greatest racer of all time was discreetly avoided. Lady Randolph had been hoisted on both. That was all that mattered. Then her happiness was complete. She was the living link between father, husband, and son. She was proud of being a woman.

Leonard Jerome's health improved considerably when he moved to Brighton. He took a suite of rooms with windows overlooking the Channel in the Lion Mansions, the fashionable boarding house. The beautiful February weather on the English seacoast was conducive to his recovery. He had never experienced such a mild winter. It was a case of dying in beauty. Dr. Chipmell attended his patient daily. On the night of March the third the faithful doctor refused to go home. "He speaks too much," he argued smiling. "He needs a watchdog." The doctor settled down in his shirtsleeves, as Leonard Jerome went to bed. He did not feel any worse. It was only that his heart was causing him a little trouble. But it would soon be over, Jerome murmured confidently. Very soon, the doctor thought. At three o'clock in the morning he pronounced his patient dead. He had breathed peacefully until a quarter to three. He died painlessly.

Leonard Jerome's body was embalmed and taken to London. The burial was at Greenwood. Randolph, attending it, lowered his head, and murmured a prayer. Then he smiled at his wife: "I'm next!"

"No!" she cried, determined still in her heartbreaking grief. "I will not have it!"

CHAPTER XX *Farewell to Politics*

Whether it was actually the impact of Egypt's majestic timelessness that mellowed and matured Lord Randolph, or whether the man now reaching forty saw the light, and needed an explanation for his conversion—the fact remains that he was from then on a calmer, quieter, and a better man. In spite of his differences with the party, and the dislike and distrust that still surrounded him in his own camp, he became a loyal and regular supporter of the government. He spoke rarely in the Commons, but always with a moderation that appeared strange in the mouth of the veteran stormy petrel. "Born and bred in the Conservative Party," he wrote in the spring of 1891, "I could never join the ranks of their opponents." He had reached the height of his intellectual power, enhanced now by wise self-restraint. Since he deliberately no longer used acrimonious words, the house gradually forgave him the excesses of his earlier years.

His next journey, on which he embarked in the summer of 1891, was neither flight nor escape. Although he pretended to go to South Africa primarily for lion-hunting, a new excitement and one of the few he had not yet tasted, he actually went as a gold-digger. Well aware of his slender life expectation, he was concerned about the future of his wife and his boys; Winston, particularly, would never be able to eke out even a miserable existence on his own.

The journey was elaborately organized. It included a trip into Mashonaland, then almost unexplored country, inhabited by the wild tribe of the Matabele. Major Gilles, a leading expert on the dark continent, was entrusted with the command of the small expedition. Hans Lee, one of the best-known hunters in South Africa, was engaged to do the shooting; Mr. Perkins, an expert mining engineer, was to search for gold. Despite the high expenses the journey involved, the enterprise was to be self-supporting. For the first and last time Lord Randolph banked on his name, after Mr. Gladstone's still the most popular with the English masses. Inspired by a pathetic, forcibly acquired sense for business, he refused the distinguished *Daily Telegraph's* more modest offer, and accepted instead the tabloid *Daily Graphic's* contract for twenty letters of four thousand words, each letter at a hundred pounds.

"Randy Pandy" as a tabloid writer was the answer to the prayers of the London cartoonists and gossip writers. The music halls burlesqued him, and the *Gaiety* stage produced such pointed songs that the Lord Chamberlain had to intervene.

Lord Randolph cared little. He set out for the vast solitudes of darkest Africa. He was entirely oblivious of the world he had left behind. A wild beard grew on his cheeks and covered his chin; it was almost entirely gray, but he did not mind that either. The days of vanity were over. He had to discharge a task, perhaps his last one. The investments he actually made in South Africa were careful and well judged. They were sold after his death for over seventy thousand pounds.

The spiteful paragraphs, the lampoons and caricatures with which the professional wiseacres of London, the London of the incipient Gay Nineties, followed her husband's sober and purposeful journey, drove Lady Randolph out of town. Since she had no longer to act as Randolph's political listening-post, she accepted an invitation to join the hunting party Baron Hirsch, the Jewish philanthropist, gave at his enormous estate, St. Johann, in his native Hungary. The Prince and the Princess of

Wales were of the party, as were Lord de Grey and his wife, the famous hostess, Lord Ashburton, and many other prominent London society lights.

Life at St. Johann was simple and healthy. Lady Randolph needed, and thoroughly enjoyed, the relaxation after the depressing times that lay behind her. Not even the torrential showers of rain that frequently "baptized" Baron Hirsch and his guests disturbed her. Indeed, she loved the rain. It was part of her love for England. Perhaps also by temperament she needed an occasional shower.

Returning from St. Johann, she stopped for a few days in Vienna. Colonel Kodolitch, once Austro-Hungarian military attaché in London, had invited her to review his Hungarian regiment. She regretted that Winston was not present. How the boy would have enjoyed the maneuvers that were displayed in her honor, and the charges *en masse* of hurdles and fences. She had the sense, and she felt the thrill, of cavalry in action.

After the review, Colonel Kodolitch and his staff squired Lady Randolph to the railroad station. "Please," whispered the Colonel, "say *Ich danke sehr* in leaving my officers."

The gentlemen lined up. "*Ich danke sehr!*" said Lady Randolph in her best German. The Hussar officers still grinned with pleasure when her train was already in Amstetten, the next stop. "*Ich danke sehr*" was the traditional salute with which Franz-Josef I dismissed the general staff after the Imperial Maneuvers. "*Du bist die Kaiserin meines Herzens....*" (You are the Empress of my heart) the Hussar officers hummed unanimously.

Hunting on Hungarian estates and reviewing red-coated Hussars, however, did not satisfy Lady Randolph any longer. The recuperation which she was so much in need of had to come from inside. It was then that the musical dilettante became the serious lover of music. She used her husband's absence to pay her first, to her unforgettable, visit to Bayreuth.

In England Wagner's music was not yet popular. The *Ring*

der Nibelungen, although a few years previously a great success in New York, had not yet reached London at all. The average opera-goer seemed proud if he could sit through *Lohengrin.* To most English people, Lady Randolph observed, *Die Meistersinger* or *Tristan und Isolde* was a concatenation of discordant sounds. At a performance of *Tristan,* indeed, she heard the lady next to her pitying Isolde for her "long wait" for Tristan in the third act, whereas, in point of fact, Van Dyck—a fat tenor, whom one could well have taken for a woman, lying on the stage, covered with a rug—had been singing for more than half an hour. On another occasion she was highly amused by the reaction of a couple next to her when, at a *Lohengrin* performance, the violins opened the overture with the long sustained note in A. "What is that noise?" asked the woman. "The gas is escaping," her companion hazarded.

To combat this widespread ignorance, Lady Randolph, eternal campaigner, arranged some lectures on the *Ring,* at the house of her sister, Mrs. (later Lady) Leslie. The lectures, delivered by a German professor who spoke with a terrible guttural accent, attracted, nevertheless, all the music lovers of London.

And so to Bayreuth. Music, in those days, was still predominantly a woman's affair. Lady Randolph's party consisted of six ladies, among them Mrs. Leslie, the famous Lady de Grey, and Mrs. Evan Charteris. All were rather spoiled society leaders, and great was their disappointment when they found in Bayreuth, then in its comparatively early years, a gathering of genuine music enthusiasts who were quite satisfied with what passed in Germany for middle-class comfort. The fashionable English ladies rapidly lost their taste for music when they were billeted in private houses, most of whose hosts could only accommodate a single lodger, and at that discharged this paid hospitality with notorious German thriftiness. But Lady Randolph crushed the dissatisfaction of her companions the very moment it appeared. She suppressed the incipient grumbling with the decree: "We will talk about nothing else in these days

but about the music we are going to hear or we have heard!"
She and her sister, it is true, had found accommodations in a
banker's house, where they were comfortable in comparison
with their friends' sorry fate. But it was not on account of this
lucky circumstance alone that Jeanette maintained discipline.
She was truly awe-stricken by Richard Wagner.

She could only express her first impression of *Parsifal* with
the German term: *kolossal*. Her little party had made it their
custom to meet between the acts and exchange opinions. After
Parsifal, however, the emotion Lady Randolph radiated became
so great that all six ladies dispersed in different directions,
avoiding one another until the performance ended and the long
night of talking it over began. Nothing could mar their almost
religious respect; neither the fact that Parsifal's wig came off
in the third act, during the Flower Maiden's song, nor the
agonies Lady Randolph suffered from a persistent toothache.

Finally a lady sitting behind Jeanette and observing her
pain-stricken face, inquired during the entr'acte if she felt quite
well. On hearing of the toothache, the stranger, introducing
herself as Mrs. Sam Lewis, the wife of the well-known money-
lender, produced a strong dose of cocaine, proving herself a
Good Samaritan. Mrs. Lewis, it appeared, carried her pain-
relieving dope constantly in her reticule. When Mr. Sam Lewis
joined the ladies, Lady Randolph understood why. He remarked that he and his good lady had just been in Rome. What
did he think of the Eternal City? Lady Randolph asked. "You
can 'ave Rome!" came the answer.

This was the only flaw in Lady Randolph's Bayreuth rapture.
For the rest she was delighted, at least for a week, with low
living and high thinking, a new experience to her.

With her habitual enthusiasm, she was now entirely absorbed
by music. At the Russian Embassy in London she neglected
her veteran and most faithful admirers to concentrate all her
attention on Abbé Liszt. He was a very old man at that time,
so blind that he ate his asparagus by the wrong end, until Lady
Randolph pointed out his error. "That is why it tasted so

strange!" he observed calmly. After luncheon, nothwithstanding his gouty fingers, he was prevailed upon to play the piano. "Alas," he said when the pathetic performance was over, "the worst of my pupils now plays better than I do." He was quite right, Lady Randolph observed. But his strong and characteristic face, so full of undimmed willpower, and so determined to go down with flying colors, struck a familiar note in her. Perhaps she was thinking of Randolph who was just fighting his way through the African bush. *"Permettez, mon père,"* she said, and kissed the gouty, white, old hands which had once performed miracles.

Rubenstein impressed her with his tossing long hair. Perspiration poured down his face as his big hands tore up and down the instrument. One could, evidently, be a fighter on the piano, too, she thought, and this would perhaps be her next battlefield.

But she was rather discouraged when a young, unknown pianist came to London, introduced to her by a mutual friend, and failed abysmally at the first private concert she had managed to arrange for him. She herself had been swept off her feet by his performance. The leading music critic, however, expressed the common opinion in the words: "Mr. Paderewski would be all right if he only left Chopin in peace."

Subsequently Paderewski's Chopin swayed Paris and New York. In the next season he returned to London, and had tremendous success. Lady Randolph was generally recognized as his discoverer in England.

Personally, she said, she had never been able to overcome her nervousness when she herself played before the public. She always felt her nerves giving way when a difficult passage approached. Sometimes she had to repeat such a movement three times, until the audience became quite familiar with it. In such cases, she frankly confessed, she was on the verge of jumping up from the piano, and rushing off the stage. But the fear of the scene such behavior would cause proved every time stronger. At the fourth attempt she mechanically played the right bars and brought the piece to the right conclusion.

Wisely, she finally decided not to make the piano her career. Lady Randolph's real greatness was not producing herself, but promoting others. Upon her return from Bayreuth, she set herself the task of popularizing Richard Wagner in England. As the years went by, she could reap the harvest. Toward the turn of the century no London concert could be given without one or more Wagnerian selections, and the *Ring*, which, at her insistence, the Covent Garden Opera had included in its repertoire, attracted huge crowds. The opera became ever more her obsession. Once at Covent Garden she sat in a box with Lord L—, who heartily enjoyed himself in whistling and humming the tunes. "What a bore that Jean de Reszke is!" Lady Randolph commented. "Why?" His Lordship asked. "Because his singing prevents me from hearing you properly," replied the dangerous woman.

With the exception of the nights she stayed in her mother-in-law's house at 50 Grosvenor Square, to attend the opera or concerts, she spent the winter in the comfortable estate at Bournemouth, which Lady Wimborne, one of Randolph's sisters, had lent the Churchills. Family life, after her husband's return in his reformed mood, was cheerful and pleasant. The boys were at home on a prolonged Christmas holiday. They romped on the cliffs of Bournemouth. Winston, although already eighteen, still tremendously enjoyed the game of hide-and-seek. His brother, aged twelve, and a cousin, fourteen, chased him. He was trapped as he stood on a bridge, his way blocked by an enemy at each end of the bridge. Nothing daunted, Winston jumped off the bridge and fell twenty-nine feet on to hard ground.

"He jumped over the bridge and won't speak to us," the boys reported to Lady Randolph.

Winston felt the taste of brandy on his lips, and looked into the stars: his mother's eyes. An eternity later eminent London specialists stood around his bed. They murmured something that sounded like: "A ruptured kidney . . . among other things."

For a year Lady Randolph nursed her ailing boy. Gradually this troubled time proved fruitful. While wrestling desperately for Winston's life, she could with a feeling of increasing comfort observe how father and son found their way to one another. Winston greatly admired his father. It was a red-letter day in his young life when he overheard Lord Randolph excusing his boy's poor scholarship in assuring a friend: "But he is a good 'un, a good 'un!" Such appreciation on the part of his father had so far been rare. Now it became more frequent.

In other ways, too, things once more seemed to go right. At the July elections South Paddington returned its veteran member unopposed. Lady Randolph successfully resumed social relations with the Salisburys. In the autumn a dinner of the four ensued, which passed most pleasantly and expressed full reconciliation. Soon afterwards the Duke of Marlborough gave a gay and exuberant all-American party at completely restored and resplendent Blenheim. Among her compatriots his Duchess felt at home, perhaps for the first time, on English soil. The Duchess of Manchester appeared *en grande tenue*. Mrs. Joseph Chamberlain still seemed to be a happy bride. All three Jerome sisters were present.

The Duke of Marlborough was the jolliest in the lot. It was no longer the enigmatic humor of the erratic Blandford. Now a business man of consequence both in England and the United States, his capriciousness had yielded to a light-hearted optimism. After his marriage he had invested heavily in Tennessee land, and had large interests in the steel and iron works in the Tennessee mountains. In London, he was chairman of the Coal and Light Electric Company, and a most enterprising member of the board of the Telephone Company. He was about to reorganize completely the prevailing system, an effort involving constant opposition against the monopoly the government wanted to introduce. Throughout the summer he had worked hard over a telephone scheme and other ventures in the city, without, however, forgetting his artistic interests. With his wife's dollars he bought back some of the old masters he had indiscriminately dispersed. Now he was a good customer at Christie's and at Seillère in Paris, where he acquired some famous bronzes. Besides, he had just introduced the American trotter to England, which caused the *New York Tribune* to comment: "The attempt to naturalize American trotters in England is one of the more innocent enterprises in which the Duke of Marlborough has been engaged. That nobleman has bought in Kentucky five very well-bred mares with the intention of forming a stud. Unfortunately, it is not likely that he will succeed. Trotters have not been bred in England because there are no places where they can be speeded, except for tracks specially constructed for that purpose. The soft roads prevailing in this country are over there almost unknown."

The party at Blenheim laughed heartily at this gloomy prophecy. Of course special tracks had been erected for the trotters.

It was one of the most amusing week ends Lady Randolph had enjoyed for a long time. On Sunday afternoon the Duke accompanied his guests back to London. The Churchills had already, for economy's sake, installed themselves in the Dowager Duchess' residence at 50 Grosvenor Square.

The Duke returned on Monday. All Tuesday he drove around his estate, basking in the autumnal beauty of Blenheim's parks and fields, and perhaps rejoicing a little in his solitude, since his Duchess had remained in town. Alone, and in good spirits, as the footman later testified, he ate an exquisite dinner. Then he went to bed, perfectly pleased with life.

On Wednesday, the ninth of November, he slept late, i seemed. The servant, finding his master asleep, returned a noiselessly as possible. An hour later he came a second time The Duke was still lying in bed. Cautiously the valet cleared hi throat. His Grace did not move from his strange position. H was lying on his back, his left arm thrown over his chest, an his right hand clenched above his heart, a serene smile on h face. The valet bent over his master. He was appalled by th pallor of the Duke's face. His death must have been due to heart failure, a little while earlier.

The family hurried to Blenheim. The Dowager Duchess was grief-stricken. Randolph was deeply shocked. Jeanette looked at the dead man. He had died a painless, enviable death, she thought. But an instant later her heart beat wildly. The dead man was forgotten. Randolph was on her terrified mind.

A month afterward, on the tenth of December, 1892, the doctors assembled in council in the house in Grosvenor Square shook their heads as they left the patient's room. The symptoms of vertigo, palpitation, and the numbness of his hands could no longer be explained with anything approaching optimism. Lord Randolph Churchill was a doomed victim of his progressive paralysis. "When?" asked Jeanette, holding herself upright. The doctors shrugged. "When it pleases God!"

The word sounded empty to her. God was too far away.

Lord Randolph Churchill was not yet quite ready to die. There was some more business to be transacted. He recovered, at least outwardly. The member for Paddington still visited the House when great decisions were at stake. Winston, an invalid, had been transported to London. There the boy managed to squeeze into the Distinguished Strangers' Gallery. He listened to his father's last attack on Gladstone. He was particularly carried away when Austen Chamberlain, Joe's son, delivered his maiden speech, and Lord Randolph immediately afterward got up, just to congratulate a promising orator "that must have been dear and refreshing to a father's heart." Winston, too, could speak to a father's heart. If Austen was allowed to follow in his father's footsteps, and if Mr. Gladstone's son, Herbert, helped the great old man at least in cutting down the oaks, why should he not be allowed to work for his father? Politics absorbed the boy much more than the preparation for his third attempt to pass the examination with what he later called a "modified" success, but he could never fulfill the wish of his heart: to become his father's assistant. It was too late.

Still determined to snap his fingers at inevitable fate, Randolph prepared for a great winter campaign that should take him all over England. Jeanette agreed to the project. Perhaps it would be a stimulant. But first, she insisted, he must collect all his strength for this effort. The doctors hoped that a cure, both in Gastein and Kissingen, might improve his health, at least temporarily. He was ready to obey. He saw his last chance, yet methodically he also prepared for the other alternative. On the eighth of March, 1893, he deposited before Solicitor Theodore Lumly his intention that his political and State correspondence, documents, and papers, which filled eleven tin boxes and were kept at the Westminster Branch of the London and Westminster Bank, Ltd., should, after the date of his decease, be handed to George Richard Pen, Viscount Curzon, M.P., of 23 Upper Brook Street, and Ernest William Becket, M.P., of 138 Piccadilly, both the County of London. Now he felt ready to resume his work or to have it immortalized.

Gastein had not changed much since the Churchills' previous visit. Again they led a quiet life with its simple routine of baths, short walks, and long drives, and for a time Randolph's health seemed restored. He wrote his mother exuberant reports about his excellent physical condition. Lady Randolph confirmed them. True, the pen shook a little in her hand. With wide-open eyes she saw that her husband's outward improvement was only belying the constant process of dissolution, advancing relentlessly.

When they proceeded to Kissingen, their trip definitely became a voyage into the past. On August the sixth, they met Bismarck. They had not seen him since their first stay in Gastein, exactly ten years earlier. It seemed a century. The Iron Chancellor's once heavy face was almost fleshless. His cheeks were hollow, his eyes were still burning, but had sunken in their sockets. He had trimmed his arrogant mustache, and the characteristic deep wrinkles in his heavy-set face were criss-crossed by hundreds of lesser wrinkles. Yet he did not look quite so worn out, quite so near an extinguishing flame as his visitor, whose overdone youthfulness (now that the South African beard was gone) told a hopeless, unconcealable story.

The Churchills had discussed at length whether they should call at the Old Castle, where Bismarck stayed. Randolph was reluctant. He rightly feared the melancholy of the meeting between two ex-potentates. But Jeanette, bent on distracting her husband, had persisted, and so they embarked upon the visit. It so happened that the Prince was not at home. Relieved, Lord Randolph left his card. The matter seemed forgotten. On the next morning the weather was showery, which induced Lady Randolph, faithful to her inexplicable predilection for rain, to go for a little walk. Randolph, of course, had to remain at home. He was just writing his mother that Jennie was, unfortunately "rather seedy" (he had not the faintest notion why) when a tall Chasseur in Prussian uniform appeared and announced Fuerst Bismarck was in his carriage at the door to see His Lordship.

Randolph hurried down and escorted Bismarck up to his hotel suite, which fortunately was on the first floor. He envied the ease with which the old man mounted the stairs, and he felt it an act of providential justice when the Iron Chancellor, the staircase negotiated, fell exhausted into the next easy-chair.

It was an entrevue of two ghosts. Both were in the same boat. Three years ago Bismarck had ruthlessly been dismissed by his "young master," whereas Lord Randolph had been dropped by Lord Salisbury. Bismarck's glorified life had entirely lost its sense. Randolph was but his own shade. Both were surviving themselves. Yet both maintained their indomitable pride. They did not admit to being has-beens at all. Imperial Germany entered into negotiations with the British Empire when Bismarck, after recovering his breath, began to speak about the healing influence of Kissingen's baths and waters. He was still the restless, high-strung talker he had been ten years before, and was as self-centered as ever. He firmly believed in Kissingen, indeed, he had come here every summer for nine years. He had soon given up drinking the waters, but the baths did him good.

"Don't you go any longer to Gastein?" Randolph asked, highly interested, since he himself had just taken that cure.

Bismarck answered with a guffaw. "Were you recently in Gastein?" he asked in return.

Lord Randolph admitted that he had just come from there. Bismarck appeared amused. "Well," he said benevolently, ready to divulge the secret. "Gastein has a peculiar water. Some people cannot stand it. Sometimes it is dangerous. Two friends of mine have just died of apoplexy while taking the baths.... My doctor told me that Gastein was actually the last resort," the old man harped on the theme. "You'd better go to Carlsbad. My old master used to go there, and I accompanied him." The memory seemed pleasant. Suddenly he turned the conversation. "How old are you?"

"Forty-four!"

"Only forty-four!" Bismarck smiled poisonously. "I am seventy-eight!" It did not sound as if he wished to comfort Randolph. It sounded rather as if he relished the thought that this young man, deadly sick to all appearances, would go before him. At least it sounded so to Lady Randolph, who stood in the door. Her husband had sent her a message to the Kursaal to return. But perhaps she was wronging Bismarck. Every word and every gesture made her suspicious. She was overstrained and felt, indeed, "rather seedy," as her husband had complained in his letter.

Her entrance changed the conversation instantly. In front of a beautiful lady the aged Prince was completely the grand seigneur. He approved of the settlement of the Siam question. He regretted the loss of M. Jules Ferry, with whom he would have established a lasting German-French friendship, which was now, unfortunately, impossible. And then they were back discussing the man whom they had already devoured in their conversation ten years before.

Mr. Gladstone was very eloquent, Bismarck admitted. But

he had always been like an ungovernable horse whom one could not curb with any bridle. This remark led to a short digression on the subject of horses. As a retired country squire, the Chancellor maintained, horseback riding was his last pleasure. But he forgot to add that now he had to use a ladder when mounting, and that his groom had to lift his right leg across the horse's back. "Do you still ride?" he ended.

Randolph was silent. It would have been unpleasant to confess that the doctors had forbidden him such exertion. But Lady Randolph lied unabashed: "Of course, every morning. Why don't we ride together? Any day you please, Your Excellency."

Bismarck murmured something unintelligible. He could, it seemed, not find quite the right English words, although otherwise his English was slow, but excellent. Probably he no longer cared to exhibit his horsemanship. Lady Randolph had boldly gambled on it. This was her round.

At home, Bismarck told his wife that this Lady Randolph was a little combative and spirited, but enchanting. He had invited the Churchills to dinner for the next day.

Lady Randolph admired the Old Castle, once a Bishop's palace. Its picturesque red roof made a distinct landmark in the flat Bavarian scenery. At dinner—a regular, old-fashioned German dinner with gray-haired domestics serving heavy food and well-tempered Rhine wines—she sat on the right side of the Prince, and while disputing her remark that the Bavarian scenery should be flat, whereas the country was indeed mountainous, he obviously enjoyed her conversation. Lord Randolph sat on Bismarck's left, next to the Princess, a feeble old lady, broken in health, who took little part in the conversation. Opposite was Herbert, the ex-Chancellor's son, and his English wife, who deluged Lady Randolph with questions about happenings in Mayfair and Belgravia. On the floor, to right and left of their master's feet, lay Tyras and Sultan, whom Bismarck called Sultl; he still felt the diplomat whose every word made history, and did not want to offend Turkey. The great Danes were grateful for every bit from their master's trembling hand, as well as for every kick with the cuirassier-boots he did not part with even at a ceremonious dinner. "I love dogs," said Bismarck. "They never want to pay back any pain one has inflicted upon them." Sentimentally he told about his dog cemetery in Varzin, where many generations of Tyras and Sultans were buried, right next to the horses. Lady Randolph was a little frightened of Tyras, who seemed to divide his dangerous attention between her and his master.

Bismarck drank a mixture of very old hock poured into a needle-glass of champagne. Randolph only sipped his. "Won't she let you?" the aged man asked, chaffing. Then he turned to Lady Randolph: "I am very glad that you don't let him drink his share," he assumed, not quite wrongly. "If he would drink more, I would have to keep him company, and then I would be half over the seas."

His great pipe was brought, already prepared for him by a venerable retainer, and lighted by enormous wooden safety-matches, to keep him from burning his shaky fingers. Bismarck leaned back in his chair, looked at Lord Randolph, and again started upon the favorite topic they had in common. Would the English people lend Mr. Gladstone to put the German finances in order? Randolph's loud peals of laughter paid tribute to this excellent joke. "The English people would gladly give him for nothing," he answered with gusto. "But you would find him a very expensive present!" Both the shades seemed highly amused.

Lady Randolph showed signs of fatigue. As she was about to leave, Tyras approached her with threatening slow steps, his eyes fixed fiercely on hers. She became alarmed. But Bismarck comforted her in a grave voice: "Don't be afraid. He is just looking at your eyes because he has never seen any like them."

After their return from Germany, her eyes were more than once red-rimmed and swollen. Randolph insisted on carrying out his planned campaign. She knew that his health was none the better for his holiday. Feverishly she tried to make him desist. She beseeched him with tenderness and patience, and sometimes she used strong arguments. He was, she said directly, for the time being no longer able to sway large audiences. Certainly he would soon recover and be able to exercise his habitual hold on the masses again. But why test his strength at an inopportune moment? "Trust the people!" was his only answer. It was a slogan he had coined many years before. It had electrified Birmingham and Manchester. But in the half-darkened rooms of 50 Grosvenor Square, where the lights had to be dimmed on account of the patient's eyesight, the magnetic word only sounded pathetic. In spite of her running feud with her daughter-in-law, which had become inevitable, since even 50 Grosvenor Square was too small for two domineering women, the Dowager Duchess strongly supported Jeanette's endeavors. This only increased Lord Randolph's stubbornness.

He was now frightfully irritable. Winston had just qualified for a cavalry cadetship at Sandhurst. The explanation was not really flattering. Competition for an appointment for the infantry, where life was so much cheaper, was keener, and consequently those at the bottom of the list were offered entry into the cavalry, for which expensive service there was considerably less scramble. However, Winston was proud of the prospect of having a horse, and of donning a magnificent cavalry uniform. In high spirits he wrote his father a letter informing him of his qualification.

The answer was crushing. Lord Randolph had already arranged for his son to join the 60th Rifles, whose colonel-in-chief, his old friend the Duke of Cambridge, was graciously ready to receive Winston. Now this chance was gone. In the infantry the boy would have to keep a man, in the cavalry a man and a horse. He answered his son's letter with a long and severe epistle, warning Winston not to become a social wastrel. Winston smiled a little at so much paternal naïveté. In the cavalry one must not keep one horse, but two official horses, and one or two hunters besides, to say nothing of the string of polo ponies.

The situation was bleak. Nevertheless, young Winston Churchill had found his way.

He was truly his father's son. Lord Randolph, for his part, did not err from what he considered his prescribed way. In spite of the now rapidly progressing disease, he looked quite optimistically into the future. His intellectual vigor had not abated. His position in the House and country was no longer contested. In a way, he felt himself the victor.

The doctors gave Lady Randolph the explanation: it was the blessing in this disease that it produced visions of optimism in its victim. There was no need to disillusion him. It was better that way. He was, as it were, mounting the ladder to heaven.

Lady Randolph understood. She even re-produced her eternal smile as she, throughout October and November, 1893, accompanied her husband on his campaign. In Huddersfield, Stalybridge, Bradford, Bedford, Yarmouth, Dundee, Glasgow and Camborn she watched, grief-stricken, but upright and motionless, how the crowds, attracted by the old appeal of Randy-Pandy's name, appeared at his meetings in masses—and how they departed shuddering at the sight of a dying man.

As every year since his early Irish days, he spent Christmas at Howth with FitzGibbon and the graying "bhoys." The whole crowd showed signs of the twenty years they had advanced since the good old days. But Randolph, in years the youngest of them, looked the oldest of all. There was not one among his life-long friends and followers who did not, broken-hearted, give up the hope of, as Lord FitzGibbon expressed it in a pathetic paraphrase, Randolph's return to power.

He was to pass away in harness. In the spring of 1894 he still persisted in his political work. Almost every week his wife was tortured by assisting his meetings in some important political center. She thanked God, who in these days of the gravest test was no longer so far away, for the delusion of paralysis in its last stage. Her husband did not realize that the newspapers, which a few years ago had quoted his most insignificant utterance word for word, now cut down their reports about his meetings to two or three paragraphs or even one. On one occasion the *Times* observed that the Hall in which Lord Randolph Churchill spoke was not filled.

Lady Randolph fully understood that there was only one thing to do: to let her husband have his way. She resumed social contacts. The Churchills again frequented the political parties at Baron Rothschild's house at Pring, where the cream of the Conservative party gathered. Winston, notwithstanding his expenses in the cavalry, acquired as a gentleman cadet a new distinction in his father's eyes. He was taken along to the Rothschilds', and met successively his father's political and sporting friends. When on leave, he was even taken to the Empire Theater by Lord Randolph, who was pathetically amused in watching acrobats, jugglers, and performing animals. Father and son were closer than ever. But no more real comradeship was to develop. Mr. Churchill recalls that his father froze to ice when he suggested that he might work as his secretary.

Perhaps Lord Randolph realized that he no longer needed a secretary. In the House he was silent. Only one day in June he alarmed the Commons, simply with an interruption. Mr. Storey was speaking about St. Peter and St. Paul as missionaries. "The Apostle Paul," Lord Randolph corrected him. These three innocent words attracted every eye toward him. His painful appearance, his ghastly pallor, his sunken eyes and extreme nervousness appeared in their stark reality. Many friends on the benches recalled St. Paul's farewell bid to the elders on the sands of Miletus. They knew in this moment that they would never see Randolph's face again. Indeed, the three words were the last Lord Randolph Churchill ever spoke in Parliament.

After this ghastly incident Lady Randolph assembled the staff of doctors in charge of her husband. "Isn't it time?" she asked. The doctors agreed. They prescribed a full year of political rest. He did not immediately accept the verdict. He would think it over, and answer on the next day.

In the evening Jeanette suggested a trip around the world.

She had found an excellent, perhaps the only possible way out. His insatiable curiosity was once more kindled. Randolph informed his doctors that he bowed to their decision.

The busy preparations for the long journey were, in a small way, a relief. A round of visits to their most intimate friends followed. All knew that Randolph was paying his farewell visit.

On June 26, 1894, Winston, just making a map on Chobham Common, received through a cyclist messenger the college adjutant's order to proceed at once to London. His father was embarking the next day on a journey round the world. Lord Randolph had telegraphed to Sir Henry Campbell-Bannermann, the Secretary of War: "My last day in England ..."

On the morning of June 27th Lord and Lady Randolph drove to Euston Station. The Dowager Duchess, the two boys, and a group of friends accompanied them. Randolph's face, his son observed, looked terribly haggard and worn with mental pain. The father patted his boy on the knee. The simple gesture was perfectly informing.

Among the friends who had come to the station to bid farewell were Lord and Lady Londonderry, Lady Jeune, Mr. Goschen, and Lord Rosebery, whose presence pleased Randolph particularly. During the whole voyage he ever again recalled the flattering fact that his Liberal opponent, whom he much admired, had taken time off so early in the morning. Perhaps this gesture indicated the possibility of a new coalition.

Lord Rosebery, heartily responding to Randolph's friendship, for his part commented later: "It was terrible. His hair was short, almost cropped, his backhead was bald, his eyes were still wide open, but they had a flickering look."

Under sentence of death, to be executed within twelve months, Lord Randolph boarded the ship. Jeanette seemed elated, as they embarked. She displayed child-like joy at the expectation of seeing the whole round world. Perhaps she could impart this joy to her husband. And when the end came it would be a mellow, gleaming sunset.

CHAPTER XXI *Journey Into Death*

The crossing of the Atlantic was stormy. Two incidents occurred. One night, the engines of R.M.S. "Majestic" suddenly stopped. Their throbbing noise, a familiar and already almost necessary nuisance, died away; instead there was the relentless blowing of the fog-horn.

Was this the end? Lady Randolph had expected it to come a little later, and in a somewhat different way. She kept aloof from the general panic. A shipwreck was perhaps the best way out. Not for an instant did she think of herself.

On the next morning the skipper thanked Her Ladyship for the exemplary calm she had maintained, thus setting a model example for more excitable passengers. True, it had been a near collision. In the dark of night some foreign vessel had almost struck the "Majestic." Well, nothing happened. And nothing would happen any more.

Lady Randolph was not quite convinced that nothing would happen. Her skepticism was soon vindicated. The inevitable concert on board was announced, and she was pressed into playing the piano. The other performers caused a din much worse than the fog-horn had done two days before. The blast and alarum offended Jeanette's musical ear, and made her positively ill. But Lord Randolph was elated. Certainly, it was only popular art. But it was good, English music.

He enjoyed everything. The nearer he came to the end, the

happier became his disposition. In a quiet hour Dr. Keith, the medical attendant, accompanying the pair, explained the miracle to Lady Randolph. Nature was applying her own medicine. The further his disease progressed, the keener the patient's senses would become. He would live the rest of his allotted time more intensely. His perception would be sharpened. Until...

"Until?"

Dr. Keith was silent.

"Is he aware ... ?" she asked.

The doctor nodded. "Very likely."

Lord Randolph was perfectly aware of his state. This was the end. It was coming early. There was still so much to do, so much to see. He had decided, it appeared from his bearing, to drink the cup of life to the brim. He had made up his mind not to think of things past. The new and changing scenes would protect him from somber recollections. Every detail of this last journey would command his interest. Indeed, on his journey into death he was the most punctilious tourist ever to visit America and Asia. Under the shadow of his rapidly approaching death he seemed oddly happy. Happier, at least, than his wife, although she watched him without showing the slightest sign of emotion. Only her hair was suddenly touched with gray. She still wore it piled high, but no longer in curls. Just one ringlet fell upon her forehead. She wore a simple traveling costume with a high-necked white blouse and a black coat with shining, big round buttons. Her expression, the photograph taken aboard the "Majestic" shows, was as intense as ever. Her face was smooth, unwrinkled. But for the color of her hair, neither time nor tragedy had marked her.

Despite its crowded, teeming streets, New York was empty without Leonard Jerome. It was no longer New York at all. A summer season in the Gay Nineties would have been unbearable to Lady Randolph. A small blood vessel in Randolph's brain broke. Undaunted, Jeanette attributed it to the heat. The thermometer recorded 81 degrees in the shade. In the

company of Mr. Chauncey Depew, an old friend and one of the
few people whom the Churchills saw, they fled the sweltering
city. It was no longer necessary to visit Newport. Bar Harbor
was just coming into its own; it would be cooler there. Mr.
Depew loaned the Churchills his private railroad car. It was her
first experience in a private car, and it proved to be a happy
one. The car was as well appointed as a small yacht. The colored
cook prepared a delicious dinner. Randolph ate with remarkable appetite. Then he had an excellent night. Jeanette, too,
fell into deep, dreamless sleep, a rare blessing for the restless
woman. A cool sea-breeze woke them. Bar Harbor was a haven
of rest.

They relished the lovely drives at a slow pace. (The days of
racing in the donkey cart along Bellevue Avenue, Newport, lay
a thousand years back.) Randolph could even venture upon
short walks. Although he did not dance, at a party at the Kebo
Valley Club he proudly watched his wife executing the Boston
which only born and bred Americans can master properly. Lady
Randolph explained the fact that her husband sat out the dancing with complete candor. Dancing had always made him
dizzy. He even had begged to be excused from the waltz at the
very ball he proposed to her. "Remember, Randolph dear?...
The Royal Yacht Squadron, at Cowes?" Very faintly he remembered. It took some exertion to conjure up the sound of
long faded music. His memory was gravely impaired.

Perpetual dressing, dinners, and dances, and what was the
horror of horrors to Lady Randolph, the leaving of cards, were
de rigueur in Bar Harbor. She met a number of pretty girls, un-
chaperoned, which astonished her a little, playing tennis all
day, without hats, another astonishing feature. This new fashion, she concluded shrewdly, was in order to bleach the hair
of the hatless brigade. She met some delightful women, whom
she immediately found congenial. There was something to the
term: compatriots, it was more than a mere word.

In his steam-yacht, Mr. George Vanderbilt took the Churchills on an excursion to East Harbor. The "volume of yearly turn-

over" of the small port interested Randolph immensely. But Mr. Vanderbilt, although a regular guest at Bar Harbor, knew little about how the "natives" in the neighborhood made their living. Then they visited his house. The young people plunged into the water, bobbing up and down, diving and swimming—without shyness, Lady Randolph observed, and without vanity. She had developed into enough of a Victorian to find female bathing-costumes not very attractive. On the other hand, the complete absence of hilarity or chaff among the bathing youth, their strict clinging to decorum, struck her as somewhat incongruous.

One night she dined with Mrs. Van Rensselaer Jones, and met at this occasion Marion Crawford, who impressed her as the personification of the best-looking American man, and more still by his remark: "People say I am idle. For sixteen years I have made my living by my pen, and have produced twenty-five novels." It was new to hear that one could make one's living by one's pen, simply by producing novels. Lord Beaconsfield, certainly a great producer of novels, had not made his living in that way. His stories of Belgravia, so true to nature, had made him one of her favorite authors. Yet now she cogitated earnestly whether this handsome young American was not the better example to follow, when she, too, would have to make a living by her pen. With Mr. Courtland Palmer, a young and inspired musician, she played on the piano. Randolph listened attentively. He had never been a very music-minded man. But now it seemed as if he were drinking in the tunes. At the piano Jeanette, her hands flying, her eyes shining, her hair disarranged by the tossing movements of her head, looked her very self. He wanted to take this picture with him.

The Churchills went on to Canada. Again they traveled in a private car. It was called *Iolanthe,* and equipped with an observation platform at the rear. It had not been easy to procure it. The President of the Canadian Pacific Railway, to whom Lady Randolph had written, proved to be, in the sharpest words of condemnation she ever used, "a broken reed." The

Pullman Company had to help out. Once more America proved the usefulness of her resources. The private car was not simply a whim of Jeanette's. She wanted it to keep her husband out of the public eye. He might collapse again. It need not be tragic, she tried to reassure herself. But it might be embarrassing in front of people. The private car was an extravagance. A year ago she would have considered that. But now money no longer mattered. Retrenchment should be forgotten. "Yes!" agreed Lord Randolph. He was above mundane worries. This sovereignity gave him a comfortable feeling. Only it became increasingly difficult to move.

Heedless of dust and cinders, they sat all day on the open platform. The fresh air did him good. But the scenery was very disappointing. It was an endless straight track, and the small pink flowers growing on both sides, which at first caught her eye, became nauseating in the long run. The aspect of the barren country would make him gloomy, she feared. She underestimated the stimulus of his disease. Everything was new and remarkable to him, even the small pink wild-flowers. The train stopped every half hour with much whistling, ringing of bells, and exchange of greetings between the engine-driver and the local inhabitants who marched or drove for hours to see the train, their only distraction and sensation in prairie life.

Lord Randolph felt the human touch of these little groups. He enjoyed the presence of the people. He observed how different they were from the English, and how they differed among themselves. Two stops, next to one another, were called Portage la Prairie and MacGregor, French and Scottish, and yet all proud of being loyal subjects of the king. One place was called Medicine Hat (after the hospital there, the conductor explained). Lord Randolph insisted on having the train stopped there. Gladly the engineer obliged. Time did not count in the Canadian prairies. Moreover, their distinguished passenger looked as if a visit to the hospital would do him no harm. Actually, it did him good. The superintendent of the hospital, where the Churchills spent an hour in careful inspection, asked his visitors to inscribe their names in the guest book. They signed right below the Duke and the Duchess of Connaught. Randolph was again in the company in which he belonged.

Winnipeg was a remarkable town. On the long ride through the prairies the travelers had quite forgotten how streets of stone houses looked. Strolling up and down they enjoyed the commotion of the great world. Even this was excitement; Lord Randolph would not miss it. Then came again two days of prairies. The horsewoman awoke in Jeanette. How she would have loved to ride through the plains. Here one could give one's horse its head and gallop for miles. She wanted to speak of it. Perhaps the idea would appeal to him. But she interrupted herself. He was no longer fit for the saddle. Her animated expression had not escaped his sharpened perception. "Amused?" he asked. "Look at all those prairie dogs," she answered with a nod. "Aren't they like hairless little squirrels with rattails?" Suddenly she thought how peaceful life in the prairies must be. Monotonous, certainly, but here, so close to nature, people find rest. Rest, she repeated silently to herself. It was a strange word.

There is no rest anywhere. The first chain of hills, the spur of the Rocky Mountains, was thickly covered with mist. It took a sharp eye to discern them. The train drove into a region almost impenetrable with smoke, so dense that one could have cut it with a knife. Randolph suffered a terrible attack of coughing. A gigantic prairie-fire was raging on both sides of the track. There was no escaping it. Even hiding inside the compartment did not help. The smoke penetrated the car. "How far is it still to Banff?" Lady Randolph asked the conductor. "Some forty miles." He would not survive them. His pale, haggard face flushed dark red with hectic spots. His body shook with the coughing fits. Dr. Keith had to give him an injection, no easy task in the vibrating and shaking car.

Banff. The scene, the snow-covered, wild, majestic Rockies

behind it was magnificent. "Beautiful," Lord Randolph said. "The most beautiful picture I have ever seen. I would not have missed this journey, not for my life. . . ." He smiled.

Banff was basking in the summer sun. They ought to have stayed in the hotel, relaxing. But neither could resist what Lady Randolph termed "the call of the wild." They had never been able to resist it. Little matter that no comfortable equipage was available in the faraway town. They climbed into "buckboards," day after day, to view the grandeur of the scenery about them. His back ached and his hands were numb. That came, of course, only from the tedium of sitting. But at least they sat close to each other, hand in hand. And so the Vermilion Lakes were twice as colorful, and twice as enchanting. Four-handed, they rowed the whole length of both lakes, eight miles. He performed all the motions, and she did most of the rowing. The skies were a lighter blue than the lakes, whose waters were so clear that one could see all the way to the bottom.

In Victoria they met Colonel Baker, the brother of their old friend and frequent guest Valentine Baker, the mystery man of Egypt. "Now that I am in the Cabinet . . ." the Colonel said. Was he in the Cabinet? Indeed, British Columbia had a government of its own. It was mostly concerned with local matters, and reminded her of a County Council rather than of Whitehall. But she was proud to be a subject of this British Empire that had its mystery men in the Near East, and by the same token its self-governing ministers near the Arctic Circle, and that these could be brothers.

Lord Randolph displayed great interest in the Parliamentary conditions in British Columbia. Who was in office, the Liberals or the Conservatives? he asked. Neither, explained Colonel Baker. There were neither Liberals nor Conservatives in this province. There were only the "Ins," who want to stay in, and the "Outs," striving to get in. *"Tout comme chez nous,"* observed the Anglo-American lady.

Admiral Stephenson, another old friend, repaid the hospitality he had so often enjoyed in House Beautiful by giving a lunch aboard H.M.S. "Royal Arthur." Randolph's table manners astonished the Admiral. His hands trembled so that he spilled the wine. "Aren't you a little fatigued from all this sightseeing?" Stephenson asked. No, her husband was by no means fatigued, Lady Randolph quickly replied. Yet good old Stephenson insisted on taking his friends back to Victoria in his own barge. He wanted to save them another exhausting railroad trip. The world was friendly, as it slowly passed out of sight.

San Francisco, the last stop before embarking for the Far East, was yes and no. The fashionable set, on hearing of the Churchills' arrival, flooded Lady Randolph with baskets of flowers. They were gorgeous, magnolias blossoming in profusion, long-stemmed roses of all kinds, white, pink, and mauve sweet peas. But the lovely California flowers, Jeanette observed, had little scent, just as the gorgeous fruit in California lacks taste. It is like a beautiful woman without brains, she commented.

The sun did not shine in San Francisco; the weather was cloudy and windy. Randolph was immediately affected by this unfavorable climate. Besides, he refused to cross the streets of the teeming, booming town. The innumerable electric trolleycars, which seemed to come from every direction at once, frightened him, he frankly admitted.

He still held to his old convictions and prejudices. His disgust of reporters had not abated. In San Francisco he was hounded by them worse even than during the years of glory in London. Yet he managed to dodge them all. Jeanette was less fortunate. When she came home, dead tired from another day—all were equally exhausting—she found a girl reporter hidden behind the curtain. Lady Randolph was ready to show the intruder the door gently, but firmly. But the girl burst into tears. Her sobs mollified Jeanette. However, she did not disclose more than that they had enjoyed their stay. The nicest thing had been the excursion to the Hotel Del Monte at Monterey, where she had chatted and exchanged stories with some old friends. "Lady

Randolph tells Good Stories on Porch of the Del Monte!"
screamed the headline. The Churchills were still headline news.

The "Empress of Japan," an ocean palace, clean and comfortable, and, much to Lady Randolph's delight, decorated with
innumerable Japanese plants and shrubs, took them to Yokohama. The talk of the ship was the Sino-Japanese War. Baron
Speck von Sternburg, leaving his post as German ambassador
at Washington for his new assignment to Japan, stridently announced that the Prussians of the East would administer a good
licking to the little Chinamen. Mr. Villiers, war correspondent
of the London *Graphic,* remained silent. There was little doubt
on which side his heart was beating, but he had to keep on good
terms with the Japanese authorities in order to be permitted to
cover their side of the front. The Chinese waiters, looking picturesque in their butcher-blue or white, smiled as they served
His German Excellency. That they occasionally spilled wine or
soup on his dinner jacket was only due to the heavy rolling of
the ship. But when his food was served late and cold, which
greatly endangered his delicate digestion, the arrogant German
complained, and when Lady Randolph by chance saw Mr. Villiers joking with the waiters, she was perfectly satisfied that the
British Intelligence Service had its hands everywhere. A few
yellow fingers even dived into Baron Speck von Sternburg's
soup plate.

She badly needed such little incidents. The seas were rough,
the skies gray and leaden, the constant rolling and pitching, besides the increasing monotony of the crossing, was wearing her
out. Amazingly, Randolph stood the difficulties of the journey
perfectly well. All his life he had been seasick, all his journeys,
far or near, had been paid for with suffering. But now he did not
mind the worst tossing. Was he, please God, recovering his
strength? Jeanette asked Dr. Keith. The medical man was not
sure. His lordship might have lost his static sense.

The harbor of Yokohama was jammed with torpedo-boats,
mines and mine-sweepers, and even submarines. This war was

not in the least like the Civil War and the Franco-German War, both of which Jeanette had witnessed in her girlhood. How rapidly the years were passing, how entirely was the world changing!

On anchoring in the harbor, a shoal of craft of all sizes and shapes, sampans and junks, swarmed around the "Empress of Japan." On a government launch, some little toy soldiers, so heavily gold-braided that they looked almost gilded, appeared to bow and hiss and scrape politely in front of His German Excellency.

The hotel proved to be the headquarters of the Western war correspondents. None of them had been able to obtain the Japanese authorities' permission to go to the front and see for himself. Only Mr. Villiers wormed his way to the battlefields by patting shoulders and greasing palms successfully. But when he arrived at the military bases, the use of the telegraph was denied to him. The reason was most flattering. The Japanese War Minister was so fascinated by Mr. Villiers' writing that he wanted himself to read every single report the gentleman would dispatch to London. Randolph, still possessed by his monomaniac contempt of the press, found nothing objectionable in so much courtesy.

The day before the Churchills arrived there had been a great Japanese victory. Even the hotel porter hastened to declare that Their Lordships would be stunned by the general popular rejoicing. Lady Randolph found no signs of it. British observers on the spot told her that the Japanese government had plunged into the war to divert the nation from internal troubles.

Yokohama was immensely interesting. But its damp heat, after the cold of the Pacific, further impaired Randolph's state of health. He refused, nevertheless, to leave before having seen more of the big Japanese town. He took Jeanette to the theater, where they sat on the floor of their so-called box and spent, like the rest of the audience, most of their time drinking tea. The play, "The Battle of Pyong-Yang," had fourteen or fifteen acts. Its performance lasted all day, and the next one, too. The audience ate and slept during the show. All had their dinners with them on little trays, loaded with bowls containing weird foodstuffs; raw fish, rice-cakes, and nameless yellow condiments. Jeanette could not touch a bit of the stuff. She demanded a drop of milk for her tea. General curiosity responded. Didn't the white lady know that one never drank milk in Japan? Why, milk has an offensive strong smell.

Meanwhile, on the stage, Chinese troops, represented by three wretched Chinamen, were incessantly being killed by twenty Japs, who trumpeted all the time, brandishing their swords, firing their rifles, and enjoying it madly. In the end came a small yellow general in smart European uniform, and made a bellicose speech to the army of twenty, in fact to the audience, which was so seized by patriotic frenzy that Lady Randolph fled, dragging with her her entirely absent-minded husband. Wata, her jinrikisha man, for the first time dared to speak to her: "Was it not a good, big play?"

On leaving Yokohama, the Churchills found the harbor in great commotion. Four Germans, bristling with weapons, on their way to watch the progress of the war in Korea, were cheered by huge crowds, who had only dirty looks for the company of English residents, bidding farewell to Lord and Lady Randolph. The Japanese were getting very much "above themselves," she noticed. This impression was confirmed by the old Japan hands in her company. Since the British government had given in over the last commercial treaty, the Japs despised the great white Queen's feeble subjects. Lord Randolph did not understand the connection. Fair trade should work both ways. But he was much too bored with politics to continue the conversation.

In Tokio, Mr. Trench, the British ambassador, tried to arrange for an audience—remarkably not for Lord Randolph with the Emperor, but for Lady Randolph with the Empress. The request of the British ambassador was most courteously received. But soon the Foreign Minister, S. Sannonyma, gave his definite reply: "I am sorry to inform you that Her Majesty the

Empress, will not be able to receive anyone, for doctor advises so do this morning. I think Lady Randolph Churchill may make a short trip, it would be better for her."

She took the snub with equanimity. The Churchills continued sightseeing. Randolph could never see enough. Kioto, the ancient capital, and still the art center of Japan, was their last stop. Its quaintness and local color was enchanting. Yet they were glad to rejoin their ship, the "Ancona," at Kobe, and leave enigmatic Japan. It had, on the whole, been an interesting expedition. But Randolph complained every day that he could not get the two typical Japanese sounds out of his ear: the tap-tap of the little pipe as it is emptied before being refilled, and the mournful notes of the reed lute which the blind medicine man plays as he walks through the streets.

In China the fatal journey reached its climax. Aboard the "Ancona" the Churchills met Mr. de Bunsen, later the British Ambassador to Madrid, who had been a young attaché at the embassy in Paris, when Lady Randolph was Jennie Jerome. "It took me years until my broken heart recovered from the shock, when Jennie ... forgive me, Lady Randolph, chose you," said Mr. de Bunsen. He smiled, but he meant it. Somehow, the words sounded soothing. Randolph only heard: recover. He refused Bunsen's invitation to visit him in Siam. He was bent on getting to Burma as rapidly as possible. Hadn't he conquered Burma? He had never seen it. He had seen nothing of his spoils. Now he was determined to last out until Mandalay. Afterward the rest of the journey would not be so very important.

Hong Kong had to be negotiated within three hectic days. There was not much to admire but the magnificent view from the Peak. A flying visit to Canton followed, and a short trip up Pearl River in a large steamer, captained by an English skipper. The first thing the skipper pointed out was a stack of rifles in the saloon, with printed instructions to the passengers to use them if necessary. River steamers, it was known, had been repeatedly attacked by pirates. The whole country was unsafe. Outraged by their defeat at the hands of the Japanese, the Chinese were in a riotous mood. White people traveled up Pearl River at their own risk. The steamer was obliged to anchor at the mouth of the river, as the channel was mine-strewn, and the Chinese pilots refused to run the risk. Menacing Chinese junks with square sails hoisted, obviously ready for immediate action, hovered about. The dark night was illuminated by constant searchlights from a near-by fort.

It was a nerve-wracking night. But both the Churchills thrilled to the danger. The next morning they insisted on sailing upstream in a sampan which their Chinese guide had prepared for them. They disembarked at Canton, where they found a row of palanquins waiting. The transparent blinds were pulled down. No Chinese lady would expose herself to the glances of the crowded streets, the guide explained. But Lady Randolph was not Chinese. She ordered the blinds pulled up. A continuous stream of people, surging by the palanquins, shouted "Frankwei"—foreign devils—and spat into the Churchills' palanquins. Another coolie-pulled cart in their company was upset by the hoodlums; the gentleman inside was beaten up. Fortunately, he did not retaliate. They would have made mincemeat of all of us, thought Lady Randolph when the danger seemed over.

But Randolph courted danger. This old trait of his was still strong. He stopped in front of a jeweler's shop that was besieged by the mob. Head erect, with a determined step, his arm firm, the proud man, with a last effort, shoved aside the yellow rascals, entered the shop, and returned, unmolested, to his wife. He brought her a green jade bangle. "To remember me . . ." he said, correcting himself immediately: "To remember this day."

In Singapore they stayed for a week at Government House. The Sultan of Johore gave them a sumptuous luncheon, lasting longer than even the generally feared Lord Mayor's banquet in London. After the meal the despot sent for his latest Sultana, a present from the Sultan of Turkey. She proved to be a very pretty Circassian of about twenty-five, but enormously fat.

Tenderly the Sultan of Johore said: "She is being fed every two hours." He liked luxurious proportions.

At the end of the week the Churchills started for Rangoon. This time Sir Frank Swettenham, the virtual ruler of the Straits Settlements, was their guide. Rangoon was the last stop before Mandalay. But Randolph was prevented from seeing the capital of the country he had annexed. Cholera was rampant in Mandalay. The plague would not have deterred him in the least. Why should it not be cholera instead of paralysis? But when Jeanette declared, and her voice left no doubt as to her serious resolve, that she would accompany him, he gave in. She thought she had saved his life once more for a little while. But Randolph felt cheated out of enjoying, at least for a moment, the fruits of his only conquest. He agreed to return to England. The boat left from Bombay. He had to be carried aboard the ship on a stretcher. He had collapsed in Bombay.

The slow, long journey back was martyrdom. In the last days of December, 1894, the patient reached England as weak and helpless in mind and body as a little child. Over four weeks he lingered on his sickbed at 50 Grosvenor Square, the Dowager Duchess' house. The paralysis had reached its final stage. Occasional semblance of improvement, even when he recognized his surrounding, and spoke to them, did not delude the doctors. At one moment the dying man asked Winston: "Did you get your horses?" He meant the commission with the Hussars. Winston nodded. He had just qualified for the Queen's commission. "Good!" his father breathed heavily.

The progress of the disease was beyond human control. Dr. Thomas Buzzard, the celebrated nerve specialist, was summoned, and the old family practitioner, Dr. Robson Roose, called back from Stuttgart, where he was spending his holiday. Their consultation with Dr. Keith led to no definite opinion. It might be a few more hours or, perhaps, another month. Sir J. Russel Reynolds and Dr. Gowers, the two outstanding authorities on nervous diseases, were called in. They gave no hope. Finally the Reverend J. Esgar Sheppard, Sub-Dean of the Chapel Royal, read prayers at Lord Randolph's bedside.

Lady Randolph, devotedly supported by the Dowager Duchess, nursed him, gave him tonics and stimulants. She plunged into the duel with death. It was she above all who achieved the miracle of sustaining his last flicker of life for thirty-one days.

Then coma set in. Attacks of syncope followed, succeeded by a collapse in which the pulse rapidly weakened.

On January 24th, 1895, Robson Roose, M.D., and George E. Keith, M.D., signed the short sentence: "Lord Randolph Churchill passed away peacefully and without pain at 6:15 this morning."

Randolph's body was taken from Paddington to Woodstock. Both his constituencies bade him a mournful farewell. The London terminus was thronged, and all Woodstock was gathered around the local station which was journey's end. Tory deputations from all over the country, labor delegations from Manchester and Birmingham, and a group of Irish friends mingled with the local people. To right and left of the bier that was carried through the archway into Blenheim Castle the Duchess and Lady Randolph walked. Lady Randolph looked straight ahead. Her face was expressionless. She had no more tears to shed.

In Westminster Abbey, statesmen and politicians of all parties attended the memorial service for Lord Randolph Churchill. Throughout his combative life he had never been as much beloved as now.

He was buried in the churchyard of Blaydon, near Blenheim, next to his brothers Charles and Augustus who had died in infancy. A plain granite cross, visible for a mile, marks his grave. A statue was erected to his memory in Blenheim Chapel. A bust of their deceased leader was set up in the House of Commons by private subscription among the members. At the unveiling,

Lord Randolph Churchill was eulogized by his oldest comrade, Sir Michael Hicks-Beach.

And so Jeanette was alone. Her heart was broken, but not her spirit. She mourned her husband deeply and for years. Yet she understood the eternal truth of human solitude. Her passions were strong. Her devotion was deep. But most powerful of all was her ineradicable zest for life.

CHAPTER XXII *Indian Summer*

Death is not the worst of evils. The worst anguish
is an empty life. Jeanette was not born to be idle. She was, she
admitted in her reminiscences—which otherwise carefully avoid
any confession of self-analysis—in a despondent mood. But her
mourning for the past, and for the man who had been her past,
could not divert her from the task of the day, and from the
tasks she was to set herself for the future.

Much of the energy she had invested in her husband's career
was now shifted to smoothing Winston's way. After his father's
death he was, in his own words, the master of his fortunes. His
mother never sought to exercise parental control over her son,
then twenty-one. But she was always at hand to help and to
advise, he gratefully remembers. "Indeed, she soon became an
ardent ally, furthering my plans and guarding my interests
with all her influence and boundless energy," to quote Winston
Churchill. "She was still young, beautiful, and fascinating. We
worked together on even terms, more like brother and sister
than mother and son. At least it seemed so to me. And so it continued to the end."

This beautiful relation found its first expression in Winston's
commission to the Fourth Hussars. The commander of the
regiment was Colonel Brabazon, a life-long friend of the Prince
of Wales, and famed as Her Majesty's "most fashionable" soldier. Besides this, he belonged to the army of Lady Randolph's

337

admirers. Certainly he had a vacancy in his regiment. He happened to be badly in need of a Sub-lieutenant. Jeanette could still tell her husband the good news in one of his brighter moments. He nodded. It was his last pleasure.

But the pleasure of seeing his son in the red and gold Hussar uniform was denied to him. Winston actually joined his regiment a few days after his father passed away. He was now a full-fledged cavalry officer, and before him lay what appeared to be an easy life. A favored child of fortune, it was Winston's good luck that the Cuban revolt flared up during his first leave. The young man in a hurry felt highly tempted to rush off to Cuba at least to watch some real fighting, which, it appeared, was no longer to be had in Europe.

But the Spanish High Command was reluctant to admit camp-followers. The chance of an English junior officer being admitted to Cuba seemed negligible. It was a clear-cut challenge to Lady Randolph. She had overcome difficulties on a very different scale. The Spanish High Command was not so formidable an adversary. After all, Sir Henry Wolff, once Randolph's right-hand man in the Fourth Party, and ever Jeanette's faithful admirer, was at that time British ambassador at Madrid. The doyen of the Diplomatic Corps, his influence was unrivaled. Sir Henry answered her appeal on behalf of her son by sending an envelope full of excellent introductions for Lieutenant Winston Spencer Churchill, coupled with the assurance that the young warrior would be warmly welcomed by the Spanish Captain-General as soon as he reached Havana.

After witnessing the realities of war in Cuba, Winston was at home on leave from India when the revolt of the wild Pathan tribesmen on the Northwestern frontier flared up. A field force of three brigades was formed under Sir Bindon Blood. It was not easy to obtain a commission. Again Lady Randolph had to go into action. Her American sister-in-law Lillian, the widowed Duchess of Marlborough, had married, for her third husband, Lord William Beresford. Jeanette had been loyal to her during the time of her persecution by her predecessor, the divorced

Duchess. Now the third husband of Winston's aunt Lillian repaid his wife's debt of gratitude. He appealed to his old friend
Sir Bindon and gave a solemn party at the Marlborough Club
for the departing young hero. Off went Winston into the most
cruel and bloody of guerrilla wars against savages in their pathless, pestiferous strongholds. He was enthusiastic at the project.

Accompanying her son to Victoria Station, Lady Randolph
smiled. She had not smiled for a long time. But now she had
every reason to be satisfied with herself. She did not let him go
penniless. She had arranged for him to write letters for the
Daily Telegraph at five pounds each. It was not much money,
but it was a great chance. Teaming up with an officer of the
British Intelligence Service, Winston regularly scooped the official news with his own reports. True, this did not endear him to
the brass hats. His book on the expedition. *The Malakand Field
Force,* in which the young subaltern criticized the faults and
blunders of the Command antagonized even the great Kitchener, although the book strongly impressed, among others, Lord
Salisbury, who was Prime Minister again, and the Prince of
Wales.

The Sirdar, however, would have nothing of the overbearing
young lieutenant when, the fighting on the Indian frontier
scarcely over, Winston's heart ached to join the expedition to
the Sudan. Sir Herbert Kitchener bluntly refused his application for a commission in the Egyptian Army, although Winston's petition had been recommended by the War Office.

The invincible Sirdar had, for once, underestimated an adversary's power. Lady Randolph devoted, Winston acknowledged gratefully, the whole of her influence to furthering his
wishes. For two months of strenuous negotiation she gave
countless luncheons and dinners, attended by most of the
mighties of the day. Still the Sirdar was mightier than all, and
entirely inaccessible. In the end, Lady Randolph, who had
known Kitchener for many years, wrote him a personal letter.
The great man's answer was perfectly polite, but it explained
that he had more than enough officers for the campaign, and,

furthermore, was overwhelmed by applications from others with far greater claims and better qualifications. The first round of the battle royal went to him.

But Lady Randolph never gave in. She played what she believed to be her trump card. She addressed herself to Lord Salisbury. In spite of the strain between the aged statesman and her late husband, the personal relations between the Salisburys and Lady Randolph had remained most pleasant.

Subsequently the Prime Minister asked Winston to come and see him. Lord Salisbury wanted to congratulate the young officer-author on his excellent book about the Indian campaign. The interview, which lasted over half an hour, and was conducted with the noblest old-world courtesy on the part of the veteran statesman, ended with his words: "If there is anything at any time that I can do which would be of assistance to you, pray do not fail to let me know."

Elated, Winston rushed home. Lady Randolph, it appeared, had won the second round. Indeed, the Premier's private secretary, Sir Schomberg M'Donnell, another of her old friends, telegraphed a day or two later to the Sirdar that Lord Salisbury would be greatly pleased on personal grounds if Lieutenant Winston Churchill's wish to take part in the impending operations could, without disadvantage to the public service, be acceded to.

Sir Herbert Kitchener wired back that he had already all the officers required. The second round ended again with noisy saber-rattling.

But in striking contradiction to the hallowed traditions of British military history, the great Kitchener won all the battles, and lost the war. The rattling saber proved a poor weapon against female diplomacy. Lady Randolph, despairing at the man-made world, enlisted another woman, one of the greatest of her day, to help her in the final assault. Lady St. Helier had long been, next to Jeanette, London's leading political hostess. Her salon was, in particular, the center of influential military circles. On Jeanette's behest she now invited to dinner Sir

Evelyn Wood, the Adjutant-General. Inevitably the table-talk turned to the Sirdar. Sir Evelyn was not too well disposed toward the mighty general. The War Office resented Kitchener's personal picking and choosing between particular officers recommended. Certainly, Sir Herbert's choice in his own sphere was absolute, the Adjutant-General admitted. But the internal composition of the British contingent, forming a part of the Expeditionary Force, rested entirely with the War Office.

Two days later Winston received laconic instructions from the War Office: "You have been attached as a supernumerary lieutenant to the 21st Lancers for the Sudan Campaign." Lady Randolph's war with Kitchener was won.

There was one last problem to be solved. Winston had to proceed at his own expense; the British army funds even refused to accept any responsibility in case he should be killed or wounded. Fortunately, Lady Randolph was on the best terms with Lord Gleneck, formerly Mr. Borthwick, the proprietor of the *Morning Post*, who had been Randolph's last journalistic supporter. This time Winston received fifteen pounds a column, three times the fee the *Daily Telegraph* had paid for his Indian reports.

To introduce Winston to society, Lady Randolph emerged out of her self-chosen seclusion. Between battles her son should have a little fun. Before the regiment embarked for India, where it would remain for twelve or fourteen years, the officers were given generous leave. Hence, Winston enjoyed from the spring to the winter of 1896 the only six unworried months of his busy life. Two or three times a week he took the underground to the Hounslow barracks, but he made his home at his mother's house. He was her constant escort and cavalier.

Lansdowne House was not yet converted into a hotel-restaurant, and no one could rent a flat in Devonshire House. Yet much of Lady Randolph's world was already gone when London still seemed to have but one concern: the Queen's Diamond Jubilee, to be celebrated the following year, in 1897.

To a great extent, Lady Randolph was fully aware, she herself had contributed to the change. Tory Democracy and the Primrose League had admitted the middle class to society. Sports were tremendously popularized, particularly by Lady Randolph, who had been one of the earliest sporting women. Racing and shooting, society's preferred sports, still had predominance. But archery and that other Victorian sport, croquet, were losing out. Sport was no longer an amusement of high life, but a hectic mass entertainment, the faster, the more popular.

Entertainment, dancing, art, and the theater were similarly changing. Lady Randolph, one of the most indefatigable dancers, equally versed in quadrille, minuet and waltz, and famous for the grace with which she led the old-fashioned dancers, had to adapt herself to the *Cracovienne* and the *Galop*. She was half sad and half amused, when the end of the century introduced the Barn Dance, the Washington Post, and a step with the horrible name of Kitchen Lancers, heralding the invasion of American jazz.

Originally, her relation to the theater had been of a social nature. With the distinct aim of creating a new center of conservative society, the young Churchills had been prominent in making the London first night a fashionable event. Now the theater was becoming increasingly popular. The new audience, however, patronized such music halls as the Trocadero, the Alhambra, the Empire, the Palace, the Pavilion, the Oxford, and the Trivoli more than the plays of Pinero, Henry Arthur Jones, Barrie, Yeats, Oscar Wilde, and G. B. Shaw, all of whom came in during the late Victorian era. As time went on, Lady Randolph succumbed ever more to the spell of the stage. Her early histrionics were sublimated into a real interest in dramatic art. The general trend to the music hall was not much to her taste.

As a young girl she had watched the last flicker of the Deuxième Empire. Now, in the prime of life, she saw Victorianism fading. Soon the Prince of Wales would succeed to the throne. He would definitely replace whist by bridge, and the old world would expire.

So much greater was her courage in marching on with unfaltering step. Yet as far as her activities for Winston allowed it, she lived in memories, sometimes in living memories. In the summer of 1895, half a year after Randolph's death, she celebrated a reunion, heavy with recollection, with Elizabeth of Austria, who once again came to England for fox-hunting. The Empress was fifty-eight at that time. But like Jeanette she was an ageless woman. Due to her rigid dieting Elizabeth had preserved her extraordinary slenderness, whereas Lady Randolph, to her secret sorrow, was a trifle plumper than at their first meeting.

Once more the Empress of Austria indulged in her maniac passion for horses. She galloped all over Cheshire and Northampton, hunting with the Pytchley under the mastership of Lord Spencer, a relative of the Dowager Duchess of Marlborough. She rented Cottesbrook Park, later the seat of Lord Combermere, and held court there. It was a gentlemen's court. Her guests were chosen from among the best hunters in England. Yet Mr. H. O. Northcote, one of the three or four most renowned fox-hunters of the day, complained: "When the hounds began to move, no hedge was too high for her. Indeed, we had to go hard to keep up with her."

During the hours she did not spend in the saddle, she declaimed the Odyssey in Greek. For both her manias, hunting and Hellenism, there was no better companion than Lady Randolph, the only woman to be offered the hospitality of Cottesbrook Park. Jeanette thrived in this atmosphere of hunting, interspersed with Homer. The two women became inseparable. They decided not to part when the Empress' holiday was over. "Again next year!" they said, embracing one another.

Next year the Empress of Austria was fifty-nine, but she was no older. She rented a hunting-box in Ireland. Again Lady

Randolph was her constant associate. They called the moors of
County Meath their prairies, and the time they spent together,
their heroic age. Elizabeth had just come from Cap Martin,
where she had visited Eugénie. She conveyed to Jeanette the
ex-Empress' heartfelt regards, and they decided that all three
of them should meet in the next autumn. In the summer Elizabeth would be required in Budapest for the Hungarian millen-
nium celebration, and Lady Randolph for the Diamond Jubilee
in London.

But the autumnal appointment never came off. On September 10, 1897, the anarchist Luigi Luccheni stabbed the Empress
of Austria, who was visiting Geneva, in the heart. The Empress
succumbed. With her died another piece of Lady Randolph's
youth.

Once more, and for the last time, Victorian society rose to
the height of its fading splendor. The background was the
uninterrupted chain of celebrations in 1897, year of the Queen's
Diamond Jubilee. The particular occasion was the fancy-
dress ball at Devonshire House on July 2. Not for almost
a quarter of a century, since the historic ball at Marlborough
House on July 22, 1874, had a ball of such magnificence been
given, nor was there ever to be another on the same scale. No
entertainment, public or private, around the Jubilee was to be
compared with this costume ball. The Duke and Duchess of
Devonshire, standing at the top of the marble staircase, received the distinguished company that thronged the beautiful
rooms. This gala topped the procession before the Queen, both
the military reviews, and even the royal garden party. It was
the greatest opportunity any woman could have to bow her
way out of society which, in spite of all its glamour, no longer
sufficed to fill a maturing and purposeful life. Lady Randolph
had a great exit from the stage she had dominated for twenty-
three years.

The event had stirred the London social world for many
months, ever since the Duchess of Devonshire had summoned

her friends to appear "in an allegorical or historical costume dated earlier than 1820." The *Times* of London commented on the preparations for the fancy-dress ball: "Never in our times has so much attention been paid to old family pictures, never have the masterpieces in the National Gallery been so carefully studied, while for weeks the British Museum has been invaded by smart ladies and gentlemen, anxious to search the paintings and drawings of the 16th, 17th, and 18th centuries." Historical books were ransacked for inspiration, old engravings were studied, people became familiar with celebrities from the past whose names they had never before heard. Solemnly, fair ladies would whisper to their score of best friends the secret that they intended to appear as Aspasia, or as Petrarch's Laura, perhaps as Frédégonde or the Queen of Cyprus. The information was, of course, strictly confidential. Nothing worse could happen than that another woman should appear in the same costume.

The guests were invited to appear as different courts, each headed by a great lady, and attended by her friends in the costumes of princes and courtiers. Readily the royal party itself fell in with this idea. In historical costumes of the 16th century the members of the royal family took their places on a dais, erected in the first drawing room, past which the whole company filed.

The invitations had been for half-past ten. Many visitors came much earlier. The Duke of Devonshire in the dress of Charles V, the great Hapsburg, wearing the collar and badge of the Golden Fleece (which the Prince of Wales had lent him for this occasion) received at the head of the staircase. Lady Randolph wondered at the striking similarity between the features of the Hapsburgs and the Cavendishes. Next to her husband stood the Duchess of Devonshire, attired as Zenobia, Queen of Palmyra. The Prince and Princess of Wales had chosen, respectively, the masks of the Grand Prior of the Order of St. John of Jerusalem, and of Marguerite of Valois. Princess Daisy Pless, accompanied by her handsome brother, Mr. George Cornwallis-West, played at being the great Queen of the East. Whether she was Cleopatra or the Queen of Sheba was not quite clear. Anyway, her entourage was so devoted to her that they had chosen to darken their faces in order to look true to whatever the choice was. Thus she beat Mrs. Arthur Pages, another Cleopatra, but with a white-skinned retinue. Lady Londonderry personified Maria Theresa. Lady Ratcliffe, Catherine the Great. Lady Ormond, Queen Ginevra. Lady Cynthia Greshem was one of the numerous Queens of Sheba. The Duchess of Sunderland was satisfied with the role of Charlotte Corday. Joe Chamberlain, the ex-radical, on the other hand, had advanced to Louis XIV. Lord Rosebery displayed his literary inclinations as Horace Walpole. A lady generally known and pitied for being on the verge of bankruptcy, was covered with gems of priceless value. At least a dozen Napoleons suffered their Waterloo when they met, and gazed stupefied at one another.

Lady Randolph appeared as Theodora of Byzantium, the circus dancer who had become the great Empress of early Christianity. Her role was a bold choice. But among the dressed-up, masked, lavishly ornamented, if poorly disguised, chatting, flirting and dancing English ladies, the Marie Antoinettes from Belgravia and the Aspasias of Mayfair, she was the only one who had indeed changed her identity and become what she played—or what really always had slumbered in her. She was indeed a Theodora, the woman in a man-made world, the restless intellect hidden behind irresistible charm, the great lady of her own making, the indomitable strength, almost toughness in a deceivingly delicate frame, the inspired woman, very much at home in a matter-of-fact universe.

Among the many pictures of the maturing Lady Randolph her likeness masquerading as the Circus-Empress was perhaps the most impressive. The dress, of course, was theatrical. She was studded with pearls. Rows of pearls crowned her head. A hoop of pearls encircled her forehead. Strings of pearls, three large and perhaps a dozen small ones, covered her neck. Two giant pearls, one black and one white, hung from them. Another enormous pearl-string around the shoulders reached below her waist. The famous Marlborough jewels had been lent her for this night.

Her trailing silk dress was richly embroidered with golden Byzantine patterns indicating mysterious signs and symbols. From her crown of pearls hung a fluttering veil of that material the Greeks used to call woven air. In her right hand she carried the Imperial Orb of the East-Roman Empire (the genuine article, borrowed from the British Museum) which prevented her from dancing; it was a welcome excuse.

She was alone. Her expression in her picture shows it. Her hair, which she habitually wore piled high, was, on this occasion, loose, streaming over her shoulders. Her eyebrows, it appeared, had grown still stronger. They arched over inscrutable dark eyes, shadowed, perhaps, by a smoke-screen of sadness. There was no photogenic smile. She looked straight ahead, calm and detached. Lady Randolph had reached her summit; now it was her turn to resign.

She had, however, to attend one more party. The Duchess of Portland invited a few intimate friends to Welbeck to bid farewell to Lord Curzon, as he was about to assume his post as Viceroy of India. At dinner, Lady Randolph sat on the right of the guest of honor. Curzon observed that she was looking sad, just after her triumph at the Devonshire ball. Why?

"It's an empty life," she confessed to her old friend, who had also been an intimate of Randolph.

"Why?" Curzon repeated. "A beautiful woman alone is a godsend in society. Certainly you may look forward to a long vista of country house-parties, dinners and balls."

And that shall be all the remainder of my life holds for me? she asked herself. She could not get the question out of her mind. Every day she pondered it. She did not wish to triumph any longer. She wanted to do something.

Out of the restless day-dreams of a lonesome woman, who had lost her husband and successfully started her son on his

way, and was now entirely on her own, too experienced merely
to play, too young to be without ambition, emerged the *Anglo-
Saxon Review:* the most magnificent, most expensive, most
high-brow magazine of the turn of the century. The *Quarterly
Miscellany* as the *Review* was called in its subtitle, was the
true expression of its woman founder. It was a museum piece
in its beauty, resembling an old master more than a product of
the rotary press, yet it dealt courageously with the questions
of the day, and its interests were all-embracing. Its particular
mission was to carry the message and mission of Anglo-American brotherhood. As the years passed, Lady Randolph became
ever more conscious of her American roots. Perhaps she sensed
the rapidly increasing importance of the country of her birth.
But this cannot have been the only explanation. Life moves in
a circle. Somehow one ages back into one's youth.

The *Anglo-Saxon Review* was only the beginning of Lady
Randolph's activities to establish more harmony between the
land that had begotten and the country that had absorbed her.
It was not yet her most important enterprise. But it was certainly the most exciting and amusing one. Also, it proved, the
costliest.

An American woman in London, Mrs. Pearl Mary Teresa
Craig, under the pen-name of John Oliver Hobbes a popular
author and playwright, became the godmother of Jeanette's
brain-child, the magazine. Lady Randolph had met her some
years before at the Curzons', and one of her habitual friendships with older women had rapidly developed. Mrs. Craig,
gentle and worldly-wise, was very much interested when she
first heard of the plan. As her salon was a literary center, she
collected the staff of the magazine-to-be around the tea-cups.
Mr. Sidney Low was acquired as assistant editor. Mr. John
Lane took charge of the cover picture, which, then a revolution-
ary idea, should be different for every issue. Mr. Cyril Daven-
port of the British Museum joined the staff, and helped in the
selection of bindings. They were to be facsimiles of celebrated
books of past centuries, mostly chosen from precious tomes in

the library of the British Museum. Mr. Lionel Cust of the National Portrait Gallery volunteered as art editor. He contributed the photogravure. Mr. Arthur Strong, librarian of the House of Lords and at Chatsworth, took the responsibility for the historical part. Mr. Knowles, publisher of *The Nineteenth Century* assumed the role of financial adviser.

To introduce "Maggie," as the *Review* was affectionately called, Lady Randolph gave a luncheon party for the most congenial crowd that had ever surrounded her. Once more a delightful and enthralling period began, absorbing her from morning till night. It was what she fundamentally needed.

Now she was no longer the wire-puller, but the responsible executive. She had to decide on the oddest and most controversial suggestions. Someone advised her to print "Maggie" in three languages. "If you want to ruin yourself immediately. . . ." Lord D'Abernon, then Sir Edgar Vincent, famed for his mixture of classical education and English common sense, commented. The first issue, it was unanimously agreed, must carry something startling. What was startling? New Ideas on Free Love? Or Sidelights on Royal Courts? Perhaps lofty poetry, preferably verses from the poet laureate? No, an essay on bimetallism from Mr. Henry Chaplin; everyone would devour it, even American housewives. "A glorified *Yellow Book,* that is the thing!" Mr. Knowles, the financial adviser, counseled.

The first volume, indeed, the herald of ten more to come, each consisting of three hundred pages, bound à la Dérome, the famous French bookbinder of the 18th century, had a gorgeous cover: the replica of Thevet's *Vies des Hommes Illustres* which had been produced in about 1604 for James I. The frontispiece was a photograph of Queen Victoria's marble bust by Edward Onslow Ford; the first picture inside reproduced Stuart's portrait of George Washington.

The introductory editorial was written by Lady Randolph. Unabashed, she began with a quotation from Dr. Johnson: "No one but a blockhead ever wrote except for money." It was a classic explanation of the exorbitant price of four guineas a year, for which the reader, however, had the satisfaction of seeing his name printed in the list of subscribers, published at the end of the year. More than two-thirds of these names were those of American readers. Thus Jeanette's dearest, life-long wish, "to render the U. S. and Great Britain more intelligible to each other," as she frequently put it, came a long step nearer to fulfillment. The exorbitant price, incidentally, the *Review* charged, was by no means chosen for speculative reasons. The idea was that the magazine should be preserved permanently, like a book. "Articles full of solid thought and acute criticism, of wit and learning, are read one day, and cast into the wastepaper basket the next," Jeanette wrote in her first editorial. To issue the copies in a more costly form meant to her lengthening their existence. Indeed, the de-luxe magazine's success in the United States was such that a New York paper ran the self-advertisement: "You pay five dollars for this magazine. It may be good, but you can buy *The World* for a cent."

The evening of "Maggie's" first publication was celebrated at a dinner in the new Liberal Leader, Mr. Asquith's, house. Mr. Asquith, a bookish man continuing in the great Gladstone tradition of mixing social progress with Homer, interrupted his meal to thumb the pages. "My acclamation!" he said.

The *Anglo-Saxon Review* had been intended as an escape for Lady Randolph. It was supposed to replace the pleasures and exertions of the great world by serious and detached work. But there is no escape for the dynamo. Jeanette, the publisher and editor, was now drafted into the maelstrom of London's literary and theatrical life. Lady Randolph had not only to go to all first nights, as had long been her habit. Now she had even to attend the rehearsals of her friend's, Mrs. Pearl Craig's, numerous plays. Since the latter was also a good musician, the two ladies played the piano together, first in private, then in public. Together with Mademoiselle Janotha they played Bach's *Concerto in D Minor* for three pianos at Queen's Hall, with an orchestra from the Royal College of Music, conducted by Sir Walter Parratt. The evening was a rousing success. Lady Randolph Churchill, the newest and most amazing editor in London, as a concert pianist into the bargain was a treat no one could miss. The ovation she received lasted longer than half an hour. "This was the only time I can remember enjoying playing in public," she recalled.

It was much more amusing than life in politics. But the omnivorous *Review* needed political articles as well, and so she had, willy-nilly, to resume her appearance in government and parliamentary society. She succeeded as well as ever. Lord Salisbury, it is true, excused himself from contributing to her magazine by his overwork, but almost all his cabinet colleagues wrote for the *Review*. Lord Rosebery, soon to become Prime Minister himself, was a most prolific contributor. Swinburne, Henry James, Max Beerbohm submitted their pieces. Cecil Rhodes, the Empire builder, wrote articles on his world-embracing field. G. B. Shaw was ready to write "A word more about Verdi," but declined to come to a luncheon party, sending a telegram: "Certainly not. What have I done to provoke such an attack on my well-known habit?" Lady Randolph replied in another telegram: "Know nothing of your habits; hope they are not as bad as your manners." Instantly a long and apologetic letter from G. B. S. arrived, and when he arrived himself to dinner—in the "worst cut tails" Lady Randolph had ever seen— he proved to be the most brilliant conversationalist at table. Subsequently he came more often to Lady Randolph's house. She remembered him as tall, thin, ascetic-looking, with wonderful, transparent eyes. His conversation was always unconventional, but that did not disturb her.

Lady Randolph's two favorite contributors to the *Anglo-Saxon Review* were a young Hussar officer, whose piece "Cavalry" early revealed the combative taste of the man who was to become England's warlord and master of prose at once, and, second, a lady who constantly changed her pen-names to protect her identity.

It was finally revealed by E. V. Lucas, whose verses in *Books of Today* started with the rhyme:

"Have you heard of the wonderful magazine
Lady Randolph is editing, with help from the Queen?"

Edward and Alexandra had already succeeded to the throne. Victorianism was a thing of the past. The *Anglo-Saxon Review* still mirrored the old world for a little while. After eleven numbers, written mostly by blue blood, and edited with Lady Randolph's heart's-blood, "Maggie" had to cease publication. Jeanette had lost her last penny on the glorious enterprise. She laughed. It had, indeed, been a wonderful time while it lasted.

For almost three eventful years the magazine had been the very life of Lady Randolph, surpassed in importance only by two events. Mr. Sidney Low, the faithful assistant, had to edit two issues of the quarterly, while his beautiful publisher was engaged on what she, looking back, called "the most thrilling experience of my life, certainly the most important public work I have ever tried to do." The other event, while thrilling enough, did not for a moment interrupt her indefatigable work; it only intensified her exertions.

The outbreak of the Boer War, although anticipated with mixed feelings for a long time, struck London like a thunderbolt. Winston went off immediately. So did John, his younger brother. Lady Randolph wanted once more to do something. She could never be altogether out of it. It was not only her passion for throwing herself into things. It was a deep and irrepressible desire for purposeful activity, increasing with the years. In moments of general stress and struggle, she felt inactivity as an actual pain. "It is like being in a country house, and seeing day after day other guests going out to hunt, while compelled oneself to remain indoors. I know nothing as depressing." It was a fashionable simile. But it expressed a deep urge.

Mrs. Blow, an American lady who had spent many years in Australia, suggested the solution. It now belonged to the ritual of American lady travelers to call upon Lady Randolph when stopping in London. Mrs. Blow arrived on an early October day in 1899. Instantly she presented her letters of introduction, and was invited to tea. Her hostess was not in the mood for small talk. She was entirely absorbed by the various movements that had been started to raise funds for the sick and wounded. She had plunged into most of them, but none seemed important enough to consume entirely her dynamic energy.

Mrs. Blow, blessed be her name and memory, had an idea. It was she who proposed to equip an American hospital-ship to be sent to South Africa. Lady Randolph listened intently. She had not yet lost the panther's scent. She sensed a great opportunity. A hospital-ship could perform a great service. More important, an American hospital-ship helping the British wounded might, by its humanitarian appeal, offset some of the bad feelings many Americans, the Irish-Americans most vociferously, expressed as to what they called the sad fate of the Boers. Lady Randolph felt that she could do a great deal for both her countries. However, a methodical woman in spite of her natural explosiveness, she asked Sir William Garstin for his opinion. Sir William was a famous Egyptologist, the next thing to an expert on South Africa Lady Randolph could get hold of at the moment. Enthusiastically he told her to go ahead. "Believe me," he said, "you will be making history apart from the excellence of the work."

History was made on October 25th at a meeting of English society ladies of American birth in Lady Randolph's house. Mrs. Blow was made honorary secretary of the committee formed on this occasion; Mrs. Adair was made vice-chairman. Jeanette accepted the chairmanship. Furthermore, the Executive Committee included the Duchess of Marlborough, the Countess of Essex, Mrs. Joseph Chamberlain, Jeanette's two sisters, Mrs. Moreton Frewen, now a handsome dark blonde *entre les deux ages,* and Lady Leslie, who looked strikingly like her father, Leonard Jerome. A score of American English-women filled the ranks.

The English people called the committee the "American Amazons." Everyone was strongly impressed by the zeal and enthusiasm with which they pursued their two aims: to collect money, and to get a ship. Both funds and ship were to be American, else the fundamental idea would have been marred. When Lady Randolph was warned of the lack of enthusiasm America showed for the British cause in South Africa, she replied undeterred: "The plea of humanity will overrun their political opinions."

On behalf of her committee Lady Randolph issued an appeal, concluding with the words: "The American women in Great Britain, while deploring the necessity for war, are endeavoring to raise among their compatriots here and in America, a fund for the relief of the sick and wounded soldiers and refugees in South Africa. It is proposed to dispatch immediately a suitable hospital-ship, fully equipped with medical stores and provisions, to accommodate two hundred people, with a staff of four doctors, five nurses, and forty non-commissioned officers and orderlies. To carry the above resolution into effect, the sum of $150,000 will be required."

Among Americans in England the response was immediate and overwhelming. American concerts, matinees, and entertainments of all kinds were organized. Lady Randolph nearly wore out her fingers on the piano. She recited verses in public, the poet laureate contributed for the occasion. She dined three times a day for the cause, although she well knew that she must watch her weight. Her old misfortune pursued her: inescapable fate forced her to be glamorous again.

At night she wrote for hours, dispatching innumerable letters, pleas and appeals to well-known American benefactors. Since the press in both countries was full of reports on the activities of the American Amazons, her epistles could be short and to the point. Yet one American multimillionaire in New York, at that an old friend of her father's, to whom she had cabled, wired back he had "no knowledge of the scheme." "You had better read the papers," she replied by cable. Another famous American philanthropist, particularly known for his generosity to libraries, refused to contribute. But the workmen in his factory collected $2,500 among themselves. Lady Randolph had asked for a sum total of $150,000. Within two months she had collected more than $200,000.

It was more difficult to obtain an American ship. She cabled to "Teddy" Roosevelt, then Governor of New York. The rough rider was distressed that he could not override the Irish vote. Unfortunately, he "could not suggest anything." Instead, Mr. Bernard Baker, President of the Atlantic Transport Company, generously proposed to the British Admiralty to hand over the "Maine" to the American Ladies' Committee. The "Maine" was a cattle-boat. At the outbreak of the South African War it had been offered by its American owners to the British Admiralty. But at that time the expenses of transforming a cattle-boat into a hospital-ship appeared too high. The "Maine" was lying unused in an English harbor when Lady Randolph produced the money to adapt it. Her committee took over the ship from the Admiralty. With true American munificence, Mr. Bernard Baker agreed to maintaining captain and crew at the company's expense, for the time the "Maine" was being used for her charitable purpose. The Atlantic Transport Company, having some experience in such matters, since they had already contributed the "Maine's" sister-ship, "Missouri," to their own government during the Cuban War, helped greatly in transforming the vessel. The staff of doctors and nurses was to be all-American. Mrs. Whitelaw Reid, the daughter of Mr. D. O. Mills, founder of the Mills School, supplied Lady Randolph's enterprise with doctors, nurses, and hospital orderlies.

All these transatlantic transactions and negotiations also concerned, in one way or another, the War Office and the Admiralty in London. Both offices were overstrained, and showed little inclination to take outsiders seriously. This indifference gravely hampered Lady Randolph. Under the impact of the first reverses the British were suffering in South Africa, general

tension in London was high. Jeanette was no less disconcerted
by the bad news than were all her friends. But difficulties always spurred her on. She visited both the Department Chiefs.
Both, Lord Landsdowne, the Minister of War, an old friend
of the Churchills, and Lord Goschen, First Lord of the Admiralty, who had been for a time Randolph's successor in
office, cut the red tape and proved extremely helpful in getting
the ship on its way.

Now Lady Randolph could carry on the drive with her
habitual speed. On November 12, when the American Amazons
met in their first general committee, she proudly pointed out
that, although the enterprise had been only a fortnight in existence, the ship, a magnificent staff, hundreds of gifts, and,
most important, much of the money, were ready. Moreover,
sympathizers in every part of the globe were working for the
cause. She carefully kept her crusade out of politics. "The
wounded are the wounded," she said, "irrespective of creed or
nationality." However, she could not refrain from remarking
that the "Maine" would probably do more to cement Anglo-
American friendship than any amount of mutual flag-waving,
and pleasant amenities. A wave of applause confirmed this
statement.

Although the "Maine" was an American boat, she needed recognition as a military hospital-ship to maintain her proper
status, and this could only come from the British government.
Lord Wolseley, commander-in-chief, was not sympathetic.
The "independence" of the American Amazons, he wrote Lady
Randolph, was so firmly established that the ladies should entirely rely on themselves.

Jeanette read the letter and hurried to the commander-in-
chief's office, looking, indeed, like an amazon on the warpath
with her burning eyes and her dangerous smile. Her conversation with Lord Wolseley is not on record. But the following
letter, she received from him, has been preserved: "I am only
too anxious to help you in this matter to show you how thoroughly our army, and indeed the nation, appreciate this evi-

dence of the interest that American ladies take in our sick and wounded."

One of Jeanette's demands had been the appointment of an English principal medical officer. Surgeon Lieutenant-Colonel Hensman was chosen, and came to her for an interview. She had enough experience with medical men to know a good doctor when she saw one. Afterwards she declared that he combined a strong sense of duty with most tactful and courteous manners. This was an indispensable attribute for an English surgeon among an American staff and crew. No one knew better than the Anglo-American woman how different the men of the two nationalities were, even when united in a common cause; it would, she feared, be no easy matter to preserve the harmony. Fortunately, her fears proved unfounded. Lady Randolph was proud that no serious differences ever arose aboard the "Maine."

The arrival of the American staff, mostly from New York, caused much excitement, not alone inside the committee, but all over London. English hospitality surpassed itself. Hotels vied with one another to accommodate the American friends at much reduced rates pending the departure of the ship. Luncheons and dinner parties and every sort of entertainment were·given in their honor. The matrons and nurses of the London hospitals took the lionized Americans to their hearts.

Princess Christian, whose great devotion to charity was well known, presented the Americans of the "Maine" to the Queen in Windsor. Victoria, a frail old woman, addressed them in a perfectly clear, if audibly emotion-shaken voice. After wishing them Godspeed on their errand of mercy, the Queen added: "I am very pleased to see you, and I want to say how much I appreciate your kindness in coming over to take care of my men."

Lady Randolph was bidden to dine and sleep at Windsor. Most graciously, the Queen spoke about Randolph, her faithful minister, whose early passing had grieved her, indeed. Then she inquired, displaying the same strong human interest, after

Lady Sarah Wilson, Jeanette's sister-in-law, who was reported to be a prisoner in the hands of the Boers. "They will not hurt her," the Queen tried to comfort Jeanette with a hopeful smile. She turned the conversation to less painful matters. She asked many questions about the "Maine," and expressed her pleasure in receiving the American surgeons and nurses. Something, however, seemed to worry her. Jeanette, accustomed to divining other people's secret worries, inquired whether Her Majesty had some other question. Shyly, the old Queen replied: "But those doctors all look very young...." "They are all the more energetic, therefore..." came the reply. The old Queen nodded. Her long and eventful years had taught her the value of human lives. "I'll see you again, tomorrow," Victoria said, dismissing Lady Randolph.

Her night in Windsor was heavy with dreams. Here Randolph had taken the fateful step, his resignation, leading to self-destruction. Four years after his death his memory was still = constantly in her mind. Her friends shook their heads that this beautiful woman, born to give and receive love, sought by many an eligible in London, should remain so utterly unapproachable. Her friends insisted she had only to stretch out her hand to become a Duchess.

The terrible news crashed into her preparation for the grand fête on behalf of the "Maine" at Claridge's. On the seventeenth of November she was visiting friends in the country to enlist their support, when, in the middle of the night, a telegram awoke her: "I regret to inform you that Mr. Winston Churchill has been captured by the Boers. He fought gallantly after an armored train in which he was traveling was trapped. Signed, Editor of the *Morning Post*."

Another telegram, dispatched by young Oliver Borthwick, a friend of Winston's and the son of the proprietor of the *Morning Post*, following immediately, was more explicit: "Deeply regret Winston reported captured by the Boers; no mention of his being wounded. He not only displayed great personal courage, but his coolness and bravery encouraged all others. Our correspondent says: Churchill, with bravery, coolness described as magnificent, got party men clear of overturned train, subsequently fighting with Dublins and Natal Volunteers, covering retreat of engineers."

Telegrams poured in from all over England, and from many friends on the continent. Empress Eugénie wired: "Sharing your frightful incertitude. Hoping for early good news." But no news came. It was a time of torture. Lady Randolph never understood how she had been able to endure the horrible suspense. The explanation seems to be that her escape mechanism functioned again: her work. The absorbing occupation with the "Maine" offered a mental refuge. She was very anxious that President McKinley should bestow an American flag upon the hospital-ship. She cabled to Washington, asking for this honor. The distinction would carry no political significance, she added prudently.

Winston was probably pacing a narrow, dirty, stifling cell with this rapid step he had inherited from her. How would they feed him in that awful place? And what about rats?

President McKinley did little to soften a mother's despair. Through Secretary Hay he refused Lady Randolph's request to send a flag for the ship, as his "motives might be misconstrued." It was very easy to guess, by whom. Had the Irish no sense of gratitude at all? Had they entirely forgotten that Randolph had been their best friend, in-and-outside the government, and that he had once gravely impaired his political existence to save the dubious honor of Mr. Parnell? Her anger against the Irish was another antitoxin against her anguish about her son. She concentrated her logical mind on the problem immediately at stake, and cabled back to Washington: "Would not red cross on flag remove difficulty? Wounded are to be tended irrespective of nationality." It was the suggestion of a compromise as she had frequently worked them out when Randolph had maneuvered himself into a deadlock. Such compromises, however, were more akin to the English nature than to the American spirit. The last word from Washington was short and did not lend itself to renewed interpretations. It read: "No!"

Now it was Lady Randolph who had worked herself into a deadlock. Never doubting that she would, indeed, receive the Stars and Stripes, she had already, through the kindness of the Duke of Connaught, asked the Queen to bestow a Union Jack which should wave next to the Stars and Stripes. Arthur Duke of Connaught informed her by letter dated December 4th, 1899, that, much to his delight, the Queen had consented to present a Union Jack to the hospital ship "Maine" as a mark of her appreciation of the "generosity of those American ladies who have so nobly come forward, and have at such great expense equipped a hospital-ship for wounded British officers and men." He himself would bring the flag down on the sixteenth, and present it in the Queen's name. On the seventeenth his Duchess and he would give a reception at the Carlton Hotel to meet the ladies, not forgetting the American nurses of the expedition.

Jeanette's confusion was indescribable. The Queen was presenting her flag under the impression that the American President was doing the same. How could she explain that this was not so? After much pondering and worrying she decided to revert to the best explanation a woman could find: to give none at all. She entrusted herself to the English sense of discretion. No one would ask an obviously embarrassing question.

On the appointed day the Queen's present, a huge Union Jack with the red cross on a white ground, was ceremoniously hoisted. Before a festive assembly of distinguished people who had come to help Jeanette, the Duke of Connaught made a most felicitous speech. Everyone was delighted. Lady Randolph replied, ending on the note that all who had been interested in this work had made it a labor of love.

The flag was then fastened to a halyard and run up by the Duke personally to the mainmast, where, after an energetic pull or two, it flew out in the breeze. The Scots Guards played *Rule,*

Britannia. Then they changed to the *Star-Spangled Banner.*
No American flag appeared. The crowd was breathless. But
not a single man, not even a woman, commented. Rapidly the
Red Cross flag climbed to the foremast. The Admiralty's transport flag followed at the helm. It all went surprisingly quickly.
Lady Randolph had managed it with her usual skill. Yet, she
recalled, she felt a lump in her throat. When all was arranged,
the much-worried but undaunted woman thanked her good
Lord with a short and fervent prayer.

She had good reason to be grateful. The day before her departure, the twenty-third of December, Winston cabled to the
Morning Post. After escaping his dungeon—which actually had
been the State Model School, a perfectly habitable building in
Pretoria—he was now safe and sound in Portuguese Lorenzo
Marquez. Of course, his mother had never doubted that there
would be a happy ending. She had never permitted herself
to be hounded by dark pictures and silly imaginations. She always had maintained her confidence in the boundless resource-
fulness and ingenuity of her own flesh and blood.

Singing, cheering, and waving, enormous crowds gathered
at the harbor to bid the departing hospital-ship Godspeed. Ten
thousand of them had inspected the "Maine" on the Sunday before. They had wrought havoc. The decks were still covered
with mud from the visitors' boots. The wards, a short time
before stables, were littered with wood-shavings, paint-pots,
ropes and all debris which the conversion of a cattle-boat into a
hospital-ship entails. The crowds were still shouting as the
steamer slowly put to sea. "Bring home Kruger! We'll eat him!"
was their resounding farewell. It was a great moment. Amazingly, Lady Randolph seemed little touched, although her
friends and relatives silhouetted on the pier faded rapidly and
the white cliffs were fast disappearing. Even embarking upon
the crowning adventure of her life, she disapproved of the
disorder around. "To say that this ship is in a state of chaos does
not quite express it!" she muttered to her personal companion,
Miss Warrender. Scrubbing brushes, soap, and innumerable

pails of water had to be produced. The lady of the "Maine" was a tidy housewife. It was the first surprise to the crew, but by no means the last.

As if every event connected with Lady Randolph had to be extraordinary and dramatic, the "Maine" ran into a full gale, lasting six days, which, according to veteran sea-dogs, was the worst experienced for many a year. For forty-eight hours the ship had to heave to. But making no headway was an impossible proposition for Jeanette. She argued with the skipper. Whether she convinced or fascinated him was hard to say. Challenging the tempest, the hospital-ship resumed her course. Everyone aboard was buffeted from morning till night and from night till morning. It was practically impossible to eat. The soup poured into one's lap, the contents of one's glass splashed into one's face. The vast amounts of goods and stores crowding the holds toppled over one another. It was chaos again. Yet Lady Randolph's ship had good luck. On January 2nd, after a topsy-turvy New Year's night, the "Maine" anchored off Las Palmas. The transport "Danton Grange" was towed to the next mooring. Water was pouring through her holes. Her engines were ruined beyond repair. With three other vessels she had gone ashore during the gale. Politely, Mr. Swanston, the British Consul in Las Palmas, informed Lady Randolph that he had been expecting her boat for a few days. Since she did not come, he had believed her to have foundered. Indeed, the brilliant green stripes, denoting the "Maine's" status as a military hospital-ship, were practically gone, many of the stanchions were bent and twisted, the ship's white paint was a foggy gray.

Lady Randolph did not allow any interruption of the journey for repairs. She would rather arrive in time to nurse the wounded of Mafeking, where, Mr. Swanston had informed her, fierce fighting was in progress, than arrive ship-shape. It was the habitual Churchill gallop. On the twenty-third of January the "Maine" anchored off Cape Town. The harbor was crowded with vessels. A forest of masts grew out of the bay. For a considerable time, every second of which was too long for her restlessness, the hospital-ship was kept rolling outside the breakwater, until the Port Commander Sir Edward Chichester, remembering many a glass of port he had had in House Beautiful, had exerted all his care and kindness to procure Lady Randolph's ship a berth inside. She stormed down the gangway. Two years before, at Bourbon, Winston had disembarked similarly dramatically, and broken his arm. But parents don't learn from their children's experiences.

She hurried to Government House. The sudden appearance of the dark woman in a white uniform, half nurse and half Royal Naval officer, tore Government House out of what seemed sleep, but was, indeed, the silent melancholy of deep gloom. No, there was no news. News was forbidden. Kitchener had ordered all officers and officials to practice the utmost discretion. Even the most harmless small talk about the war was strictly ruled out. Cape Town was overrun with spies and traitors. Many of the inhabitants were disloyal. Valuable information was being continually transmitted to the enemy. Under such conditions any questions would have been impolite, and answers impossible. Even the parrots Lord Milner, the host, kept in Government House were mute.

After dinner, to which Lord Milner had invited his entire staff, Lady Randolph knew all she wanted to know. The siege of Ladysmith continued. General Buller had crossed Tugela. But the whereabouts of Lieutenant Winston Spencer Churchill was not revealed. No one could say on just which warpath the amazing young officer-correspondent could be found. Could mother and son both be in South Africa at the same time without meeting? Everything was possible in the Churchill family.

On January 25th, the authorities dispatched the "Maine" to Durban. There the ship was to be filled with patients and wounded from other hospital-ships and sent back home immediately. Lady Randolph did not care to return so quickly. She had a specially trained and equipped staff of American doctors who were ready to deal with complicated cases, not just with patients who had been treated already on other ships and half restored to health. The authorities did not listen to such arguments. So Lady Randolph made once more the rounds of powerful old friends. Sir Redvers Buller, commander of the Expeditionary Force, was one of them. His word was decisive. The "Maine" was permitted to remain in the harbor of Durban. The most interesting medical cases from the whole battlefront were sent down.

Among the slightly injured officers was Lady Randolph's younger son, John. He had to walk with a crutch, yet he, a Churchill, if the only inconspicuous one, would rejoin the South African Light Horse in a few days. Winston? No one knew his latitude and longitude. In a rather resigned mood Lady Randolph decided to use the two days John still had to avail herself of an invitation from the Governor of Natal, Sir Walter Hely-Hutchinson, to visit with her son Pietermaritzburg. The train was moving out of the station when, breathless, but happily smiling, Winston jumped on to the running board. He had two days off. Of course he wanted to spend them with his mother.

It was a happy reunion, yet, in some way a departure. A mother feels the moment her son has definitely outgrown family life. Since his escape from Pretoria, which he would, if very much urged, relate with oratoric magnificence—his father's heritage—he was the most lionized young man in South Africa, and not in South Africa alone. In England the ditty made the rounds:

> "Then there is Winston Churchill
> And all I want to say
> He is the greatest and the latest
> Correspondent of the day...."

and an infinite number of men's choirs (an English institution taking the place of the American barbershop-quartet) were already rehearsing: "See the conquering hero comes..." duly to receive the jailbreaker from Pretoria. From New York came an offer for a lecture tour through the U. S., ten thousand dollars guaranteed. Winston was definitely on his own. His mother had helped him greatly. Now, she felt, she should retire. The intimate personal relation remained entirely unchanged. But somehow, one may assume, Lady Randolph felt that she was alone.

She spent her motherly feelings on many boys. On the afternoon of her return from Pietermaritzburg the first ambulance train arrived; a batch of eighty-five men was carried aboard the "Maine." Thus far, Lady Randolph had known the armed forces primarily in the embodiment of drawing-room generals, commanders of Expeditionary Forces, and glittering, medal-studded military attachés. Now she met Tommy Atkins. The British soldier, she was immediately aware, is a fine fellow. She heard hundreds of instances of his courage and self-sacrifice on the field and in action related, but never by the silent or bashfully grinning wounded man himself. Out of his uniform she found him a big child, who wants to be kept in order, and not too much coddled. Yet the American staff of the "Maine" was inclined to do just that. Her advice to the doctors and nurses was "to give the men a higher ideal of cleanliness and comfort than they ever had before." Moreover she saw to it that family ties were closely kept. She wrote innumerable letters dictated to her by her patients. Invariably, they began the same way. "Dear father and mother, I hope this finds you in the pink, as it leaves me." Then came a great scratching of heads and biting of finger nails, until Lady Randolph suggested a description of how they were wounded. Now their story poured out. Lady Randolph's hands were stiff by the time she had taken down the first two dozen reports. Every time she concluded with the question: "Won't you send your love to anyone? . . . Not outside the family, I mean?" she added sternly. One gallant Tommy, who lay with a patch over his left eye, fixed his right on her, and asked to add to his letter: "The sister who is a-writing of this is very nice."

A few days later came the second batch of ten wounded officers and ninety men. Now the "Maine's" wards were crowded.

The parties had been transported all the way from the hospitals
of Frere, Estcourt, Mooi River, and Pietermaritzburg. The fame
of the American hospital-ship had swept the country like wildfire. Every hospital wanted to entrust their critical cases to the
care of Lady Randolph and her celebrated medical staff. Surgi-
cal and operating cases were everywhere treated according to
the knowledge of contemporary science. But antiseptic dressings, the frequent use of electricity and gymnasium apparatus
as well as massage, all imported from New York, were new
medical devices.

Lady Randolph herself was hard at work. Officially, she contented herself with the role of a nurse, but her familiarity with
the science of medicine amazed the doctors. Surgeon Lieutenant Colonel Hensman asked her whether she had studied
medicine as a girl. "No," she replied. A fleeting cloud overshadowed her eyes. "But, I believe, I have had some experience." She proved it. It was she who organized the functioning
of the service in every detail. She assigned the doctors to their
dressings and duties in the morning, one of them in daily rota-
tion, being appointed as orderly medical officer, whose job it
was to make a thorough inspection of everything, report any
flaw he might discover, and listen to complaints. Lady Randolph personally supervised the nurses responsible for carrying
out the doctors' orders. The medical stores were managed by
non-commissioned officers. Lady Randolph insisted on a daily
report on the supplies available. Soon she was known as the
Angel of Durban. Paradoxically, the new 4.7 gun, to which the
Boers had no answer, was christened after the angel. *Lady
Randolph* helped considerably to decide the outcome of the
war. But Lady Randolph had done more to mitigate its terror.

The return journey, favored by delightful weather, helped
the sick and wounded to recover at least their morale. They
sang all day and discussed their further destinations and plans.

On the last evening of the journey a dozen of her officer-
patients handed her, on behalf of all the wounded aboard, a
letter of gratitude. Some of the signers were maimed, disabled,

and ruined for life. Yet their letter ended with the truly English sentence: "We hope the next voyage of the ship will be as pleasant to you, as this one has been to all of us."

On an early April morning a salvo of guns greeted the returning American Amazon at the port of Southampton. It sounded like a formidable reception. She alone knew that it was the salute of farewell. Lady Randolph was about to go.

The Queen, in the last year of her life no longer able to grant audiences except in cases of supreme necessity, had sent a message through Princess Louise, Duchess of Argyll, who desired to say that Her Majesty was much gratified to hear what good work the "Maine" had been doing among the wounded in South Africa, and wished to express her great appreciation of this generous undertaking. Their Lordships from the Admiralty followed suit. Even Mr. Elihu Root, Secretary of War in Washington, "begged to convey the thanks of the army of the United States for the human and effective service" the ship (minus the Stars and Stripes) had rendered. The good ship sailed a second time to South Africa, and was subsequently dispatched to Chinese waters. Finally, after the "Maine" had been in commission for fifteen months, Mr. Baker, the President of the Atlantic Transport Company, presented the ship to the British Government, the American Amazons giving all the hospital equipment into the bargain. In accepting the gift, King Edward said "the fact that it had been intended for my beloved mother makes it specially valued, and the culminating present of the ship to the British Government will always be remembered as a lasting link of friendship between the two countries."

Lady Randolph played only a modest role in all these celebrations. Quietly, she refused to appear at the numerous festivities, which were still an important part of public life. She lent a helping hand in preparing the "Maine's" second sailing to Cape Town and the Chinese expedition. But she joined neither of the journeys. She was, as Winston had called his father, a victor without the spoils.

She secluded herself in the office of the *Anglo-Saxon Review*, and appeared to be once more entirely absorbed by her editorial work. "Life continues. Life must go on!" she repeated again and again. Whether she was referring to herself or to the magazine that had to struggle with increasing financial difficulties, remained undisclosed. At the summit of her success, at an age in which her beauty was fully matured, in the late spring of 1900, the turn of the century and of her own life too, she wanted to get away from public affairs. She did not retire into solitude. She spent much of her time pleasantly in the company of a tall, handsome young man: Mr. George Cornwallis-West.

On the seventh of July, 1900, Winston left the army to devote himself entirely to politics. He was already contesting Oldham, a notoriously fickle constituency which he conquered with a vengeance. He was well on his way to fame. No longer was he —a fact that greatly counted—a financial responsibility to his mother.

Now her path was clear. A few days after Winston's resignation from the army his mother renounced her entire past. In her wedding gown she stood before her mirror and said goodby to Lady Randolph. Her new name, considerably less famous, would be Mrs. George Cornwallis-West. It was not difficult to bid farewell to her first life. It had been a rich life, but now it was fully accomplished, and it should not last beyond its time. Exit Lady Randolph.

But there is no exit, there is no end. Every change is but transformation into another sphere. Every end is a new beginning.

AMONG THE BOOKS CONSULTED ARE:

BICKNELL, ANNA L. *Life in the Tuileries.* New York: The Century Company.

BROWN, HENRY COLLINS. *New York of Yesterday.* New York: Henry Collins Brown.

BUSCH, DR. MORITZ. *Bismarck in the Franco-German War.*

CHURCHILL, WINSTON, *Lord Randolph Churchill,* London: Macmillan & Co.

CHURCHILL, WINSTON. *A Roving Commission.* New York: Charles Scribner's Sons.

CORDOVA, R. J. DE. *The Prince of Wales' Visit in the United States of America.*

CORNWALLIS-WEST, MRS. GEORGE. *The Reminiscences of Lady Randolph Churchill.* New York: The Century Company.

COWLEY, EARL OF. *Secrets of the Second Empire.*

ESCOTT, THOMAS H. S. *Lord Randolph Churchill as a Product of His Age.* London: Hutchinson & Company, Ltd., 1895.

—— *Platform Press, Politics, and Play.* London: Simpkin, Marshall, Ltd., 1895.

—— *Social Transformations in the Victorian Age.* London: Seeley, Service & Company, Ltd., 1897.

HASWELL, CHARLES H. *Reminiscences.* New York: Harper & Brothers, 1896.

LABOUCHERE, HENRY. *Diary of the Besieged Resident in Paris.*

McALLISTER, WARD. *Society As I Have Found It.* New York: Cassell & Company, 1890.

O'SHEA, JOHN AUGUSTUS. *An Iron-Bound City.*

371

PERUGINIA, MARK EDWARD. *Victorian Days and Ways*. London: Hutchinson & Company, Ltd., 1936.

QUENNELL, PETER. *Victorian Panorama*. New York: Charles Scribner's Sons, 1937.

ROBB, JANET HENDERSON, *The Primrose League 1883-1906*.

ROSEBERY, LORD. *Lord Randolph Churchill*.

STRACHEY, LYTTON. *Queen Victoria*. New York: Harcourt, Brace & Company, 1924.

TSCHUPPIK, KARL. *Empress Elizabeth of Austria*. New York: Brentano's, 1930.

QUEEN VICTORIA. *Leaves from the Journal of Our Life in the Highlands*. London: John Murray.

YOUNG, G. M. *Victorian England*. New York: Oxford University Press, 1936.